Where the Boys Are

THE HAYMARKET SERIES

Editors: Mike Davis and Michael Sprinker

The Haymarket Series offers original studies in politics, history and culture, with a focus on North America. Representing views across the American left on a wide range of subjects, the series will be of interest to socialists both in the USA and throughout the world. A century after the first May Day, the American left remains in the shadow of those martyrs whom the Haymarket Series honors and commemorates. These studies testify to the living legacy of political activism and commitment for which they gave their lives.

Where the Boys Are

Cuba, Cold War America
and the Making of a New Left

◆

V A N   G O S S E

VERSO

London · New York

First published by Verso 1993
© Verso 1993
All rights reserved

Verso
UK: 6 Meard Street, London W1V 3HR
USA: 29 West 35th Street, New York, NY 10001-2291

Verso is the imprint of New Left Books

ISBN 0-86091-416-x
ISBN 0-86091-690-1 (pb)

'One Thousand Fearful Words for Fidel Castro' appears in Lawrence Ferlinghetti, *Starting from San Francisco*. Copyright © 1961 by Lawrence Ferlinghetti. Reprinted by permission of New Directions Publishing Corp.

British Library Cataloguing in Publication Data
A catalogue record for this book is available from the British Library

Library of Congress Cataloging-in-Publication Data
A catalog record for this book is available from the Library of Congress

Typeset in Minion by NorthStar, San Francisco, Calif.
Printed and bound in Great Britain by Biddles Ltd., Guildford and King's Lynn

For my parents,
Anthony Gosse and Dey Erben Gosse,
who taught me about fair play

Contents

Acknowledgements

There are many debts acquired in writing this book that can only be paid in this insufficient form. In the History Department at Rutgers, I had a very supportive dissertation committee of Jackson Lears, John Leggett and James Livingston. My advisor, Norman Markowitz, was a fount of knowledge of US policies and politics, and an example of historiographical gravity.

I remain in other ways in debt to Rutgers. The History Department provided exceptionally generous support in the form of a fellowship and later a teaching assistantship. The most important intellectual training I received there was in women's history, and I owe much to the feminist professors and students who made it such an exciting place in the 1980s, especially to Judith Walkowitz and my mates in her seminar. In another way, Jim Livingston, while I wrote my dissertation and after I completed it, has helped me see the totality of US history in a materialist fashion, deepening my convictions about history as a way of learning and a guide to practice. He and Patricia Rossi and Vincent and Julia Livingston have also been very good friends over some tumultuous years.

My one year of teaching at Wellesley College provided much-needed space and time to finish my research and begin to revise, and I am grateful to the History Department there for the appointment. The department's chairpersons, Katherine Parks, Jon Knudsen and Paul Cohen, and its secretaries, Helen Atkins and Thelma Pellagrini, made me feel at home and facilitated my research in many ways. I also express thanks for a grant from the Committee on Faculty Awards, which enabled me to employ several research assistants. Of these, Amy Mayer displayed notable competence and was also a good friend and fellow activist.

Various scholars took the time to carefully read my dissertation as I began revising it for publication, and they have my thanks. David Oshinsky and Paul Buhle helped me to rethink and rewrite the book's beginning, and encouraged me to overcome an indulgence in polemics for their own sake throughout.

ix

Keith Haynes and Steve Rosswurm wrote detailed commentaries – in the latter case virtually page-by-page, a great kindness – that spared me from many mistaken assumptions and easy ellipses. All four of these readers forced me to clarify my arguments, and if I have not sufficiently answered all their objections, this book is still much better for their constructive criticisms.

I would never have embarked on a dissertation that took on a life of its own and led to this book if Verso had not seen fit back in 1988 to commission from me (and immediately announce!) a history of the Central American solidarity movement. I still owe them the latter book, and am extraordinarily grateful for the confidence they showed in a novice scholar. Throughout these years Michael Sprinker has been the most tolerant of editors. He also read with a searching eye and gave me valuable advice on how to finish the book when I needed it. Steven Hiatt edited and produced the final text with great dispatch, sympathy and professionalism.

One always leaves the most personal to the last in these matters. First, I want to thank all those who talked to me or corresponded about their own involvement with the Cuban Revolution, especially Berta (Green) Langston, Neill Macaulay, Richard Gibson, Saul Landau, Asher Harer, Alan Sagner, Victor Rabinowitz, Joanne Grant, Betty Millard, Marvin Gettleman and Don Soldini; a special thanks to Michael Myerson, who first introduced me to the history of the Fair Play for Cuba Committee back in 1988, when I assumed that there had been no solidarity with the Cuban Revolution in its earliest days and went to him for guidance on later matters.

Next, I want to thank my comrades in the Committee in Solidarity with the People of El Salvador and related organizations over the past eleven years. We did not talk much about my research in the later eighties when I was in graduate school. There wasn't time, and usually I had more than enough to say about the present. But most of my understanding of what solidarity is, and how politics works in this country, comes from what we did together. I will always be in their debt, and honored by the association. Adelante, *compañeros!*

Finally, there are Eliza Jane Reilly and Johanna O'Mahony Gosse. Johanna is too young to check copy, but she is all the proof I need that grace and beauty and a sense of justice (and a saving lack of respect for authority) are inborn in all of us. She grew up with this book, as with all the phonebanks and 'district collective' meetings she slept through, and I hope she likes it.

With Eliza Jane Reilly, it is hard for me to begin, or to know where to end. She has really been my chief editor, as well as dear friend and companion. Often she understood the implications of my work better than I did, and talked me through its necessary linkages and conclusions. That she did this, patiently and lovingly, while attending graduate school in the same department and putting up with the indignities visited upon a female scholar *cum* spouse, is a testament to her solidarity with me and this project. I hope that I can repay my debt to her in a like solidarity.

One must note here the distortion of history which is being widely pushed both in Latin America and among the less responsible intellectuals of the United States. This is that the current of trade and investment, being 'dollar diplomacy', was merely a purposeful establishment by the United States of an 'informal empire'. ... The argument is not entitled to intellectual respect. Eras move in their own times. From 1900 at least until 1933, Cuba had only three possible alternatives. She could be a colony, she could be an independent entity living within the only trade system then current, or she could starve. Of the three, the second alternative was obviously the most advantageous. The intellectuals who now irresponsibly use the strictly propaganda word 'imperialism' are men who never experienced real 'empire'. In point of fact, Cuba was as free to develop her life, moral structure and social forms as any small country at the time – perhaps as any small country can be.

Adolf A. Berle, Jr

The undergraduates were delighted. They saw in him, I think, the hipster who in the era of the Organization Man had joyfully defied the system, summoned a dozen friends and overturned a government of wicked old men.

Arthur Schlesinger, Jr

The tragedy of American diplomacy is aptly symbolized, and defined for analysis and reflection, by the relations between the United States and Cuba from April 21, 1898 through April 21, 1961. The eruption of two wars involving the same two countries in precisely the same week provides a striking sense of classical form and even adds the tinge of eeriness so often associated with tragedy.

William Appleman Williams

Introduction

Confronting a Revolutionary World: Cuba as End and Beginning

In its simplest terms, this book deals with what Fidel Castro and the Cuban revolution meant to the many North Americans who cheered the bearded hero before and after the fall of Fulgencio Batista on 1 January 1959. It has a particular focus on those who kept cheering even when the hero became a demon to everyone else, and who thereby helped spark the era of renewed social and political struggle known as 'the sixties'.

In excavating this forgotten foundation of the New Left, my goal has been to show how *fidelismo* was a destabilizing and eventually radicalizing force in the United States, as well as in Cuba. The initial terrain for this destabilization, however, had nothing to do with radical politics, which makes this book more than a story of the left, old or new. The grounding of Yankee *fidelismo* was the extrapolitical world of spontaneous action for its own sake, what Norman Mailer defined as Hipsterism. This fertile space was opened up to Castro's 26th of July Movement in 1957 and 1958 not by leftists, who evinced very little interest in the Cubans, but by a diverse alliance of liberal journalists, activists, and fervent anti-Communists like Henry Luce, who believed they could defuse a hostile Third World by appropriating the appeal of rebellion for both domestic and foreign consumption. At a delicate conjuncture of the Cold War, Fidel became their Rebel With a Cause on a grand scale, but his popularity in the US, especially among young men, exceeded expectations. In this context, I trace how the collapse and reinvention of traditional boyhood and manhood provided the raw material for behavior that was not subversive or oppositional in any political sense, but simply nonconformist. Thus also the book's title, taken from a novel that accurately (and riotously) showed how collegiate *wanderlust* might sketch a short line between libidinal urges and joining Fidel's boys in a 'tropic, coeducational Valley Forge'.

Besides making an argument about the Cold War's politics of culture, however, I also examine a largely unexplored area within the more prosaic culture of politics, specifically the tripartite (albeit grossly unequal) relationship of US

1

foreign policymaking, organized liberalism and organized radicalism in the decade between the fall of Joe McCarthy and the Gulf of Tonkin Resolution. With the advantage of hindsight, one can see that during this period the US began 'slipping from its Olympian position', in Thomas Paterson's formulation, as a series of crises foretold the decline of hegemony abroad and the unraveling of the political order at home apparent by the early 1970s.[1] Nothing more signified the tragedy of that coming apart, as William Appleman Williams wrote a few months after the Bay of Pigs invasion, than the response to Cuba and Castro by North American liberals, and their inability to offer an Open Door for social revolution in the postcolonial world.[2]

My final purpose, then, is to demonstrate that the defeat at Playa Girón served as 'a firebell in the night', as Thomas Jefferson called another decisive moment, for all those committed reformers and imperial democrats who followed John F. Kennedy onto that beach as they would later follow Lyndon Johnson into Vietnam. From the defeat in Cuba one could discern the first outlines of how a radicalized liberalism and the reshaped, decentered 'old' left would combine, when thrown together by circumstance and a common enemy, to become *a new left*. That left, whose death has been prematurely announced many times over the past thirty years, persists in an awkward symbiosis with mainstream liberalism through the present, despite considerable efforts at disentanglement on both sides. In the end, therefore, like the war with Vietnam that it presaged, the Cuban revolution was not only a powerful catalyst across the Third World, but also resonated in the US with an anarchic force, shaking up the body politic and, for a few days in late April 1961, stripping it bare. That is, after all, what revolutions are supposed to do.

But to understand any of these points, it may be more useful to offer a sketch of the real story here, the 'personal politics' of America's romance with Fidel. This courtship, once well publicized, abruptly faded from sight for reasons that require some consideration.

History Missing

Years before *The Port Huron Statement* was issued in August 1962, even before black students started sitting down at Southern lunch counters in February 1960, disparate US citizens — gun-toting teenagers, diehard liberals, excited reporters, stray adventurers, even Errol Flynn — had taken up the revolutionary cause championed by CBS News in a primetime May 1957 special called 'Rebels of the Sierra Maestra: The Story of Cuba's Jungle Fighters'. In contrast to those team-playing organization men who were the fifties' explicit role models, the ragged *barbudos* led by Fidel Castro, chomping their cigars and darting down green mountain slopes to ambush Batista's garrisons, were every teenage boy's dream of gunfighting, personal heroism and nose-thumbing at

2

received authority. Two years of enthusiastic US press coverage and solidarity both vicarious and practical climaxed when Batista fled Cuba on New Year's Eve, 1958, leaving an entire column of would-be Yankee guerrillas stranded in Miami.

The popular fascination in the US with Castro hung on, even as official hostility congealed, so that Fidel himself was greeted by ecstatic crowds in New York and Washington, D.C. and at Princeton and Harvard during his triumphal US tour in April 1959. But as tensions steadily heightened over the rest of that year, all the voices that had once hailed Cuba's liberation rapidly stilled, and Castro became the latest case study in Latin betrayal and instability. As Cuba refused to accept North American dictates and the revolution defined itself, the Fair Play for Cuba Committee (FPCC) was organized across the country during 1960, a campaign that took place spontaneously and conspicuously outside the traditional divisions within the US left's shrunken ghetto. Over the next two years, thousands of people were pulled into the orbit of FPCC and related efforts to defend the Cuban revolution, as best symbolized by C. Wright Mills's runaway bestseller, *Listen, Yankee*.

Beyond its considerable reach, this 'fair play movement' encompassed not only principal New Left theorists like Mills, I. F. Stone, William Appleman Williams, Paul Sweezy and Leo Huberman; but also the most celebrated Beats and bohemians of the day – Allen Ginsberg, Norman Mailer and Lawrence Ferlinghetti; many key black radicals and early nationalists, including LeRoi Jones, Harold Cruse, the once-notorious Robert F. Williams and even Malcolm X; and the radical wing of a renascent pacifism led by Dorothy Day and Dave Dellinger. Perhaps even more important, a cadre of student activists came to the fore at a handful of campuses like Berkeley and Madison, many of whom would in the next decade play leading roles in the antiwar movement and the revival of the intellectual left. In sum, virtually every current of the later sixties upsurge briefly cohered around the defense of Cuba.

Yet the excitement and admiration generated by Fidel Castro in the US in 1957–59, let alone the existence of the Fair Play for Cuba Committee in 1960–62, are completely absent from the accounts published after the downturn of 'the Movement' in the mid 1970s, and only recently have diplomatic historians noted the evidence of pro-Castro sentiment in assessing US policy towards Batista.[3] If the Fair Play for Cuba Committee is mentioned at all, the reference is usually to the claim made immediately after President Kennedy's assassination that Lee Harvey Oswald was a card-carrying member, and to the widespread anxiety on the left that there would be a new witchhunt for anyone who had manifested pro-Castro inclinations.[4]

It is important therefore to stress that the Cuban revolution was not always seen as extraneous to the formation of the New Left, just as the latter was not always defined as it is now, as a movement consisting solely of white college students. In one of the earliest books on the 'new radicalism', Paul Jacobs and

Saul Landau noted in 1966 that

> by 1960, this new generation was throwing itself against American society, both
> literally and figuratively. They found a new hero in Castro, the man of action, the
> man without an ideology, whose only interest seemed to be bettering the life of the
> Cuban people. They responded to the youthful Castro with enthusiasm and de-
> manded 'fair play' for the Cuban Revolution.[5]

Similarly, in that same year the SDS veteran Jack Newfield published his influential *A Prophetic Minority*, which like others placed the Cuban revolution
near the center of events:

> A New Left then began slowly to take root, nourished by the pacifist and socialist
> British New Left of the Aldermaston Marches and the *New Left Review;* by the Beats'
> private disaffection from and rage at the Rat Race; by the Cuban Revolution; and by
> the writings of such men as C. Wright Mills, Albert Camus, and Paul Goodman.[6]

As late as 1976, Ronald Radosh edited a book-length collection, *The New
Cuba: Paradoxes and Potentials,* that documented from a 'critically supportive'
position the relation of 'the North American and Western European Left' to
Cuba. In the introduction, he remarked with a distinct note of pride that 'this
small and often isolated Left had raised the banner of solidarity with the Cuban revolution at an earlier moment, the era of the Bay of Pigs.'[7]

Of all those who once pointed to Cuba's influence in the US, however, only
the historian and activist Staughton Lynd hinted that this inspiration predated
the appearance of a New Left in 1960: by any measure, that was the year when
North American youth, black and white, first embarked on mass action,
thereby spurring a revival on the noncampus left. Writing at the height of the
sixties, he linked the twin crises of informal apartheid and informal empire in
defining this movement in the United States. After detailing the events
touched off by Khrushchev's indictment of Stalin and the Soviet invasion of
Hungary in 1956, he pointed out that

> That same year ... contrasting New Left charismas were launched in the Western
> Hemisphere. Fidel Castro and his handful of followers landed from the *Granma* to
> conquer their Cuban homeland, and Martin Luther King led the successful
> Montgomery bus boycott.[8]

The question of what happened between 1956 and 1960, which Lynd describes
accurately as an 'incubation period', becomes crucial, and the Cuban revolutionary struggle, including Fidel Castro's sheer 'charisma', comes to the fore as
one of several circuitous routes towards radicalization.

My objective is to understand why the first effects of the Cuban revolution
were felt in the US well *before* any idea arose of a 'new' left, and not coinciden-

4

tally before Castro was seen as a direct threat to US interests. The evidence suggests that Cuba's influence was felt primarily among those most insulated from political discontent: middle-class youth, especially males, in their teens and twenties, for whom World War II was at most a faint memory and the Affluent Society was the overwhelming tangible reality. Most of these young people had no practical idea of what the left had been or could be, outside of the stylized paranoia of J. Edgar Hoover's *Masters of Deceit*. Nor had they inherited any vibrant traditions of cultural opposition, as both the 'people's culture' of the Popular Front left and the various avant-garde bohemias had been subsumed into the new high culture championed by repentant leftists, from Sidney Hook to Clement Greenberg. For many of these young men, Cuba became an important early interstice between 1956 and 1960, akin to the struggle of African-Americans in the demands it placed upon Cold War ideology. Ironically, it was certain Cold Warriors' very investment in Fidel as a 'safe' guerrilla warrior that positioned Cuba as a wedge of radicalization; when the main body of North American liberals pulled back from the revolution in 1959–60, not everyone retreated with them. It is therefore not sufficient to look merely at the Fair Play for Cuba Committee, the events leading up to the Bay of Pigs, and the revelation of Kennedy's great-power cynicism as influences upon a New Left. Solidarity with Cuba in the early 1960s must be judged in the light of Fidel Castro's indisputable popularity in the US before the fall of Batista.

Closing the New Frontier

Having sketched the major events in this narrative, it's worth pointing out that the significance of Fair Play for Cuba, let alone the foreign correspondents and teenage soldiers-of-fortune who earlier headed for the Sierra Maestra, is likely to remain controversial. There are many to whom the familiar narrative of the late 1960s – mass politicization via Vietnam and a student movement whose hopes rose and fell with the Students for a Democratic Society – remains their story. To those waves of white college students radicalized between 1965 and 1969, a generational cohort with a distinctive worldview, the Cuban revolution and the Bay of Pigs came and went before their involvement, and they may feel that this was not really part of the sixties as they remember it, and deserves only the most minor recuperation. One can see the logic of this perception. FPCC disappeared very early and left few public tracks other than Oswald's shocking presence. In fact, well before 22 November 1963, tolerant treatment of Castro had been banished from all but the most left-wing discourses, with the exception of the *Catholic Worker* and some black newspapers. In June 1962, SDS held its now-legendary conference at a United Auto Workers summer camp in Port Huron, Michigan, and could manage only the opaque equation of Castro with South Vietnam's Diem as a 'dictator'; Cuba was already an accomplished fact for those who pinned their hopes on reconstructing a 'participatory democracy' within the US before any serious challenge to foreign policy.[9] Not for another five years, following the rise of Black Power and growing awareness that the war in Vietnam was no aberration, did Cuba surface again as the symbol of a still rebellious socialism.

The lack of a public memory does not efface two plain facts. First, it is self-evident that the Bay of Pigs was the first great defeat of the US in its confrontation with a revolutionary Third World. Second, this defeat hardly slipped by unnoticed at home, as the administration's lies and Cuban popular commitment to the revolution were both revealed in the ignominious collapse of the CIA's 'exile brigade'. President Kennedy, like many Democrats then and later, was most concerned about thunder on his right, but a measurable noise was also heard to his left, as basic Fair Play for Cuba arguments assailing US diplomacy as immoral and hypocritical were momentarily validated among wider circles.

This shock and outrage constituted a premonitory crack in the Cold War consensus that had bifurcated domestic perceptions of the world into them and us, thereby neutralizing the potential elements of any coherent radical coalition. For the first time since World War II, the dividing line between Cold War liberalism and everything to its left was no longer how one stood on the question of the USSR's menace or promise or, by extension, where one stood with regard to the Communist Party USA and the old Popular Front. Instead, for a small but measurable number of older liberals, churchpeople and academics, for many younger 'radical-liberals', independent socialists, pacifists, antipolitical Beats and African-Americans fed up with the caution of their elders, Cuba's right to self-determination superceded the US claim to defend a Free World. On this basis, all the varieties of incipient New Leftism made common cause with the surviving battalions of the existing Old Left, forging the pattern of a fundamentally polycentric radicalism that has endured ever since.[10]

Of course, the 'fair play movement' was small by later standards, as were all efforts at opposition in those days. At its peak in the spring of 1961 FPCC could mobilize only some thousands instead of the millions who were in the streets by the end of the decade. Yet by any standard relevant to that time, it was astonishingly successful, rapidly attracting thousands of paid-up members and a national network of local chapters in a few short months, an unheard-of feat for an independent radical initiative during the high Cold War years, especially one under continuous government pressure.

More important, though, is how the surprising diversity of those who chose to side with Castro called up a larger political tempest within the most dynamic force in US politics, the Cold War liberals who believed themselves the heirs of Franklin Roosevelt's New Deal and victory in World War II. The problem of Cuba's reclaimed nationhood after 1959 clarified the extent to which many of these liberals no longer supported the elemental rights of self-determination and juridical equality between peoples. As articulated most famously in Woodrow Wilson's Fourteen Points, this had been one of the great talismans of modern US politics in claiming superiority over the European powers, with their endless competition for colonial booty. In April 1961, the convenient fictions that had papered over CIA coups in places like Guatemala and Iran were missing, and an avowedly liberal president, who only lately had compared Castro to Simón Bolívar, defended a Great Power's right to make and break law as it saw fit, with no reasonable excuse of national self-preservation. The central justification for *realpolitik* since World War II had been the Soviet Union's real or implied threat in many parts of the globe. But in Cuba this threat did not obtain – there was as yet no major Soviet military presence, nor any public commitment to socialism, nor even much of an organized Cuban military. On the face of it, Castro in the months leading up to the Bay of Pigs invasion was no more a Soviet 'client' than any number of non-Communist Third World nationalists, from Nasser in Egypt to Sukarno in Indonesia, all of whom the US tolerated and even wooed. There could be little doubt that Castro's major sin lay simply in being Castro, and 'only ninety miles away'.

The scale of the defeat at the Bay of Pigs exposed for the first time how anti-Communism had bred a commitment to empire. It was a painful but salutary awakening for many. Before then, there had been no meaningful domestic opposition to a foreign policy framed entirely in East–West terms, and the word 'imperialism', much like the word 'capitalism', had 'belong[ed] to the vocabulary of demagoguery, not to the vocabulary of analysis', in the pithy phrase of the historian Arthur Schlesinger, Jr, then a special assistant to the president.[11] In a mixture of repulsion at what Senator J. William Fulbright later called 'the arrogance of power' and a residue of genuine good feeling for what the Cubans were trying to accomplish, the first silhouette of a new and wider political spectrum began to appear. In this context, the anathema pronounced in C. Wright Mills's famous telegram to a Fair Play rally on 24 April 1961, 'Schlesinger and Co. have disgraced us morally and intellectually', has a prophetic quality: Schlesinger himself felt compelled to reprint it in his New Frontier memoir, *A Thousand Days*. The interaction of Cuba, its revolution, and the movement for fair play thus has a double significance. It shows us 'what was' circa 1960–61, and also indicates what was to be – the inevitability of a popular challenge to what William Appleman Williams called 'empire as a way of life'.

The Sixties and the Myth of Declension

Reinserting the Cuban revolution into the early history of the New Left clarifies how anti-imperialism, and a concomitant 'international solidarity', defines the history of US radicalism over the past generation. Such a thesis, however, constitutes a sharp break with current paradigms regarding that history, specifically the themes of failure, decline and closure in the historiography of the sixties, and the periodization of that history within sharply defined chronological limits.

For many scholars the move in the late 1960s towards confronting US imperialism in solidarity with the armed peasants of the Third World was a grievous and willful error and defines the closure or 'death' of the New Left. In this telling, a promising mass democratic movement shattered itself on the rocks of blind allegiance to totalitarians, leaving no radicalism worth discussing. Even among left-leaning historians, the dominant historiographical tone regarding the sixties is one of lessons learned and misguided sympathies to be avoided: the development of organized, self-conscious 'solidarity movements', when addressed at all, is used merely to confirm the declension from untarnished idealism circa 1960 to an infatuation with 'picking up the gun' circa 1970.[12]

This book presumes a different vision not only of the Eisenhower-Kennedy years, but of what came after. In general terms, I see the period from the late 1950s through the fall of Nixon as the beginning, and not the end, of struggle across the widest imaginable field of class, race, gender, and empire, a struggle no more resolved in the 1990s than it was in 1972 or 1981. This is, after all, the working assumption of most conservative political strategists, and one that makes evident sense to students whose earliest political memory is of Jimmy Carter. I do not mean to diminish the importance of the multifarous social movements born in the sixties, but merely to point out that the true significance of that era is a great legacy of unresolved social, political and cultural divisions.

In this context, it is worthwhile to examine why so many different radical currents in the US have felt a necessity to stand together across borders with Third World revolutionaries, especially those in the Americas. This book is a beginning, examining the first major instance of this common stand, which is not a point that the New Left arrived at, but rather one of the bases upon which it rests. In a later study, I will examine both the differences and the continuity between the solidarity movement with Central America during the 1980s, the antiwar and 'anti-imperialist' movement circa 1970, and the civil rights and 'fair play for Cuba' movements in 1960.

My working conception is that the many different radicalisms of the past generation are linked together, however disassociated from each other they appear. Like others, I see a great going-out into the world by young white North Americans that 'began in McComb, Mississippi and led to the Mekong Delta', in Todd Gitlin's powerful phrase. But, unlike Gitlin and many others, I do not see this spiritual and physical emigration as climaxing in 1969 or 1971, since with less fanfare it continued unabated into Latin America, extending towards Cuba, the Caribbean and the Southern Cone in the 1970s, and Nicaragua, Guatemala and El Salvador (as well as South Africa) in the 1980s. The root impulse of this journey has been a search by middle-class people 'bred in at least modest comfort', in the famous opening lines of *The Port Huron Statement*, for existential fellowship, for authenticity, for personal meaning and community – for solidarity. Preceding formal politics, it is the desire to overcome the consumption-driven alienation characteristic of late capitalism by reaching 'the people', those who instead of enjoying a culture of abundance must struggle to produce their own subsistence: the poor walled off in ghettos, sharecroppers' shacks and mountain valleys, inside and outside Fortress America.

Characterizing the root impulse of the New Left as a quest for community and fellowship, even describing this as 'solidarity', is hardly unheard of. In his perceptive 1973 intellectual history, *The American Left in the Twentieth Century*, John Diggins summed up the entire experience of Northern students in the civil rights movement in one sentence: 'Their crusade became a "back-to-the-people" movement in which youths could struggle in interracial solidarity to overcome their isolated existence.'[13] In Kirkpatrick Sales's vastly influential *SDS*, published at the same time, this generational move was likened to a similar move 'to the people' by Russian bourgeois youth at the high tide of imperial complacency and reform-from-above.[14] Closer to home, the Abolitionist movement before the Civil War, which led young white Northerners 'of the better sort' to support and officer black regiments in the Civil War, and after the war inspired thousands to go South to teach ex-slaves in Freedmen's Bureau schools, is a comparable phenomenon, as Howard Zinn noted back in 1965 in casting the Student Non-Violent Coordinating Committee as 'the New Abolitionists'. There are also valid comparisons with the settlement house movement of the Progressive Era, which recruited thousands of college-educated native-born youth to live in the tenement neighborhoods created by Southern and Eastern European immigrants, with the Peace Corps, or with SDS's quixotic Economic Research and Action Projects among the Northern poor in 1964–67. Clearly, diverse political and emotional tendencies reveal themselves in these episodes, from clear-eyed support for revolutionary change to bourgeois *noblesse oblige*, from the Social Gospel to social control; the sole overarching continuity is what James Gilbert has called 'a common element of moral perfectionism' rooted in Protestant culture.[15] The reader should keep in mind, however, that analyzing the varied impulses of guilt, altruism, romantic hubris, machismo, raised consciousness and paternalism embedded in struggles for 'Abolition' or 'Fair Play' does not imply an indictment. I find nothing contemptible in the search for solidarity, however fraught that quest may be.

To understand the radicalism of the 1970s and 1980s, therefore, I argue that the 'sixties' should be treated as an open-ended beginning, rather than as a

9

~~finite moment hermetically sealed off from what came before – the so-called Old Left – and what has come since.~~ The recovery of a continuous line of solidarity with Latin America from the late 1950s through the present suggests a new trajectory for our understanding of radicalism in the United States during the Cold War – a change over time in political consciousness that does not fit any simple model of movements rising and falling.

But beyond theories about what does (or does not) tie the Cold War left together, the most damning indictment of the thesis tying the putative suicide of the New Left to its anti-imperialism is the evidence presented here that anti-imperialism and an enthusiastic solidarity were foundational to that New Left. Rediscovering the importance of Fidel Castro and the Cuban revolution to young North Americans at the dawn of the New Frontier not only calls into question our understanding of radicalism in the sixties and after. It calls upon us to consider whether now, after the Cold War, there can be any opening for fundamental change in the United States unless we again consider the necessity of an Open Door for revolutions: can we be for social and political democracy here and not everywhere?

Notes

GENERAL NOTE: The reader will notice the use of the term 'North American' throughout this book to indicate citizens of the United States, following common Latin American practice. While this may be offensive to other peoples and nations also present in North America, it is preferable to simply calling US citizens 'Americans'. Also, while Spanish words and names are properly accented here, I have not added those accents to English texts that did not include them in the original.

1. Thomas G. Paterson, 'Introduction: John F. Kennedy's Quest for Victory and Global Crisis', in Paterson, ed., *Kennedy's Quest for Victory*, New York: Oxford, 1989, p. 8.

2. Williams's note on the inside cover of the second edition of *The Tragedy of American Diplomacy*, New York: Dell, 1962, specifies that it was revised during December 1961, and from the tone throughout it is clear that the Bay of Pigs had a profound effect upon his thinking.

3. See Morris Morley, *Imperial State and Revolution: The United States and Cuba*, Cambridge: Cambridge University Press, 1987, and Jules Benjamin, *The United States and the Origins of the Cuban Revolution: An Empire of Liberty in an Age of National Liberation*, Princeton, N.J.: Princeton University Press, 1990. Although both authors agree that the US decision to embargo arms to Cuba in March 1958 did signify a conscious undercutting of Batista, they have different emphases. Morley refers to 'a minor groundswell of legislative concern' on the issue by some liberal Democrats, while underlining the State Department's deep-rooted hostility to Castro throughout (p. 60). Benjamin attaches greater significance to the tensions in domestic politics, specifying that 'the assault on Washington's Latin America policy came from within', beginning with Adlai Stevenson's raising the antidictatorial banner in the 1956 campaign (p. 137). Abetted by 'a general mood in the North American press', he finds that 'to much of the North American public, the issue was clear. The United States should not be arming an unpopular dictator who was using the weapons against his own people' (pp. 150–51).

Neither author discusses in any detail why Castro appealed so strongly to the US press and public, and how this popularity pressured policymakers. To understand how the US dealt with the Cuban revolution, I suggest we go beyond the parameters of diplomatic history, and factor popular, nonelite politics into the making of foreign policy. One major attempt to do so, with a wealth of data covering ground similar to this book, is Richard E. Welch, Jr's *Response to Revolution:*

10

The United States and the Cuban Revolution, 1959–1961, Chapel Hill, N.C.: University of North Carolina Press, 1985. The latter's periodization and focus differ markedly, however, so that in the end we tell different stories.

4. In current historiography of the New Left, the Cuban revolution and its North American partisans have essentially disappeared. There is no reference to Fair Play for Cuba in James Miller's *Democracy Is in the Streets: From Port Huron to the Siege of Chicago,* New York: Simon & Schuster, 1987, or in Tom Hayden's memoir *Reunion,* New York: Random House, 1988. In Maurice Isserman's *If I Had a Hammer: The Death of the Old Left and the Birth of the New Left,* New York: Basic Books, 1987, which directly addresses this same period, Cuba's effect on both the 'old' and 'new' left is hardly mentioned, and the only FPCC reference is to the Oswald affair. Todd Gitlin's massive *The Sixties: Years of Hope, Days of Rage,* New York: Bantam, 1987, repeats this treatment. The book begins with memories of watching Batista's fall televised on New Year's Eve 1958, and seeing Castro at Harvard a few months later, but Gitlin underlines that this meant little to him personally.

For exceptions to the omission of Cuba in recent accounts of the sixties, see Fredric Jameson's essay, 'Periodizing the 60s', in Sohnya Sayres, Anders Stephanson, Stanley Aronowitz and Fredric Jameson, eds, *The 60s Without Apology,* Minneapolis, Minn.: Univ. of Minnesota Press, 1984, pp. 178–209, which situates the wave of anticolonialism after 1955, from Africa to the US South, as the sixties' true 'beginning'. Regarding Cuba, he remarks that 'for many of us, indeed, the crucial detonator – a new Year 1, the palpable demonstration that revolution was not merely a historical concept and a museum piece but real and achievable – was furnished by a people whose imperialist subjugation had developed among North Americans a sympathy and a sense of fraternity we could never have had for other Third World peoples in their struggle, except in an abstract and intellectual way' (p. 182). The other recent recognition of Castro's role is in John Patrick Diggins's *The Rise and Fall of the American Left,* New York: Norton, 1992: 'Young, bearded, defiant, Castro became the symbol of rebellious young Americans in search of a John Wayne of the Left, a guerrilla who could shoot his way to power and at the same time remain virtuously uncorrupted by the temptations of power' (p. 237).

5. Paul Jacobs and Saul Landau, *The New Radicals: A Report with Documents,* New York: Vintage, 1966, p. 12.

6. Jack Newfield, *A Prophetic Minority,* New York: New American Library, 1966, p. 15. See also Martin Kenner's preface to the first US collection of Fidel Castro's speeches in 1969, which specifies how taking sides with Cuba at a critical moment served to radicalize the incipient New Left: 'Students in the early sixties reacted to two major events: the sit-ins in the American South and the revolution in Cuba. The role of noted liberals like John F. Kennedy, Adlai Stevenson, and Arthur Schlesinger, Jr. in the United States' attempts to crush the revolution, pushed more and more students out of the liberal wing of Democratic politics into protest politics. ...' Martin Kenner and James Petras, eds, *Fidel Castro Speaks,* New York: Grove Press, 1969, p. *ix.*

7. From the Introduction in Ronald Radosh, ed., *The New Cuba: Paradoxes and Potentials,* New York: William Morrow, 1976, p. 9. Paul Lyons's essay, 'The New Left and the Cuban Revolution', effectively demonstrates connections from the New Left's earliest days in 1959 through what he describes as its collapse in 1970. Lyons suggests that the Cuban revolution moved through successively 'humanist', 'populist', 'socialist and anti-imperialist', and finally 'Communist-Leninist' phases that paralleled the evolution of radicals here who repeatedly looked to Cuba for inspiration. His argument is in many respects convincing, though colored by the disillusionment of the early 1970s. Yet even Lyons ignores the grassroots response in this country to Castro's revolution in 1957–58, without which the organized solidarity of 1960–62 appears to have been written on a blank slate.

8. Staughton Lynd, 'Towards a History of the New Left', in Priscilla Long, ed., *The New Left: A Collection of Essays,* Boston: Extending Horizons Books, 1969, p. 3.

9. The otherwise comprehensive *Port Huron Statement* avoids discussion of Cuba almost completely, though in the early 1960s it was one of the most sensitive issues in US politics. SDS leaders were undoubtedly aware of how the Bay of Pigs had torn apart the liberal-left a year before, and given their domestic focus, it is understandable that they did not want to stand or fall on the issue of Castro and Cuba. See *The Port Huron Statement* [Appendix] in Miller, *Democracy Is in the Streets,* p. 349, for a single, critical reference to the Bay of Pigs invasion ('the colonial peoples of the world wondered whether our foreign policy had really changed from its old imperialist ways') and pp. 359–60 for the comment that 'to support dictators like Diem while trying to destroy ones

WHERE THE BOYS ARE

like Castro will only enforce international cynicism about American "principle", and is bound to lead to even more authoritarian revolutions, especially in Latin America where we did not even consider foreign aid until Castro challenged the status quo.'

10. I use the term 'polycentric' to underline my disagreement with histories of the sixties that assign the leading role to a single organization, or to a single area of struggle. In this sense, James O'Brien's early insight that 'at no time during the decade had any organization been able to maintain hegemony over the movement' remains underappreciated (see O'Brien, 'The Development of the New Left', *Annals of the American Academy of Political Science* [May 1971], p. 24). The historian's task does not become, however, the pursuit of decentered spontaneity, always 'from the bottom up', but the illumination of relationships between many different centers of insurgent action, with competing organizational practices and worldviews.

11. Quoted in Peter Novick, 'Historians, "Objectivity", and the Defense of the West', *Radical History Review* 40 (Winter 1988), p. 14.

12. This declension informs most recent studies, including the major books by Gitlin, Miller and Isserman cited earlier. Individually and collectively, these treatments add considerably to our understanding of the period. From Miller, we gain a powerful sense of *The Port Huron Statement*'s complex intellectual roots, and how it became so compelling a manifesto for parts of its generation, as well as the inner life of the original SDS cadre. Isserman brilliantly illuminates the left's history before and after the Communist Party's 1956 crisis, particularly the complexity of 'anti-Stalinist' politics in the 1940s and 1950s. Gitlin's is the most ambitious, as a personal memoir intertwined with the first panoramic view from a later vantage point. However much one might disagree with its emphases, it is the most complete statement regarding what happened and what went wrong.

13. John P. Diggins, *The American Left in the Twentieth Century*, New York: Harcourt Brace Jovanovich, 1973, p. 169.

14. Kirkpatrick Sale, *SDS*, New York: Vintage, 1973, p. 95.

15. James Gilbert, 'New Left: Old America', in Sayres et al., eds, *The 60s Without Apology*, p. 246.

1

The New Empire and the Old Anti-Imperialism

Given the long history of US hemispheric hegemony, with its roots in the Monroe Doctrine and the expansionism of Southern slaveholders, is there a parallel history of domestic opposition to our informal empire in the Americas? No: instead of any institutional continuity, there are disconnected surges of public activism spread through the administrations of Presidents McKinley, Theodore Roosevelt, Taft, Wilson, Harding, Coolidge, Hoover and Franklin Roosevelt. In the era of Truman and Eisenhower, there is an almost total break. The left in the United States, which might have provided connections over time, had its own continuity repeatedly checked. Once the Cold War closed in, almost all sectors of organized liberalism acquiesced to empire, while the old Popular Front left that had allied with that liberalism was no longer in any position to rally a hemispheric front as in the 1930s and 1940s. For all these reasons, we can reasonably conclude that there were no direct political origins for the 'fair play movement' to defend the Cuban revolution in 1960–62, much less for the earlier unorganized popular enthusiasm in the US for Fidel Castro.[1]

There were, however, suppressed precedents and half-forgotten traditions as well as certain personal ties stretching back before the Cold War, and it is the purpose of this chapter to outline them briefly. My emphasis here is two-fold: first, to give some sense of the interval between the world wars, when US liberals and radicals cooperated successfully with each other and their Latin American counterparts in promoting Good Neighborism (if not always anti-imperialism) in the Americas; second, to delineate the birth of the Cold War, when US policy in the Americas and indeed the world found its fitting climax with the cool, professional scuttling of Guatemalan democracy in June 1954. The absence of any effective opposition to that project across the entire spectrum of US liberalism and its smothered leftwing forms the immediate backdrop for the honeymoon between the 26th of July Movement rebels and the North American public, which began less than three years later.

Mexico, Nicaragua and Liberals on the 'American Front'

By the 1920s, North Americans had already lived through a generation symbolized by Teddy Roosevelt's carefully staged ride up San Juan Hill during the 'splendid little war' of 1898, and his subsequent presidential evocation of the Big Stick in the Americas, formalized by the Monroe Doctrine's Roosevelt Corollary pronouncing the right of the US to unilateral intervention in the hemisphere. This open imperialism also provoked considerable opposition. At the turn of the century, old New England Radical Republicans (piquantly characterized by Lenin as 'the last of the Mohicans of bourgeois democracy') led the broadly based Anti-Imperialist League.[2] During the teens labor radicals, Socialists and the Industrial Workers of the World organized major campaigns against US intervention in the Mexican revolution; several groups of Wobblies even abortively tried to join the fight with Emiliano Zapata's peasant forces. Most intriguingly, a coalition of mainstream Protestant denominations actively supported the moderate *carrancista* wing of the revolution through an intensive lobbying effort led by missionary leaders based in Mexico.[3]

After World War I, the United States only grudgingly accepted that Mexico would have a nationalist, anti-imperialist and, for a while, quasi-socialist government. Intervention remained a distinct possibility, as tensions over Mexico's internal and external policies continually surfaced through the next two decades. Counter-revolution had a mass base in the US, as suppression of the Catholic Church aroused intense ire in the North American Church's hierarchy and much of the laity.[4] In these same years, however, the liberal intelligentsia came to a new awareness of imperialism and the variety of it practiced by the United States, thanks to such famous books as Scott Nearing and Joseph Freeman's *Dollar Diplomacy* and Parker Moon's *Imperialism in World Politics*.[5] And, while many writers, artists, academics and journalists of diverse backgrounds went to Europe in the twenties, many others went south. As Irene Rostagno has described it,

> Mexico had become a second Paris, a place one could go to escape the platitudes of American individualism and industrial blight. Paris offered culture and sophistication; Mexico mystery and closeness to 'the origins' ... the opportunity to participate simultaneously in a millenial culture and a progressive revolution.[6]

From new forms of engaged scholarship and journalism, and contacts based on travel, expatriation, and long-existing mission programs, an alliance of church and academic liberals came together in the 1920s to press for a 'genuine pan-Americanism'. They were spurred by the hope that their country would choose a path different from that of the European empires, and their common goal became to explain the Mexican revolution to North Americans, offering understanding and critical support. In many ways they served as fore-

14

runners of Roosevelt's Good Neighbor Policy of the 1930s, which claimed to respect Latin American sovereignty.

Among many well-known figures in this milieu, the most exemplary was Samuel Guy Inman. A brief description of his career as missionary, revolutionary educator, university lecturer, amateur diplomat, author and interlocutor for Latin Americans throughout the first half of the century indicates the scope of liberal solidarity before the Cold War. Born in Texas in 1877, Inman was a lifelong partisan of the Social Gospel, creed of Protestant humanitarianism. He served for ten years as a Disciples of Christ missionary and teacher in Mexico, during which he became a close friend and political ally of General Venustiano Carranza, the eventual victor in the revolution's internal struggles. Inman was the first Secretary of the Committee on Cooperation in Latin America, founded in 1916, which united thirty Protestant mission boards in opposition to US intervention in Mexico. In 1919, he published a major study of the revolution's progress, *Intervention in Mexico,* and gave the first-ever course in the US on inter-American relations, at Columbia University. Over the next decades, Inman wrote numerous influential books calling for a 'spiritual entente' in the hemisphere through government-sponsored cultural exchanges and an end to traditional enmities. Eventually, he was called upon to smooth the way for Secretary of State Cordell Hull at a series of inter-American conferences in the 1930s.[7]

Yet Inman pulled few punches, even while serving in a diplomatic capacity. In the same 1937 book, *Building an Inter-American Neighborhood,* in which he reported on his work as a US delegate to the recent continental conference in Buenos Aires, he showed no hesitation in calling for the 'transformation of a policy of economic imperialism' that had characterized the past forty years of US policy towards Latin America.[8] He and the other anti-imperialist liberals in the Committee on Cultural Relations with Latin America (CCRLA) organized annual 'Seminars in Mexico' from 1925 until at least 1935, bringing together North American academics with important Mexican revolutionary intellectuals and administrators, including Marxists and Communists like Vicente Lombardo Toledano and Diego Rivera.[9] This ecumenicism, as in Inman's description of his own country's imperialism during one seminar as 'this tremendous juggernaut', stands in sharp contrast to the atmosphere of postwar decades, when liberals could not have attended such meetings or expressed such opinions without being branded as – at least – 'fellow-travelers'. It also underscores the breadth of good-neighborliness among those who believed that 'continental solidarity' – often defined in nineteenth-century terms that saw the Monroe Doctrine as a defence of sister republics against Europe – had only recently been corrupted by short-sighted US policies. For Inman and others, Roosevelt's anti-Nazi alliance was the fulfillment of a life's faith, and by 1942 he would declare that 'the unity of the American continent is the hope of the world.'[10]

Before the rise of fascism's global threat, advocating a nonimperialist policy towards the Mexican revolution had already acquired a larger significance. During the 1920s, attitudes towards Mexico were closely linked to the US occupation of Nicaragua, and successive US administrations feared that 'Mexican Bolshevism' would ignite Central America. While liberals like Inman and their allies in Congress supported the quiet rapprochement of Wall Street and Washington with revolutionary Mexico, they also joined in an open fight when a guerrilla war against the US evoked startling domestic sympathies with the Nicaraguans.

The intense involvement of New York banking interests in Nicaragua had led to the occupation of that country by US Marines from 1912 to 1925; effectively it was a North American protectorate for a generation, like Cuba, Haiti, the Dominican Republic and Honduras. The failure of a US-brokered settlement between Nicaragua's traditional factions led to yet another occupation in 1926, but this time something quite unexpected developed. Instead of permitting himself to be bought off, Augusto César Sandino, an officer in the Liberal Party forces opposing the latest US protégé, took to the hills with an Army of National Sovereignty, vowing to expel the Yankees at all costs. To the consternation of the US State Department, Sandino excited a worldwide admiration that infected surprisingly large numbers of North Americans.

Sympathy with the Nicaraguan guerrillas, and disgust at the brazen North American occupation, was hardly confined to the radical fringe. Even before anyone had heard of Sandino, the installation of the unpopular Conservative Adolfo Díaz as president in late 1926, and Coolidge's threats to Mexico because of its support for Díaz's Liberal opponent Juan Sacasa, had caused considerable outrage. Influential groups like the National Council for the Prevention of War and the Federal Council of Churches mobilized; the *New York Times* and Senator William Borah of Idaho, chairman of the Senate Foreign Relations Committee, expressed their opposition; Senator George Norris called the intervention 'a blot on the national honor'; even the Ku Klux Klan and Southern Democrats weighed in because of their sympathy with Mexico's vehement anticlericalism![11]

Coolidge backed down and committed himself to a negotiated solution in Nicaragua and maintaing peace with Mexico. He sent the senior diplomat Henry Stimson to Nicaragua in the spring of 1927 to broker a deal between the rival Liberals and Conservatives that would permit US-managed elections to take place the next year and bring an end to disorder. Meanwhile, a new, purportedly nonpartisan National Guard was quickly trained by Marine officers. Sandino was derided as just one more venal bandit by the North Americans, despite his fierce warnings, an international outcry, and the flow of peasant recruits his cause attracted. Then, on 16 July 1927 the Sandinistas fought a major engagement with the Marines at Ocotal, which included unrestricted bombing and strafing by US planes that killed hundreds of Nicaraguan civilians. The pot boiled over. Governor Edward Dunne of Illinois wrote Coolidge an open letter in which he declared:

> In all of U.S. history there has been no action of such indecency as we now see in Nicaragua. ... The slaughter of 300 Nicaraguans by the Americans is a blot on the United States, and for this reason I request the demotion and punishment of General Feland who ordered the bombardment.[12]

The State Department was outraged by Sandino's 'stealthy and ruthless tactics which characterized the savages who fell upon American settlers in our country 150 years ago', and the Hearst newspapers vilified Sandinista 'atrocities'. A recent scholar notes: 'U.S. intellectuals found Sandino [and] the general public had an unusually strong appetite for news about Sandino, perhaps because he seemed to fit the mold of the heroic individual in a manner not dissimilar to the style of Charles Lindberg.'[13]

In short, one more Latino rebel received his fifteen minutes of fame, in this case as a short-lived cultural icon of the Roaring Twenties, the dashing Latin cavalryman in a clean white shirt with the nerve to take on the US Marines. That he possessed a gift for riveting aphorisms should not be ignored: 'The sovereignty of a free people is not to be discussed; it is to be defended with gun in hand.' Even a Marine first lieutenant in Nicaragua was reported to have said, 'I am an Irishman at the service of the United States, and I say as an Irishman that General Sandino is a patriot. ...'[14]

New generations of radicals, grappling with the complacent, hostile US of the 1920s, took up Sandinismo in this original incarnation. The black press, from Marcus Garvey's *Negro World* to the NAACP's *Crisis*, edited by W. E. B. Du Bois, gave extensive and favorable coverage to the rebels, and Garvey's Universal Negro Improvement Association had a significant pro-Sandino membership on Nicaragua's Caribbean coast.[15] In his *Memoirs*, the longtime Puerto Rican radical Bernardo Vega recalls the eclectic character of US solidarity with Nicaragua in New York City in these years:

> One of the many protests against the invasion was a large rally held on February 19, 1928, at the Labor Temple on 14th Street and Second Avenue. The principal speakers were Scott Nearing, the well-known author of *Dollar Diplomacy*; Leon Ganett, editor of *The Nation*; John Brophy, president of the International Mineworkers' Union [Brophy was actually an opposition leader in the United Mine Workers]; Juan De Jesus, president of the Philippine Club; Ricardo Martinez of the Union Obrera Venelozana; H. C. Wu of the Chinese Writers' Society. ...[16]

The manner in which Sandino became known to ordinary North Americans in his own words, outside of the stock calumnies of the US government and the sensationalism of the yellow press, is worth particular notice here, as does the man who 'found' him. Perhaps the most memorable episode of

North American solidarity in these decades, clearly presaging what would later happen in Cuba, occurred when a young Yankee newsman went into the back country of Central America in 1928 after Sandino had been reported dead, made contact through the rebels' underground in several countries, and finally located the General of Free Men in his remote mountain headquarters, very much alive. The resulting lengthy and sympathetic interviews, serialized in *The Nation*, were an enormous sensation. They made Sandino a much more real and formidable figure than he had been before, and made the interviewer famous in his own right.

That reporter was Carleton Beals, and he was, with Inman, the most representative figure of this era among the North Americans active in Latin America. While the latter participated in an institutional church and academic network, Beals embodied a tradition of intrepid journalism-*cum*-activism that, precisely because it was personal and not institutional, could survive as a memory and a political practice into the Cold War, providing the only relevant example at the outset of the Cuban revolution. Holed up in the Sierra Maestra in January 1957 with all of eighteen men, already declared dead and buried by at least one major US wire service as well as his government opponents, Fidel Castro's most urgent need was a North American journalist; surely he had the famous story of Beals and Sandino in mind when Herbert L. Matthews was smuggled through Batista's patrols.

A short outline is sufficient to indicate the flavor of Beals's life. As a young Berkeley graduate and draft-resister, he joined the many disaffected gringos going south. Settling in Mexico City as the new government was consolidating itself, he witnessed the building of revolutionary power at close quarters. By 1928 he had established himself as a writer on the region's politics, so *The Nation* commissioned his search for Sandino, and Beals's career was made. Though he never repeated such a scoop, from the 1920s through the 1960s, in over two hundred magazine articles and more than two dozen books, he persisted as the most consistent voice on Latin America in US liberal-left circles, and beyond; by 1938, even *Time* cited him as 'the best informed ... living writer on Latin America'.[17]

Given his once-considerable prestige, Beals's florid language and unashamedly gringo outlook seem quaint and ethnocentric from this end of the century. His writing is filled with detailed comments on the torrid heat and smells of railway cars, what he had for breakfast, the swelling bosoms and buttocks of Mexican, Cuban or Guatemalan women and their flashing or downcast black eyes, the greasy hair and corpulent features of soldiers and officials, and so on. His books abound in incidents and dialogue that anticipate the fictionalized extremes of 'new journalism' as practiced in the 1960s, as much Tom Wolfe as John Reed. Here is a typical Beals meditation on 'The Raw Tropics', connecting excessive courtesy, North American profiteering and dead meat:

Life in tropical countries ceases to have dignified significance. Dignity among southern peoples is a protective coloring. A false note invades it; the plumage is too gaudy. Fierceness, brooding, alternating with abandon, rhythm, passion – these are the deeper qualities. Courtesy with us is a normal attitude; with the Latin of the hot countries it is a bright embroidery; it must be exaggerated. ... The pleasure-loving upper classes are quite unconcerned about the misery of those beneath, doubly so because they often represent a different race. Universal lack of sanitation is one of the symptoms. This lack, however, lays its finger of death not only on the lower classes but upon the whole community.

Foreign experts usually mess things up. Salvador, at fantastic cost, borrowed money from American bankers that Americans might at a fantastic price pave the streets of the capital, where much dust carried germs. The result is an American customs collector and other meddling humiliations. ...

In contrast to her smart paved streets, San Salvador has a *rastro*, or slaughter house, which is a foul blot on mankind. It emits a frightful stench; streams of blood and patches of flesh rot everywhere; even the fence posts are daubed up. Women come out with fresh meat dangling over their shoulders or carrying it in baskets on their heads, the red juice running down over their heads and faces. The meat is exposed to all the germs of the air. Buzzards swarm.[18]

Interspersed with these picturesque interludes, however, Beals also captured the minutiae of poverty, political oppression and the imperial hand in terse, almost cinematic prose. His *The Crime of Cuba* (1933), with a grim photo essay by Walker Evans, dramatized the terror of Gerardo Machado's regime and US complicity at the very moment of a popular uprising; it was cited for decades. He communicated not contempt but admiration for Latin Americans who were trying to remake their countries, and targetted with unforgiving precision the mercenary, vulgar North Americans he found everywhere looking for an easy dollar. After 1945, opposition to empire often amounted to no more than this: speaking out on behalf of those who were different. During the Cold War years, Beals was almost the only writer of repute outside the quarantined left who refused to bow to the new anti-Communist orthodoxy and still asserted the traditional anti-imperialism, though his readership shrank to journals like *The Christian Century*, *The Progressive* and *The Nation*. He was thus the obvious choice as honorary co-chairman of the Fair Play for Cuba Committee, along with Waldo Frank.

Communists as 'Good Neighbors' on the Popular Front

Besides the activities of liberals like Inman and uncategorizable radicals like Beals, the Depression and World War II years were the heyday of the Communist Party USA and the larger Popular Front left within which it moved. The connection of North American Communists to Latin America (and Latinos living here), and the contradictory relationship between anti-imperialism and antifascism in the Americas, require some attention.

From 1930 on, the CPUSA dominated left-wing politics in the US. By the end of the decade it had built a small but well-organized mass base, with a membership of 100,000 and an active periphery five or perhaps even ten times greater. New York was the heart of Communist strength, where it elected party members to the City Council and was a visible organization with tens of thousands of supporters concentrated in neighborhoods like Harlem, the Lower East Side and sections of Brooklyn and the Bronx. New York also retained its centrality as the hemisphere's most important city, a gathering place for the left as well as business executives and bankers.

The CP's role in supporting Sandino plus its active solidarity with Cubans rebelling against Machado, revived militant internationalism within the Latino colony in the United States and raised the credibility of the then-vehemently anti-imperialist US party.[19] Radicals among the expatriate Spanish-speaking community in New York were attracted to the openly multiracial and multinational Communists. Close relationships developed between Puerto Rican and Cuban members of the CPUSA and their countrymen and women who led parties in the Caribbean.[20] Top leaders like Juan Marinello, the Cuban writer and first Communist government minister in the Americas (under Batista in 1940), and Francisco Colon Gordiany, president of Puerto Rico's General Workers Confederation, spoke at major rallies in New York.[21] Often these prominent Latin Americans shared the stage with East Harlem Congressman Vito Marcantonio of the American Labor Party. The latter was for many years the left's most eloquent tribune in Washington, until finally defeated by the combined forces of the Democratic, Republican and Liberal parties in 1950. Among his many battles, 'Marc' led a losing fight to grant independence to Puerto Rico from the thirties on, and defended Puerto Rican rights on the mainland throughout his career. As a consequence, for years 'not an electoral campaign went by which failed to raise the ridiculous charge that thousands ... were being shipped in from Puerto Rico to cast their votes for Marcantonio.'[22]

The relationship of the CPUSA to its Latin American sister-parties in these years is still obscure. Hemispheric activities were coordinated at various times from New York – for example, through the Socorro Rojo Internacional (SRI), a legal aid and propaganda organization that sent advice, literature and small stipends to parties in various Latin American countries.[23] After the declaration of a United Front Against War and Fascism at the Communist International's Seventh Congress in 1935, CPUSA General Secretary Earl Browder acted as a hemispheric 'adviser'.[24]

Most important, from 1935 to 1945, Browder's party was linked in the US to a considerably larger and ideologically looser Popular Front left that shaded into mainstream liberalism, and under his guidance similar developments took place throughout the hemisphere (with the intense sympathy felt for the

Spanish Republic serving as a common bond, one kept alive by the refugee diaspora after 1939 throughout the Americas). In effect, the New Deal was Latin Americanized, and following the US lead, all the American Popular Fronts became part of a even more powerful political coalition after 1941, though hardly 'left' in any possible construction of the word, when the US and the Soviet Union allied against the Axis Powers during World War II. What Browder dubbed the Democratic Front flourished, and most leftists became the staunchest supporters of the Allied war effort and of their own governments if the latter cooperated. Batista, Somoza and Trujillo, dictators who all received Communist support at least briefly, did not resemble FDR. However, this policy of alliances allowed very heterodox groups of liberals, trade unionists and radicals in many countries to cooperate in supporting democratization, antifascism, friendship with the Soviet Union and the official US Good Neighbor policy.[25] For that brief but still controversial period, none of these political aims appeared contradictory, because they were all tied together by the glue of antifascist unity. Anti-imperialism took a back seat, and was even repudiated in favor of a 'way to freedom through an alliance with the United States in this war that threatens the whole continent and the democratic ideals of the New World.'[26] In this context, the phrase 'inter-American solidarity' was widely used by both the government and the left, with highly ambiguous connotations.

The ambiguous reach of the all-American Popular Front is demonstrated by the US organization set up to facilitate its efforts. In late 1938, an impressive array of middle-class liberals and New Dealers, with covert CP backing, convened a Conference on Pan-American Democracy to popularize 'cooperation for democracy' against the Nazis' efforts to promote fascism throughout the hemisphere.[27] The long list of sponsors of this conference, which created a permanent Council for Pan-American Democracy (CPAD), included a most impressive range of names: Sidney Hillman, Bennett Cerf, Paul Douglas, John Haynes Holmes, A. Philip Randolph, Roy Wilkins, Upton Sinclair and George Soule; its 'Good Neighbor Dinner' was chaired by Assistant Attorney General Thurman Arnold, one of FDR's key advisors, with Senator-elect James Mead as the keynoter.[28]

In practice, and not surprisingly, those who actually maintained the CPAD were less well-known and rather further to the left.[29] But, despite the twists and turns of international politics, with renewed anti-war activity and anti-imperialism during the Soviet detente with Hitler in 1939–41 rapidly succeeded by pro-US and pro-war exhortations when the USSR was invaded, the CPAD continued to attract prominent academics like the anthropologists Ruth Benedict and Franz Boas, both of whom served as officers, and cultural figures such as Fredric March and Lewis Mumford.[30] Its delegations, diplomatic receptions, banquets, theater benefits, art exhibits and public appeals to break with Franco, commute the sentence of the Puerto Rican Nationalist leader Pedro Albizu Campos, and pressure Trujillo, Vargas, Perón and other dictators to free their political prisoners received serious attention from both the press and policymakers. A sense of real cultural shock is still evoked by the *New York Times*'s respectful coverage of a 1943 'Night of the Americas' ('Linked by Nature and Welded Together by a Common Will to Victory'), held at the Martin Beck Theatre on Broadway, where Lombardo Toledano and the great Communist poet Pablo Neruda, who was then Chile's consul-general in Mexico, were greeted by stars of stage and screen.[31] Like so much else, this civil treatment ended abruptly once the war was over. Soon, the CPAD was placed on the US Attorney General's new list of subversive organizations and the organization promptly disappeared, one more small and obscure 'Communist front'.[32] In its time, though, this front reached far beyond the Communist Party and other radicals, and in doing so it exposed both the benefits and limits of a Popular Front approach to solidarity in the Americas.

Cold War Liberals and 'Democratic Solidarity'

Things changed. After World War II, the antifascist front in the Americas vanished, leaving hardly a trace. An anti-Communist apparatus arose to take its place, including a self-proclaimed 'Democratic Left' of liberals, business unionists and conservative socialists who organized outwards from the US throughout the hemisphere to oppose 'threats of totalitarianism both from the right and from the left'.[33] The postwar change in political climate was so complete that support for the CIA's 1954 coup against Guatemala's bourgeois-radical government was nearly unanimous. Among the supporters of this application of John Foster Dulles's dream of rolling back the Reds were liberals like the ex–New Deal 'brain truster' Adolf A. Berle, Jr; trade unionists like AFL President George Meany; and social democrats like *New Leader* editor Daniel James, author of the authoritative treatment of how Guatemala was saved, *Red Design for the Americas*, which proclaimed apocalyptically that 'the battle for the Western Hemisphere has begun.'[34]

A half-century later, it is easy to see that the New Deal and war-time alliance of liberals and radicals was not destined for long life. Its unity was mile-wide as 1945 dawned, but fragile enough to begin shattering once FDR died and a mushroom cloud appeared over Hiroshima. The United States was the pre-eminent world power at war's end, with only the Soviet Union as a potential rival. For a brief time, many people, from Earl Browder to 'one-worlder' Republican Wendell Willkie, believed that the mutual understanding of the Teheran and Yalta conferences among Stalin, Roosevelt and Churchill should be preserved, allowing a democratic capitalism and a pragmatic socialism to cooperate to achieve economic prosperity and world peace. The only alternative seemed to be another world war, as posed by Browder's old nemesis and successor in 1945 as CPUSA leader, the hard-bitten William Z. Foster. Eventually, a minority of Roosevelt Democrats left their party to back former Vice President Henry Wallace for president in 1948. They believed that peace with the Soviet Union was absolutely necessary, in the face of the Marshall Plan and President Truman's enunciation of a bipartisan doctrine of worldwide 'containment'. In confusion, the CP also backed Wallace, despite its leadership's certainty that war with the Soviet Union was imminent. Neither of these sections of the old Popular Front could imagine the duration of what John F. Kennedy later dubbed 'the long twilight struggle'. They assumed that, one way or another, the struggle between the Soviet Union and the US would be played out in direct confrontations. While wars of national liberation in the developing world were important, the question of peace between the superpowers was the transcendent issue. Few on the left in this country contemplated that revolution and counter-revolution in the Third World would soon set the pace of history.

Far more prescient were the architects of the new Cold War liberalism. Although corporate interests, Southern Democrats and Republicans all supported Truman's 'get tough' policy, it was card-carrying New Dealers who made a new liberal creed the cutting edge of anti-Communism, including Eleanor Roosevelt herself, the various husks of the old Socialist Party, CIO leaders such as President Philip Murray, and AFL craft unionists. Not only did this new political force quickly recognize the domestic exigencies of the Cold War, it also saw that in this war, every corner of the world was a potential arena. In the end, anti-Communist liberalism proved to be genuinely internationalist in a way that the Henry Wallace Progressives, including the Communists, were not.

Two years after Wallace's ignominious showing in the polls, within months of the outbreak of the Korean War and Joe McCarthy's famous speech in Wheeling, West Virginia, during which he waved a list of 'known Communists' in the State Department, US trade unionists and liberals moved to forge a Grand Alliance in the Western Hemisphere. They hoped to steal a march on the Communists, simultaneously isolating the latter and defeating the numerous military dictatorships that refused to distinguish between Red and anti-Red opponents.[35] On 12–15 May 1950, academics, legislators and exiles from fifteen countries gathered in Havana to form the Inter-American Association for Democracy and Freedom (IADF). The US delegation included four US congressmen; the AFL's Latin America Representative Serafino Romualdi; Ernst Schwarz, secretary of the CIO's Latin America Committee; and leading anti-Communists like Norman Thomas of the Socialist Party, Roger Baldwin of the American Civil Liberties Union, the historian Arthur Schlesinger, Jr, Clarence Senior of the League for Industrial Democracy, James Loeb of the Americans for Democratic Action, and the NAACP's Walter White.[36] Resolving to 'demonstrate inter-American democratic solidarity against every form of totalitarianism', they planned a continental headquarters in Uruguay and a federation of national committees.[37] However, the only organization that ever functioned was the North American Committee, run from New York by Frances Grant, secretary-general and motivating spirit of the IADF for the entire thirty years of its life.

Over the next decade the IADF functioned as a much-needed solidarity organization for liberal and socialist (but anti-Communist) refugees. These were the years in which Trujillo in the Dominican Republic and the Somozas in Nicaragua were joined by new *caudillos* like Generals Marcos Pérez Jiménez in Venezuela, Rojas Pinilla in Colombia, and Manuel Odría in Peru, as well as the peripatetic Cuban Fulgencio Batista, who seized power again in 1952. For a host of once-and-future leaders, from the Bolivian Victor Paz Estenssorro to the champions of anti-Communist social democracy in Latin America, José 'Pepe' Figueres of Costa Rica and Rómulo Betancourt of Venezuela, Frances Grant was 'kind of a Red Cross'.[38] Around such men, often harassed by US officials bent on cooperation with authoritarian governments, the IADF's small, well-connected world of diplomatic intrigue steadily functioned: private briefings with sympathetic journalists, testimonial dinners and press conferences, letters to the *Times*, lobbying at the UN and the State Department, reports from new exiles on conditions at home, a regular bulletin called *Hemispherica*, even attempts to meet with Eisenhower.[39] In sum, the IADF constituted the domestic voice for a hemispheric loyal opposition, agitating against misguided US support for despotism that played into the hands of Communists or anti-US radicals. They were right, of course, as the past forty years have shown, but in unintended ways the IADF also anticipated the growth of a liberal anti-interventionism that would later reject the logic of empire. This precursive role sprang from the contradictions built into the IADF's politics. However 'antitotalitarian', in the fifties it naturally focused on those regimes that were persecuting its members and friends. When the US fulsomely praised the dictatorships as Good Neighbors, the IADF effectively displayed the dark side of *realpolitik* as a foreign policy. Its legacy became not a more effective version of reformist anti-Communism, but the less complicated message that tyrants are unworthy of US support.

The Left Implodes

In contrast with a dynamic Cold War liberalism, the old radical-liberal coalition disintegrated after its last gasp with the 1948 Wallace campaign. Over the next two years, the structures of the left collapsed as the Progressive Party fell apart, the CIO expelled eleven left-led international unions, and the Communist leadership was convicted of conspiracy to advocate the overthrow of the government of the United States. The CP sent hundreds of its best cadres into a disastrous underground in 1951–56, preparing for clandestine struggles against the Fascist Leviathan they believed to be just around the corner, while deliberately excluding thousands of ordinary members. Any organization or institution that resisted the anti-Communist imperatives of foreign and domestic policy was proscribed, whether or not party members were involved. A few kept going, but the political and personal costs were enough to keep them small and limited in effectiveness. While the left was being efficiently quarantined, it responded by dispersing itself, and 'became more and more an undefined ghetto' of a low-key liberalism on the one hand, and the private vision of worldwide class struggle on the other.[40] That Communists and their one-time allies played both of these hands, simultaneously submerged in and far outside what they called the 'mainstream', only made the time more confusing for all who had once collaborated to build a New Deal for America and a better world.

No politically active person in the decade after 1945 could ignore the demands for independence and armed rebellions in the chain of European possessions stretching across Africa and Asia. But against the bloody epic of Indian independence, the Chinese revolution, the Mau Mau rising in Kenya, the mass Defiance Campaign in South Africa, and French defeat at Dienbienphu, Latin America dwindled to near invisibility. The 'Afro-Asian' anticolonial upsurge, signaled by the emergence of the nonaligned nations at the 1955 Bandung Conference in Indonesia, was applauded; neocolonialism in this hemisphere remained obscure. Most North Americans found the endless succession of coups and so-called 'revolutions' to the south incomprehensible and ludicrous, and those who once agreed that Latin America was the foundation of the US empire forgot that fact in the glare of hot and cold global wars. Until the Cuban revolution, the whole region seemed to be a seedy backwater, not only in the North American popular imagination, but among the political classes on the right, the center and the collapsed left.

In this context, only a few Communists and like-minded anti-imperialists continued to speak out regularly on Latin American affairs; it may be that they alone had the personal or interparty relationships to present a cohesive viewpoint based on actual facts. A few examples illustrate the trend towards ignoring the region, and the exceptions. In its first three years of existence, the *National Guardian,* the expression of surviving Progressive Party left-liberalism with the largest circulation of any radical paper, hardly mentioned Latin America.[41] In 1951 Elmer Bendiner, an associate editor close to the CP, took on the hemisphere as a permanent beat. His first article, on 21 November 1951, denounced the lack of interest in Latin America among US progressives and called for solidarity, declaring, 'It's Time for Americans to Learn About the Americas', and from then on he covered the region first-hand, and was sometimes jailed for his pains.[42] Similarly, *Monthly Review,* the important 'independent socialist magazine' founded in 1949, gave almost no space to the

Americas in its first years, though it later played a central role in publicizing Third World revolutionary strategies.[43] These were, after all, the years of the trial and execution of Julius and Ethel Rosenberg, and when the CP announced that it was 'five minutes to midnight', many on the left agreed. Perhaps understandably, they had little time for struggles in the 'banana republics'.

Given the political atmosphere at the time, it is especially surprising that a small group sympathetic to the CP managed to found a Latin American Research Bureau in 1950 in New York, and after several years of publishing a mimeographed newsletter, *Latin American Facts*, graduated to a printed bulletin, *Latin America Today* in March 1953. Betty Millard, an experienced writer with the defunct *New Masses* who had spent years working in Europe with the Women's International Democratic Federation, became editor. From then on, *Latin America Today* cut an impressive path in nuanced frontline reporting on diplomatic conferences, hidden repression and political change, as well as exposure of US business interests and presentation of analyses by Latin Americans themselves, anticipating the North American Congress on Latin America of the late sixties. (The Aesopian language required at that time can be seen, though, in its self-description as 'the only liberal publication in the world dealing solely with the problems of Latin America and inter-American relations'!)[44]

It is notable that during the 'scoundrel time' of the mid-fifties, in the left's memory a period of foglike conformity and pervasive repression, *Latin America Today* not only survived but advanced. Perhaps its experience parallels that of the Civil Rights Congress and other black-led organizations in these years, which had a clear and present wrong to right and thus were less easy to dispose of. It could not have hurt that *Latin America Today* usually inveighed against the same dictators and the same policy of appeasement as the liberals of the IADF, however little their paths crossed otherwise. Unfortunately, it succumbed to exhaustion at the end of 1956 just as a series of dramatic events — the Twentieth Congress of the Communist Party of the Soviet Union, where Khrushchev denounced Stalin as a criminal, the national-Communist uprisings in Poland and Hungary, and the Soviet invasion of the latter — catalyzed a new era internationally, forcing radical rethinking within US radicalism.

The Siege of Guatemala

Before the Cuban revolution, North Americans woke up only once to the potential for trouble in Latin America. And that instance — Guatemala, 1954 — was as blatant a case of conspiratorial manipulation as has occurred in US history. Aroused by the threat of mild land reform, the United Fruit Company, in the habit of operating as a government throughout Central America, sent into action a corps of lobbyists and publicists to poison the reputation of Guatemala's quite limited democratic reforms. From 1950 on, respectable newspapers, moderate congressmen and reputable Latin Americanists studied in great depth the 'problem' of Communist infiltration in the government of President Jacobo Arbenz. In the eighteen months before Colonel Carlos Castillo Armas's pathetic Liberation Army crossed into Guatemala on 18 June 1954, a siege mentality was induced in the US: no other image but that of a fortress under fire conveys the tone of defensive lines barely holding. Arbenz's government was a 'beachhead of international communism', declared Spruille Braden, spokesman for United Fruit and former assistant secretary of state for Inter-American Affairs, in early 1953. By that fall *Life* and *U.S. News & World Report* were discussing 'The Red Outpost in Central America', and posing the question of the Caribbean as 'A Communist Lake?' In December, the National Planning Association, a purportedly nonpolitical think-tank, issued a report suggesting that 'the Communists are so deeply entrenched that it may no longer be possible to eliminate them by peaceful means', while Assistant Secretary of State John Moors Cabot referred to Guatamala as a 'center of infection'. In January, the new US ambassador, John Peurifoy, told *Time* that the US might be compelled 'to take some measures. ... We cannot permit a Soviet Republic to be established between Texas and the Panama Canal', and Alexander Wiley, chairman of the Senate Foreign Relations Committee, called Guatemala a 'dangerous bridgehead of international communism in this hemisphere'.[45]

Rather than exposing the exaggerations of Communist influence in Guatemala, the role of United Fruit, or the climate of fear induced by CIA disinformation, the liberal and social democratic networks played a central role in this campaign of defamation and disinformation, as United Fruit's brilliant publicist, Edward Bernays, had intended from the first. Notable in this regard were Daniel James and *The New Leader*: United Fruit heavily subsidized the journal, and James's denunciations of Arbenz appeared in due course, making 'a vivid impression on the US liberal community'; a CIA-funded publisher published James's book, which was widely distributed to the press.[46] Meanwhile, Robert Alexander, a leader of the IADF, worked with the State Department to have the American Federation of Labor publicly denounce 'the growing influence of the Communist elements in Guatemala'.[47]

Given this torrent of abuse from the main forces of organized liberalism and labor, hardly any mainstream voices had the stomach to denounce the calumniation of Arbenz's government before the invasion, or to protest its rapid denouement in which Ambassador Peurifoy, backed up by CIA bombing raids, pressured the Guatemalan army to depose Arbenz. Samuel Guy Inman's closely reasoned and amply supported 1951 pamphlet, *A New Day in Guatemala*, arguing that the New Deal–style government was firmly in the camp of the West, made the most explicit comparison with the earlier clamor for intervention in Mexico, but Inman's time had passed, and none of his old allies answered the call.[48] The IADF, ostensibly set up to protect elected governments against external subversion, simply wavered for several years. Finally, in early 1954, a headline in *Hemispherica* declared that 'Guatemala Betrays Itself', and after Arbenz's fall, these partisans against dictatorship could only bring themselves to say that the US-sponsored invasion was 'a confession of hemispheric failure' in which 'democracy lost by default'. At no point did the IADF condemn the coup or the ensuing repression. By early 1955, *Hemispherica* would refer to Castillo Armas's takeover as a 'revolution' against a 'communist-infiltrated regime', and in Frances Grant's résumé of a decade's worth of activism at the 1960 conference, the events of 1954 in Guatemala simply disappeared. Indeed, at the IADF's annual banquet in 1958, at which Adolf A. Berle, Jr was the honoree, Guatemala's ambassador to the United Nations presented the award.[49]

Futilely, the remnants of the Popular Front left declared Guatemala 'A Second Spain' and 'Guatemala's 1776'. In a question that was unfortunately revealing, the National Committee of the CPUSA asked, 'Will the American people stand aside and permit the Hessian hands of our ruling class to drown in blood the young democratic republic of Guatemala?' and *The Nation* suggested that the 'town bully attitude' of the US 'hardly differ[ed] from the attitude of Russia toward one of its lesser satellites.'[50] Only in New York was any action beyond journalistic appeals reported. In March 1954 a Provisional Committee on Latin-American Affairs held an indoor rally of over a thousand people, with Bendiner, Paul Robeson and a few other progressive luminaries. In late June, as the United Nations debated Guatemala's appeals for an internationally supervised cease-fire, the American Peace Crusade (which, the *Times* noted, 'is cited on the Attorney General's list of subversive organizations') organized a large picket outside; in San Francisco someone painted 'Viva Guatemala!' on City Hall.[51] Alone within labor and foreshadowing his union's break with the AFL-CIO mainstream during the Vietnam War, United Auto Workers' Secretary-Treasurer Emil Mazey spoke out against the intervention as it took place, calling for a new US policy in Latin America.[52]

Guatemala represented perhaps the highest point of North American triumphalism in the postwar era, and was celebrated far beyond the terms required by US national interest. In late 1955, as bloody reaction reigned, Castillo Armas was welcomed in the US as a conquering hero and honored with a ticker-tape parade, a medal and a Waldorf-Astoria banquet on his forty-first birthday by New York's liberal mayor, Robert Wagner; he also received an honorary degree from Columbia University and special praise from Francis Cardinal Spellman, the most powerful Catholic prelate in the US.[53] After 'rejoicing' (his own words) over Arbenz's fall, the AFL's Romualdi spent months in Guatemala, hoping to rebuild a 'free' trade union movement, until he finally tacitly admitted that the new ancien régime had no interest in unions of any sort.[54] Only the CIO, after endorsing the original intervention, denounced the mass repression of all trade unionists.[55] A world-weary tone permeated the left's post-mortems on Guatemala. Irving Howe, editor of the new *Dissent,* who personified high-minded socialist melancholia, bemoaned the absence of an anti-Communist left outside 'the West' that the US could disinterestedly aid; Howe saw Guatemala as 'a classical example of how *not* to fight Stalinism.'[56] Meanwhile, a small letter-writing campaign was waged by *Latin America Today* to save captured cadres of the Partido Guatemalteco de Trabajo, as the CP there was known, from the firing squad.[57]

Amid a general pillorying of Reds, the events of 1954 in Guatemala served as one more housecleaning, like Joe McCarthy visiting a factory town where the United Electrical Workers hung on to a local, or adding another organization to the Attorney General's list. In most ways, the farcical 'revolution' meant nothing to North Americans. Guatemala was just a spot on the map where, assisting freedom, the US had triumphed over the International Communist Conspiracy. The ensuing decades in Guatemala itself have seen a terrible, drawn-out slaughter to stamp out any dissent, though armed rebellion has persisted. In the wider world, the heritage of this intervention was twofold. It provided the US with a permanent model for counter-revolution and counter-insurgency. But Latin Americans (including an obscure Argentine doctor then living in Guatemala named Guevara) also learned a hard lesson in the meaning of national sovereignty. Ultimately, the question of who had profited most from the example of Guatemala was settled in Cuba, at the Bay of Pigs.[58]

Notes

1. The one major exception to the discontinuity in North American anti-imperialism is the role of the US as the traditional rearguard for hemispheric exiles of every stripe. In this respect, political links reach back before the Civil War, especially between New York and the Caribbean. The Cuban-American connection was particularly strong and very important to the anti-Batista revolutionaries of the 1950s; see Chapter 3.

2. V. I. Lenin, *Imperialism, the Highest Stage of Capitalism,* New York: International Publishers, 1939, p. 111. The League's understanding of the nation's future direction is captured in this statement by its president, former Senator and Abolitionist George Boutwell: 'The republicanism of our fathers is assailed by the doctrines of imperialism as they were maintained by George III', from Boutwell, *In the Name of Liberty* [pamphlet], 15 August 1899, reprinted in Philip S. Foner and Richard C. Winchester, eds, *The Anti-Imperialist Reader: A Documentary History of Anti-Imperialism in the United States,* vol. 1, *From the Mexican War to the Election of 1900,* New York: Holmes & Meier, 1984, p. 298.

3. See Deborah J. Baldwin, *Protestants and the Mexican Revolution: Missionaries, Ministers and Social Change,* Urbana, Ill.: University of Illinois Press, 1990.

4. A vivid example of this clerical outrage is Bishop Francis X. Kelley's *Blood-Drenched Altars,* Milwaukee, Wis.: Bruce Publishing Co., 1935. In this 500-page diatribe covering all of Mexican history from the perspective of the Counter-Reformation, Kelley devotes one chapter to denouncing the 'American Front' of venal bankers and diplomats hoping to swallow Mexico whole, Masons, 'parlor pinks', bought journalists, Samuel Gompers, and especially 'Liberals' and Protestants like Carleton Beals, Samuel Inman, Hubert Herring and Ernest Gruening – all described below.

5. Scott Nearing and Joseph Freeman, *Dollar Diplomacy,* New York: B. W. Huebsch and the

Viking Press, 1925; Parker Moon, *Imperialism and World Politics*, New York: Macmillan, 1926. Many of these books were published by the Vanguard Press from 1926 to 1936 as 'Studies in American Imperialism', a series funded by the American Fund for Public Service (see the editor's introduction by Harry Elmer Barnes to Leland Jenks, *Our Cuban Colony*, New York: Vanguard, 1928, p. *xii*).

6. Irene Rostagno, 'Fifty Years of Looking South: The Promotion and Recognition of Latin American Literature in the United States' (Ph.D. dissertation, University of Texas at Austin, 1984), p. 20. Among the writers who went to Mexico, Rostagno lists Jack London, John Reed, Anita Brenner, Katherine Anne Porter, Hart Crane, Lincoln Steffens, D. H. Lawrence (via the US), and Waldo Frank, for decades the best-known exponent of Latin American literature in the US, who played a crucial role in legitimizing the Fair Play for Cuba Committee.

7. The editor's preface by Harold Eugene Davis to Inman's last, posthumous book, *Inter-American Conferences*, Washington, D.C.: University Press of Washington, D.C. & the Community College Press, 1965, includes a short biography. Inman's other works include *Problems in Pan-Americanism*, New York: George H. Doran Co., 1921; *Ventures in Inter-American Friendship*, New York: Missionary Education Movement of the United States and Canada, 1925; and *Latin America: Its Place in World Life*, New York: Harcourt, Brace, 1942. See also Baldwin, *Protestants and the Mexican Revolution*, pp. 70, 122–4, 131–2, 140–49, 162–5 for a detailed account of the lobbying campaign, the significance of the Social Gospel in missionary work, and the role of Inman and others as emissaries of a particular vision of the Mexican revolution.

8. Samuel Guy Inman, *Building an Inter-American Neighborhood*, New York: National Peace Conference, 1937, p. 13. Exactly what meaning Inman and liberals like him attached to terms like 'economic imperialism' requires further examination – certainly he was not here referring to Lenin's thesis that imperialism is the highest stage of capitalism, leading, ineluctably, to socialist revolution.

9. Two books were published from these seminars, *The Genius of Mexico*, New York: CCRLA, 1931, edited by Hubert Herring and Katherine Terrill; and *Renascent Mexico*, New York: CCRLA, 1935, edited by Herring and Herbert Weinstock. The two volumes include notable North American scholars, like Robert Redfield, Frank Tannenbaum, Mary Austin and Ernest Gruening, who later as a US senator cast one of two votes against the Tonkin Gulf Resolution in 1964.

10. Inman, *Latin America: Its Place in World Life*, p. 18.

11. Quoted in Neill Macaulay, *The Sandino Affair*, Chicago: Quadrangle Books, 1967, p. 31. See also Bryce Wood, *The Making of the Good Neighbor Policy*, New York: Columbia University Press, 1961, pp. 17–22; Gregorio Selser, *Sandino*, New York: Monthly Review Press, 1981, pp. 51–61; and Robert Freeman Smith, *The United States and Revolutionary Nationalism in Mexico, 1916–1932*, Chicago: University of Chicago Press, 1972, pp. 238–40. Smith notes the enmity of US diplomats towards Inman, Tannenbaum and others of the CCRLA. Borah and Norris were among the congressional leaders of that Western and Midwestern anti-imperialism later stigmatized as 'isolationism'.

12. Quoted in Selser, p. 81.

13. Quoted in Wood, p. 35; John A. Britton, *Carleton Beals: A Radical Journalist in Latin America*, Albuquerque, N.M.: University of New Mexico Press, 1987, p. 69. See also Macaulay, p. 84.

14. Selser, *Sandino*, p. 83; Macaulay, *The Sandino Affair*, p. 145.

15. Ted Vincent, 'Sandino's Aid from the Black American Press', *Black Scholar* (May/June 1985), pp. 36–42.

16. *Memoirs of Bernardo Vega*, New York: Monthly Review Press, 1984, p. 153.

17. Quoted in Britton, *Carleton Beals*, p. 123. The reader should note that Beals was hardly the only representative of the reporter-activist type. He was preceded by John Reed and, even earlier, John Kenneth Turner, who wrote *Barbarous Mexico* in 1911 as part of Mother Jones's campaign to free the Flores Magón brothers, Mexican anarchist leaders imprisoned in the US. Over the following four decades, there were probably hundreds of political travelogues and potboilers on Mexico. Other prominent 'internationalist' journalists include Edgar Snow, Anna Louise Strong, Agnes Smedley, Harvey O'Connor and, as an apotheosis, Ernest Hemingway.

18. Carleton Beals, *Banana Gold*, Philadelphia: J. B. Lippincott, 1932, pp. 102–3.

19. Nicaragua had been especially important to the first wave of Marxist-Leninist organizing in the Americas. Latin America remained a low priority in the worldwide strategy of the Communist International (CI) until 1928. As a consequence, in most of the hemisphere only tiny parties

formed during the twenties; their development was unsystematic and received little support. The first collective act of these clandestine grouplets was to found the All-American Anti-Imperialist League (AA-AIL) as a continental organization in 1924. The league had affiliates from Argentina to the US and a newspaper in Mexico City, *El Libertador*, edited by Diego Rivera. Its main focus was organizing militant solidarity with Sandino, until the CI broke with him in 1929. In the United States it raised money for medical aid to the guerrillas, held protests, and worked closely with Sandino's brother Socrates, a carpenter who lived in Brooklyn; see Socrates Sandino, 'My Brother, Gen. Sandino', *New Masses* (July 1928), p. 4. Thanks to Randy Slotkin for this information.

20. New York was, of course, not the sole center for North and Latin American solidarity within the CPUSA's orbit. The Party also had a significant presence among Chicano and Mexicano workers in the Southwest. See Vicki Ruíz, *Cannery Women, Cannery Lives: Mexican Women, Unionization, and the California Food Processing Industry, 1930–1950*, Albuquerque, N.M.: University of New Mexico Press, 1987.

21. Besides Vega's autobiography, the other readily available source for New York's Latin American left is Jésus Colon's *A Puerto Rican in New York and Other Sketches*, New York: Mainstream, 1961, drawn from the column that Colon wrote for the *Daily Worker* after 1955. Before that, he headed thirty Spanish-speaking lodges of the International Workers Order.

22. Vega, p. 186. One whole section (pages 374–439) of the commemorative collection of Marcantonio's congressional speeches, debates and writings, *I Vote My Conscience*, New York: The Vito Marcantonio Memorial, 1956, documents his speaking out on behalf of 'the most exploited victims of a most devastating imperialism' in Puerto Rico (from a speech, US House of Representatives, 11 May 1939 in *I Vote My Conscience*, p. 374). See also Gerald Meyer's *Vito Marcantonio: Radical Politician, 1902–1954*, Albany, N.Y.: State University of New York Press, 1989, on Marcantonio's appeal to the cultural pride of despised peoples, including El Barrio.

23. The Salvadoran Communist leader, Agustín Farabundo Marti, worked in the New York offices of the SRI and the All-American Anti-Imperialist League in 1928, before returning to head the former's Salvadoran section and plan the famous insurrection of 1932: see Thomas P. Anderson, *Matanza: El Salvador's Communist Revolt of 1932*, Lincoln, Neb.: University of Nebraska Press, 1971, pp. 25–6, 37, 65.

24. Robert Alexander, *Communism in Latin America*, New Brunswick, N.J.: Rutgers University Press, 1957, p. 38. The best-known incident occurred in 1937, when the Mexican Communists became estranged from Lombardo Toledano, head of the Confederation of Mexican Workers. In interviews with Alexander (23 March and 1 April 1950, transcripts of which the latter kindly showed me), Browder said that both sides came to New York and then Browder himself went to Mexico City and brokered an end to the split. See also Harvey Levenstein, 'Leninists Undone by Leninism: Communism and Unionism in the United States and Mexico, 1935–1939', *Labor History* (Spring 1981), pp. 237–69.

25. This alliance had some concrete manifestations. Browder told Robert Alexander he intervened with FDR to save the life of Argentine party leader Victorio Codovilla, about to be deported to Spain in 1943. Within a few days of Browder's appeal, Roosevelt indicated that the Argentine government had reconsidered.

26. From the preface to Vicente Lombardo Toledano, *Fifth Column in Mexico*, New York: Council for Pan-American Democracy, 1943.

27. The quote is from the *New York Times* article announcing the conference in advance, 21 November 1938.

28. 'Call to a Conference on Pan-American Democracy at the Hotel Washington, in Washington, D.C., to be held on December 10th & 11th, 1938' and 'Agenda for Conference on Pan-American Democracy', in Frances R. Grant Papers, Special Collections, Alexander Library, Rutgers-The State University of New Jersey (afterwards FGP).

29. David Efron, a professor at Sarah Lawrence College, was executive secretary and an important figure throughout the CPAD's history. Its first officers did include Gardner Jackson of Labor's Non-Partisan League as chairman and George Soule (editor of *The New Republic*) and Upton Sinclair as vice-chairmen. Within a few years, however, the chairman and secretary-treasurer, respectively, were two pillars of the Popular Front: Clifford McAvoy, a New York City official and leader of the American Labor Party, and Abraham Isserman, a prominent left lawyer, whose clients included the CP.

30. The perambulations of the Popular Front in the antiwar period, hardly irrational in their

own terms, can be followed in the 'Report to the National Board of the Council...', (late 1939), 'Press Release, March 8, 1941', *Inter-American Review* (April 1941) and 'Statement of Principles' (24 May 1941), all in FGP. The salient themes include the danger of US arrangements with the British Empire to take over its colonial possessions, repudiation of the Good Neighbor Policy regarding strict nonintervention, and above all 'to keep the Western Hemisphere free and clear of involvement or participation in this war in Europe.' Cordial references are made repeatedly to Mexico, Batista and Chile's Popular Front government. By 1942, in contrast, the CPAD was denouncing perfidious 'neutralist' regimes like that of Argentina that repressed 'anti-fascists' trying to aid the United Nations ('Dear Friend' letter, 8 May 1942, in FGP), and hailed Lombardo Toledano's meeting with US war production chief Donald Nelson in Washington ('Noticiero Especial', 2 April 1942, in FGP).

31. See *New York Times*, 22 December 1940; 25 May, 22 July and 25 September 1941; 18 October 1942; 14 February and 17 July 1943; 11 and 28 June, 19 and 27 October, and 2 December 1945.

32. The 'front' reference is in Robert Alexander, *Communism in Latin America*, p. 340, the only scholarly mention of the CPAD.

33. 'Preliminary Memorandum', Organizing Committee for the Inter-American Conference for Democracy and Freedom, in FGP.

34. Daniel James, *Red Design for the Americas: The Guatemalan Prelude*, New York: John Day, 1954, page 11.

35. At a meeting of future organizers of the Inter-American Association for Democracy and Freedom, including Frances Grant, German Arciniegas (former Colombian minister of education), Robert Alexander and Serafino Romualdi, one speaker 'pointed out the necessity for quick action in organizing the Conference, because of his conviction that if the forces in defence of Human Rights do not mobilize, other groups may organize to further totalitarian movements which are now under way' (from Minutes, Special Meeting of the Latin America Section, International League for the Rights of Man, 14 June 1949, in FGP). In his memoirs, Romualdi credits Rómulo Betancourt, just exiled from Venezuela and living in Washington, D.C. with the original idea for the Havana Conference.

36. The conference's North American 'Sponsors' who did not attend ranged from Eleanor Roosevelt to Congressman Richard M. Nixon (for details, see 'Aid for Democracy Set Up in Havana, *New York Times*, 15 May 1950). In his revealing memoirs, Romualdi, who functioned as the *éminence grise* of this peculiar form of solidarity movement, mentions soliciting 'a generous grant' from his good friend Nelson Rockefeller to subsidize travel expenses for a massive US presence (see *Presidents and Peons: Recollections of a Labor Ambassador in Latin America*, New York: Funk & Wagnalls, 1967, p. 441). As the archetypal 'corporate liberal', Rockefeller acted as a behind-the-scenes backer of cooperation and cooptation in Latin America from the 1940s through the 1970s. His first job in government was as special coordinator of Inter-American Affairs under FDR during the war. Both Romualdi and Alexander were employed in his office's Labor Relations Division (*Presidents and Peons*, pp. 20, 36).

37. The quote is from Romualdi's *Inter-American Labor News* (Monthly Bulletin of the Inter-American Confederation of Workers), June 1950. Interestingly, the 'first official act' of the IADF was to call on Secretary of State Dean Acheson 'to use his influence in halting a proposed Export-Import Bank loan to Franco Spain' (Press Release, 8 June 1950, in FGP).

38. Interview with Robert Alexander (longtime vice-chairman and later chairman of the IADF's North American Committee), 16 June 1989.

39. A useful summary is the 'Report of the Secretary General, 1950–1960', in *Report of the Second Inter-American Congress*, New York: IADF, 1961, pp. 44–76. See also Minutes of the US (or North American) Committee of the IADF, 11 June 1952, 24 February 1956, and 11 January 1957, in FGP; 'U.S. Urged to Guard Freedom of Latins' and 'Uruguay's Envoy Is Honored Here', *New York Times*, 16 April and 9 October 1955; Charles Ameringer's *The Democratic Left in Exile: The Antidictatorial Struggle in the Caribbean, 1945–1959*, Coral Gables, Fl.: University of Miami Press, 1974, pp. 222–34.

40. Cedric Belfrage and James Aronson, *Something to Guard: The Stormy Life of the National Guardian, 1948–1967*, New York: Columbia University Press, 1978, p. 155.

41. Only two major articles on Latin America appeared in the *National Guardian* from late 1948 to late 1951: a 13 December 1948 story on the new dictators ('Violence Spreading in Latin

America'), and an 8 August 1949 article promoting the left-led peace movement's foray into the hemisphere, 'Peace Crusade Moves to Mexico'. The latter may have been what the IADF's founders were concerned about forestalling.

42. For Bendiner's various articles and scrapes, see the *National Guardian* of 9 January, 2 and 16 April, 8 May, 5 June, and 21 August 1952, which mostly focused on building a Latin American peace movement. In 1953, he was joined by Kumar Goshal, who covered the global anticolonial struggle.

43. Other than a pungent critique of the Puerto Rican Nationalists by an anonymous special correspondent ('Puerto Rico: The Necessity for Socialism', February 1951) and a few articles about Jamaica in early 1952, the region was ignored until the Guatemalan crisis. A little better was *The Nation:* lying across the fault-line between the left and liberalism (and under constant attack in these years for its 'softness' on Communism), it published a range of viewpoints, from the anti-Communist Flora Lewis, then of *The Economist* ('The Peril Is Not Red', 13 February 1954) to Julio Alvarez del Vayo, former foreign minister of Republican Spain and a thorough anti-imperialist.

44. The limitations of the 'progressive' and Communist perspectives can be seen, also, in how the *National Guardian* and *Latin America Today* described the 26 July 1953 uprising in Cuba, led by 'the young Ortodoxo lawyer' Fidel Castro, as an 'adventurist putsch' by 'Orthodox (conservative) youths' whose main effect was to legitimize Batista's crushing of the Communists. Fidel's epochal 'History Shall Absolve Me' speech at his trial went unreported, though *Latin America Today* noted without comment his self-identification with José Martí (see the 31 August 1953 issue of the former, and the July/August and October issues of the latter). The only protests against the bloody repression in Cuba after the Moncada attack were undertaken by the Civil Rights Congress, which sent delegations to the Cuban consulates in New York and Detroit and the Cuban embassy in Washington, D.C. and staged a large picket at the UN (*National Guardian,* 24 and 31 August 1953; *Latin America Today,* September 1953).

45. *New York Times,* 13 March 1953; *Life,* 12 October 1953; *US News and World Report,* 6 November 1953; Theodore Geiger, *Communism Versus Progress in Guatemala,* National Planning Association, December 1953; *Time,* 11 January 1954; United Press, 14 January 1954; all quoted in *Latin America Today,* November 1953 and January/February 1954 issues, along with a detailed examination of United Fruit's close ties to the national security apparatus, and details of the brewing invasion as accurately reported by the Guatemalans.

46. Stephen Schlesinger and Stephen Kinzer, *Bitter Fruit: The Untold Story of the American Coup in Guatemala,* Garden City, N.Y.: Doubleday, 1982, p. 89. See this book (especially pp. 79–97) and Richard Immerman's more comprehensive *The CIA in Guatemala: The Foreign Policy of Intervention,* Austin, Tex.: University of Texas Press, 1982, on the tight coordination between United Fruit and the liberal establishment, including the Council on Foreign Relations, the *Christian Science Monitor,* the *New York Times,* leading Democratic insider Thomas Corcoran, and former Senator Robert LaFollette, Jr.

47. From the AFL's 'open letter' to Arbenz, quoted in the *New York Times,* 7 February 1954. According to Alexander, he suggested this letter to Jay Lovestone, who headed the AFL's foreign operations (Lovestone had been CPUSA general secretary in the late twenties, and for long after was its most implacable enemy). Then and later, Alexander acted informally on behalf of Lovestone in Latin America (interview with Alexander, 19 January 1989). Richard Immerman documents the interaction of the US embassy in Guatemala City, the State Department and the AFL at this time, including Alexander (*CIA In Guatemala,* p. 232n14).

48. S. G. Inman, *A New Day in Guatemala: A Study of the Present Social Revolution,* Wilton, Conn.: Worldover Press, 1951.

49. *Hemispherica,* January/February and June/July 1954. In the intervening March/May issue, Alexander wrote a rather tortured analysis of the 'necessary and healthy' Guatemalan revolution that had somehow gotten entwined in Communist tentacles, which did suggest that direct North American intervention would be 'disastrous'; also ibid., June/July 1958 for Berle dinner.

50. *Political Affairs,* July 1954; *The Nation,* 29 May 1954.

51. *National Guardian,* 8 March 1954; *Latin America Today,* March/April 1954; *New York Times,* 25 June 1954; *Latin America Today,* August 1954.

52. *Latin America Today,* August 1954, quotes Mazey's speech to a Michigan CIO convention in early June: 'We have to change our foreign policy from what is good for American business to one of lining up with people in these countries on a basis of peace in the world.' It also noted

approvingly that Democratic Senator Dennis Chavez of New Mexico, debating Joe McCarthy on 20 May, before the invasion, asked, 'But what about the enslavement by United Fruit Company?'

53. *New York Times*, 5 November 1955.
54. Romualdi, *Presidents and Peons*, pp. 240–44.
55. *Latin America Today*, September 1954, quotes several articles in the *CIO News*.
56. *Dissent*, Autumn 1954.
57. *Latin America Today*, December 1954; June, September, and October 1955.
58. This connection between Guatemala and Cuba, Arbenz and Che Guevara, and all the larger implications of this point, are thoroughly documented in Immerman, *The CIA in Guatemala*, pp. 187–201.

2

Have Gun, Will Travel:
The Mystiques of (Counter) Insurgency

The nearly universal triumphalism attending the overthrow of Arbenz in Guatemala gave little reason to hope that the US government, much less a know-nothing public, would approve of revolutions of any sort in Latin America: the campaign against Arbenz had demonstrated how easily even the mildest reformism could be labelled 'Communist-inspired' and defined as a threat to national security. Yet less than three years later, a much more audacious and radical undertaking, the Movimiento Revolucionario 26 de Julio (the 26th of July Movement, named for the date in 1953 when a small force of ex-student militants had tried to seize an army base in eastern Cuba and set off a popular uprising) was promoted by some of the most ferociously anti-Communist bastions of the US press, and even more surprisingly, began attracting an almost cultish following among young people. The basis for this unlikely phenomenon was a fortuitous combination of imperial exigency and lowbrow desire.

To begin with, the larger context for the US response to Castro was the US need in the 1950s to define itself as somehow anti-imperialist, and in Latin America as antidictatorial. Throughout the decade, US foreign policy as directed by Eisenhower and the Dulles brothers had frankly embraced feudal oligarchs and military autocrats as a means of garrisoning the system of alliances and ententes known as the Free World. Banking on reaction was highly effective in the short run, but as with maintaining segregation at home, it carried heavy political costs in the larger ideological competition with the socialist bloc for the loyalty of the 'emerging nations'. The more liberal (and out-of-power) sectors of the political establishment believed that the US had to prove its capacity to export democracy along with capitalism, if necessary by replacing the regional satraps who had faithfully guarded the anti-Communist perimeter. Typically, State Department and CIA personnel dressed up authoritarians in democratic and populist sheep's clothing, like Ramon Magsaysay in the Philippines, or the Catholic tyrant Ngo Dinh Diem in 'South' Vietnam. There were always hopes, nonetheless, for a real democrat, a genuine revolutionary for the US to befriend, and at an opportune time Fidel appeared to fill that bill, with his carefully ambiguous manifestos and supposedly overwhelming bourgeois support within Cuba itself.

In addition, the figure of the bold Latin American revolutionary had, in however shallow and patronizing a fashion, been historicized within North American popular culture prior to (and therefore outside of) the Cold War definition of revolution as 'attempted subjugation by armed minorities or outside pressures'.[1] The traditions of Bolívar, Juárez, Villa, Zapata, and even the long-running armed struggle in Cuba itself had all been authenticated at one time or another by the US film industry and were available for recall when Castro appeared on the scene.

Finally, the late 1950s happened to be a singularly propitious moment for Castro as a movie-hero come to life. Beginning in 1955, rebellion and the fall of old orders were in the air – or, at least, on the airwaves. The distinctively 'alternative' (using Raymond Williams's formulation) youth culture that had been brewing in the US since the end of World War II sprang into public consciousness. Great anxiety attended the arrival of the mumbling, alienated teenager – the 'rebel without a cause' who had no visible means of engagement with society other than driving fast cars and listening to the 'jungle music' from the wrong side of the tracks that was belatedly dubbed 'rock 'n' roll'. Meanwhile, the Montgomery bus boycott signaled a more purposeful insubordination, an unstoppable but nonviolent mass movement of ordinary people, assaulting an entire 'way of life' in the name of Christian love and the US Constitution. Abroad, alongside the final break-up of the old colonial empires, the Hungarian revolution of 1956 resurrected primal images of civilian resistance: paving-stone barricades, Molotov cocktails and a city in flames, which, however demoralizing they were for the traditional left, inspired many others to question authority.

Amid this milieu of rebellion, Fidel Castro came off as uniquely the right stuff for many in the US and an alternative to the hipster's nihilistic lust for sheer experience without consequences. Others talked of freedom and democracy. Against all odds, the 'Lawyer' and 'Fanatic' Castro, the 'Rebel Leader' (as the US press dubbed him) *acted*. Like Martin Luther King, Jr, his revolution appeared to be more than anything a personal, moral decision to stand up against of the tyranny of the status quo. At a time of no politics, the 'political' could at first be reclaimed only as the 'personal', and so, at first, solidarity with the Cuban rebellion could express itself only in the most subjective terms.

Good, Bad and Ugly Americans: Dealing with Dictators

Beyond the contradictory US relationship to revolution in Latin America since the nineteenth century, the imperatives of world competition with the Soviet

Union shaped the US response to the Cuban revolution. Since World War II, Communism had been periodically contained through subversion of nationalist governments and installation of friendly despots, like Castillo Armas in Guatemala and the Shah in Iran. Rather more often, the US simply turned a blind eye to repression by governments deemed friendly, and kept the aid dollars flowing. This know-nothingism was particularly identified with the Republicans, whether of the bland Eisenhower variety or the rabid McCarthyites with their charges of selling out Chiang Kai-Shek. Committed to a global version of reform-from-above, and trying to successfully counterattack on Cold War terms, liberals in the later 1950s (urged on by their silent partners in the remnants of US social democracy) baited the ruling Republicans as shortsighted Babbitts whose incompetence, insensivity to other peoples, and coddling of dictators would hand the underdeveloped nations to the Soviets on a platter. What was needed were genuine democrats in the Third World, popular leaders who could steal the Communists' thunder. To succeed, however, the latter needed systematic, long-term US support, integrating economic, political and military strategies into a single plan: *counter*-insurgency, the mirror-image of guerrilla war.

All of these liberal arguments, as well as the sense of imminent crisis as colonies throughout Africa and Asia freed themselves and evinced skepticism over US claims, were stated forcefully in one of the bestsellers of 1958, *The Ugly American*, whose title has endured ever since as the emblem of public awareness that 'we' have a problem with 'foreigners'. It began on an ominous note:

> This book is written as fiction; but it is based on fact. The things we write about have, in essence, happened. They have happened not only in Asia, where the story takes place, but throughout the world – in the fifty-nine countries where over two million Americans are stationed.[2]

The book is about Sarkhan, 'a small country out toward Burma or Thailand', in the mid 1950s. At its outset, the entire argument about the wrongheadedness of US foreign policy is made to a young North American from Wisconsin, John Colvin, as he is held at gunpoint by an old Sarkhanese friend, Deong. The two had fought the Japanese together as guerrillas only a decade earlier, but now the world has changed. On his own with no help from the US embassy, Colvin has set up a free milk-distribution center, hoping to convince the Sarkhanese to take up dairy farming, but Deong intervenes to ruin his plan by dosing the milk with a powerful emetic. In an exchange along the lines of the traditional 'As long as you're going to kill me, tell me why you did it' convention in gangster films, Deong explains the world-historic necessity of giving the mothers and children of Sarkhan acute diarrhea:

You can't make an omelette without breaking eggs. ... Look, John, I told you that milk is part of history. If you get this crazy milk and cattle scheme of yours going, it could in time change the economic balance of Sarkhan. ... It's a good idea. Out in the bush we've talked it over a lot. But you're the wrong person to be permitted to do it. If it succeeded, the Sarkhanese would believe that America was their savior.[3]

This sequence introduces the themes of imperial disarray, which authors Burdick and Lederer pound home for the rest of the book. The United States has grown complacent and arrogant. In the great global struggle even the most innocent act has political implications. Ideologies like Marxism have hardly ended but are central to human behavior, and require deep study to be effectively combatted. Finally, the nonwhite peoples must be appealed to in terms of their own self-interest and cultural values. Soon the moment of truth arrives: 'Deong, you're a Communist', says Colvin. But this betrayal of an unselfish friend and ally, both Colvin personally and all the good Americans, is explained as highly rational:

'As if there were a choice', Deong replied softly. 'Look, John, you took me off the back of a water buffalo and taught me about the big outside world. And I learned that the side with the most brains and power wins. And, John, that's not your side anymore. Once it was, but not now. America had its chance and it missed. And now the Communists are going to win.'[4]

Colvin's attempts at rebuttal make no headway:

'No, you haven't got the power or the will or anything', Deong said, and his voice was rock hard with assurance. 'You've done nothing but lose since the end of the war. And for a simple little reason: you don't know the power of an idea. The clerks you send over here try to buy us like cattle. You people are like the fable of the rich man who was an idiot.'[5]

The rest of The Ugly American reprises these themes through a gallery of characters representing 'good' US officials, soldiers and private citizens, who are selfless, innovative and nonracist, versus the 'bad' Americans, who are venal, bigoted and provincial. At virtually every turn, the wily Russians, who speak Sarkhanese and are schooled in local mores, outwit the clumsy Yankees.[6] The novel also features a side-trip to Hanoi, and a biting sketch of French military blindness and racial arrogance just before the fall of Dienbienphu to underline how those who do not learn from history are condemned to repeat it. Its denouement comes when the James Bondish Ivy League man who is the new ambassador to Sarkhan sacrifices his career by demanding that the secretary of state restructure the entire Foreign Service on the Russian model.

The need for a Leninist cadre, in fact if not in name, is made especially explicit by the presence of the novel's truelife hero: Colonel Edward Lansdale (his name barely modified), the legendary North American avatar of counter-insurgency who had befriended Magsaysay in the Philippines and worked with him to defeat the Communist-led Huk guerrillas, and would go on to play a crucial role in the early counter-insurgency war in Vietnam. Like the Russians, but none of the other Yanks, 'Hillandale' is fluent in local languages, eats Asian food with enthusiasm, and even respects national customs (in Sarkhan, palm-reading). Above all, he knows how to charm the natives. His nickname in the book is 'The Ragtime Kid', based on his virtuosity as a harmonica-player, and indeed there is a Pied-Piperish aspect to both the real and the fictionalized Lansdale.

For good reason, then, Richard Slotkin has called this period leading up to and encompassing John F. Kennedy's brief presidency the 'Green Beret mo-ment in foreign affairs', emphasizing how 'the mystique of the Special Forces' and of the whole theory of counter-insurgency, 'involved almost from the start a peculiar kind of identification with the enemy'.[7] But this mimetic trading places with national liberation struggles so as to appropriate their appeal could ultimately become confusing, even self-defeating. If North American liberals argued that guerrilla warfare was good, provided the right people led the guerrillas, they legitimated armed struggle in all its forms. If they de-nounced Washington's support for tyrants like Franco, Trujillo and Batista as both immoral and impractical because blind reaction provoked social revolu-tion, they unintentionally made an argument for noninterventionism as the most moderate course: 'let the people decide'. Finally, given the impossibility of finding pro-US radical democrats capable of carrying out massive social reform without damaging US business interests, they created impossible ex-pectations. Thus Cuba began the process of deconstructing liberal-imperial ideology that the war in Vietnam completed. Once Fidel Castro came along, claiming he would accomplish all the goals of pro-US democratization and development, who was to tell the North American people not to believe him? In effect, the Cuban revolution disarmed the US with its own words played back, and Fidel acquired a transient authenticity as the greatest liberal of them all, a true liberator of the 'humanist' revolution. On these and a host of other contradictions, liberal imperialism as ersatz-revolution defeated itself long be-fore it was destroyed in practice by the Vietnamese Communist application of the strategy of 'prolonged people's war'.

'Hate Thundered out of the Cactus Fields...': Hollywood's Primitive Rebels

In addition to the new thinking about counter-insurgency current at the end of the 1950s, revolution in Latin America, at least as civil rebellion in the old-fashioned sense, preserved vestiges of a popular face in North American mass culture quite different from the reception accorded Asian or African struggles. From their earliest days, Hollywood film studios had marketed sexually charged depictions of savage, romantic Latin America, and intermittently included in these were portrayals of rebels and revolutionaries, usually downgraded to 'bandits'. This practice survived into the 1950s when scenarios of rebellion anywhere else became suspect, because the films made money and appeared part of the bucolic, 'Western' past rather than the tense international present. At the height of the Cold War this appeal also allowed Latin America to function as a site for allegorical and even critical treatments of Cold War themes. Young people growing up in the postwar US were thus exposed to a primitive vision of heroic insurgency in one particular Third World backwater sharply at odds with other, racially charged depictions of nonwhite peoples; this vision proved an indispensable discursive opening for a revolutionary movement in Cuba. As a cinematic residue of familiarity, it reflected not only the low priority of Latin America in the average North American's worldview, far below Europe, Asia or even Africa, but ironically the force of racial and cultural stereotypes older than the Russian revolution:

> From the Frito Bandito to Chiquita Banana, views of Latin American men and women have remained static since 1900. Nowhere is this more true than on the American screen where the dated conceptions of the Middle Ages and the Enlightenment rather than the current realities of the South American continent shape the filmic image of the Latin American.[8]

As Allen Woll has shown, Hollywood's fascination with the physically accessible drama and violence south of the border has deep roots. As far back as the early years of the Mexican revolution, when the revolutionary general Francisco (Pancho) Villa was an international celebrity, the Mutual Film Corporation paid $25,000 for the exclusive right to film his battles and produced an approved film biography, *The Life of Villa*. Interest in a genuine revolution, however, was submerged for many decades when 'Hollywood ... appeared at a loss, as though unable to depict a Mexican in any other occupation than bandit or lazy peasant'.[9] Both stereotypes were prominent in MGM's 1934 blockbuster *Viva Villa!*, a comic opera of *campesino* bloodletting dominated by Wallace Beery's hammy Irish charm as a most unlikely rebel chief, with the revolution's actual progress left to a series of title cards:

> Chaos hit Mexico and at the head of the chaos rode Pancho Villa with a cry of vengeance. ... Somebody had stolen their revolution and hate thundered out of the cactus fields. An army of vengeance arose out of nowhere to recapture the land stolen from their fathers.[10]

Until World War II, though, even this small amount of historical exposition was avoided in favor of a succession of easily exploitable male and female stock characters into which all Latin Americans were merged: the Greaser, the Gaucho, the Latin Lover, the Mexican Spitfire.

The advent of European war in 1939 cut off Hollywood's foreign markets and made Latin Americans its main external consumers. An influx of German films and the urgency of corralling the hemisphere's strongly anti-imperialist peoples into a US-led front combined to force a sudden change in the presentation of Iberian America's revolutionary history. As Latin dance music replaced swing at the top of the pop music charts, a surfeit of pan-American oriented films promoted the equality and cultural complimentariness of all Americans, north and south. These were the years when bandleaders like Desi Arnaz and Xavier Cugat became national stars, and Carmen Miranda took Broadway and then Hollywood by storm. However sentimentalized, the war against fascism did promote Good Neighborliness in North American films and broader reaches of popular culture towards the peoples of Latin America, distinguishing them from other US allies in that they were deemed to be 'like us'. In this vein, too, their struggles to be free of European interlopers and despots, from Spanish grandees to Napoleon III to Nazi conspirators, were justified in democratic terms that were explicitly associated with the revolutionary traditions of the US. Perhaps the best example of the latter is the carefully researched, big-budget *Juarez* (1939), in which Paul Muni portrayed Mexico's Liberator Benito Juárez as consciously emulating Abraham Lincoln. In contrast to the Mexican government's hostility to earlier films, *Juarez* premiered in Mexico City's Palace of Fine Arts.[11]

The strength of this validation of revolution in Latin America by even hard-headed Hollywood producers can be seen in its survival right into the 1950s, a time when the slightest hint of overly egalitarian liberalism in earlier films was queried for evidence of International Communism's invisible hand. The most influential example of this odd legacy, carrying forward the long tradition of Mexican revolutionary biographies, was *Viva Zapata!* (1952), starring the young Marlon Brando as another simple son of the soil who takes up the gun to defend his people. The film's ancestry stretched back to the days of the Popular Front. After World War II, a new screenplay was prepared by the leftwinger Lester Cole, but then promptly dumped when Cole became notorious as one of the 'Hollywood Ten'. Finally two ex–Popular Fronters moving rapidly to the right, Elia Kazan and John Steinbeck, were engaged as director and screenwriter by 20th Century Fox's Darryl F. Zanuck. Through many tortured reworkings, the martyrdom of the guerrilla leader became in their hands a paean to North American–style liberal democracy instead of social revolution. A wary Zanuck insisted on inserting explicit references to the US as the model for which the *zapatistas* fought, and gradually built up the sinister intellectual Fernando, played by Joseph Wiseman, as a premature Stalinist manipulator. A vague call to trust in the people and gradualist reform instead of leaders who will end up either corrupt or dead was substituted for Zapata's program of armed struggle to expropriate land for the landless.[12] Yet it remains indisputable that, as in the preceding *A Streetcar Named Desire* and the subsequent *On the Waterfront* (another parable of Cold War liberalism pitting a self-abnegating, individual hero against the venality of institutional leaders), Brando under Kazan's direction was a riveting figure, and a far more believable 'fake Latin' revolutionary leader than any Hollywood leading man before or since. His martyrdom at the end of *Viva Zapata!* was double-edged in ways that the filmmakers could hardly anticipate, and in that sense it turned out to be more 'real' than filmed. Despite themselves, Kazan and Steinbeck heroized the entire Mexican revolution as a utopian peasant insurgency, permanently selfless and glorious via the film's cult status on campuses in the next two decades, as a 'modern' film with a quintessentially postwar star and sensibility.[13]

Just a few years earlier, a much-less-remembered movie indicated the relative strength of prewar cultural memories and images dramatizing not just Latin American history, but specifically bloody revolution in Cuba. In *We Were Strangers* (1949), John Huston directed John Garfield as a professional revolutionist named Tony Fenner, who goes to Cuba to aid the anti-Machado underground of the early 1930s. The plot is simple enough: Garfield and his comrades tunnel into a cemetery to blow up the dictator during the funeral of an official they have assassinated. Ultimately, the plan is discovered and Garfield dies, tommy-gun in hand, but at that moment the streets of Havana fill with an aroused citizenry as the final insurrection begins. In many respects it resembles films made during the previous war about European resistance to the Nazis, with its somber realism and motifs of common suffering, as well as the hero's death at the moment of victory. Little wonder that the film is barely known compared with Huston's preceding and succeeding efforts, *The Treasure of the Sierra Madre* and *The Asphalt Jungle*.

We Were Strangers never became a free-floating cultural agent like *Viva Zapata!*, remolded by later viewers for their own purposes. Yet it still tells us something about the long-term acceptance in the US of images of Cuban rebellion, even in the year that China 'fell' to Communism. This point hardly needs to be made for those old enough to remember the Batista-Mafia alliance that ran Cuba in the 1950s, or earlier, the butchery of the Machado regime as recounted by Carleton Beals and denounced on the floor on the Senate. As Huston himself noted about the film,

> Years later, a revolution did come to Cuba and in a way it was somewhat prophetic. All the conditions in Cuba certainly indicated that a revolution was required, regardless of the form it took. It was, at that time, just about as corrupt a place as there was in my experience of the world. Everybody was corrupt in Cuba.[14]

For most North Americans, Cuba and Castro have been synonymous for so long, however, that to find *We Were Strangers* on late-night television twenty or thirty years later is still a distinct cultural shock. That Hollywood would sanction the primal site of modern revolution in the Americas, even if accidentally and before the fact, still seems amazing, akin to seeing *North Star,* the comic-book-style epic of the Soviet people versus the Nazis, though Huston's film is far more subtle. At the time, *We Were Strangers* was blasted by right and left as either 'the heaviest dish of Red theory ever served to an audience outside the Soviet', or 'capitalist propaganda', though the middlebrow critics of *Time* and *Colliers'* were relatively impressed.[15] Recently, Robert Sklar has shown how *We Were Strangers* overlooked the reality of US involvement in Machado's replacement, arguing that the film is an

> early example of a genre that has become more and more prevalent in Hollywood's present-day response to Third World liberation struggles: the film that abhors tyrants but is decidedly ambivalent toward movements that oppose them, and is most interested in the tragic fate of Americans that get in the way.[16]

Still, it is hard to imagine such a film about revolutionary conspiracy and terror in any other non-European country being released in the US in 1949. Hollywood found no profit in dramatizing the independence struggles of Asia or Africa, or for that matter the antifascist partisans of World War II, once the war had ended – for the obvious reasons that in the former case the dramatis personae were people of color, and in the latter mainly Communists. US filmmakers stayed away from rebels of all sorts in these years, but perhaps because Huston had just made the very successful *Treasure of the Sierra Madre* (itself an exceptionally realistic drama of Latin America), combined with the remaining acceptability of the subject, a 'prophetic' film about revolution in Cuba could be released in the US only seven years before the core of Castro's Movimiento 26 de Julio landed in a mangrove swamp in Oriente province.

While the fifties saw no more films looking at Latin American rebellion from the inside out, a related genre developed addressing how North Americans should respond to anti-imperialist insurgency through a return to Mexico, Hollywood's traditional setting for the chaos of revolution. Over many decades, Mexico was a convenient stand-in for all those harsh, tropical lands beset by indistinguishable banditti and rebels, corrupt officials, brutal soldiers, idealistic reformers and rapacious Europeans – for the entire Third World at a safe, pre-Soviet remove. In the postwar period, it became the homeland for a new genre, dubbed by Richard Slotkin the 'Mexico Western', which 'tells the story of a group of American gunfighters who cross the border into Mexico during a time of social disruption or revolutionary crisis to help the peasants defeat an oppressive ruler or warlord, or a vicious bandit.'[17]

Via this formula, US filmmakers were freed to comment upon, critique and otherwise depart from orthodox, post-1945 conventions of how 'Americans' should behave in the contemporary world. Whereas any Yankee protagonist placed in 1950s Berlin, Istanbul – or, for that matter, Mexico City – was by definition a committed Cold Warrior, the 'heroes' of a Mexico Western were typically mercenaries and opportunists, who move in and out of the action as free agents, getting what they can for themselves and getting out with little concern for ideology.

By the end of the 1950s, however, with the rise of wars of national libera-tion as a threat to US global power, the depiction of the gunfighter gone south of the border became a primary metaphor for the new cult of committed but ruthless counter-guerrillas: 'The Green Beret entered the imaginative world of his home-front fellow citizens wearing the clothes of the gunfighter'. In the enormously successful *The Magnificent Seven* (1960), 'a group of American gunfighters – professionals and technicians of violence, rugged individualists all' rediscover themselves in saving a poor Mexican village from the local war-lord, acting out the new kind of fighting *cum* civic action necessary to combat armed movements in Indochina, or post-Castro Latin America.[18]

Yet even this triumphalist remaking of an old story could be turned inside out, and end up celebrating something hardly identical to the intentions of Washington policymakers. As Slotkin points out, by the end of the next dec-ade, Hollywood used this same frontier mythology and filmed history to make its most savage comment on the slaughter in Southeast Asia in Sam Peckin-pah's *The Wild Bunch* (1969), suggesting how useless was the professionalism of the gunfighter or the Green Beret cut off in a deeply foreign land not at all like movie-Mexico, or movie-Vietnam.

On a more prosaic level, since the 1960s Latin America, especially Mexico and Cuba, has remained the movieland of choice for picturesque revolution. Sometimes these stories are B-movies with a political gloss, as in 1970's *100 Rifles*, featuring second-level stars (Raquel Welch as a fiery Indian revolution-ary girl, Burt Reynolds as 'Yaqui Joe', a pleasure-loving half-breed, Jim Brown as a tough black lawman) in a potboiler that assumes a virtuous 'people' and the virtues of insurrection. Or they can be glossily portentous romances, like *The Old Gringo* (1989) and *Havana* (1990), in which the disorder of revolu-tion serves as a backdrop for North Americans seeking themselves. In the end, few such movies have much to tell us about the actual countries they are set in, or their revolutions, but they continue to be produced – a fact that may be more important than any single film's political content or lack thereof, and that in itself raises some interesting questions.

After all, it cannot be said that North American moviemakers have ad-vanced a positive view of revolution in this hemisphere. The Mexico Western routinely conflated the bandit leader sacking towns with the guerrilla chieftain attacking government garrisons, and from *Viva Villa!* in 1934 to *Che!* in 1968 to *Salvador* in 1986, actual revolutionaries were turned into caricatures, occa-sionally heroic but almost always brutal. These images are so easily parodied as to be ridiculous, as in Woody Allen's *Bananas* (1974), in which a North

American nebbish becomes Maximum Leader of a two-bit banana republic, simply by gluing on a false beard and wearing fatigues. Yet even the most didactic, formulaic and repetitive mass cultural products can get away from their producers and take on a life of their own, mutating into something new or even subversive. Perhaps the most important aspect of Hollywood's treatment of insurgency in Latin America is how it reverses an old axiom. In this case, contempt has bred familiarity, and with the latter has come a lowering of racial passions and xenophobia, the 'otherness' that has always justified US imperialism. And so when Fidel Castro first appeared in news magazines and on television, he could easily be seen here as a re-appearance of the Man on Horseback, alternatively an idealist of the Brando/Zapata type or a 'strong man', like so many others who had arrived at power through coups dubbed 'revolution'. Despite considerable evidence that the Cuban revolutionary war was a Latin American revolution of a new type, these two stereotypes of the idealistic 'bearded fanatic' and the macho 'bearded *caudillo*' persisted well into 1959, until Castro's anti-anti-Communism and fierce anti-imperialism clarified matters. By then the Cubans had already crossed through the window of opportunity that various North American illusions and mythologies had created for them, and spun off their own current of sympathy among young *yanquis* who wanted to go beyond the self-referential pleasures of playing 'the rebel' via stance and artifact.

'The Hungary of the Americas'

Besides a lingering pop-cultural tolerance for Latin American revolution and increasing discomfort with the Cold War's contradiction of maintaining dictatorships in the 'Free World', a spectrum of political developments after 1955 were crucial to Cuba's attraction as the site of a non-Communist Latin revolution. Suddenly, from deepest Dixie to Eastern Europe, new rebellions and insurgencies sprang up everywhere, evoking the democratic traditions of the United States. At that time, before the revelations and disappointments of the 1960s, it must have seemed to North American liberals and reformers, young and old, that truly history favored them – and Cuba became a particular extension of this hope. In turn, this historical frame peculiar to the later 1950s had a special meaning, given Cuba's status as one of two Latin republics that figured strongly over decades in North American culture and daily life; the other, Mexico, had already had its revolution, of course. Demands for clean and representative government, for a government of laws and not of men, in short for a sweeping moral reform, all had a combustible and loaded quality in the US; given Cuba's unique function as the offshore recipient of North America's libido, it would be not only Cuba that would be reformed. This produced a situation that, as the *New York Times* pointed out with considerable understatement in May 1957,

> borders on the bizarre. There is one-man dictatorial rule ... an organized guerrilla resistance movement. Yet it is a haven for American tourists who fly there in a jiffy for a happy vacation.[19]

The legitimacy the Cuban guerrillas quickly acquired in the US therefore needs to be set within two contexts: that of Cuba historically vis-à-vis the United States, and the general political terrain in the second half of the 1950s, from the global to the domestic. In the US, the Cuban struggle against oppression reminded many of the challenge just opened against white supremacy in its Deep South heartland, with overtones that reached deep into US history. A century earlier, millions of young Northern whites imbued with the spirit of Protestant moral reform had come to see the slave states as what the historian Ronald Walters has called the 'Erotic South', the site of depravity and unrestrained excess.[20] In the 1950s, white America was beginning to wake up from its long indifference to the Jim Crow system, and again young people of conscience found everything that was wrong with their country rooted in the pathologies of segregation, and above all its institutionalized immorality – denial of human feeling and the Golden Rule.

A similar burden of conscience existed, on a smaller scale, regarding Cuba. There is no serious study of the 'entertainment industry' in Cuba, or its relationship to US organized crime and public awareness in the US of this famously unholy alliance, but what Havana once meant for North Americans surfaces now and again in popular memory, and occasionally in film. Francis Ford Coppola's *The Godfather, Part II* effectively depicts the deal-making that went on even in the shadow of the revolution's imminent triumph, with a Meyer Lansky-like character in charge ('Hyman Roth', played by Lee Strasberg), and Richard Lester's *Cuba* gives a good account of the decadence of the old regime in its last throes. If someone old enough to remember is asked why he or she readily supported Castro, the answer is invariably along the lines of 'Batista was so bad, and my God, everybody knew the Mafia was running Cuba!' Behind these comments, usually unspoken, is the knowledge that Cuba was where respectable North Americans went to gamble without restraint, to see live sex shows of the most inventive character, to indulge without fear of discovery in whoring with partners of either sex, to drink and eat cheaply, to be waited on hand and foot – all in an environment as close at hand as Miami, and completely geared to servicing their tastes. There were other places in the Americas with widespread prostitution and the like (the role that Tijuana plays in the popular memory of the Southwest comes to mind), but nowhere was the cornucopia of forbidden pleasures so total and ostentatious as in Havana. In Cuba, far more than in other Caribbean islands or Latin American countries, North Americans therefore had seen for themselves the consequences of US friendship for a rapacious dictatorship, and had further seen how ordinary US citizens took advantage of Batista's pimping of his own country.

If Cuba, like Mississippi, seemed embarrassingly at odds with the crusading spirit of a missionary anti-Communism, the last losing battles of European imperialism reinforced the message that the old order was passing away, and would no longer be tolerated by once-colonial peoples. From Malaya to Kenya, the British Empire was successfully waging quiet, dirty counter-insurgency wars, but much more visible was its acquiescence in the 1957 independence of Ghana, Africa's first postcolonial nation, under Kwame Nkrumah's pan-Africanist leadership. Meanwhile, the deepening war of independence in Algeria following the French defeat in Indochina would shortly destroy the Fourth Republic and bring De Gaulle to power. More than any other single event, however, the Suez Crisis of 1956 signaled that the white man's right to rule peoples of color no longer obtained. When Egypt's upstart president Gamal Abdel Nasser moved to nationalize the Suez Canal, combined French, British and Israeli forces invaded the country and quickly drove for Cairo. But the United States (which had not been consulted before the invasion) recognized the global political stakes involved and forced the withdrawal of the Middle East's traditional colonial powers in abject humiliation. In all these cases, most of the world and at least a good part of the US public saw the moral battlelines clearly drawn, as even the Eisenhower administration grudgingly recognized with its belated intervention in Egypt and Eisenhower's decision to move the National Guard into Little Rock, Arkansas in 1957, the first use of federal power to protect black rights since the 1870s.

Less famous or less remembered than any of these events, there was also a specifically Latin American subtext to the Cubans' strategy to use their historical position as a small country in a great power's sphere of influence to assert a claim to national independence. At the time, the Cuban revolution in every respect seemed like only the latest, most dramatic stage in a continental restoration of democracy and the rule of law. As dictators toppled across the hemisphere, the rebels in Cuba gave their struggle a particular piquancy by claiming a special identification with the uprisings against Soviet domination in Poland and Hungary. The result was a weak and vacillating response by the Eisenhower administration to an obviously dangerous situation, in which public support was withdrawn from Batista at a crucial moment and the political initiative was ceded to the insurgents and their friends in the US.

Given the following decades, in which a pervasive fear of Castroism has produced successive waves of 'democratization' and dictatorship accompanied by systematic repression throughout Latin America, it is hard to remember the string of uprisings and resignations-under-fire that from 1955 on overthrew a host of notorious despots. At the time, many observers heralded what seemed like a decisive return to democracy throughout the hemisphere, while *Time* noted plaintively that the US had 'an unhappy knack of appearing to back the dictators.'[21] The fall of Juan Perón in Argentina in 1955 was followed by the departures of Generals Manuel Odría in Peru in 1956, Gustavo Rojas Pinilla in Colombia in 1957, and Pérez Jiménez in Venezuela in 1958. This trend towards liberalism and civilian rule cast the most sympathetic light on the multiclass civilian insurgency in Cuba: Fulgencio Batista's fall seemed ordained by history. Not only did the Cubans benefit from a 'bandwagon' among North Americans like those in the Inter-American Association for Democracy and Freedom (IADF) who concerned themselves with the region, but to a larger audience here the antidictatorial impetus highlighted the continued, egregious existence of the remaining *caudillos* – especially those closest to home like Trujillo and Batista.

What was the content of these various changes of government? In the case of Argentina, it was an outright military coup, albeit one followed by elections. In other countries, notably Venezuela, there were urban uprisings, with streetfighting and the creation of popular militias. In the last case, the opposition that overturned Pérez Jiménez ranged from the Catholic Church to the Communists, and at first all political tendencies were represented in the insurgent junta. Initially, then, the Cuban civil war appeared relatively moderate as a variation on a theme, and until the very last moment many North American experts predicted that Castro would have no choice but to compromise with key elements of the regime, especially the army.

In a more pointed fashion, from early 1956 through most of 1957, a scandal erupted in which Caribbean tyranny spilled over into the United States, stimulating US citizens and even liberal politicians to directly confront the policy of supporting rightwing dictators. While Castro's men trained in Mexico, the need for armed rebellion against Latin tyranny (even from exile within the US) was brought home by a notorious case involving Generalissimo Rafael Trujillo of the Dominican Republic, the longest-serving autocrat of them all, and his kidnapping of a prominent, certifiably democratic Latin émigré on a busy Manhattan street. The victim was Jesús de Galíndez, a leader of the anti-Communist wing of the Spanish Republic-in-exile also prominent in the IADF. In March 1956, he was teaching at Columbia and had just completed a doctoral dissertation exposing in great detail the misdeeds of Trujillo (for whom he had once worked). Like several earlier enemies of 'the Benefactor' who had found New York no haven, Galíndez was evidently murdered; he was never seen again.[22]

Attacked this close to home, the liberals' solidarity network swung into action. With Norman Thomas as spokesman, the IADF mobilized its allies, including the American Catholic Trade Union Committee, the American Civil Liberties Union, the Committee for Cultural Freedom and the AFL-CIO, to denounce Trujillo (with ample sympathetic coverage by the *New York Times*).[23] The Eisenhower administration was publicly embarrassed, and was eventually forced to take action, as the scandal stretched out over the rest of 1956 and well into 1957. New and tantalizingly gory revelations kept it alive, from New York detectives inspecting the boiler of a Cuban ship into which Galíndez allegedly was stuffed, to a pro-Trujillo crowd picketing the Columbia commencement at which he received his doctorate *in absentia*, with signs 'printed in red, white and blue and complemented with United States and Dominican flags [that] proclaimed that Dr. Galindez was a poor Roman Catholic, a foreign agent, a thief and a Communist.'[24]

The Galíndez case was a high watermark for the IADF in terms of successfully pillorying one of the 'Democratic Left's' worst enemies, but it also revived a long-dormant public revulsion against Caribbean despots and widespread sympathy for those who opposed them – as long as they remained anti-Communist. Its staying power as a scandal was a powerful stimulant to rising North American sympathy for Castro. One example of this close connection is Edward R. Murrow's radio exposé, 'The Galíndez-Murphy Case: A Chronicle of Terror', broadcast on CBS Radio in May 1957, the same month as the first major television report on Castro, also on CBS. The furor over Trujillo also provoked a ground-breaking congressional attack on US Latin America policy by freshman US Representative Charles O. Porter, a Democrat from Eugene, Oregon, whose constituent Gerald Murphy was apparently murdered by Trujillo's police after piloting the plane that flew Galíndez to the Dominican Republic. Porter was quickly taken up by the New York crowd and their friends throughout Latin America as a new-found champion, provoking virulent attacks from segregationist Dixiecrats who closely identified with the likes of Batista and Trujillo – which in turn fed into the sense of a new liberal crusade linking the different fights for democracy throughout the hemisphere, from Alabama to 'Ciudad Trujillo'.[25]

Eventually, official discomfort and the retreat from a formerly unchallenged policy of backing strongmen were brought to a head in May 1958, when Vice President Nixon's South American tour provoked massive riots and direct attacks on the vice presidential motorcade. In the wake of this shock, an antidictatorial stance became quasi-official, as Nixon himself told Tad Szulc of the *Times* that he saw

> the problem of dictatorships in Latin America as a ball and chain around the neck of the United States. ... He feels that the United States must be extremely careful not to appear to be trying to keep the dictators in power. ... His formula is that for dictators the United States should have only a handshake and for free governments a warm embrace. If good and evil are treated equally, he thinks, the evil is favored.[26]

Galíndez's disappearance and the subsequent cover-up, in the context of a continental tide of prodemocratic insurgency, tantalized US journalists and provoked a backlash within which pro-Castro sentiments became acceptable and even fashionable. But in these same months, another violent struggle half the world away provided the most explicit language with which *fidelismo* justified itself and demanded support from North America. Just weeks before the *Granma*'s landing party was nearly wiped out in early December 1956, with only Castro and eleven others reaching the Sierra Maestra, another poorly armed citizen insurgency had also defied a brutal professional army. While few in Cuba or the US would choose this analogy today, the Hungarian uprising of October and November 1956 was a forceful example of national pride-in-arms with worldwide repercussions transcending the existing polarities of left and right, East and West. Almost overnight a legendary aura grew up around it among young people in the US through books like James Michener's *The Bridge at Andau;* the unequal battles in the streets of Budapest between students with Molotov cocktails and Russian tanks recalled for a moment the tragic moral clarity and stirring imagery of the 'good war' against the Nazis for a generation that had known only a Cold War whose half-measures were laced with imperial ambiguity. The exaltation of the 'freedom fighters' and excoriation of the Soviets' brute might and *raison d'état* by the Western media easily transmitted into admiration for other proclaimed democrats with hunting rifles and patriotic dreams.

The Cuban revolutionaries and those North Americans rallying to their support wasted no time in making the linkage explicit. At first the *barbudos* ('bearded ones') and their Cuban-American supporters simply likened themselves to the Hungarians. Early reportage of the exiles' street protests repeatedly cites their placards and banners describing Cuba as 'the Hungary of the Americas' and asking, if 'Cuba's Dictatorship Is As Vicious As Russia's', why was the US arming Batista? This anger was widespread, not only in the US but in Cuba. One young US journalist traveling around Cuba in 1958 found out how deeply felt was this invidious comparison when he observed Cubans watching US Information Service films at a schoolhouse in the mountains:

> The second film is called 'Memories of Hungary'. It is about the Hungary that was before the Communists. After the film, the USIS man makes a brief speech in Spanish in which he tells how all of this was destroyed by the Communists. He hands out small comic books to the children (most of whom are 7 or 8 years of age!) which depict in typical comic-book detail the Russians mowing down the Hungarian freedom-fighters. One of the Cuban teachers comes up to me after the film and asks why the American government admits Hungary's freedom fighters but deports Cuba's. I tell her to ask the USIS man. She says it will do no good. Later I have dinner with the USIS man and tell him what the schoolteacher has said. 'I hear that all the time', he says.[27]

This theme of hypocrisy was also readily seized upon by North Americans outraged by solid US support for a ruler as crudely oppressive as Batista. A characteristic letter to the *New York Times* denounced the Eisenhower administration for 'supplying a regime whose disregard for basic human rights equals in every respect the record of Iron Curtain countries.'[28] Even more pointed was the degree to which those North Americans who chose to actually fight in Cuba justified their actions in terms of the Hungarian example – as we shall see below. At the height of the war, when he had become the object of much attention by the North American media, Fidel himself put it adroitly, indeed unanswerably, to his interlocutor: 'Why be afraid of freeing the people, whether Hungarians or Cubans?'[29] A few years later, a Berkeley activist in the first-ever book on the new youth politics used the same formulation, but from a North American perspective, 'Does it help to think of the Russian crimes? Do you think we can think of Hungary and not remember Cuba?'[30]

Rebels, Then Causes: 'A Bad Boy from a Good Family'

It could be argued that at any time after 1945 residual pro-insurgent sympathy for Latin America might have inclined the US public towards toleration for a non-Communist revolution in Cuba. North Americans liked to think of themselves as having a special relationship to the Cubans dating back to 1898 and the Spanish-American War's original conflation of liberation with domination. While skewed by paternalism on the one hand and a submerged national rage on the other, there was clearly a close connection based on the island's proximity. Regardless of the Cold War, the US remained as always the staging ground for exile conspiracies and invasions in the Caribbean. The resulting intimacy predisposed people in the US to cast a neutral eye on one more escapade by hot-blooded Latins. Yet it is doubtful that a tiny guerrilla *foco* in the Sierra Maestra could have sparked the same excitement in the US before the events of 1956, let alone the same display of even-handedness and even tentative covert support from some lower-level elements of the US government (just as the 26th of July Movement would never have been so canny without the example of the CIA coup in Guatemala).

Only in the later 1950s did a cultural space unfold to smooth the way in the US for the Cuban revolution. Beyond the passing of the old order, from Suez to Montgomery, this was the coming-of-age of a whole generation of young white people, and their shift into a stance of halting but highly visible 'difference' – at its summit represented by James Dean and Elvis Presley, but also including Anthony Perkins, Jerry Lee Lewis, Maynard G. Krebs, Alfred E. Newman and a hundred other freakish, often unmanly boy-men.[31] In these same years, events from Eastern Europe to the Americas helped give insurgents of all stripes a new authority, but just as important to incipient solidarity with Cuba's rebels *and* the later rise of a radicalized student movement in the US was the new youth culture that rejected adult standards in favor of the music, dress, style and, most important, the values of otherwise-despised subaltern groups. Here, long before the organizational germination of SNCC or Fair Play for Cuba or SDS lay the seeds of a new sensibility, for these were the actual 'receptors' of the Free World's cacophony.

Whether US teenagers after 1955 actively sought a Robin Hood, a swash-buckler who would steal from the rich and give to the poor, is impossible to say. Obviously enough, they were seeking images of dissonance, or creating their own out of what was available. As James O'Brien has pointed out, the 'worst mistake' one could make about US youth in the fifties would be to 'confuse the students' acquiescence in the life patterns of corporate America with enthusiasm for those life patterns.'[32] Of course, debates about different strategies of containment in the Third World hardly mattered except to a few from self-consciously political families. The majority of young people lived in a time easily characterized in a television series of the 1970s as *Happy Days*, or by a serious historian in the 1980s as the ultimate *American High*. However traumatic the rise of Joe McCarthy and the execution of the Rosenbergs was for children of the Popular Front, or how bastardized the middlebrow national culture appeared to a few would-be mandarins at the elite universities, the uncontested character and felt abundance of daily life for the much larger numbers in the new middle class was real, and remains remarkable.

There was a problem nonetheless with the all-encompassing narrative of the Free World and the American Century: it quickly became very boring. Not only did 'we' never lose, the 'we' was transparently the world of the fathers, of older male authority. The character of state power in this period was so thor-oughly associated with the restoration of patriarchal rule and stability, epito-mized by the figure of Ike, and the containment of subversive sexual currents and unorthodox family arrangements, that one can speak of a distinctly *patri-archal imperialism* (with the cultural offensive of the 1980s centered on Ronald Reagan as its faux, Indian Summer version).[33] Yet, as in any tale involv-ing fathers and sons, great struggles were inevitable, especially when the actual, everyday dad's authority was effectively undercut by the symbolic fatherhood of the corporation and the corporate state.

At first Middle America's young men did not set out to overturn their parents and remove the dead hand of the past. How could they, when on all sides this was pronounced the best of all possible worlds? Instead, their separation was pro-claimed via a cult of otherness and marginality, which developed a weird attrac-tion beyond all previous youth fascinations with the outsider and directly challenged received ideas of contemporary manhood. For millions of clean-cut, hard-working 'fellas' moving down the track from age fourteen to twenty-one, at the end of which adulthood loomed as career or marriage, a series of defiant 'bad boys' who were neither good nor well-groomed nor even very cheerful were in-tensely fascinating. These mean, moody, often physically unprepossessing youth had been around in films since the war, as had the sinuous, honking black dance music that, refashioned as 'rock 'n' roll' and played by both whites and blacks, changed the structure of the entire culture industry. It was not until 1955–56, however, that the bad boys hit their stride fully as a 'dominant trope', with an impact that linked the overlapping youth, bohemian and popular cultures of the 1950s, and has since acquired mythic status: the films *Rebel Without a Cause, The Wild One, Blackboard Jungle;* the latter's theme song, Bill Haley's 'Rock Around the Clock', first chart-topping breakthrough of the new 'rock 'n' roll'; the surge to stardom of the Hillbilly Cat, Elvis Aaron Presley, summing up the subversive possibilities of style for style's sake; the Beat sub- or counter-culture's arrival through the success of Allen Ginsberg's *Howl!* and Jack Kerouac's *On the Road,* each suggesting that young men had other things to do with their time than compete with other men.[34]

Yet, like the 1913 Armory Show, or Martin Luther King, Jr's 'I have a dream...' speech, or the Declaration of Independence, the ubiquity of each of the above as a disposable 'postmodern' referent obscures their significance as not merely vulgar, but perilous developments for a Victorian culture entering its final crisis. In our time, they are treated as material artifacts and 'kitsch' carefully segregated from the political, as with Dean and Elvis, or have aged into a famous obscurity, as with Ginsberg and Brando. At that time, this eruption of the new, the loud, the gross and fantastic was treated like the arrival of the Visigoths. The still-powerful voices of antimodern reaction saw rock 'n' roll and its associated products (juvenile delinquency, premarital sex and the rest) as paired with integration in a grand Communist conspiracy to unhinge White Christian America. The hundreds of thousands of middlebrow, college-educated *New York Times* and *Saturday Review* readers, those semi-intellectuals accustomed to arbitrating taste, deplored the erosion of standards and the Western Tradition as they have ever since, sensing the threat that the cultures of nonwhites, the untutored and the deviant posed to a canon based on the lives of a certain kind of white man.

Indeed, virtually everyone – except perhaps the tiny number of orthodox Marxists – recognized the political consequences of the linguistic, sartorial and visual noise produced by the new consumers, so to ask *if* 'popular culture' is related to 'radical politics' in the 1950s, to proclaim these as separate spheres of thought and feeling within advanced capitalism, is to beg the question. We do not need to ask if there is any connection between, say, James Dean and Fidel Castro. The question becomes what form this connection takes: how do we reconstruct a continuum of 'bad boys' that extends beyond the celebrity of the performing self and encompasses the radical new identity of selflessness articulated by Cuba's revolutionary youth, while recovering that portrayal too as a performance?

The path that leads from the cult of 'the rebel' (whether the book by Camus or Nick Adams in his Confederate Army cap on the TV Western of the same name) to the beginnings of a cult of Fidel begins with 'desire' in its rawest form, and both its politics and its lack of politics. The bad boys, in tandem with their millions of admirers and imitators, portrayed variants on an outlaw sensibility keyed only to the recovery of pleasure, and a rejection of the fierce will to repression with which American men in the postwar period had become identified – Elvis Presley being the preeminent example of this escape. The recovery of desire through pleasure and the body, whether the kind of public teenage sexuality dormant since the heyday of the young Frank Sinatra, or that which had always been unseen, like Ginsberg's homosexuality, was crucial to the watershed of the mid 1950s.

All too often, however, this turn to the physicality of the present is cleaned up in hindsight and presented as wholly liberatory and joyful, a categorical expression of newfound power and defiance as 'natural' in a generational sense as the passing of the seasons. Teenagers did push themselves forward as autonomous agents in the democracy of participatory consumption; this is the side of fifties youth culture remembered with such tremendous nostalgia ever since George Lucas's 1972 film *American Graffiti* heralded the dawn of the long, post-sixties era. But for others this turn to the Hip – that terrain permeated by the trappings of rebellion we associate with parodies of fifties rockers, Beatniks and 'juvies' – reflected disgust, despair, rootlessness and anger, *Waiting for Godot* rather than *Happy Days*. This is the world of the 'white Negro', anatomized by Norman Mailer in a 1957 *Dissent* essay still bracing in its apocalyptic invocation of

> ... the American existentialist – the hipster, the man who knows that if our collective condition is to live with instant death by atomic war, relatively quick death by the State as *l'univers concentrationnaire*, or with a slow death by conformity with every creative and rebellious instinct stifled ... why then the only life-giving answer is to accept the terms of death, to live with death as immediate danger, to divorce oneself from society, to exist without roots, to set out on that uncharted journey into the rebellious imperatives of the self.[35]

Because of the author's characteristic hyperbole and calls 'to encourage the psychopath in oneself ... one is a frontiersman in the Wild West of American night life, or else a Square cell, trapped in the totalitarian tissues of American society', it has been assumed that Mailer was interested mainly in the Hip as the amoral embrace of pure feeling, 'relinquishing the pleasures of the mind for the more obligatory pleasures of the body', which he identified with 'the Negro [who] had stayed alive and begun to grow by following the need of his body where he could'.[36] But 'The White Negro' is in fact ultimately a consideration of politics and the lack thereof, in the presence of numerous rebels and no causes, as underlined by Mailer's quoting of the psychiatrist Robert Lindner's *Rebel Without a Cause: The Hypnoanalysis of a Criminal Psychopath*, which frankly describes how this particular kind of rebel is like 'an agitator without a slogan, a revolutionary without a program'.[37] Throughout Mailer refers to himself as a 'radical humanist' hoping for a more propitious moment, who sees the Hipster 'with his adoration of the present' not as a New Man, but as the product and reflection of the political collapse of the 1950s:

> ... these have been the years of conformity and depression. A stench of fear has come out of every pore of American life, and we suffer from a collective failure of nerve. The only courage, with rare exceptions, that we have been witness to, has been the isolated courage of isolated people.[38]

The bulk of 'The White Negro' Mailer devotes to delineating the mores, the language and milieu of Hipsters as the rise of antipolitics, or at best a 'politics of style', which on its face seems very far from the wild idealism evoked by the derring-do of Castro's *muchachos*. Yet embedded in this voracious examination of life lived for its own sake is its flipside, the alternate, wholly political reality of choosing 'to accept the terms of death, to live with death as immediate danger, to divorce oneself from society, to exist without roots...' – the option, in other words, of making revolution. Of course, by the summer of 1957 when 'The White Negro' first appeared, this is exactly what Fidel Castro and his Rebel Army were already doing, and thanks to a small but powerful phalanx of solidarity in the US press, their private war was already famous, so it can be presumed and even demonstrated that others, if not Mailer himself, had begun comparing their own desperate stasis with the state of grace newly achieved by a few young men in nearby Cuba.

The distance between the Hipster, the rebel without a cause (what Mailer called the 'sexual radical'), and the rebels in Cuba did not appear very great at the time. Castro was popularized here in the most colloquial terms – one young freelance journalist described him as 'a combination Robin Hood, George Washington and Gregory Peck', and the famous *New York Times* correspondent Herbert L. Matthews summed up his first impression of Fidel with the telling words, 'this was quite a man'.[39] As we shall see in greater detail, it was Fidel's virility as much as anything else that the Yankee press cheered on, but even more revealing is the considerable consternation in some quarters. Were the *barbudos* nothing but wild men, kids with guns, frontiersmen in the Wild West of American night life – which taken literally was a rather precise definition of the role Cuba played as the extremity of North America's culture of consumption? Did they believe in anything? It is hardly incidental that in his first examination of Castroism for *The Nation*, Carleton Beals damned what he saw as the amoral adventurism of the 26th of July Movement under the headline 'Rebels Without a Cause'.[40]

Indeed, the connection, unmistakable in terms of how Castro was 'read' here, lies precisely in the crises of gender identity rendered indelibly in *Rebel Without a Cause*. Publicity for the film claimed that it was about the problem of 'teenage violence', with its posters featuring the famous still of a coolly grinning James Dean in jeans, a white tee-shirt and a red jacket, leaning against a wall with his legs crossed, and the slogan 'A BAD BOY FROM A GOOD FAMILY'. Another poster restates the message with a sardonic leer, placing over a still of Dean and Natalie Wood holding each other the caption '... AND THEY BOTH CAME FROM 'GOOD' FAMILIES!'

But, as every kid knew who saw the picture, it wasn't 'Jim', the eponymous character played by Dean, who was 'bad', but the whole rotten world around him, and most centrally the absence of viable models for manhood, and the failure of the father. The plot begins on this note, with no great subtlety, as a drunken Jim yells 'Why can't you be a man?' at the father (Jim Backus), who has come to pick him up at a police station. The latter is the perfect man of his time, kindly, placid and indulgent – a type usually depicted with sympathy in the new 'situation comedies' that rapidly came to dominate television's depiction of family life as quintessentially suburban (for instance, Carl Betz in *The Donna Reed Show* or Robert Young in *Father Knows Best*).[41] But unlike such reasoning, reassuring figures, Jim's dad is also wholly ineffectual, dominated by a harridan wife and mother-in-law, always worried about what people will think, and incapable of understanding his son's need for a man he can emulate, admire and obey. The father's only response to Jim's desperate pleas for attention by getting into 'trouble', as in the opening scene when he has been picked up for drunkenness, is to buy him things or to give him a 'new start' by moving to a new town. This failure of parents as men and women, and therefore of the entire hypocritical, go-along-to-get-along adult world is underlined by each of the other teenage characters. In an exact reverse of Jim's situation, his girl's family features a domineering father who literally pushes his daughter away, and a weak mother unable to offer protection or guidance. Most pointed, of course, is the pathetic, doomed rich kid 'Plato' (Sal Mineo), whose fundamental masculine identity is crippled by his effective abandonment; in scenes with clearly homoerotic overtones, he turns to Jim as a surrogate father or brother. Given the collapse of the natural order that each of these harrowing 'families' represents, the only recourse becomes the apparently aimless violence that accompanies Jim wherever he goes: the knife fight, eventually the famous 'chicken run', all of which prove Jim's heroic and virile capacities, and highlight how redundant the hero or rebel has become. The film's ending is hardly a resolution. After a brief idyll hiding out together, Plato is killed by the police despite Jim's courageous, desperate attempt to save him. Jim's dad promises to try harder, but the film's true resolution is crystal clear: to be a man now, you can count only on yourself, be unafraid to break the rules, and become an outlaw if necessary.

In this sense, ordinary life in the US (or how it was talked about and filmed and pondered) proved to be much more of an 'open text' than it must have seemed at the time. In their own infantile fashion, the products of Hollywood, Madison Avenue and Tin Pan Alley were full of dissident themes that, even when commoditized, proved to have uncontainable resonances. Consider the whole cult of marginal men and islands-unto-themselves that made this the heyday of the TV Western, the angry loners, cool killers and odd dandy tricksters played by Steve McQueen in *Wanted: Dead or Alive*, Gene Barry in *Bat Masterson*, Hugh O'Brian in *Wyatt Earp*, James Garner in *Maverick* and Richard Boone in *Have Gun, Will Travel*, among many others. Or to put it simply, when the 'rebel' as the trope of manhood renascent is as wildly commoditized as it was from 1955 on, it becomes remarkably easy for new and different commodities to enter into the marketplace. This is the dialectic of advanced capitalism that has long been recognized (albeit with considerable discomfort on the left) by everyone who takes popular culture seriously. It is also the only means of appreciating Fidel's ready appeal for youth here, and his positioning not as a 'politician' but as a fighter, or in the now-hackneyed phrase, 'a man of action'. To all those boys who wanted more than the local, individual kicks of snarling along to 'Hound Dog' and 'Whole Lotta Shakin' Going On' or practicing the slouching and mumbling of a Dean or a Brando, who felt the exaltation of the Montgomery bus boycott, or the contrary restlessness of Dean Moriarty, or who simply liked the idea of going into the hills with a .22 rifle and shooting at cops, Cuba offered a satisfyingly violent, quasi-political alternative. At least some put their admiration into action, but many more cheered along – enough to provide a new and distinct base for solidarity in the very months that full-blown US governmental hostility, culminating in invasion, were being turned upon Cuba in 1960–61.

Remembering the Ricardos: Too Close to Home

The importance of Cuba's physical closeness to the US recurs throughout this story, as a marvelously cheap and permissive getaway spot, as well as a dictatorship too near to be ignored. Both light and dark sides of the island's life combined in a most perverse appeal when revolution brewed, as we shall see. But it's worth underlining that ultimately the meaning of 'Cuba' for the Yankees transcended the island of Cuba itself, and resided here in the US, just as many of Cuba's cities increasingly resembled a Spanish-speaking offshore colony with their mainland radio and television shows and farm clubs for major league baseball. As the Cuban-American historian Louis Pérez, Jr has demonstrated, the familial character of the two countries' relationship, and the ways that Cubans embraced North American mores, achieved a unique intensity by the 1950s. 'Cuba was beginning more and more to sound and look like the United States', he writes, spawning 'a consumer culture without counterpart elsewhere in Latin America', and in turn a consumption crisis because the dependent economy based on sugar production simply could not keep up with Cubans' desires.

57

Yet it was not only Cubans who took a foreign presence to their bosoms in ways that were, wholly without intention, destabilizing. Perhaps the best way to unravel the curiously 'homey' and intimate welcome the Yankees gave Fidel Castro as one of their own is to remember that, before Fidel, the best known Cuban by far was a character as American as apple pie – Lucy Ricardo's lovable bandleader husband on the most popular television comedy of that era, *I Love Lucy*. It is easy to dismiss any larger resonances attached to Desi Arnaz as Ricky Ricardo; he seems such an everyday, familiar presence as a straight man, so un-Cuban given how the island's revolution and Castroism dominate our retrospective memories. All the more reason to remember Ricky – he was both foreign and funny, with his endlessly imitated bellow 'Loooo-seee!', and very much one of our own. Stressing that the 26th of July Movement's founders came 'from those quarters of historical proximity with the North Americans', Pérez concludes that 'North American influences in Cuba served to release the forces that would eliminate the North American influence in Cuba.'[42] As it turns out, that influence itself cut both ways – the paradox of Yankee cultural hegemony was that it validated a Cuban presence in the United States that *also* 'served to release the forces that would eliminate the North American influence in Cuba'.

Notes

1. President Harry Truman's famous formulation, in his 1947 speech to a joint session of Congress inaugurating the global policy of containment known as the Truman Doctrine.
2. William J. Lederer and Eugene Burdick, *The Ugly American*, New York: Norton, 1958, p. 7.
3. Ibid., p. 23.
4. Ibid., p. 23.
5. Ibid., pp. 23–4.
6. At points this picture of Machiavellian Soviet guile is unintentionally droll:

> At the Moscow School for Asian Areas, both Ambassador-designate and Madame Krupitzyn went through two years of rigorous studies to prepare them for their new job. They learned to read and write Sarkhanese. They learned that the ideal man in Sarkhan is slender, graceful and soft-spoken; that he has physical control and outward tranquility; that he is religious (Buddhism is the prevalent religion); and that he has an appreciation of the ancient classical music.
>
> The Ambassador-designate molded himself into this pattern. He dieted and lost forty pounds; he took ballet lessons. He read Sarkhanese literature and drama, and became a fairly skillful player on the nose flute. ... (ibid., p. 35)

7. Richard Slotkin, 'Gunfighters and Green Berets: *The Magnificent Seven* and the Myth of Counter-Insurgency', *Radical History Review* 44 (April 1989), pp. 86, 75.
8. Allen Woll, *The Latin Image in American Film*, revised edn, Los Angeles: University of California, Los Angeles, Latin America Center Publications, 1980, pp. 4–5.
9. Ibid., pp. 10–13, 30.
10. Quoted in ibid., pp. 47–8.
11. Ibid., p. 61. My account of this period is indebted to George Black's *The Good Neighbor: How the United States Wrote the History of Central America and the Caribbean*, New York: Pantheon, 1988, a unique and stimulating blend of cultural analysis and pictorial documentation.

12. See Paul J. Vanderwood, 'An American Cold Warrior: *Viva Zapata!* (1952)' in John E. O'Connor and Martin A. Jackson, eds, *American History/American Film: Interpreting the Hollywood Image,* New York: Ungar, 1979, pp. 183–201.

13. Ibid., p. 198.

14. Gerald Pratley, *The Cinema of John Huston,* South Brunswick, N.J. and New York: A. S. Barnes, 1977, p. 74. In any number of films of the 1930s and 1940s, Cuba represents the domain of vice, corruption, pleasure and desire. See Michael Curtiz's *Out of the Fog* (1940) with John Garfield, and Huston's 1948 *Key Largo* with Humphrey Bogart, as well as that year's *The Breaking Point,* also with Garfield.

15. Quotes from *Hollywood Reporter* and *Daily Worker* in William F. Nolan, *John Huston: King Rebel,* Los Angeles: Sherbourne Press, 1965, p. 77.

16. 'A Second Look', *Cineaste,* vol. 15, no. 3 (1987), pp. 56–7.

17. Slotkin, 'Gunfighters and Green Berets', p. 66. Slotkin lists thirty-five such films during 1954–70, beginning with *Vera Cruz,* in which Gary Cooper and Burt Lancaster played charming freebooters and Civil War veterans who cross the Rio Grande.

18. Ibid., pp. 66, 76.

19. *New York Times,* 20 May 1957.

20. I thank my friends Lynn Mahoney and Charles Ponce de Leon for this comparison.

21. *Time,* 10 March 1958. See also Tad Szulc, *Twilight of the Tyrants,* New York: Henry Holt, 1962, for a representative treatment of this period.

22. A good short description of the case is Russell H. Fitzgibbon's preface to the belated English-language publication of Galíndez's dissertation, *The Era of Trujillo,* Tucson, Ariz.: University of Arizona Press, 1973, pp. *xi–xviii.* The Spanish-language version was published in Chile to great acclaim throughout Latin America only a few months after Galíndez's disappearance.

23. As reported in the *New York Times* of 21 March 1956, these and other groups sent a telegram to Attorney General Herbert Brownell, urging an FBI investigation. The *Times* described Galíndez as an 'anti-Communist journalist'.

24. *New York Times,* 7 June and 4 July 1956.

25. See letter, Frances R. Grant to Rep. Porter, 3 June 1957 (written from San Juan, Puerto Rico): 'You have already become a Legend here. ... One of the providential happenings in the cause of Inter-American relations, especially as they concern the evolution of democracy, has been your coming to Congress and your courage in attacking the problem of our attitude to the Latin American dictatorships. For this we are all indebted to you. ...', in FGP; also Charles O. Porter, 'The Struggle Without End', *New Leader,* 14 April 1958, 'My mail, my visitors and my reception on four trips to Latin America in 1957 make it clear that I enjoy wide popularity on that continent'.

26. *New York Times,* 15 May 1958.

27. Harold Flender, 'Cuba Libre', *The New Leader,* 3 March 1958.

28. *New York Times,* 5 May 1957. The bullish naiveté and fragility of such solidarity is suggested by the writer's suggestion that US citizens should aid Cuba in the spirit of 'the volunteers of '98'.

29. *Look,* 4 February 1958.

30. David Horowitz, *Student!,* New York: Ballantine Books, 1962, p. 9.

31. Without question, the 1950s crisis of gender affected both young men and young women, but it was represented at first almost entirely through male characters. This reflected the relative degrees of cultural repression: anxieties about male performance and autonomy lay barely below the surface of almost every popular text, partly because they fit more readily into pre-existing narrative patterns, as already seen in the 'Mexico Western'. Anyone wanting to understand the 'male revolt' of the fifties, to which I offer here a small coda, must consult Barbara Ehrenreich, *The Hearts of Men: American Dreams and the Flight from Commitment,* New York: Anchor/Doubleday, 1983.

32. James Putnam O'Brien, 'The Development of a New Left in the United States, 1960–1965' (Ph.D. dissertation, University of Wisconsin, 1971), p. 53.

33. See Elaine Tyler May, *Homeward Bound: American Families in the Cold War Era,* New York: Basic Books, 1988, for a fine reading of how empire was gendered into the fabric of America's homelife.

34. The idea of a 'dominant trope' for male film stars of a given era is drawn from a talk by Robert Sklar at Rutgers University in May 1990, in which he examined the group of 'city boys' – James Cagney, John Garfield and Humphrey Bogart – whose gendered class position (and personal

politics) defined a dominant Hollywood trope in the 1930s and 1940s. In moving this device forward, note that the figure of the violent anti-hero who fascinates women in spite of themselves was of course age-old, but suddenly reappeared after World War II in performances by Gregory Peck (*Duel in the Sun*, 1946), Montgomery Clift (*Red River*, 1949), and of course Marlon Brando. In music, white kids' fascination with the newly electrified African-American 'rhythm and blues' also dated from the late 1940s. As early as 1951 the Cleveland disc jockey Alan Freed dubbed it 'rock 'n' roll' in a tremendously popular show aimed at this new audience; Freed was only one of a number of white entrepreneurs and promoters around the country who contributed to the movement from below that went public on a massive scale after 1955.

35. Norman Mailer, 'The White Negro', reprinted in Gene Feldman and Max Gartenberg, eds, *The Beat Generation and the Angry Young Men*, Secaucus, N.J.: Citadel Press, 1984 (1958), p. 344.

36. Ibid., pp. 344–6.

37. Quoted in ibid., p. 349.

38. Ibid., p. 343. Mailer's analysis of the position of the black man (once one gets beyond the embarrassing references to jazz as 'the infinite variations of joy, lust, languour, growl, cramp, pinch, scream and despair of his orgasm. For jazz is orgasm') is equally precise and polemical: 'he has been living on the margin between totalitarianism and democracy for two centuries' (pp. 344, 346).

39. J. L. Pimsleur, *The New Leader*, 30 September 1957; Herbert L. Matthews in the *New York Times*, 24 February, 1957.

40. *The Nation*, 29 June 1957.

41. See David Marc, 'Comic Visions of the City: New York and the Television Sitcom', *Radical History Review* 42 (September 1988), pp. 49–63. Marc describes how the existence of race and ethnicity were effaced in the mid fifties in favor of 'a kind of Eisenhower Walden where adolescence and moral ambiguity were trotted out each week and proven to be no match for the paternal instincts of a rational whitebreadwinner' (pp. 53–4).

42. Louis A. Pérez, Jr, *Cuba and the United States: Ties of Singular Intimacy*, Athens, Ga.: University of Georgia Press, 1990, pp. 210, 226, 234.

3

The Yankee Fidelistas

In one sense, the development of solidarity with the rebellion in Cuba was purely fortuitous. Latin America's special place as a beneficiary of benign neglect on the part of the US before and during the Cold War set the larger context. Events from the Montgomery bus boycott to the streetfighting in Budapest to the Galíndez affair framed a distinct moment. Guilt over Cuba as a running scandal provided a motive. Yet this degree of determination would have been meaningless without the coming together of a radical shift in the subjectivity of one sector of North American society with the Cubans' own agency, which, like all impulses to self-determination, remained also a highly contingent, subjective 'human' factor. And this contingency itself was a decisive element in the historical interaction between a 'new' left waiting to be born and the Cuban Revolution, because it was the rebels' insistence on themselves as the subjects of their own history, even in the streets of North America, that made them so magnetic to their would-be cousins and *compañeros* in the North.

From the end of 1956 through the flight of Batista in the early morning hours of New Year's Day 1959, the Cuban insurgency was a major 'story' for North Americans, attracting consistent attention as a bit of offshore exotica – the beards, especially – and a more intense identification from a minority. This fascination with revolution in Cuba was as intensely personalized then as it is now. Fidel Castro appeared to sum up everything that was attractive about the uncategorizable insurrection, just as in later decades he was the convenient vehicle for the demonization of the revolutionary process. For young people and older liberals as well he became a kind of Latin American White Knight – a real-life 'Zorro' or 'Cisco Kid', the freelance idealist of violence made genteel by his Hispanicism. As President Eisenhower's own brother and key advisor put it, with unintentional irony, Castro was 'a symbol of a noble revolution'.[1] Many narrators would stop the story there, assuming a one-to-one correspondence, usually seen as malignant, between the tensions within US culture and the lemming-like tendencies of youth (towards drugs, orgiastic revels, and false gods like Fidel and Ho Chi Minh). Indeed it has often seemed that the only people in the US who retain a strong memory of Castro's popularity here are vengeful Tories like George Will or Patrick Buchanan. I intend to go beyond sketching a possible conjuncture, which by itself demonstrates nothing but contingency, and show how the solidarity of 1957–58 was constructed, not as a conspiracy, but by often uncoordinated responses to serious political contradictions affecting a wide range of North Americans and Cubans.

First to be considered is the massive support of the Cuban-American community, which produced most of the concrete aid (recruits, munitions and organized publicity) emanating from the US, and which recruited individual North Americans into everything from public relations to gun-running. Second is the way in which this involvement of US citizens merged with the enthusiasm for Castro along a wide front of the North American press, and how this zeal also translated into concrete political actions within mainstream politics. Finally, the phenomenon of that small but highly visible number of North Americans who enlisted as guerrilla fighters is explored through a variety of media – television documentary, combat memoir, oral history and popular fiction.

The Exiles and the Pull of Cuban History

The agitation by Cubans in the United States for their country's liberation had an exceptionally long history, stretching back into the nineteenth-century struggle against Spain. For Castro, Batista and thousands of other Cubans on all sides of the political wars of mid-twentieth-century Cuba, the mainland remained the place to return to, and return from – a home away from home. An awareness of how intimate and almost claustrophobic were these relations from a Cuban point of view is therefore essential to understanding the Cuban revolutionaries' strategy towards the US, both when they sought the favor of the North American public, and when they finally declared Cuba's first real independence. Hugh Thomas comes closest to summing up the Cubans' historical perspective in the 1950s. In his words, Castro originally 'fought as a political leader driven to take up arms but willing to make concessions and gestures to all. As in previous Cuban civil wars, liberal North Americans helped the Cuban rebels to the best of their considerable ability.'[2]

The long-term salience of this geographical/historical relationship is indicated by Fidel's own experiences, and those of many of his comrades, long before anyone outside Cuba had heard of them. Like many Cubans of his class, the US was the first place he turned for refuge, leisure or outside political support in his prerevolutionary career, and even later. On retiring from the presidency in 1944, Fulgencio Batista himself had moved to Daytona Beach,

Florida.[3] Castro first came to the US on his honeymoon with Mirta Díaz-Balart in 1948, the year that Batista returned to Cuba and began planning his return to power. Only a year later, however, Fidel was back in the US as an exile. An outspoken student leader, he fled the *bonches* or 'action groups' then terrorizing Cuban politics, and lived at 155 West 82nd Street on Manhattan's Upper West Side for several months, while considering graduate study at Columbia University.[4] The latter was hardly an unusual choice for young Cuban intellectuals. If Fidel had enrolled at Columbia in 1950 instead of returning to Havana to pursue a political career with the reformist Partido del Pueblo Cubano (the so-called 'Ortodoxos'), he would probably have met Manuel Pineiro, later head of the Americas Department of Castro's remade Cuban Communist Party; in these same years Vilma Espín, a key female leader later married to Raúl Castro, studied engineering at the Massachusetts Institute of Technology; and Camilo Cienfuegos, later apotheosized as a revolutionary saint after his untimely death in 1959, worked in a Chicago tailor shop.[5] But young Cubans did not just go to the US for pleasure, refuge, work or an education. Some served in the US Army, acquiring experience they would later put to revolutionary purposes, like Isaac Santos, who trained the volunteers for the attack on the Moncada Barracks in 1953.[6] Quite a few played baseball here, including one of the eighteen men Herbert L. Matthews met when he 'found' Fidel in February 1957; Castro himself had spent several weeks at a Washington Senators 'tryout' camp in 1944, soon after being named the top high school athlete in Cuba.[7] Even Ernesto Guevara, whom the Cubans would later dub 'El Che', somehow found his way to the US in 1952, though perhaps even then more to inspect the enemy than for pleasure, spending an ignominious month in Miami when his funds ran out during a hemispheric tour.[8]

Beyond these personal and anecdotal histories, the statistical evidence compiled by Louis Pérez, Jr suggests that it was quite usual for middle-class Cubans to visit the US often, if only to shop in New York and Miami.[9] More important for poorer Cubans was the large North American presence in Cuba itself – the mining companies, oil refineries, hotels, casinos and sugar plantations run or managed by US citizens, the missionaries scattered around the island, and, of course the huge military establishment at Guantánamo. Indeed, Havana was long a favorite port-of-call for the US military, famed as a truly wide-open place and 'the best liberty town in the world', as a young ex-airman named LeRoi Jones remembered it a few years later. For *habañeros*, therefore, if not for the rural proletariat who formed Cuba's silent majority, Yankees were tourists – 300,000 a year by the mid 1950s – usually looking to gamble, drink and pursue the exceptional range of sexual entertainments unavailable in the States.

Besides the Cuban bourgeoisie's attachment to the US, and the island's special status as playground and investment-site for North Americans, there was a third aspect to the relationship: the historic working-class Cuban communities in Florida and the Northeast, traditionally organized around cigar-making. Since José Martí's time, this was where money and recruits were raised for insurgent expeditions, and in the 1950s stateside support remained crucial in Cuban politics. Even while in jail on the Isle of Pines in 1954, Fidel was issuing instructions detailing how the Ortodoxo clubs in New York should commemorate the first anniversary of the Moncada attack.[10] Upon Batista's amnesty for the Moncada survivors, Castro and a core of men went to Mexico, but the question of consolidating the Cuban-American base came first, before training men, buying weapons, or making alliances.

In October 1955, Fidel embarked on a seven-week tour covering the eastern US from Tampa, Key West and Miami to New York and the nearby Cuban communities in Bridgeport, Connecticut and Union City, New Jersey. In recognition of the past and to emphasize the gravity of his intentions, Fidel's staging of his own coming-to-America had a ritualistic aspect, intended to remind the immigrant communities of the long fight not yet completed for national sovereignty – praising the Acción Civica Cubana in New York for having the 'spirit of the club of émigrés of 1868 and 1895', and telling a New York audience that 'we are getting some things done among the émigrés here just as our Apostle Martí did in a similar situation.'[11] Everywhere, he spoke to large crowds at banquet halls and theaters, on occasion displaying his young son to the crowd (little Fidelito attended school in New York until the revolutionary victory), and speaking in dramatic terms of his duties as a father and a patriot. Always a hat was passed, and the audiences gave substantial sums for the invasion unequivocally guaranteed for the coming year: 'I can tell you with complete confidence that in 1956 we will either be free men or we will be martyrs. That means that in 1956 we will be fighting in Cuba.'[12]

This tour was no one-shot affair. There were many others vying for the political allegiance of the Cuban-Americans, many with more money and name recognition, if less respect, than the young and penniless Castro. As an essential aspect of establishing hegemony over the anti-Batista forces, from those like ex-President Carlos Prío Socarras scheming for the *status quo ante* to the good-government Ortodoxos he had left behind, Castro organized a network of six Patriotic Clubs, which rapidly expanded; the United States ultimately had sixty-two branches of the 26th of July Movement.[13] Later, a high-level Exile Committee headed by a prominent anti-Communist Cuban academic, Mario Llerena, was added, provoking endless internecine feuding over who had Fidel's personal blessing. These groups continued to function through 1959 (and at least in the case of New York have organizational descendants to the present day), providing crucial support to the revolution in terms of weapons, new soldiers and most of all, eye-catching publicity.[14] Indeed, the exile front in the US was so important that Fidel almost certainly would have visited the US again if he could, to exercise the personal direction for which he became famous as a head of state. But the Cuban government protested angrily against his 1955 tour, and eventually persuaded the US to deport him with a ban on further entry (he did slip into the US once again before the victory, swimming the Rio Grande to meet with Prío Socarras in McAllen, Texas in September 1956).[15] A further measure of Castro's desire for close supervision came in late spring 1958, after the disastrous attempt at a general strike and insurrection in Havana. Haydée Santamaria, one of two women among the inner circle of Moncada veterans (the other was Vilma Espín), was sent to supervise the US fundraising campaign and weapons shipments in Miami, the by-then notorious hotbed of rearguard intrigue, which *Time* magazine gleefully referred to as a 'hive of revolutionaries ... the revolutionary headquarters of the Americas'.[16]

It is really the high-profile notoriety of the émigrés' support for the 26th of July Movement that concerns us here. Caribbean political exiles have used the US to plot their return, publish newspapers, hold banquets and run guns into and out of their respective islands since the last century; they continue to do so today, yet rarely do their activities make the front page. But widespread anxiety about Batista's regime so close to home, in tandem with Castro's personal charisma and carefully directed discourse of constitutionalism and economic development, impelled both liberal and not-so-liberal observers in the US to give the revolutionaries a rare forum. Within this space, or helping to widen it, was the 26th of July Movement's stateside network, which broke the usually insular pattern of émigré organizing by cannily staging a series of dramatic 'media events' designed to appeal to North America's sense of moral superiority and enjoyment of novelty: running up the 26th of July Movement's flag at Rockefeller Center or the Statue of Liberty while singing the Cuban national anthem, special masses held by the 'Catholic Ladies of Cuba' at St Patrick's Cathedral 'in memory of all victims massacred in Cuba under the Batista regime', and constant pickets and protests, even breaking into a televised World Series game at Yankee Stadium by showering the stands and the field with leaflets – it is not incidental that this last, most spectacular incident was dreamed up by a young Staten Islander, Donald Soldini, while nursing wounds won in battle with Raúl Castro's column in the Sierra Cristal.[17] Most controversial, of course, were the often-abortive expeditions with men and weapons from both Florida and Texas, which led to charges by Batista that the US government's interdiction was insufficiently aggressive, and counter-charges by many Cubans and their North American friends of pro-Batista interference against rightful, however nominally illegal, activities.

The climax of the 26th of July Movement's work in the US came early – too early – revealing how closely this work was tied to strategies implemented in Cuba. In the early spring of 1958, Castro began to publicly warn of a general strike in Havana over the clandestine *Radio Rebelde*, as the first stage of a mass insurrection and final offensive. As it happens, the plan failed abysmally, apparently due to the slapdash habits and middle-class student character of the *fidelistas* in the capital, the collaborationist position of the trade unions and, most important, the concentration and efficiency of Batista's repressive apparatus exactly where the revolution was weakest, in Havana.

In the US, however, the tempo of organizing mounted to a high pitch, as Batista was denounced on the floor of the US Congress and the Eisenhower administration suspended its military aid (though that which was already in the pipeline kept flowing, leading to considerable Cuban bitterness). In the week before the expected shutdown in Havana, the Patriotic Clubs and the Exile Committee timed a whole series of actions, both public and covert, towards the final push when they expected Batista to totter and call on the US for help. Not all worked as intended, but the net effect was intense publicity.[18] On 27 March Arnoldo Barron, the head of one New York grouping, was arrested with thirty-four of his men in Brownsville, Texas as they prepared to embark for Cuba. The next day, hunger strikes began in New York and Miami, and on 29 March a flag was hung from the Empire State Building in New York and a pro-Castro march was reported as far afield as Hollywood. On 31 March three North American bombmakers were arrested in Brooklyn, and the earlier US arms cut-off was officially announced, while two days later, a Rochester, New York company was indicted for illegal arms sales to Castro. On 3 April while massive coverage focused on the advance of Castro's forces in the eastern part of the island and final preparations on both sides in Havana, a full-dress press conference was held in New York attended by all the major news agencies and television networks, where the Exile Committee's top bourgeois spokesmen emphasized that Cubans were 'fighting for freedom, civil liberties and individual rights ... in most clear and absolute terms, we want to express our group's rejection of Communist cooperation.' Then, over the next few days, prominent New Yorkers came forward. Congressman Adam Clayton Powell, Jr, Castro's most ardent supporter among US politicians, denounced Batista's 'assassins' sent here to kill exiles, and Inter-American Association for Democracy and Freedom leader Frances Grant endorsed Castro at a huge banquet held at the Belvedere Hotel.[19]

What was the net effect of this intense mobilization of the Cuban-American community, in hindsight so incongruous when even the words 'Cuban-American' have violently anti-Castro connotations? It is impossible to tell how much of the 26th of July Movement's munitions came from the US: Herbert Matthews later reported that the volume of guns arriving from the US rearguard was exaggerated, since only 40 percent got past the US Coast Guard and the FBI. On the other hand, the presence of Haydée Santamaria in Miami, and the urgent encouragement given Yankees like Donald Soldini, Neill Macaulay and Frank Fiorini in their gun-running suggests that the US pipeline was crucial to the armed struggle.[20] As is often the case, the moral and human aspects may have been as significant as the material factor – even when stymied, the quixotic efforts of the exiles got attention as old-fashioned melodrama with a patriotic edge. Cuban-Americans graphically demonstrated that Castro, and not Batista, enjoyed popular support verging on mass adulation, and this fact confirmed the reports of journalists and returning tourists. With their calculated stunts, and in myriad less-visible ways, they humanized the connection between the US and Cuba, and between the US government and Batista, for all those North Americans who usually paid little attention to foreign news; one still meets people who remember the fervor with which the Cuban waiters staffing Manhattan's nightclubs and bars continually raised money for Fidel.

Still, no matter how agile their tactics, born of long experience with the vagaries of US politics, by themselves neither the Cubans in Manhattan nor those in the hills of Oriente could dictate the kind of attention, much less sympathy, they received from the Republic of the North. They needed an interlocutor, and at the right moment they found not just one, but a whole circle of willing interpreters. The ensuing press coverage amounted to a public relations campaign that, however tinged by naiveté and condescension, vigorously celebrated Fidel Castro and his revolt against all the dead hands of the past.

Our Man in Havana: The Journalist as Activist

Since the dawn of the Cold War, few Third World figures of any sort have received such sustained, sympathetic coverage from the journalistic establishment in the US as did Fidel Castro in the two years before Batista fell. This attention was radically different from the post-1959 caricatures of Castro as a long-winded tyrant, or even the treatment of him as a colorful and charismatic, albeit undemocratic figure, notably during the 1970s. Instead, North American observers portrayed Fidel rather as Hollywood had presented Benito Juárez at a similar time of international uncertainty, certifying him as a Western-oriented individualist committed to a nebulous conception of 'liberty', whose main desire was to emulate 'America'. And while his prowess as a World War II–style partisan leader was often cited, US reporters in 1957–58 paid equal attention to Castro's landowning, middle-class origins, his status as a lawyer and an intellectual, and his Spanish – and therefore racially pure – parentage, Herbert L. Matthews noting in his first scoop that Castro's father, like Francisco Franco, was a 'Gallego', or Galician. The social composition of the revolutionary forces and their program of radical reform was usually ignored, and sometimes willfully misunderstood.

The sensational three-part interview with Fidel Castro that appeared from 24 to 26 February 1957 in the *New York Times*, conducted by its editorialist and retired foreign correspondent Herbert L. Matthews, has been mostly excoriated since the 1960s. Indeed, even a generation later, it seems as if conservatives think no Third World revolution could ever come to power without the toadying appeasement and credulity of crypto-leftists among the US press, with Cuba and the *Times* a particular sore point. The 1960 *National Review* cartoon of a satanically grinning Fidel squatting on a subjugated island labeled 'Police State of Cuba', over the caption 'I Got My Job Through the *New York Times*' captures these sentiments perfectly, and remains a classic piece of liberal-baiting.[21] Still, there is no question that the *New York Times*, as the most powerful arbiter of mainstream opinion, was indispensable in bringing Fidel into the minds and then the hearts of the informed North American public. For all these reasons, any discussion of how insurgent Cuba was received in the US in the 1950s must place Matthews and the *New York Times* at its center. But the *Times* was hardly alone in its enthusiasm for the *fidelista* revolution. As Matthews pointed out in 1961 when he was made a scapegoat for the left turn of the Cuban Revolution, 'a great many other American journalists were writing the same things'.[22]

Rather than treating Matthews as an isolated aberration or quirk of history, it is therefore more accurate to focus on the network of reporters who collaborated with each other in bringing a measure of the Cuban reality to US readers. And the first thing one notices when going beyond the famously 'liberal' *Times* is how eclectic were the politics of those beating the drums for the Cuban Liberator. Matthews's closest rival for Fidel's ear was Jules Dubois of the *Chicago Tribune*, a paper seen for decades as the national mouthpiece of the anti–New Deal, pro–Joe McCarthy Old Right. Andrew St George, writing in *Coronet* and *Look*, was an anti-Communist Hungarian exile almost certainly working for US intelligence services.[23] Robert Taber put Castro on CBS during prime time, but had no defined politics other than prior experience with and sympathy towards Algeria's nationalist rebels. The semi-legendary woman photojournalist Dickey Chapelle, who spent three weeks with Fidel during the final offensive in late 1958 and hailed the rebels in the archconservative *Reader's Digest* as late as April 1959, had made her name chronicling the exploits of the Hungarian Freedom Fighters.[24]

Perhaps the most graphic example of how widespread were pro-Castro sympathies is the handling of the Cuban revolt by the Time/Life company, the empire of Henry Luce, foremost promoter of 'the American Century'. Despite (or because of) their muscular, omnipresent anti-Communism and aggressively pro-imperial stance, Luce's publications championed the 'Rebel Leader' early and often. In the two years before Batista fell, his weekly *Time* – then probably the most broadly influential news voice in the US – ran thirty-one stories on the rebellion in Cuba, almost all focused on Castro as the kind of man North Americans could like and even respect.[25] Announcing the insurgency in December 1956, even before the *Granma*'s landing was known abroad, he was 'Lawyer Castro ... the well-born, well-to-do daredevil of 29'.[26] From then on the tone of admiration for Castro's Hemingwayesque virility and martial highmindedness rarely flagged. Rather than the revolution, the dominant emphasis was always on the personal struggle between the shrewd, swarthy dictator Batista and the 'swashbuckling young lawyer Fidel Castro' at the head of his 'wily, determined rebels', the 'strapping, bearded leader of the never-say-die band of anti-Batista rebels who strike and run.'[27] Of course, this unselfish fearlessness was always in implicit or explicit contrast to the 'fleshpot city of Havana', where 'roulette wheels spin in the casinos, and saucy chippies flirted in the nightspots'.[28]

Only occasionally was Castro's 'bootless, unremitting violence' deplored instead of celebrated, usually when the rebellion appeared to flag.[29] It appears that for *Time* Castro's stock rose or fell as his *machismo*, rather than his politics, was praised or found wanting. By far the most negative characterization of the revolutionaries appeared in late April 1958 after the failed general strike in Havana, when *Time* briefly turned on the rebels, sneering that they were 'soft-handed amateurs'. A week later, under the headline 'Agonizing Reappraisal', it was announced that 'the days of blind Fidelismo were over', since it was now clear that Castro had a 'weakness in practical organizing ability' – weakness of course being the last attribute formerly assigned to the 'Rebel Chief'.[30]

Above all, *Time* writers delighted in the impeccably middle-class character of the revolution. Reporting a secret interview with leaders of the civilian underground in Havana, their reporter sneered at Batista's claim that the rebels were all Communists, sardonically quoting his hosts' claim that 'we are bourgeois', and noting that 'the only proletarians were the help'. His conclusion, echoed many times by North American journalists, was unequivocal: 'this is not a social revolution', since the assassination of one of the anonymous aristos funding Castro would be 'about like killing Lyndon Johnson'.[31]

Like the rest of the world's press, *Time* hit its rhetorical peak after face-to-face encounters with what it dubbed 'This Man Castro'. Following Herbert L. Matthews's exploit, eyewitness reports from the Sierra Maestra became a rite of passage. Contributing Editor Sam Halper's report in the 14 April 1958 issue of *Time* on 'The bearded Rebel Castro' and 'his ragtag, fanatic force' captured virtually all of the major factors in the revolution's favorable presentation to North American audiences: crusading idealism offset by anti-Communist moderation, *machismo* qualified by self-sacrifice. Halper began by noting approvingly that 'Castro is a fighter; 16 months ago he invaded Cuba from a yacht. But he is also an articulate man interested in words, manifestoes, books (he treasures a volume of Montesquieu) and the language of ideas.'

After quoting Fidel on 're-establishing the constitutional rights and freedoms of the people', Halper notes that he had once 'hotheadedly espoused a series of student-radical notions, e.g. nationalization of Cuba's U.S.-owned power and telephone companies.' Castro is then quoted again, to reassure the reader of his maturity: 'I am still the same revolutionary, but I have had time to study the political and economic factors. I understand that some ideas I used to have would not be good for Cuba. I do not believe in nationalization.' *Time* then certifies that 'almost to a man', the Rebel Army is made up of ardent

Roman Catholics 'who wear religious medals on their caps or on strings around their necks.'

Turning from Castro as an individual, Halper effectively sketches the less-than-impressive condition of Castro's 'disorganized, barebones partisan army'. Pointing to their lack of food, equipment and training, he reports plainly that 'nothing about the appearance of Fidel's force would lead me to think it could fight'. But then he quotes Castro: 'If they had been fighting for an ideal, [Batista's troops] could have beaten us 30 times. But no man is supposed to die for $35 a month.' The article concludes on this stirring, suggestive note: 'Castro's men have a cause. They believe in him (and hate Batista) fanatically; they believe they are fighting for their country's freedom. Their real strength lies in the fact that they are obviously willing to die – and for nothing a month.'

Though *Life* did not cover Fidel on a more-than-monthly basis like its sister publication *Time*, the Luce empire's flagship of photojournalism provided powerful images, adding to the Castro mystique. Its big spreads on the Castro boys went all-out for dramatic effect, from the 14 April 1958 montage of Fidel the 'unbending rebel' in close-up, talking and gesturing with his ever-present cigar, to a series of articles on the four dozen US businessmen and military personnel taken hostage by Raúl Castro's column in July 1958 as a shield against Batista's air attacks. From the vantage point of earlier and later US responses to hostage crises, whether the punitive war against the Barbary pirates in the early nineteenth century or the agonies of the Carter and Reagan administrations, it is instructive to survey the sweet reason lavished on this incident in *Life*'s 14 July issue – but then the hostages themselves were the best possible propaganda for *fidelista* virtue. The general tone of 'mutual admiration' (as recorded by *Life*'s photographer) resembled a hunting and drinking party in the woods more than a tense diplomatic imbroglio – indeed the prisoners and their guards reportedly held a Fourth of July celebration, and a US airman exclaimed, 'I am just like one of them.' A week later, the battle-seasoned *Life* team focused on Raúl, the smiling 'Longhaired Leader', and his comrades, 'just like a band of kids'. The presence of the comely 'Deborah' (Vilma Espín) posed with her submachine gun received special attention, as did her impeccably liberal sentiments: the next leader of Cuba should be someone like Adlai Stevenson, she declared.[32] Eventually the remaining hostages were released in a public gesture of deference; the US had invaded Lebanon for anti-Communist purposes, and Raúl Castro declared grandiloquently in a letter to the US admiral commanding at Guantánamo,

> Because of the measures adopted by your nation in the face of the latest international events – taking into account the need your army has for each one of your members in these moments – the Military Commands of the 26th of July Revolutionary Army in the 'Frank País' Second Front have decided to order the immediate release of all the sailors who still remain in our liberated territories.[33]

When examining these old magazines, one finds it easy to denigrate how much their approval meant to the rebels. It was not just that, with rare exceptions, the US press did not Red-bait Fidel. Even the conservative, cautious *US News & World Report*, which displayed little interest in Cuba until the revolution came to power, noted that the 'real fight is being made by non-Communists and nongangsters', and approvingly quoted 26th of July Movement leader Faustino Pérez: 'Of course we're not Communists. I am a practicing Catholic. So are Fidel and the rest. ...'[34] This forbearance alone would not have saved the Cuban Revolution from comparative oblivion, a silence in North America from which the revolution in power would have drawn no sustenance. Instead, leading US magazines and newspapers offered widespread exposure, a relatively unrestricted forum and explicit respect, which became in its effects and its self-consciousness a kind of solidarity unique in the annals of Cold War reportage. As one of the Yankees who actually fought with Castro noted years later, sketching the subtext of his short passage from US Army lieutenant to an officer of the *Ejercito Rebelde*: 'Joining the Cuban Revolution seemed like a good idea. I'd followed its progress in *Time* magazine during my fifteen months in Korea.'[35]

Animating and directing this solidarity was the *New York Times*, the true voice of the vital center, of a determined but cautious liberalism as the natural party of government in the Cold War era. Over two years of guerrilla war, repression and diplomatic maneuvers, its detailed coverage of the 26th of July Movement had an exceptional impact in Cuba as well as in the US and repeatedly gave the *batistianos* apoplexy. In Herbert Matthews's words, describing the effect of 'the most powerful journalistic instrument ... in the free world' on Fidel Castro's rise: 'I turned the spotlight on him. He has held the center of the stage ever since. ...'[36] This was, however, Matthews's more circumspect version of events, when he was being held personally accountable for Cuba going Communist. At the time, writing for his colleagues in the bulletin of the Paris Overseas Press Club, the note of masculine triumph was palpable: 'We hit General Batista so hard we knocked him down and almost knocked him out ... it hit the President and his Government like an atomic bomb.'[37]

This note of confrontation was introduced early on, when the Cuban government's initial response to Matthews's interview was to cable the rival *New York Herald-Tribune* that it was a 'chapter in a fantastic novel'; they had been proclaiming, and perhaps believing, that Castro was in his grave since the *Granma*'s disastrous landing.[38] In response, the *Times* ran a grainy photo of Matthews and Castro smoking cigars together on a jungle slope with a signed and dated note from Fidel, and from that day on – the world's most powerful newspaper having taken sides – the war in all senses had truly begun.

What is usually remembered about this instantly famous and later infamous feat of reporting is the effect of Matthews's articles within the US. Certainly Matthews made Castro into an overnight celebrity-hero, causing journalists to flood into Cuba looking for this charismatic new man of mystery. Yet the impact of what Matthews justifiably called 'the biggest scoop of our times' was greatest in Cuba itself, given the context of repression, censorship and an overwhelming Yankee cultural and political presence. It is this part of the story that has been ignored. Latter-day commentators speak as if Fidel suborned Matthews personally in a Machiavellian move to manipulate North American public opinion, but what really interested the rebels was obtaining coverage from an authoritative source that would be read in Cuba – in Che Guevara's words, this was 'more important for us than a military victory'.[39] As soon as he knew that the interviews would appear and prove that Fidel was alive, Mario Llerena flew to New York from Miami and assembled a team to reprint several thousand copies of the articles and mail them back to a selected audience on the island (he used the Havana telephone directory and Social Register for addresses). The effect was immediate. Matthews himself reported that only a week after the initial story, his article was 'rapidly becoming a national issue', and there is ample evidence to back up his claim.[40] Batista's government did everything it could to discredit the stories, including cutting up all copies that reached the island, until Matthews trumped them with his photo. In Miami the newspaper was rapidly bootlegged among the exiles, while from both Cuba and the mainland telegrams, letters and boxes of cigars flooded Matthews's office at the Times.[41] Even the US embassy's Richard Cushing wrote him a 'personal' note of congratulations, reporting that he had 'caused a lot of seething indignation in high quarters', and that 'I (and others) thought your series was a dandy.'[42] Eventually, Mario Lazo, then the leading Cuban lawyer for North American interests, became so concerned about Matthews's influence on public opinion that he flew to New York to see Harry Guggenheim, former US ambassador to Cuba, hoping that the latter could intercede with the Times.[43]

The results of Matthews's scoop, whether in Cuba or in the US, have been debated (and assailed) for a generation by everyone from neoconservative pundits to George Wallace during his 1968 run for the presidency, and need not concern us too much here.[44] What has not been examined seriously, in terms of delineating the peculiar contours of solidarity with the Cuban Revolution, is how Matthews himself saw his actions, given that for a long time he was a hero to his colleagues and liberal public opinion in general. It is most notable now that, from the first, Matthews wrote nearly as much about the significance of his reporting, with himself cast as another protagonist, as about Cuba itself. The stirring 'lead' paragraphs of his 24 February 1957 New York Times story established the dramatis personae quite explicitly: 'Fidel Castro, the rebel leader of Cuba's youth, is alive and fighting hard and successfully in the rugged, almost inpenetrable fastnesses of the Sierra Maestra. ... No one connected with the outside world, let alone with the press, has seen Senor Castro except this writer. ...'

With this one article, the aging reporter gave Fidel the stature of a legendary figure, at a time when the latter still had only eighteen men actually under arms in the 'Rebel Army'.[45] But Matthews not only did this for Castro, he told his readers he was doing it, and then proceeded to document the remarkable effects of his own agency. Cubans of all sorts reacted: the magisterial voice of North America had spoken, assuring them that not only was Castro surviving, but that he would win. From then on Matthews saw himself, and was seen by many, as a vital player in the revolution, a subtext in the *Times*'s subsequent coverage made quite explicit in a 1957 internal memo:

> ... the role we have been playing since February is of far greater importance to Cuba than that of the State Department. The articles on Fidel Castro and the Cuban situation which I did in February have literally altered the course of Cuban history. ... At the same time I believe that because of the truly extraordinary effect of anything I do or anything that we print editorially on Cuban affairs at this extremely critical point, we must be very careful to remain within the bounds of strict journalism. ... I think we can feel proud of the extraordinary power which *The New York Times* possesses in a situation like this. ...[46]

Reporting upon himself was no one-time affair. During a visit to Santiago de Cuba in June 1957 in what he described as 'a glare of publicity', Matthews found evidence of his own agency everywhere, and duly put that evidence on the front page. In fact, along with his by-now unabashed hero-worship of Castro, Cuba's appreciation of the *Times* is the major focus of his three-day series. Every stratum of local society lined up to meet with the reporter plenipotentiary – the Rotary and Lions clubs, the mothers of boys tortured by Batista's Military Intelligence Service, the Archbishop. Even the anonymous masses felt his solidarity, and were moved to gratitude: 'Dozens of humble persons accosted me on the streets and elsewhere to shake hands. ... Everybody I saw was convinced that the police authorities had orders from Havana to refrain from any act of terrorism during the three days I was here. ... The *Times* gets credit for giving Santiago de Cuba three days of peace, such as this tormented city has not known for many months.'[47]

Eventually Matthews's ardent partisanship brought down a firestorm of abuse from middle-class Cubans who believed that the revolution had been betrayed, and from North American conservatives looking for who 'lost' Cuba. He produced a defiant defence in 1961, *The Cuban Story*, in which he unselfconsciously boasts of his private interventions as a high-level go-between for the 26th of July Movement, as when he helped save the lives of three captured rebel leaders, Armando Hart, Javier Pazos and Antonio Buch: 'This was the way the rebellion had its links to the United States. ...'[48]

Throughout, Matthews's self-portrayal is deeply contradictory, revealing the unreconcilable impulses felt by a certain kind of liberal at that time. Unlike most, Matthews faced these conflicts in himself, even if he never managed to resolve them. Repeatedly in *The Cuban Story* and his later autobiography he insists that his professional duty as a journalist impelled him towards this great 'story', and that he was only history's impersonal agent in making Castro famous and the revolution possible. Anxiously, he assures his readers in 1961 that if Castro is truly 'subverting and stirring up' the hemisphere, 'then he and his regime will have to be destroyed.' Yet elsewhere the subjective identification with Fidel is explicit: he speaks of how 'I was moved, deeply moved, by that young man', and at one point even describes the Cuban Revolution as 'my triumph, along with others'.[49]

Those commentators who avoid imputations of either treachery or lunacy have characterized Matthews's championing of Castro as an old man's foible, the typical sentimentalism of the bleeding heart. At best they concur with his fellow *Times* correspondent Tad Szulc that Matthews sought a 'vindication of the Spanish tragedy' and 'felt almost paternal about this movement of young people. ...'[50] Matthews himself was not immune to offering this alibi. He often chose to balance the discrepancies between the hard-nosed foreign correspondent and the old man refighting the good fight by making himself Castro's Dutch Uncle, a trusted friend and outside arbiter: 'Fidel and I always spoke frankly to each other and he took criticism from me that no one else would have dared to utter. He knew that I was sympathetic, understanding and a friend. ... He is normally a poor listener, but he used to listen to me. ...'[51]

But like so much of the writing on revolution in Cuba, this fetishization of the purely subjective has effaced the actual politics of the situation. Matthews's claiming of a purely personal friendship, sidetracked from the political responsibility of taking sides, cannot obliterate his concrete efforts at solidarity, which the Cubans took seriously indeed. The private documents and reminiscences of that time, even of the fighters in the Sierra Maestra, are full of references to him couched in respectful terms.[52] In the end, as the US right has correctly understood, Matthews's actions speak louder than his carefully chosen words, as does his evident lack of regret and the deference paid in Cuba when they no longer needed his help, despite his always-critical support of a revolution that has never suffered criticism lightly. As late as the mid 1970s, a prominent Sierra Maestra veteran echoed Matthews's oft-repeated references to Fidel and the revolutionary leaders as his 'friends' when he told a North American writer, 'We know that Mr Matthews does not agree with many things we do, but we consider him our friend.'[53]

It is in that gray area of friendship, covering both great commitment and an imprecise distance, that we must leave Matthews's journalistic and personal solidarity, with its gentlemanly and Jeffersonian ethos. What mattered most is that he tapped into, represented and unleashed a larger, unspoken discontent. The cohort of newshounds who followed him built a pathway into North America without which the history of the Cuban Revolution might have been quite different. In later life, Herbert L. Matthews remained the man who assured the US that Castro was not a Communist, exemplifying how treacherous the Third World could be and what to avoid. In less well-publicized ways, he was also an augury of what would come for North American liberalism on the horns of future imperial dilemmas.

Because it did so much to spark the subsequent North American fascination with Castro, however, the significance of Matthews's intervention in early 1957 and thereafter tends to obscure how the *Times* as a whole granted a special dispensation to the *fidelista* movement, not just in Cuba but also in the US. Before anyone had ever heard of the Sierra Maestra, Fidel Castro was given unusual prominence. The *Granma*'s landing in early December 1956 was reported at the top of the front page, along with a photo of a beardless, suited Fidel, the 'exiled student leader', looking like a respectable young lawyer.[54] Three days later the first in a long, regular series of reports on the local New York activities of the 26th of July Movement's 'Club Patriotico' appeared, noting that 200 Cubans had picketed at the United Nations and the Cuban consulate in support of the revolutionary upsurge. Over the next two years this coverage continued, amounting often to free advance publicity: sometimes the *Times* announced meetings in advance, and committee addresses and meeting places were often noted for those seeking further information. Castro's US spokesmen were quoted respectfully, and indeed whole stories were many times little more than interviews with one or another prominent new exile – whether Judge Manuel Urrutia, named by Fidel as Provisional President-in-exile, or dissident army officers, they always came first to New York.[55] Even when US politicians denounced Castro because of the July 1958 kidnapping of North Americans, and editorial cartoonists quickly reverted to caricatures of bloodthirsty bandit-rebels, the *Times* refrained from condemnation.[56]

The Cubans in the US made their gratitude very clear, underlining the symbiotic character of this relationship. One of their largest demonstrations was a rally of appreciation outside the newspaper's offices on West 43rd Street in Manhattan. Four hundred Cubans from New York, New Jersey and Connecticut marched with US and Cuban flags, presenting a signed album recording their thanks for Matthews's articles, all of which was reported in the *Times* in tones of quiet self-congratulation.[57] Thus not only did the *Times* validate the revolution in Cuba, but even more decisively, the solidarity of Cuban-Americans and the sympathy of North Americans, whether public and legal, as in press conferences denouncing Batista's abuses, or private and illegal involvement in fundraising, arms procurement and even fighting.

Similarly, in Cuba itself, the relationship of the *Times* to both the 26th of July Movement and the US government went well beyond Matthews's flying visits and 'personal' connections. Ruby Hart Phillips, who had been reporting from Cuba for decades, regularly acted as a go-between, not only setting up clandestine meetings with embassy staff for rebel emissaries, but also interceding with both Batista and Castro personally on various occasions.[58] And, as when Matthews corresponded with Foreign Service officers or met with Secretary of State Dulles, Phillips clearly did so as a highly placed institutional representative, not as some sort of lone wolf.

Yet a generation's worth of conservative outrage has been directed solely at Matthews, ignoring how the *Times* itself systematically publicized the 26th of July Movement's active solidarity and presented the rebels' doings and their perspective to the Cuban people; perhaps the breadth and complexity of North American support for Castro is simply incomprehensible in certain quarters.[59] As with the assumption that Matthews somehow hypnotized *Times* owner Arthur Ochs Sulzburger and his fellow editors, none of them radical in the least, the fury towards him as an individual deviant has obscured rather than exposed the influence that this institution and others exerted to formulate a new antidictatorial policy in Latin America and the rest of the Third World, with Cuba as a test case.

The 26th of July Movement's prestige among stateside anti-Communist liberals was not simply an obsession of Herbert Matthews and one or two other journalists, one that unaccountably caught on with the public, as if the *New York Times* or *Time* were not part of a particular political superstructure of East Coast opinionmakers and intellectuals. This solidarity went considerably further than frank and therefore helpful press coverage and behind-the-scenes mediation by a few. Across a rather wide front, Democrats and Republicans, college professors and trade unionists, liberals, conservatives and even some parts of the national security bureaucracy took sides on behalf of a revolution in Cuba that they felt was connected with the fight against dangerous reaction and obscurantism at home. In this extragovernmental campaign, the press was simply part of a larger 'lobbying' process, as when Jules Dubois brokered Batista's condemnation as 'not democratic' by the prestigious Inter-American Press Association, while Republican Senator Jacob Javits was successfully urging Secretary of State Dulles to have Matthews brief the new US ambassador to Cuba, Earl E. T. Smith.[60]

Most tellingly, the only people who stepped forward to defend Batista were the same figures defending white supremacy at home, like Senator Allen Ellender of Louisiana, who held a press conference at the US embassy in Havana a few weeks before Batista's fall, at which he denied there was a civil war going on other than that 'bandits are burning sugar plantations', and urged the restoration of US military aid.[61] On this issue as on many others, such as the desegregation of Southern schools, the Eisenhower administration ended up rather uncomfortably in the middle until by late 1958 it moved towards a queasily reformist position of supporting Batista's removal by moderate forces that could block Castroite radicalism. Backing Castro, therefore, became in the context of the times and discarding the false lens of hindsight, a small but worthwhile success in the vital center's battle for a more worldly, self-critical

and modernizing America, an America taken away from the provincial Babbitts with their White Citizens Councils and the Jenners, Eastlands and other
epigones of Joe McCarthy who, along with the most famous Mafia figures,
shared a cronyish fondness for the likes of Batista. After all, Castro was a man
of 'surprisingly moderate views' that added up to 'a kind of welfare-state liberalism', as the *Washington Post*'s editorial writer Karl Meyer found after visiting
with Fidel in 1958.[62] Over and over again, the exiled middle-class leaders who
spoke for him in the US (themselves latecomers to the 26th of July Movement) gave reassurances of his anti-Communism, and on occasion Fidel himself offered proof that he could be trusted – though usually in deliberately
ambiguous language.[63] In any case, the 26th of July Movement's themes of
national sovereignty and self-respect, and the implications of its fealty to
Martí, were simply so much boilerplate to North Americans, who assumed
acquiescence in US hemispheric leadership.

The best way to demonstrate the mechanics of anti-Batista, pro-Castro liberal pressure is to outline the connections between private and public action.
Not surprisingly, the Inter-American Association for Democracy and Freedom
played a role in the marshalling of liberal and centrist forces. At the time,
1957–58 must have seemed like the IADF's and the 'Democratic Left's' vindication. As the Galíndez campaign revived old antidictatorial sympathies towards Latin American democrats, IADF founder Rómulo Betancourt returned
to power in Venezuela, and Batista appeared to be next on the list of dictators
to fall. IADF Secretary General Frances Grant established a close working relationship with the 26th of July Movement's Exile Committee, unreservedly
hailing the revolution at numerous press conferences and banquets. When
Manuel Urrutia, the provincial judge whom Castro named as provisional
president, came to New York to denounce Batista for encouraging 'gambling
and contraband in narcotics', his press conference was held at her office, and
Grant stood beside him to announce that her organization was preparing a
report to the United Nations on terrorism and human rights violations in
Cuba.[64] But it is the IADF's more behind-the-scenes efforts, overlapping with
the work of the Exile Committee, that serve to indicate how a revolution in
Cuba got a respectful hearing among elite sectors in the US.

Herbert Matthews is the premier example of how farflung and effective the
IADF's network could be in the right circumstances. He was a 'de facto' member of its US Committee, working closely with Frances Grant to influence US
policy in alliance with sympathetic members of the Foreign Service since he
was appointed the *Times*'s editorialist on Latin America in 1950.[65] As he put it
in his autobiography, the forgotten State Department people were so grateful
that the august *Times* would pay attention to their region that 'the Inter-
American Bureau was put at my disposal'.[66] Long before meeting Castro, Matthews had made a practice of denouncing dictators and promoting the
perspective of the IADF in the *Times*, as in the Galíndez case, and more than

once he had forced the release of innocent democrats, in one instance even smuggling himself into an Argentine prison.

Matthews was hardly the IADF's only vehicle for securing entrée to influential North Americans on behalf of the various émigré causes. Its leaders, especially Grant and Norman Thomas, performed this service for Cuban oppositionists in a variety of ways: writing to officers of Americans for Democratic Action, senators like Jacob Javits, and of course to Secretary Dulles.[67] Meanwhile, working through the 26th of July Movement's registered 'foreign agent' in Washington, Ernesto Betancourt, and aided by the IADF's connections and unexpected support from various quarters, Mario Llerena found himself in great demand as Castro's US spokesman. Betancourt arranged meetings with the State Department and with Congressman Charles Porter, who had already made his name denouncing Trujillo, and who wanted to go to Cuba to meet with Castro. Llerena in turn hoped to bring Porter a letter from Fidel, which the latter could then make public under advantageous circumstances, but for reasons he never discovered, these proposals excited little interest in the Sierra.

Most curious, and still unexplained, was how Llerena and Fidel secured their most outspoken backer in the US, the flamboyant Harlem Congressman Adam Clayton Powell, Jr, whose speeches on the floor of the House backed up with confidential documents Llerena had been sent by the military attaChe at the Cuban embassy 'caused no little commotion in Washington official circles'.[68]

In his telling, Llerena was introduced to a man named Arnold Johnson by Manolo Couzeiro, a 'beatnik' Cuban painter who had already excited Llerena's suspicions by reporting offers of aid he claimed to have received from US Communists. Johnson, who claimed Cuban parentage, in turn introduced Llerena to Representative Powell as well as 'a number of influential blacks with whom he was acquainted – professionals, journalists, radio commentators, businessmen.'[69] From this encounter came Powell's 20 March 1958 speech followed by Porter's further attack on 26 March and a few days later the administration's admission that on 14 March it had held up a Cuban government shipment of 1,950 Garand rifles at the New York docks, effectively signaling that the US no longer wanted to risk too much on Batista. Soon after, in an eerie replay of Borah's denunciations of Machado a quarter of a century earlier, Senator Wayne Morse even demanded an investigation of Batista's abuses by the Senate Foreign Relations Committee – all this in the context of a mounting wave of public agitation by the Cuban community in the US, as noted earlier. But Llerena's account of his alliance with Powell as 'the most significant development that took place while I was the 26 of July's delegate', and Arnold Johnson's central role, is oddly tantalizing, as if there was some mystery or conspiracy involved that he could not fathom: he specifies that Johnson 'could have been acting on behalf of some group or party, though I have no knowledge that he belonged to any.'[70] This mystery is clarified to some extent by reports of Johnson's encounters with others. He visited Norman Thomas and Frances Grant a few months later to urge action against Batista, and Thomas's letter to Grant explains the basis of Llerena's suspicions, and points to a surprising willingness on Thomas's part to cooperate with the 'Democratic Left's' arch-enemies:

> A man named Arnold Johnson, a Communist who used to be a very good man before he was a Communist and who has had some experience in Cuba and with Cubans, came to see me urging some kind of statement on the subject of the Batista dictatorship. I thought he had some knowledge that I lacked and suggested that he put on paper what he thought would be good. I enclose the result.
>
> I want to raise the question with you whether it would not be good for our Inter-American Association to make a statement on the Batista dictatorship which we might possibly get outsiders of importance to sign for purposes of publicity. None of those outsiders should be under any suspicion of communism. I do not suggest this draft as a model for such a statement although it seems to be reasonably worded. ...[71]

Whether Johnson was acting on his own, using the personal contacts that black Communists retained in black circles, whether some discreet intervention was attempted at the behest of the Cuban CP (the Partida Socialista Popular), which was in early 1958 negotiating an alliance with Castro (or whether Johnson was a 'Communist' at all), remains unclear. Leftists concerned with Latin America remember considerable disagreement as to whether Castro was a revolutionary or just an adventurer, and enthusiasm for him among the anti-Communist US press could only have fueled apprehensions among those used to being out in the cold.

The ramifications of supporting Castro produced myriad strange cohabitations. As we have seen, some intensely anti-Communist and usually rightwing voices found much to cheer in the new 'strong man', though there were always those who saw any kind of rebel as a likely Red, and rumors of the Castro brothers' past ties to the Marxist left periodically had to squelched by the 26th of July Movement's anti-Communist US representatives. But even among Fidel's putative allies on the IADF's antidictatorial front, the latter's endorsement of the 26th of July Movement provoked a split. Serafino Romualdi, who as the AFL and then the AFL-CIO point man on the Americas had helped organize the IADF, had close political and personal ties to Eusebio Mujal, the pro-Batista boss of the Confederación de los Trabajadores Cubanos (CTC). Indeed, Mujal cited his ties with Romualdi in denouncing the *New York Times*'s pro-Castro coverage.[72] As late as March 1958, Romualdi led a top-level AFL-CIO delegation to Havana for the opening of the Havana Hilton, while claiming that this was 'solely to honor the achievements of a trade union organization' – a union pension fund had underwritten the hotel's construction – and when the general strike failed in part due to the CTC's opposition, the AFL-CIO resisted demands from 'Castro sympathizers' to denounce its brother federation. Subsequently, Romualdi and the AFL-CIO worked closely with Mujal to make a deal with Batista and bring in a provisional government that would forestall the 26th of July Movement.[73]

What was apparently an intramural dispute among anti-Communist social democrats spilled over into the letters column of *The New Leader*, when Romualdi objected to a critical review of his friend Robert Alexander's book *Communism in Latin America* by Daniel James. In rebuttal, James waxed acerbic about the 'Democratic Left' championed by Alexander and Romualdi and in passing anyone who supported Castro, asking:

> Where, finally, is the 'democratic Left' in the current fight against President Fulgencio Batista in Cuba? As far as one can make out Fidel Castro is by no means a democratic (or any other kind of) leftist. Nor do there seem to be other kinds of leaders or parties of a democratic leftist coloration as active as Castro in that struggle. On the other hand, it is a shameful fact that the leader of Cuban trade unionism, Eusebio Morales [sic] – who has long been a power in the Inter-American Regional Organization of Workers alongside Romualdi – is one of the bulwarks of the Batista regime.[74]

James proved to be rather in the minority in finding no 'democratic left' in Cuba. Spurred by a complex of intentions and needs on both sides, sections of organized political opinion in the US actively functioned on behalf of the 26th of July Movement, both in assigning a discourse of liberty, democracy and freedom to the *fidelistas* in their struggle against Batista, and in periodic *sub rosa* mediations. This is hardly a new story. As David Brion Davis has recently pointed out, it is wrong to posit, as do many New Left–influenced historians, that since its own revolution in 1776 the United States has viewed all other revolutions with suspicion, if not actively counter-revolutionary hostility.[75] Rather, the US has oscillated between two responses, depending largely on the reception (and therefore the presentation) of a particular revolutionary movement domestically. To the extent that a movement is seen as directly confronting US national interests, as in Guatemala a little earlier and Vietnam throughout this whole period, it must wage an uphill battle for any legitimacy within all but the left periphery of US politics. On the other hand, if a movement is depicted or displays itself as wishing to emulate US democratic traditions, it has a good chance of receiving the enthusiastic favor of significant sections of the US population. Witness, besides the 26th of July Movement in 1957–58, a wide range of Latin American struggles, from the original Cuban rebels against Spanish tyranny in the 1890s to Sandino, as well as Filipinos (whether Aguinaldo circa 1900 or Aquino in 1986), and most recently, the belatedly ecstatic reception accorded Nelson Mandela at the end of the 1980s.

In sum, Castro was not the beneficiary of aberrant dupes in the media who undermined the US government's attempt to steer clear of the Cuban morass, as conservatives later tried to claim. The favorable depiction of the Cuban Revolution went well beyond individual peccadillos or mere journalism. It was part of the long-running debate over how to deal with the non-European world, and whether to see it in strictly East–West terms involving traditional alliances with the established forces of order, or to develop a new approach based on structural reform and popular support – at least the facade of 'revolution' and 'progress', however rare the substance. But if the sum of pro-Castro activity in the US was certain private networks that worked to assure a level playing field for the Cuban guerrillas, then this would be a straightforward tale of political sympathy and schism – as it has been described ever since, in the various passing references noting how Castro went from folk-hero status to a bête noire in two short years.

The efforts of individuals and groups within the established intelligentsia fed off another, less containable dynamic. From early in 1957, there was a noticeable tendency for a variety of 'ordinary' North Americans (neither journalists nor political activists) to join or otherwise materially support the rebellion in Cuba. This latter phenomenon provides much of the color and sheer oddity of Yankee *fidelismo*, as we shall see, and is crucial to explaining how enthusiasm for the Cuban Revolution could transcend the extreme hostility of the US establishment after 1959.

The Yankee Fidelistas in Action

In the first place, the sense that the Cuban rebels were doing what 'we' would do in similar circumstances was fostered most strongly by the anonymous US citizens who kept asserting this equivalence. As one of the hostages exclaimed upon his release in July 1958, 'These people are fighting for freedom!' In addition, a recognizable handful of North Americans went beyond empathy and joined the fight directly, bolstering the 26th of July Movement's status as nothing else could. Their numbers were never very great, nothing like the thousands who had gone to Spain twenty years before, or the tens of thousands who 'accompanied' the movements in Central America in the 1980s. Indeed, at no time were more than a few actually fighting in Cuba, however many tried to get in, and the most effective practical backing came in the form of gun-running and related munitions-gathering in the US, often with a mercenary tinge. Yet this entrance into revolutionary conspiracy and guerrilla combat seized the imagination of many at home, most obviously that of a generation who in the late 1950s felt that they had missed their war and chance for heroism.

Three very different texts reveal the full flavor of this spontaneous, ingenu-
ous solidarity during 1957–58. First is the sensational 19 May 1957 CBS Special Report by Robert Taber, 'Rebels of the Sierra Maestra: The Story of Cuba's
Jungle Fighters', which stands on its own as the purest distillation of early
North American enthusiasm for the 26th of July Movement, and has a double
significance in that Taber went on to found the Fair Play for Cuba Committee
three years later. This half-hour documentary was built around the appealing
imagery of idealistic boys and girls, including three North Americans, banding
together for liberty in the green hills of Cuba; it also presented a much gentler
Fidel than anything later seen. In contrast, Neill Macaulay's memoir *A Rebel in
Cuba* traces the Cuban Revolution's powerful lure as sheer derring-do and
gunplay for footloose gringos, minus most of its politics. A contrast is provided, however, in the oral history recounted by Don Soldini, who went to
fight in Cuba before Macaulay, and for rather different reasons. Soldini demonstrates that for some at least the quest for personal experience could also be
melded to some deep if inchoate political identity.

Taber's filmed expedition for CBS in the spring of 1957 was hardly unique
– there was a race on to find and 'capture' Castro after Matthews's scoop in
February. Indeed, Matthews had brought Mario Llerena to CBS, and getting
Taber and his cameraman Wendell Hoffman into the Sierra and out again with
usable film became the priority for the 26th of July Movement's strategy of
reaching beyond the *Times* to build broader journalistic support.[76] Besides the
prestige of CBS as the premier broadcast news operation, Taber had another
great advantage over any print reporter. He was able to bring directly into
stateside living rooms the guerrillas, Fidel himself, and most important, the
three servicemens' sons from the base at Guantánamo who had joined the tiny
Ejercito Rebelde, thereby setting a high-minded tone for all the later US volunteers. With the camera's illusion of a natural intimacy, he introduced the *barbudos* as at once strange and strangely comforting, like and unlike, titillatingly
alien and yet vaguely familiar to all those North Americans seeking to reassure
themselves of their own authenticity in a changing world. Whereas Matthews
and his colleagues sought dramatic effects in their writing, Taber could actually cast and direct the play, choosing his own effects and posing his actors.

As it happens, Taber's staging was hardly subtle. The film opened with a
montage of Castro and his men frozen as in a diorama behind tree branches
and foliage, sternly pointing their rifles at nothing at all, while flamenco music
played on the soundtrack. In the recounting, this opening may sound as if it
signals the most one-dimensional portrayal possible – a revolution of stick
figures. But the effect was actually quite the reverse because the rebels' willingness to pose, to play themselves, signaled their sincerity and obvious commitment. From there on, all of the film's action was symbolic and quite explicitly
acted for Hoffman's camera. Not for these boys the formal austerity and felt
distance of Ho Chi Minh or Mao Tse-tung; with the US camera crew and

whatever audience they envisioned in North America, they were clearly at home. Equipped with this troupe, the Sierra Maestra became for Taber and CBS News the platform for a morality play about kids finding themselves through an otherworldly defiance and being rather than doing: there is no fighting in 'Rebels of the Sierra Maestra', no contact with anything outside the jungle, nor even any discussion of Cuban history and how Batista's tyranny had driven the rebels to take up arms.

In truth, there was very little of Cuba at all in the film, which hardly detracts from its 'you are there' effectiveness: Taber and CBS recognized that North Americans were hardly interested in the troubles of a steamy Caribbean island, but were fascinated by *fidelismo* as the revival of romantic rebellion, a throwback to an earlier age. If the Cubans themselves felt any need for an explanation, it is absent from the film.

Signaling at the outset that this was a transparent tale of discovery, Taber in voice-over tells the viewers that he was in the Sierra 'not to explore the maze of Cuban politics', but to find 'a man the government says isn't there, the Rebel Leader Fidel Castro.' From then on, short episodes of narrated exposition were balanced with live 'speech' by the protagonists (Fidel and his three North American teenage volunteers) and plotless montages of daily life among the rebels, as the camera's eye travels ever deeper into the mountains. The Sierra is constructed visually as a pastoral idyll beyond mundane cares, a verdant utopian counterpart to the colonial 'heart of darkness' simultaneously sought and feared by white men. In this jungle space, with sunlight slanting through the trees, Taber's rebels seem completely and joyously alone, and their rebellion appears as a quixotic removal from temporal violence and decay. In fact, much of the film's power derived from this subtext of the 'real' Cuba, never shown but known to most North Americans as the Mafia's Caribbean sewer. In contrast, Taber's pictorial anecdotes of a brotherly (and sisterly) asceticism must have been especially arresting, and reassuring, almost like a Scout camp: hammocks strung between trees, primitive cooking fires, Taber himself bathing in a stream without soap, the generous sharing of cigars, canned sardines, milk and honey from a split log, the women who 'carry their own guns ... the only concession to their sex is the wild gardenias in their buttonholes.'

In one sense, Taber and his editors at CBS took a cue from Matthews, foregrounding the experience of the North Americans in their journey towards Castro. But they also evoked the long tradition of journalists-as-explorers in trackless 'native country', going back to the nineteenth century and the journalist Henry Morton Stanley's famous search for Dr Livingston in the heart of Africa. Repeatedly and portentously, the narrator underlines how Taber and Hoffman 'walked a hundred-fifty miles into jungle to get this story.' After the initial sequence of guerrillas posed for battle, and then a moment to establish context (a smiling, white-suited Batista superimposed on a map of the 'lush volcanic island one hour by plane from Miami'), the camera follows the two journalists on their long climb into the Sierra guided by fatigue-clad women (actually Haydée Santamaria and Celia Sanchez), to the accompaniment of dubbed-in bird calls and miscellaneous jungle sounds. After much exertion, they find the rebel camp and are greeted by Camilo Cienfuegos, an impish Raúl Castro and the rest. The camera roams over the smiling group, as the landing of the *Granma* and their literally exalted position is described: 'With Fidel Castro here are former clerks, technicians, students, townspeople and the simple campesinos, natives of these hills ... inside the mountains they are untouchable; outside the mountains they are outnumbered a hundred to one. ...'

After pausing briefly on the figure of 'Doctor Fidel Castro, thirty-one, holder of four university degrees', it moves on to the main event, three barely mustachioed North American boys with straw hats, bandoleros and big cigars, sitting on a log and earnestly inspecting their weapons.[77] Each is described in terms of his military duties: 'Michael Garvey, fifteen, the youngest man in camp', is 'assigned to a light machine gun with Fidel's rear guard', and just like any fellow at home, 'on the rifle stock Mike had carved the name of a girl-friend back at the base.' Taber asks the boys why they have come to this outlandish place. A shy, drawling Chuck Ryan, at twenty-one the oldest, acts as spokesman and explains their strange quest in language repeated many times over the next two years:

> Well, we came to do our part for the freedom of the world mostly. We just heard so much about how, uh, about how Batista was so cruel and he was a dictatorship [sic], and how with the war in Hungary and the people fighting for freedom there, we just felt moved to come here, so we made contacts with Cuban friends and asked them is there anything we can do to help the revolution, to help them get freedom, so here we are. ...[78]

Another of the boys, Victor Buehlman, stoically concurs: 'It's a rough life, but I believe I'm doing it for a good cause.' Then Chuck addresses a plea to the other boys' parents: ['They should be proud of their sons. ... I only hope that they can try to realize what their boys are doing. Their boys are fighting for an ideal ... for their country and the world. This is for world peace. ...']

He ends shaking his head, apparently choked-up: 'I just want my parents to trust me and have faith.' As if cued, Fidel enters the scene a little awkwardly and sits down next to the three boys. Queried by Taber regarding the new recruits' performance, the commander of the Rebel Army answers in a high, soft voice, his English tentative but precise: 'I am very happy and grateful to them. They have learned very much here. They are brave and I am certain that they will be good soldiers. ... ' Rather than the combination of mastery and threat Castro has projected to North Americans for a generation, the resonances of this brief appearance, his first for North American television audiences, are of a diffident if well-bred colonial schoolmaster entrusted with the care of valuable foreign students, and anxious to please.[79]

Taber's own intervention then follows, affirming the dual role of North Americans as guarantors and monitors of the revolution's behavior. Noting that he is a parent himself, and extending the motifs of paternal guardianship established in the joint interview, he reports that he convinced Castro to 'honorably discharge' the two youngest boys so they can be returned to their families; new names will be carved on their rifle stocks. Then, after a series of atmospheric vignettes fleshing out camp life, the film climaxes with the guerrillas ascending Pico Turquino, Cuba's highest point, to pray before a shrine to José Martí and sing Cuba's national anthem. Fidel is interviewed again, sitting at the foot of a statue of Martí and speaking his quiet, careful English. After denouncing Batista's lies and praising the US reporters who have 'made him a fool ... he will be furious', Castro explains how his tiny group holds off the entire Cuban Army:

> It is not the same to fight for liberty as to fight against it. All the people of the Sierra Maestra are with us. Hundreds of men are watching the enemy movements day and night. ... We gladly suffer cold and rain and the hardship of life in the mountains that the Batista soldiers can't when they come up here.

In language strikingly similar to the speeches he made in the US announcing the revolutionary invasion, Castro sums up his goals: 'We have struck the spark of the revolution, the Cuban Revolution. We have demonstrated that the tyranny is incapable of defeating the fight for liberty.' The film finishes with the whole ragtag band beaming and shouting 'Viva!', waving their guns and the Cuban flag in the air.

The significance of Taber's film, hard on the heels of Matthews's discovery, is that North Americans who had been shown only rebels minus causes, as a pose or a form of social 'delinquency', now had a full-fledged rebellion playing itself out in their living-rooms, at the center of which were their own teenage compatriots. Jules Dubois noted the effect of these first volunteers in his 1959 book:

> The news that three youths from the Guantanamo Bay naval base had joined Castro awakened the imagination and desire for adventure of many another young American throughout the United States. Volunteer after volunteer tried to establish contact with the rebels. Many wrote letters to me. ...[80]

And if the prospect of fifteen-year-old US citizens joining a Third World guerrilla band seems only a picturesque oddity, consider what its import would have been in other circumstances – in Vietnam, the Philippines or El Salvador – if 'army brats' from a US base had crossed over, and even more unlikely, if such an event had been foregrounded respectfully on network television, in effect celebrated. There has been nothing like it before or since, and it is not merely a question of relative naiveté – the Cubans and Fidel Castro in particular really did break through to pull towards their cause North Americans like Matthews and Taber as well as others whose activity was more directly partisan.

The case of the three boys may have been only a nine days' wonder in the spring months of 1957, but in conjunction with the well-oiled publicity machine of the New York liberals and the constant hunger strikes, pickets and seagoing escapades of Cuban-Americans, it set a precedent for North Americans' personal involvement. If nothing else, here was a human-sized war, a respite from the Cold War's geopolitics and brinksmanship on a scale dwarfing any individual intervention.

By the summer of 1958, the presence of US citizens fighting with the 26th of July Movement was an established part of the ongoing 'Cuba story', and hopping a plane to Cuba (which required no passport) became an attractive option for would-be soldiers of fortune. For some, it was remarkably easy to join the fight, as described in the one published account, Neill Macaulay's *A Rebel in Cuba*. That August, a recently demobilized US army lieutenant, the young Macaulay found the home address of the 26th of July Exile Committee's coordinator in a New York newspaper article, dropped by the man's house and left a note offering weapons for 'the noble cause of Dr. Fidel Castro Ruz', hoping the Cubans would take him along with his guns.[81] He quickly found out that there was no shortage of gringos itching for some action. Visiting the Exile Committee's office at 305 Amsterdam Avenue in Manhattan, he discovered two other 'college-age Americans' already there. Don Soldini, another North American returned from fighting with Raúl Castro's column, explained the situation: 'They wanted to join up. ... A lot of guys like that come up here. Especially in the summer. Some say they want to join up but they've got to be back in the States in September when school starts. ...'[82]

Macaulay was eventually accepted because of a service background he rather exaggerated – in Korea, the command of a Post Exchange. But he was from a traditionally military South Carolina family (his grandfather was 'a yeoman sergeant in the Confederate Army'), and he had graduated from the exclusive military academy, the Citadel. He flew to Havana, met his contact and waited to go into the hills, spending his time with friends from South Carolina in Cuba to drink and whore. After some weeks, he was sent to a new guerrilla column in western Cuba, far from Castro's base in Oriente. Their work, described in chilling detail very different from Taber's peaceful setting, was to deny Batista's army control over the region, while liquidating the informers who threatened the revolution's peasant base. In practice, this meant irregular ambushes of convoys and the taking of small guardposts. More regularly, it included tracking down and hanging *chivatos*, or spies.

After the revolutionary victory, Macaulay was made an officer and commanded a heavy-weapons platoon that functioned as an execution squad for the numerous *batistianos* found guilty of war crimes. Demobilized once again in March 1959, just in time to forestall losing his US citizenship, he applied for the land due a rebel veteran under the Agrarian Reform and brought his wife and newborn son to Cuba. Over the next year, they developed a profitable operation, growing tomatoes and cucumbers for the south Florida market. Then disaster, or rather the onset of Cuban socialism, struck:

> But by the end of the 1959–60 crop year, it became obvious that private export agriculture – and practically all individual enterprise – was doomed. ... [This] convinced my wife and me that the kind of life we wanted was no longer possible in Cuba. ... [83]

Macaulay and his family slipped out in July 1960, illegally bringing their car and household appliances. After 'a brief stint as military commander' of one of the two hundred-odd anti-Castro organizations' in Miami, he was frozen out of the Bay of Pigs: 'the CIA wanted nothing to do with me ... or, for that matter, any native Cuban liberals. They preferred the manipulatable right.'[84] He entered graduate school during the same month as the invasion, became a historian of Latin America, and wrote the first scholarly book in English on Sandino before publishing this pungently told tale of youthful opportunism.

At no point in Macaulay's deadpan reminiscences of his time as *A Rebel in Cuba* does he give a 'political' explanation of his motivation for risking his life under a foreign flag. Early on, he quotes Soldini's comment that 'he could tell that I was a guy just like him – a guy who liked a good fire-fight.' He notes elsewhere in passing that 'it was a good cause ... and I had nothing better to do.'[85] Clearly, he felt some personal attraction to the war against Batista, because he makes numerous allusions to his antisegregationist Southern liberalism, and his awareness of the campesinos' oppression is the most visceral aspect of the book. While expressing compassion for Batista's small-fry, who were executed more or less summarily, Macaulay sees this revolutionary justice as the inevitable wages of repression, and in a letter left behind in case he was captured, he angrily denounced how the US 'has too often aided even the most odious dictatorships.'[86]

Yet by no stretch of the imagination was Macaulay, in the old phrase, a 'man of the left'. As he remembered it later, to look for ideological motivation in his Cuban adventure was a fool's errand: his liberal sympathies were 'the antithesis of ideology. Freedom requires no intellectual defence.' More to the point,

> Adventure, living comfortably and independently amidst the beauty of rural Cuba, the excitement of developing export agriculture and making lots of money – that's worth killing for (provided it's killing, as Judge Roy Bean would say, people who need killing), but not dying for. Of itself, military adventure is like sex in the age of AIDS: not worth dying for, but worth risking death for – to one degree or another,

depending on the individual and his tastes.[87]

In this willingness to search for the game with the highest stakes, Macaulay and others like him seem to have belonged to the nineteenth-century genre of mercenary-heroes, having more in common with the protagonists of the Mexico Westerns and with real-life 'filibusters' like William Walker (who briefly seized the presidency of Nicaragua in the 1850s) than with the Communist 'internationals' in Spain or the 'faith activists' making a witness for peace along the Nicaraguan border in the 1980s.[88] Indeed, the closest parallel is to those earlier Yankees who joined the Cuban insurrection against Spain just before the US intervention in 1898 from a similar blend of adventure-seeking and generalized sympathy.[89] In his own frank telling, Macaulay explained to his parents that he was off to Cuba 'to make my fortune', and he also remembers unblushingly his intention to 'rise to power with the revolutionary forces ... by the end of the semester ... I should have acquired a home and a livelihood' (he had eloped just before leaving for Cuba).[90] Only the filter of subsequent decades, when Cuba was a prime antagonist, makes the actions of Macaulay and like-minded daredevils seem incongruous.

How many North Americans collaborated with the Cuban revolution? Culling the US press, Cuban reminiscences and other sources, one finds numerous references. The *New York Times* later reported a total of twenty-five had actually fought in Cuba, and apparently some were killed by Batista's police.[91] After Ryan, Garvey and Buehlman's fifteen minutes of fame in early 1957, by far the best-known was another US veteran, Captain (later Major) William Morgan of Toledo, Ohio, who received considerable attention when he was discovered leading the 26th of July Movement's rival, the 'Second Front of the Escambray'. Morgan stayed in the public eye in Cuba and at home, first as the rebel commander who took the city of Cienfuegos on New Year's Day, 1959, then as the hero who worked with Fidel to foil a counter-revolutionary conspiracy in August 1959 and was hailed on Cuban press and television; he was shot as an accused anti-Castro conspirator in 1961 while maintaining his innocence. According to Matthews, with whom he corresponded, he was a convinced if politically unsophisticated rebel, 'a tough, uneducated young American ... the interesting thing about Morgan, which entitled him to a passing fame as a child of our times, was that he had ideals.'[92] A 1958 statement entitled 'Why I Am Here' proclaimed the antidictatorial, anti-Communist sentiments widely associated both with Castro and the Yankee *fidelistas:*

> Here are men who are fighting for liberty and justice in their land and I am here to fight with them. ... Over the years we as Americans have found that dictators and Communists are bad people with whom to do business. Yet here is a dictator who has been supported by the Communists and he would fall from power tomorrow if it were not for American aid. And I ask myself why do we support those who would

destroy in other lands the ideals we hold so dear.[93]

There are other enigmatic snapshots of North Americans in action, enough to suggest that more remain undiscovered, like the passing reference to a 'gringo' demolitions expert in a letter from Raúl Castro to his older brother, the *New York Times* correspondent Ruby Hart Phillips citing 'a boy from Iowa' with Fidel's column in the summer of 1957, or the *Life* feature after Batista's flight that included a grim-looking young Chicagoan named Jack Nordeen, 'disabled by polio but [who] manages to stand guard at a rebel post'. At one point, the Cuban police caught a US Navy enlisted man, Robert Franklin Riggs, 'in an attempt to smuggle arms and ammunition to the rebels', and turned him over to his superiors at Guantánamo for court-martial.[94] Another sailor from Guantánamo, Charles Bartlett, explained his desertion in the simplest human terms: 'I was on liberty in the city of Guantánamo when I saw some soldiers, for apparently no reason at all, beat up some civilians. I couldn't stomach it and thought it was an injustice. So I decided to join the rebels.'[95]

By 1958, the constant publicity was clearly having an effect on young people in the US, especially the college-educated. The prestigious Yale Political Union debated the resolution that 'The United States Should Allow Its Citizens to Give Support to Fidel Castro', and even before young men began showing up at exile offices, wanting a little revolution with their summer vacation, Carlos Franqui had noted in an internal report that besides 'great sympathy from the entire press' and 'possibilities of reaching universities, labor unions, outstanding personalities, and some political sectors', there was discernible 'sympathy among the youth'.[96] Mario Llerena remembered the urge to action during his speaking engagements on US campuses:

> At Columbia University, the Massachusetts Institute of Technology, and the University of Chicago, among others, my lectures were followed by question-and-answer periods. Almost invariably some student would write me later to request further information on the Cuban revolution or to inquire how he or she could help.[97]

A report from Cuba itself confirms both the potential numbers of would-be 'jungle fighters', and the range of their motivations. When Harold Flender, yet another freelance writer looking for Castro, ended up in early 1958 at the US consulate in Santiago de Cuba, the 'harassed, tired, nervous' staff told him that

> there have been quite a few Americans who have tried to join with the rebels recently. They have all been caught by the Cuban Army before making it to the hills. The Americans, explains the Consulate official, fall into three categories: (1) ex-World War II paratroopers who are intrigued with the idea of fighting; (2) professional adventurers who feel they will be awarded large sums of money when Castro takes over Cuba; (3) idealistic teen-agers who want to fight dictatorship and estab-

lish democracy.[98]

In this context, it is especially intriguing to discover that well before the full tide of pro-Fidel press coverage and news of the three Guantánamo runaways, a few young men in the US already imagined themselves as rebels in Cuba. And these youth had less of a purely theatrical or mercenary tinge to their adventurism, and something closer to a serious political interest in a 'revolutionary with a democratic philosophy'. The first story here is of intentions unfulfilled, but it has considerable significance because of who the would-be rebel shortly became. The second story is that of the quintessential Yankee *fidelista,* Don Soldini.

On 9 March 1957, only two weeks after his interview with Fidel Castro broke, Herbert L. Matthews received a letter from an undergraduate at Berkeley named Hank di Suvero. After complimenting Matthews on one of his earlier books, di Suvero explained matter-of-factly that

> a group of friends and I got into a planning mood, and mapped out an expedition to go to Cuba, and help Fidel Castro. We would be eight. We would have two jeeps. We would go from Key West to Havana. We would be a combination cultural anthropology & uranium prospecting group; our destination would be somewhere in the Province of Oriente, preferably in the Sierra Maestras. We would then join & aid Fidel Castro. We are all honor students at the University of California. We have all been student leaders. Some of us have spent a summer with the American Friends Service Committee in Mexico. We consider ourselves liberals. Lastly, we are all highly adventurous.
>
> Now to the questions: (1) What kind of a man is Fidel Castro? Is he another Cuban warlord, or is he really a revolutionary with a democratic philosophy? (2) Would eight men and two jeeps be of any help to him? (3) Would we have a hard time getting into Oriente? (4) Is mail from Cubans (in Cuba) to Cubans in the United States (as in Berkeley, California) censored? (5) If we leave July 1, could you be of further help to us regarding Cuban contacts etc?[99]

Matthews immediately wrote back in a discouraging vein, and apparently that was that for this naive plan. Besides its self-confidently manly and businesslike tone, typical concerns regarding Fidel's character and the assumption that the revolution can wait until the Berkeley expedition has finished the spring term, the greatest import of this letter lies in what di Suvero did after failing to get to Cuba. Later that year, he helped found SLATE, the independent student political party that was the basis for Berkeley's legendary activism, and the exemplar of revived leftwing campus politics for activists throughout the country as the sixties began.[100] Here, then, is at least one concrete link between the appearance of a New Left among the youth of Cuba and a similar impulse in the US.

Of course, no future Berkeley radical ever did make it into the Sierra, nor were any of the gringos who actually took up arms college students, as far as is known: the 26th of July Movement was looking for military experience not summer interns, and, as we shall see below, students tended to have second thoughts when the moment came to commit themselves. Di Suvero and his friends were not alone, however, in locating their enthusiasm for Castro and the revolution in a political response more sophisticated than the equation of Batista with the Russians in Hungary. Don Soldini, a young Staten Islander from a self-consciously proletarian background, had made up his mind to join this particular 'good fight' before Herbert L. Matthews made Castro world-famous. Even in the briefest outline, his Ping-Pong-like tale, back and forth between the US and Cuba, in and out of combat and prison cells, is odder and far less predictable than fiction.[101]

At the end of 1956, only eighteen, Soldini had just returned from hitchhiking across the US and Mexico. He had dropped out of high school two years before and bummed around, working docks and shipyards. Half-Irish and half-Italian, he retained a familial memory of radicalism – a Wobbly grandfather on his father's side deported in the 1920s, Irish Republican Army sympathies on his mother's. These memories, plus an intense reaction against Joe McCarthy ('I hated his fucking guts') evidently left Soldini waiting for something to happen, or something to do:

> I was always the internationalist. When Israel invaded Egypt, I was highly indignant and I went to the Syrian Embassy and enlisted in their army! I was looking for a cause, a good fight. If it was 1938, I would have been in the International Brigade.

As he tells it, a recruiting sergeant at the Staten Island Ferry terminal who was 'kidding around' said, 'I figure you were in Mexico, you would have joined that guy who invaded Cuba', and this jibe set him off on frenzied reading, even digging out maps of Oriente in the public library. Then Matthews's articles confirmed that Castro was still alive, and Soldini made up his mind to join up. By June 1957, he had hitched his way to Santiago and stayed in a hotel for a month putting out feelers that finally led to an 'interview' with the local underground. Able to lie about military service because of his extensive knowledge of guns, Soldini was on line for the Sierra, but his joining the massive demonstration after 26th of July Movement leader Frank País was killed led to deportation. Back in New York, he joined Arnoldo Barron's faction of the Exile Committee and became involved in publicity schemes while training in the wilds of Connecticut and northern New Jersey for another invasion.

In November 1957, Soldini returned to Santiago on his own, and this time he managed to stay. For some months, he lived in a safe house, helping smuggle arms into the mountains one step ahead of the Servicio Intelligencia Militar. Then, in April 1958, nearly all of the 26th of July Movement's urban cadre left the city to join Raúl Castro's new column in the Sierra Cristal. There Soldini took part in numerous battles, was promoted to corporal and wounded in the neck. Eventually he had a falling-out with Raúl that nearly led to his hanging. The immediate cause was his vociferous objection to the summary execution of prisoners, but the real reason for Raúl's threat was that this particular tendency among the rebels 'did not take well to Americans'. To get out of a bad situation, Soldini accepted an assignment to locate guns in the States, with the promise of a lieutenancy when he returned to Cuba. Back in New York once again, he took up gun-running efforts that involved not only the Cubans and the IRA, but even the Algerian rebels. While trying to assemble this exile arms consortium, Soldini was nearly caught in an FBI sting outside a Third Avenue bar in Manhattan in September 1958. He thereupon hooked up with Neill Macaulay, and used the latter's money to get to Mexico, where he met Castro's two sisters. At this point, the most interesting as well as harrowing part of his narrative ensues, in the months before Batista's fall.

Soldini went back to Havana, where he found the underground largely smashed in the aftermath of the general strike. Broke and friendless, he tried to get through Batista's lines by bus, dressed as a Cuban and pretending muteness, but was arrested as what government troops called a 'mau-mau', and taken to the *cuartel* run by Colonel José Maria Salas Canizares, the infamous 'Butcher of Oriente'. Beaten continually with rifle butts, forced to dig his own grave, taken out at night and told to 'camine, puta' in the headlights (the age-old Cuban method of shooting a prisoner), his cellmates beaten to death or shot, trying to eat or flush away letters to Fidel from his sister Lidia ('all of the papers just stood on the water') – Soldini's capture at this point resembles a formulaic B-picture set in the tropics. What apparently saved him from immediate execution was a strenuously repeated claim that his uncle was a famous Italian restaurateur in New York and Batista's personal friend. Taken to Havana for a higher level of interrogation, he shared a cell with another Yank, who had been arrested at the airport 'because he had combat boots' and who was about to be deported. Just as Soldini's last escape bid failed (when his guard fell asleep and he almost made it through the gates), his cellmate's promise to contact his family led to the State Department's intercession and deportation.

Back in Miami, Soldini began smuggling guns via the Key West–Havana ferry and Fort Lauderdale airport, and incidentally met one more US veteran-turned-*fidelista*, Frank Fiorini, better known later as 'Frank Sturgis'.[102] By this point, however, Soldini had larger plans. He talked to Haydée Santamaria, Fidel's delegate in southern Florida and got permission to do something with the 'avalanche' of North Americans applying to fight in Cuba as it became apparent that Castro would win. With the encouragement of Provisional President Manuel Urrutia, he sifted through hundreds of letters and contacted the most likely candidates, telling them to get themselves to Miami and wait for an expedition. Not surprisingly, there were few political criteria other than actually showing up and an ability to fight:

> Most of the guys were Korea vets and whatever. I wasn't even interested in why they
> wanted to do it. ... . It was a bunch of assholes, really. Let's be honest about it. I
> wanted my *own* column now, right. And of Americans. I wasn't really looking at
> them, if they were willing to pay their own expenses and wait. I figured the more
> numbers I had the more power I had in getting the Cubans interested.

By the end of December, he had 'sixty or seventy guys sitting in rooming houses', and went to New York to arrange a plane. And here the story of Yankee *fidelismo* ends rather abruptly, with no denouement, as Soldini was awakened on New Year's morning with a shout over the telephone from Miami: 'Batista se fué!' The would-be North American column of the *Ejercito Rebelde* went up in smoke, before they could even be trained, one of the more fantastic what-ifs of recent history. Soldini could already feel himself redundant. He organized the New York exiles' ecstatic return on a commandeered Cubana airliner, claimed his officer's status, and enjoyed several months of triumph as a companion of Fidel himself, appearing on the Jack Paar Show and turning down book and movie offers. But he could not stay out of trouble, and voluntarily went to jail for months when a North American friend was arrested on flimsy charges of being a spy for Wall Street. By September 1959, Soldini had said an emotional goodbye to Castro, and was back in New York, studying at night for his high school equivalency degree and working as a cheese salesman by day. After going to university in Mexico, he got an Alliance for Progress–funded job with the Mexican government (though the FBI continued harassing him until 1966). Since then he has been a successful international business consultant, occasionally involved in promoting better relations with Cuba.

Soldini's tale puts into high relief how in the case of the Cuban Revolution the quest for adventure fused with political conviction. Moreover, it encapsulates the whole career of US solidarity with the Cuban guerrillas before their victory: from him alone responding to the obscure but dramatic 'invasion' of the *Granma*, to the would-be *comandante* riding herd on his own column, preparing an airborne invasion that would never come. The difference between Soldini and many other gringos remains that he was and is quite unapologetic about this particular subjectivity, which Cubans and North Americans (not only men but men especially) do seem to share. As many men are in talking to those who have never seen combat, he is reticent about the fighting itself, but the undeniable excitement of it all still comes through, the sense of an epiphany:

> Anyway, I loved it. I truly loved it. This was the greatest thing that ever happened to
> me. With all the privations – hunger, thirst, dysentery. One time I didn't even have
> shoes. But to me it was the greatest. There's never been another experience I've ever
> had in life. ... I mean this is pure idealism, pure passion. Batista the bad guy, Fidel

the good guy – I'm on the side of the good, how great can you go?

The Yankee Fidelistas in Fiction

If only because Cuba was so close, observing the revolution – or joining in, and the distinction could be a fuzzy one – was a tangible possibility as nowhere else; many thousands of North Americans of all ages routinely flew down for the nightlife and the sun, including such prominent cosmopolitans as New York Mayor Robert Wagner, who received a medal from Batista during his New Year's Eve visit in 1956, and Senator John F. Kennedy, who spent Christmas 1957 with his friend, Ambassador Earl E. T. Smith.[103] The widest resonances of this tantalizing prospect, the revolution-as-vacation fit for both idealists and funseekers, are best found not in memoirs or press accounts, but in a novel, Glendon Swarthout's *Where the Boys Are*, published in 1960 but set in late March 1958. This light-hearted detailing of student angst and hijinks, in which one plotline involves a gang of kids trying to invade Cuba, illustrates in pure, unironic form how the revolution became a convenient shorthand for both individual commitment and sheer exotica, an emblem of a nascent bohemia. It is a strange piece of middlebrow popular fiction, the kind of bestseller that is remembered mainly because it marks a certain moment in time. Joseph L. Mankiewicz's big-budget 1961 film version has survived as a high point of Hollywood kitsch: it introduced a whole crop of sixties ingenues, including Jim Hutton, Paula Prentiss, Delores Hart and Yvette Mimieux, and featured George Hamilton, Frank Gorshin and (acting and singing the hit title song) Connie Francis. But by 1961 the political atmosphere had so changed that Castro and Cuba were entirely obliterated from the movie, leaving only sexual contestation as a main theme, although in watered down form.

In the book, a varied cast of Northeastern and Midwestern college students converge on Fort Lauderdale during the famous spring break frenzy, hoping to make temporary or permanent sexual and class alliances and briefly enjoy themselves before adult responsibility comes crashing down. The sensible narrator is a smalltown girl named Merrit, who meets and beds an assortment of boys: flamboyant collegiate empresario TV Thompson; heptalking jazz musician Basil Demetemos; snooty Ivy Leaguer Ryder Smith. The main plot line, as elaborated in archly self-conscious youthful slang, involves Merrit's sleeping with all three, and trying to make up her mind which she likes most; at the end of the book she discovers she is pregnant by one of them, and achieves a rueful self-knowledge. Along the way, however, Castro's revolution becomes a convenient vehicle (since they are in Florida) to provide both wacky adventure and a whiff of idealism.

The nagging presence of the Cuban revolt as an attainable challenge is raised in the first chapter. Introducing herself as if this were a long chatty letter, Merrit talks about the wonder of being on the ocean for a Midwestern girl like her, with

> ships sailing to and from romantic places like Cuba and Port-au-Prince and Galveston and coming over the water ... you could hear the sounds of gourds and voodoo drums and steel bands, though from Cuba it might have been firing since it seemed to me I'd read they were putting on a revolution.[104]

Next she meets Boy #1, the restless hustler TV Thompson ('the Mike Todd of Michigan State'), who mentions an disturbing incident on the drive down, 'a semiadventure I haven't been able to sublimate':

> Outside Knoxville at night there was this hitchhiker and I'd promised myself isolation. But he stood there in my headlights too proud to thumb. All he had was a sign on his suitcase. Havana. That stopped me. We took turns driving and talked all night. He was very sharp, a Phi Bete from Minnesota and about to graduate this June. But you know where he was going? Miami to Havana to Santiago to be in on the revolution! Think what he was giving up, a degree in three months, a suburban future, the works, just to go to Cuba and shoot up the sugar cane fighting for a country not even his own and possibly be killed! How many kids at the U do you know would do a thing like that? He'd given away all his clothes, packed one bag and taken off with no message to the school or his parents. I really rebutted this character, I argued with him all the way to the airport in Miami, which is where I dropped him, but he took the ball on downs. I can't shake that crazy guy. He's been raising hell with my Id or something ever since.[105]

Once inserted, these essential themes of spontaneity versus conformity ('with no message to the school or his parents') and adventure ('fighting for a country not even his own and possibly be killed') versus the guaranteed success of purely Economic Man or Woman ('a suburban future, the works'), surface continually throughout *Where the Boys Are,* but like the random copulations littering the text, Cuba as the trope of youthful rebellion is ultimately a *deus ex machina.* The real importance of Cuba, and of TV Thompson as the would-be Yankee *guerrillero*, is to serve as male foils for the central protagonist Merrit, and her inward-directed quest to overcome alienation. Like her, TV is looking for something, but he can't figure out what it is. His attraction to the idea of Cuba functions as the gender equivalent of her sexual experimentation and uncertain liberation. Explaining how as a high school junior she tried gamely 'to join the Deflorated Daughters of America', Merrit describes a 'decision to give my maidenhood away for the sheer exaltation of it':

> I made up my mind not to be seduced because that meant playing the role of victim, which I despise, in sex or life or anything else, so among the lads of Carter City High I soon became known as the Babe Didrickson of the Back Seat. A hundred times I fought the good fight and won. Then my attitude altered. What was mine was mine

and I would damn well dispose of it any way I wanted but above all else I would have freedom of choice.[106]

At the end of the book, the failed, foolish but ultimately gallant expedition to Cuba is quite explicitly the counterpart of her pregnancy – a sign of commitment and experience, of wisdom hard-earned. 'We had proved to ourselves that ... given a colorful cause we would fight', explains Merrit with some satisfaction.

The students' eventual entry into rebel politics comes in improbable fashion. While getting blind drunk in a nightclub, they meet an underwater dancer and sometime stripper named Ramona, who is a committed Castroite – with a speech impediment. She lures them to the gorgeous sin palaces of Miami Beach and there explains about 'the revolution':

> 'What revolution?' we demanded.
> She rose melodramatically, bent over us, exposed to the boys her terrific lungs, blazed her baby-blue eyes, extended a shapely arm toward the window, pointing over the cabanas and pool to the black ocean.
> 'There!' she hissed.
> Then we remembered. They were having a revolution in Cuba. Most of us had seen stuff about it in the papers but had paid no attention because we were making our own current events.
> 'So?' Ryder said. 'They're always having one. Local color, pulls in the tourists.'
> 'Ooooo!' Ramona swayed down savagely. 'Yoo out hoonting igoonas and two hoondred miles from here young booys are dyin' for freedoom and demoocracy!' She made us huddle. She told how an intrepid band had landed on Cuba's coast, how their ranks had been augmented by hundreds of youthful patriots, boys and girls both, how they were holed up in the mountains of Oriente Province, lashing out in guerrilla raids, retiring to bury their dead and grow beards, sometimes having nothing to eat but python meat. She made it as picturesque as a tropic, coeducational Valley Forge.[107]

'Sort of despite ourselves, not because of *Fidelismo* or the boy from Minnesota ... ', the college kids are recruited into a madcap fundraising scheme, as Ramona explains to them the secret world of 'the overseas headquarters and arsenal of the revolution' in Miami, where 'oodles of Americans help, too.'[108] They perform as a glee-club in a nightclub benefit where the marimba band plays 'Castro's Cha-Cha-Cha', and later act as respectable shills, betting on a fixed jai-alai game and then a dog race until $1,500 has been raised. Then TV drops a bombshell. Like the 'Phi Bete from Minnesota' who has been obsessing him, he is off to Cuba. In no time, the wily Ramona is evoking Schweitzer, Bolívar, Pilsudski, Lafayette and above all, the value of good publicity. In response to her suggestion, the enamored TV has a brainstorm – 'The Lauderdale Legion ... give them an alternative to going back to school'! The next day he stages a march up the beach, with 'three boys abreast, striding erect in their swim trunks, with heads bandaged like The Spirit of Seventy-Six' and signs reading 'SPEND SPRING TERM IN CUBA! ... LET'S BOMB BATISTA! ... ENROLL IN REVO-LUTION 202! ... SEEK YOUR IDENTITY IN ORIENTE!'

TV makes a great speech to a gang of 300 assembled kids and some news-papermen:

> We've had a ball down here, all of us, but they're about to lower the boom of time on us. It's back to the ratrace. But I clue you in, you guys can have that slush. As for me, give me sun or give me death! ... So that's why this meeting. I won't give you any hard sell. This revolution in Cuba may be rancid but it's the only one available. And let's face it, Batista is the bottom of the human barrel. Now a couple hundred of us could go over there and soak up more sun and some frozen daiquiris and clean up the whole Caribbean in a couple of weeks. How are they going to keep us down on the campus after we've seen Havana? I mean, you want to live forever?[109]

TV's recruitment pitch is a disaster, but after a few more diversions, a large party of enthusiastic kids, laden down with weapons, do set sail on Ryder's uncle's yacht – and promptly crash into a dock. At book's end, with lessons learned, Merrit is left lying on the beach, planning to return home and have her baby. Cuba, like any other questions of where the 'boys' are, has disap-peared, and she is left older, wiser, and necessarily alone.

In Like Flynn; or, The Swashbuckler's Return

There is a last, too-good-to-be-true epilogue to the story of how Fidel Castro's revolution was aided from the US. As we have seen, admiration for his exploits grew from the collapse of old political identities, fears about male agency among boys and young men, and the whipsawing effects of popular culture. To demonstrate these connections, I have evoked the vast store of movie and television lawmen (or 'good men') who are forced to stand outside the law, all those driven heros and anti-heroes fighting a corrupt world by any means necessary, from Terry Malloy to Paladin to Shane. Implicit in this analysis is the assumption that Fidel was aware of these Wild West overtones to his ad-ventures; his supporters in the North American media were clearly conscious of how to promote him using the tropes of gunman-as-reformer.

Now, despite the literary and anecdotal evidence provided to substantiate this submerged folk-memory, my thesis may still seem somewhat overblown, a 'new journalistic' confusion of metaphor for fact minus any smoking gun. As if to demonstrate that there was nothing subtle about Castro's appeal in purely popular terms outside the realm of politics, enter the ultimate Hollywood Male of the Golden Age, the star of *The Adventures of Robin Hood*, *The Charge of the Light Brigade* and *They Died with Their Boots On,* Errol Flynn, whose offscreen legend as a drunken satyr was at least as powerful as his screen heroics. In this case, Mohammed did not have to go to the mountain. On his last legs, the fifty-year-old actor and his fifteen-year-old girlfriend Beverly Aadland hit Cuba in October 1958. It was a natural place for a man of Flynn's appetites, the 'Best place to get drunk', as he wrote on a Havana menu, and from all reports he was attracted by Castro's reputation for derring-do in the old style.[110] Once there, he became known as a *fidelista,* this tidbit being picked up by the Yankee press as one more bit of Cuban exotica. What really happened is unclear. It is highly doubtful that Flynn, afloat in a sea of vodka, ever picked up a gun and fought with the Rebel Army, though he apparently liked to hint about gunplay to journalists and hangers-on. It is indisputable that he joined Castro's entourage, and was present at rebel headquarters near the city of Santa Clara on 31 December 1958, the night Batista fled Cuba.[111]

But beyond simply being there to lend his dubious prestige, Flynn did attempt a sincere contribution to the revolution, which unfortunately is remembered, if at all, as a butt of ridicule. In early 1959, while turning out articles on Cuba for Hearst's *New York Journal-American,* he began his last film, released later that year as *Cuban Rebel Girls* (sometimes known as *Assault of the Rebel Girls*). Perhaps the title, with its faintly pornographic air, or the casting of Flynn's underage girlfriend as the star, have led to this movie's pathetic reputation. Undeniably, it lacks the production values of even a competent Hollywood B-movie, and poor Aadland had not a shred of talent. Yet like *Where the Boys Are,* it is a telling artifact. Rather than sensationalist or 'sexy', *Cuban Rebel Girls* is as doggedly unironic and earnest as Robert Taber's 'Rebels of the Sierra Maestra', and it too aspires to documentary status. Rather than playing a character, Flynn the on-screen narrator is modestly himself, quasi-journalist, quasi-adventurer, quasi-star. His main story is not actually about Cuban 'girls', but rather concerns how an all-American platinum blonde working in a New York beauty salon (Aadland) might somehow end up as a rebel in Cuba. It's simple: she is terribly worried about her American boyfriend, Johnny, a beefy US Army vet à la William Morgan, who's with the 26th of July Movement. It so happens that a Cuban-American friend and co-worker has a brother with the rebels, so the two go to Cuba to help out and end up embroiled in the guerrilla war, marching through the woods, singing patriotic songs, and talking about the evils of Batista and the importance of unselfish sacrifice. An avuncular, grizzled Flynn shows up periodically as an engaged reporter, making wry jokes in the voice-over about how he is no longer recognized. The plot is tissue-thin, but Flynn, a political amateur and certainly no radical, apparently felt that North American audiences might accept it and him because of the story's importance – that there were still some young people in the world with ideals.

By itself, Flynn's presence on the fringes of the insurgency is mainly bizarre, hardly equivalent to a major male luminary of the day like Rock Hudson, Tony Curtis, Charleton Heston or Kirk Douglas palling it up with Fidel in the Sierra. By the late 1950s, he was no longer a serious star, but rather an outlaw figure and an embarrassment with his defiant, alcoholic hedonism. Not for nothing did he call his scandalous autobiography, dictated that same year, *My Wicked, Wicked Ways,* and the Cubans who saw Flynn in the first days of victory remember him wandering bottle in hand through celebrating crowds.[112] He would die before 1959 was over of a heart attack. In a different way, however, Errol Flynn did serve to validate Fidel, in that personally and cinematically he recalled a bygone era of flamboyant individualism and pure gallantry, the 'Robin Hood' that was his first and lasting screen persona as well as the most common metaphor applied to Fidel. A companion subtext to his revels in Havana was that this was the place for men who truly did not give a damn. As Norman Mailer would surely have agreed, the unrepentant boozer as much as the hipster was a kind of rebel.

So adventurers of all sorts went to Cuba to be with Castro, if not in actuality, at least in their own minds. If chance encounters with men in their teens circa 1958 are any indicator, it seems more than possible that a large percentage of boys between junior high school and college in the US at that time fantasized about taking off for the Sierra Maestra. Two unprompted anecdotes substantiate this premise. In one case, two fifteen-year-old 'hoods' caused a sensation in their high school in Connecticut when they stole a service revolver, a car and $100 from one of their fathers and tried to drive to Cuba to fight with Castro. Of course, they were apprehended at a tollbooth before escaping the state, but the attempt made them local heroes. In another case, a whole group of undergraduates at Temple University seriously discussed joining Fidel. However, only the most ardent of them acted – but instead of going to Cuba, he joined the Marines, only to later regret it.[113] Neither of these stories have much to do with 'politics', of course, but they do indicate how widespread was the equation of Castro with disciplined masculinity in a good cause. All of these boys, above everything else, desperately wanted to be known as 'a guy who liked a good fire-fight.' As we shall see, the image of Fidel Castro as his own man survived for a remarkably long time, given the vilification that began here soon after the revolutionary victory. It would be two years before a significant number of young men (and women too) from the United States would go to Cuba, with much larger numbers accompanying them in spirit, but some essence of Castro's manly charisma and the mystique of his insurgency surely was implanted before 1959, which like a seed falling to the ground in winter, would bide its time unseen.

Notes

1. Milton Eisenhower, *The Wine Is Bitter*, New York: Doubleday, 1963, p. 255.
2. Hugh Thomas, *Cuba: The Pursuit of Freedom*, New York: Harper & Row, 1971, pp. 1479.
3. *New York Times*, 11 August 1957.
4. Tad Szulc, *Fidel: A Critical Portrait*, New York: William Morrow, 1986, pp. 85, 183, 191–2. According to Lionel Martin, Castro had already read *The Communist Manifesto* and several key works of Lenin, but bought his first copy of *Capital* during the honeymoon (*The Early Fidel: Roots of Castro's Communism*, Secaucus, N.J.: Lyle Stuart, 1978, p. 64).
5. Szulc, *Fidel*, p. 72; Brennan, *Castro, Cuba and Justice*, New York: Doubleday, 1959, p. 78.
6. Szulc, *Fidel*, p. 236.
7. Herbert L. Matthews, *The Cuban Story*, New York: George Braziller, 1961, p. 35.
8. Szulc, *Fidel*, p. 334.
9. Pérez, *Cuba and the United States*, p. 208.
10. Letter, Fidel Castro to Carlos Franqui, 18 June 1954, in Carlos Franqui, *Diary of the Cuban Revolution*, New York: Viking, 1980, p. 79.
11. Letter from Fidel Castro, 25 September 1955, and speech, 30 October 1955, in Franqui, *Diary of the Cuban Revolution*, p. 95.
12. Quoted in Franqui, *Diary of the Cuban Revolution*, p. 96. See also Castro's article in *Bohemia*, reprinted in translation in Jules Dubois, *Fidel Castro, Rebel: Liberator or Dictator?*, Indianapolis, Ind.: Bobbs-Merrill, 1959, pp. 103–5.
13. Kevin Beirne Tierney, 'American-Cuban Relations, 1957–1963' (Ph.D. dissertation, Syracuse University, 1979), p. 29. Though southern Florida and the New York City area were undoubtedly the main exile centers, Chicago also saw considerable activity; see *The Independent*, edited by Lyle Stuart, for September 1964, in which he describes his temporary assistant during a Cuban press junket, Gloria Marsan (formerly Robert Taber's secretary), who had been a militant with the 26th of July Movement in Chicago for two years: 'She broke into diplomatic receptions to distribute handbills. She glued 26th of July posters to the doors of the Batista embassy' (presumably he means the consulate).
14. See Mario Llerena, *The Unsuspected Revolution: The Birth and Rise of Castroism*, Ithica, N.Y.: Cornell University Press, 1978.
15. Matthews, *The Cuban Story*, p. 146; Szulc, *Fidel*, p. 366; Teresa Casuso, *Cuba and Castro*, New York: Random House, 1961, p. 112.
16. Szulc, *Fidel*, p. 443; Llerena, *Unsuspected Revolution*, pp. 231, 241; *Time*, 22 Sept. 1958.
17. See the *New York Times*, 4 August 1957 and 6 April 1958, 21 April 1958, and 26 May 1957 for these specific incidents, and note 55 below for many more, in the context of the *Times*'s treatment of this protest campaign; see Dubois, *Fidel Castro, Rebel*, p. 318, for evidence of the World Series attempt; and interview with Donald Soldini, 3 June 1992.
18. What looked like coordinated efforts from the outside concealed an intensely factionalized internal dynamic, as revealed with considerable anger in the memoir by Castro's titular chief delegate in the US, Mario Llerena. The legacies of old feuds, Castro's whirlwind recruitment trip in 1955 and myriad personal backchannels into the Sierra meant that in New York there were three or even four separate groups 'perpetually quarreling', and that two separate 26th of July Movement support structures were replicated in each city with a large Cuban population from Chicago to Los Angeles. These 'personalistic clans' were often, as with Barron's club in New York, simply the old Ortodoxos renamed (see Llerena, *Unsuspected Revolution*, pp. 130–31, 133, 144, 219, 225).
19. For all of the above, *New York Times*, 28, 29 and 30 March; and 1, 2, 3, 4, 6 and 9 April 1958; also Llerena, *Unsuspected Revolution*, p. 228.
20. Matthews, *The Cuban Story*, p. 146. On the Yankee *fidelistas* like Soldini et al., see below.
21. Reprinted in Black, *The Good Neighbor*, p. 105.
22. Matthews, *The Cuban Story*, p. 81.
23. Thomas, *Cuba: The Pursuit of Freedom*, p. 938.
24. For Chapelle, see R. Hart Phillips, *Cuba: Island of Paradox*, New York: McDowell and Obolensky, 1959, pp. 388–9. She was killed by a mine in Vietnam in 1965.
25. *Time*'s choice was hardly random, as it had earlier given a 'stamp of acceptance' to Batista's coup by putting him on the cover of the 9 April 1952 issue (see Thomas, *Cuba: The Pursuit*

of Freedom, p. 789).

26. *Time*, 10 December 1956.

27. *Time*, 25 February 1957 and 4 March 1957. Note that by 28 October 1957, the rebels still merited that distinctly North American accolade 'wily', but now they had grown in size and become 'six hundred wily sharpshooters' – it's a wonder that Batista's men were not called Redcoats or Hessians!

28. *Time*, 20 January 1958 and 25 March 1957.

29. *Time*, 17 February 1958.

30. *Time*, 21 and 28 April 1958.

31. *Time*, 9 December 1957.

32. *Life*, 21 July 1958. The article did mention an 'ominous cloud' on the horizon concerning Raúl's reported 'Red' ties, but hardly let it overshadow the larger story of youthful hijinks and newsworthy Yankee sympathy. See also the 14 July 1958 *Time*, which described Raúl Castro as a 'captor and genial host', and quoted the hostages referring to him as 'a swell guy, that Raúl Castro', who had provided 'good food and plenty of it, and beds with clean sheets.' Besides, they said, 'We are all rebel sympathizers anyway'.

33. Quoted in Dubois, *Fidel Castro, Rebel*, p. 277. For Ike's very restrained response, see his press conference as reported in the *New York Times*, 3 July 1958. While the Navy apparently wanted to send in the Marines, wiser heads prevailed. The peculiar position of the 'Democratic Left' is revealed in how the CIA and State Department had IADF friend Adolf A. Berle, Jr ask Pepe Figueres and Rómulo Betancourt to pressure Fidel for the hostages' release (see Jordan Schwarz, *Liberal: Adolf A. Berle and the Vision of an American Era*, New York: Free Press, 1987, p. 322).

34. *US News and World Report*, 29 March 1957. In fact, Perez was a well-known Presbyterian, casting doubt on this reporter's competence.

35. Neill Macaulay, 'I Fought for Fidel', *American Heritage* (November 1991), p. 80.

36. Matthews, *The Cuban Story*, pp. 53, 67.

37. Copy of Overseas Press Club bulletin article, FGP.

38. Minister of Defence Santiago Verdeja, quoted in Phillips, *Cuba: Island of Paradox*, p. 300. When the UPI's Francis McCarthy published the story of Castro's supposed death in December 1956, it was widely believed. Thus, US journalists both consigned the revolution to oblivion and rescued it (Szulc, *Fidel*, p. 378).

39. Quoted in Thomas, *Cuba: The Pursuit of Freedom*, p. 1039.

40. Llerena, *Unsuspected Revolution*, pp. 430; *New York Times*, 1 March 1957.

41. The correspondence files for 1957 in the Matthews papers at the Butler Library, Columbia University, are filled with missives from across the spectrum of Cuban society. Even now, the ardor and gratitude of these communications is striking, from Havana's Americanized bourgeoisie to proletarian exiles stranded in New York with little money or English. See also the 27 February 1957 letter from William M. Porter, lawyer for the 26th of July Movement in Miami, which gleefully reports a 'black market in the Sunday edition' and asks Matthews to give a speech; in Herbert L. Matthews Papers (hereafter HLMP).

42. Letter, Richard G. Cushing to Matthews, 26 February 1957, in HLMP. He noted that 'This is a personal letter, of course. I'm in a strange position here', presumably referring to the feud pitting the US embassy's pro-Fidel political and CIA officers against the pro-Batista military attachés and political appointees, Ambassadors Arthur Gardner and Earl E. T. Smith (see Thomas, *Cuba: The Pursuit of Freedom*, pp. 964–7; Mario Lazo, *Dagger in the Heart: American Policy Failures in Cuba*, New York: Funk and Wagnalls, 1968, pp. 139–40, 233–5; Morley, *Imperial State and Revolution*, pp. 66–71). It is important to stress here that only US personnel in Cuba itself were ever certifiably 'pro-Castro'; see, for example, James Reston's comment to Herbert L. Matthews about the embassy's chief political officer, John Topping, 'who was as you know enthusiastic about the Castro revolution' (letter, Reston to Matthews, n.d. [apparently 24 February 1960], in HLMP). The ranking State Department officials in Washington, such as William Wieland and Roy Rubottom, were liberals but sought throughout 1958 to forestall Castro by convincing Batista to resign in favor of a 'moderate' coalition government (see the account by Wayne S. Smith, *The Closest of Enemies: A Personal and Diplomatic Account of U.S.-Cuban Relations Since 1957*, New York: Norton, 1987, pp. 20–21, 36–7).

43. Lazo, *Dagger in the Heart*, p. 116.

44. Thus in 1967 a senator interrogating the *Times's* Harrison Salisbury after his unprece-

dented trip to Hanoi, which had effectively rebutted various US claims about the war, 'Did the Matthews visit to Cuba induce you to try to make a scoop in North Vietnam?' (quoted in Herbert L. Matthews, *World in Revolution: A Newspaperman's Memoir*, New York: Scribner's, 1971, p. 298).

45. See Szulc, *Fidel*, pp. 401–11 for a detailed account of the 'guerrilla theater' involved in convincing Matthews of Castro's strength, with the same column repeatedly marching through the camp.

46. Reprinted in Matthews, *The Cuban Story*, pp. 309–10.

47. *New York Times*, 10 July 1957. The next several days' articles continue in this vein – his first article reproduced in the thousands, traveling to Pinar del Rio and again being cast in the role of a protector, receiving civic delegations and grieving parents. Jules Dubois received similar treatment on his visit to Santiago later the same month. He was honored at a dinner given by the city's leading citizens, at which a place at the table was left conspicuously vacant for Fidel (Dubois, *Fidel Castro, Rebel*, pp. 163–4).

48. Matthews, *The Cuban Story*, pp. 61–3; see also Szulc, *Fidel*, p. 429, and Franqui, *Diary*, p. 281, detailing the US ambassador's and the CIA's efforts within Cuba to prevent the executions.

49. Matthews, *The Cuban Story*, pp. 40, 88, 276.

50. Szulc, *Fidel*, p. 407. Matthews had made his name originally as a highly engaged *Times* correspondent during the Spanish Civil War, which he always affirmed as 'a political and moral conversion for me' (*World in Revolution*, p. 11).

51. Matthews, *The Cuban Story*, p. 121, also p. 133 for similar language; and *A World In Revolution*, p. 294: 'We have been friends. ...'

52. See Ernesto 'Che' Guevara, *Episodes of the Revolutionary War*, Havana: Guairas Book Institute, pp. 36, 40–41; also letters from Castro to Celia Sanchez, 5 July 1957, and Armando Hart to Castro, 16 October 1957, referring to Matthews, in Franqui, *Diary*, pp. 192, 241; also, Armando Hart to Mario Llerena (when the 26th of July Movement withdrew from the Miami-based opposition junta in December 1957): 'We want you to explain the whole situation to Mr. Matthews on behalf of Fidel', in Llerena, *Unsuspected Revolution*, p. 165. The volume of official 26th of July correspondence to Matthews from inside Cuba confirms that he was seen not only as an emissary but as a powerful ally, a position shared by Dubois.

53. Martin, *The Early Fidel*, p. 261.

54. *New York Times*, 1 December 1956.

55. See *New York Times*, 4 December 1956 and 13 January 1957 (pickets at the White House and Cuban Embassy protesting the Cuban interior minister's visit); 20 May 1957 (600 watch Robert Taber's CBS Special at the Palm Gardens in Manhattan, also pickets in New York and Washington); 9 June 1957 (another UN protest); 10 August 1957 (a dissident general from the Cuban Army interviewed in New York); 5 September 1957 (Democratic Workers Committee of Cuban Emigrés, on West 64th Street in Manhattan, selling revolutionary 'Bonds of Honor' to raise money for combattants' families); 22 September 1957 (picket at UN with US and Cuban flags); 28 October 1957 (Charles Ryan, North American veteran of Sierra, speaks at Manhattan Tower Hotel, Broadway and 76th Street, raises $1,000); 21 December 1957 (thirty-one *fidelistas* arrested at docks, trying to stop rebel stowaway from deportation); 23 February 1958 (announcement of upcoming 26th of July Movement meeting to formally endorse Urrutia, with time and place); 24 February 1958 (900 people at rally for Urrutia, with a photo of the latter and another leader in front of a huge portrait of Castro); 15 March 1958 (another picket at the docks).

56. For these cartoons featuring Castro as a tiny devil in fatigues, all beard and teeth, see the *New York Times*, 6 July 1958, along with Matthews's article reporting the possible shift to disapproval of Fidel, who 'until now had considerable sympathy in this country'.

57. *New York Times*, 1 July 1957.

58. Phillips, *Cuba: Island of Paradox*, pp. 325, 364–5, 372–4, 386–7.

59. Scholarly treatments that represent this myopia about the *Times*'s actual role include William E. Ratliff, 'The *New York Times* and the Cuban Revolution', and John P. Wallach, 'Fidel Castro and the United States Press', in William E. Ratliff, ed., *The Selling of Fidel Castro: The Media and the Cuban Revolution*, New Brunswick, N.J.: Transaction Books, 1987, pp. 1–37, 129–55. The articles that comprise this book were presented at a Washington, D.C. conference sponsored by the Cuban American National Foundation, leading anti-Castro lobby in the US, on 16–17 November 1984.

60. Dubois, *Fidel Castro, Rebel*, pp. 179–80. Like Matthews, Dubois was seen by Cubans as

an influential mediator. After the *Granma*'s landing, Ortodoxo leaders appealed to him to arrange a truce for the survivors (Dubois, *Fidel Castro, Rebel*, p. 143). Franqui's *Diary* reproduces a 25 July 1957 letter from the banker Justo Carrillo to Fidel, referring to 'a certain person very close to you, the highly qualified Jules Dubois' (p. 211).

61. Quoted from an English-language Havana newspaper in Dubois, *Fidel Castro, Rebel*, p. 333.

62. Quoted in Szulc, *Fidel*, p. 455.

63. See the letter from Mario Llerena in the *New York Times*, 12 November 1957: 'When are those who are responsible ... going to realize that helping the Latin American dictators means preparing the ground for the bad seeds of Communism?'

64. *New York Times*, 15 January 1958. See also Statement of Dr. Manuel Urrutia, 'For Release Tuesday, January 14th ... ', and 'Remarks of Frances R. Grant, Secretary General of the Inter-American Association for Democracy and Freedom, at the Meeting of the Committee-in-Exile of the 26 of July Movement, to celebrate the "Grito de Baire", February 23, 1958, at Palm Garden, New York City', in FGP.

65. See Letter, Frances Grant to Herbert Matthews, 16 July 1956, in which she proffers 'the unanimous invitation' to join the IADF's US Committee: 'You are already a "de facto" member and we would like the privilege of calling you such.' Matthews's reply of 5 August explains that 'I have found in this work that I am more useful to people by being sort of uncommitted. As you say, I am already a "de facto" member and I will always remain so and do whatever I can but anyone in an editorial position is more effective if it cannot be claimed that he is *committed* to any particular line', in FGP. Matthews had won the IADF's annual award in 1953, one of the few North American honorees in its history.

66. Matthews, *World in Revolution*, p. 226.

67. See Letter, Frances Grant to David C. Williams, Americans for Democratic Action, 17 September 1957, asking that he meet with Roberto Agramonte, Ortodoxo presidential candidate in the aborted 1952 elections and briefly a cabinet minister in 1959; letter, Jacob Javits to Norman Thomas, 21 March 1958, explaining why a planned meeting with a delegation led by Urrutia had fallen through due to a secretary's mix-up; letter, Frances Grant and others to Secretary John Foster Dulles, 27 March 1958, protesting 'almost daily, shiploads of arms, tanks, etc. ... to swell the military defenses of General Batista, the Cuban dictator.'

68. Llerena, *Unsuspected Revolution*, p. 182. See *Congressional Record, House of Representatives*, 20 March 1958, p. 4948, where Powell declared that the US was 'a partner with the dictator of Cuba, Fulgencia Batista, in the killing of close to 4,000 Cubans so far.' He then listed in detail from embassy records the arms shipped to Cuba and placed a memorandum from Llerena in the record. Powell climaxed with a bloodcurdling letter from a Cuban imprisoned by Batista, a former US citizen who had resigned his lieutenancy in the Cuban Navy because of the savage atrocities he had witnessed. Rep. Charles Porter followed up the next week with a speech entitled 'Let's Stop Intervening in Cuba', in which he likened the situation to the French using US planes to bomb Arab villages in Tunisia. In the interest of not 'being a party, on any side, to this deplorable fratricide', he urged total withdrawal and support for UN-mediated elections, and closed by inserting a Jules Dubois article in the record (*Cong. Rec., House*, 26 March 1958, p. 5496).

69. Llerena, *Unsuspected Revolution*, pp. 177–8. Mark Naison, in *Communists in Harlem during the Depression*, New York: Grove Press, 1983, refers to how Johnson 'achieve[d] prominence as Adam Clayton Powell's righthand man in the Harlem jobs movement of the late 30's', (p. 123).

70. Ibid., p. 179.

71. Letter, Thomas to Grant, 23 June 1958; Grant's reply of 26 June 1958 dismisses Johnson's draft statement and suggests, 'As the Cuban situation now seems at an impass [sic], I think it might be a good [sic] to wait for the next incident and then consult with the Cuban leaders as to what would be more effective in helping their cause', in FGP.

72. *New York Times*, 19 June 1957 (telegram from forty-six 'labor chiefs' on how Cuban workers are apolitical and happy with the status quo); *Times*, 21 June 1957 (letter from Mujal, citing labor conference including Romualdi).

73. Romualdi, *Presidents and Peons*, pp. 197–8, and this entire chapter, 'Mujal and Batista', pp. 180–201. At the time of the Bay of Pigs invasion, Romualdi was further angered when his 'competent and experienced' *mujalista* friends (and therefore him) were excluded from the Cuban Democratic Revolutionary Labor Front through the machinations of 'a group of U.S. labor

subleaders, most of whom were associated with the CIO before the merger and who had a reputation of being "democratic leftists'" (p. 225).

74. *The New Leader*, 24 March 1958.

75. David Brion Davis, *Revolutions: Reflections on American Equality and Foreign Liberations*, Cambridge, Mass.: Harvard University Press, 1990.

76. Llerena, *Unsuspected Revolution*, pp. 95, 103.

77. Their presence was not a complete surprise to the viewing audience: see *New York Times*, 8 and 24 March, 22 April and 10 May 1957; also *Time*, 11 March 1957 on 'Castro Convertibles' with school photos of three 'young zealots'.

78. From the beginning, the boys' action was projected as consonant with 'American' traditions. The 24 March 1957 *New York Times* included their special oath:

> I swear in the name of our people and the people of Cuba, which I want to serve, that I am inspired in [sic] the same ideals of liberty and democracy that drove the founders of the United States of America to declare their independence on July 4, 1776 ... that I am proud to be useful to the cause of liberty in Cuba in the same way that our countrymen were in Europe and Asia during the last two world wars and in the same way that in the past century hundreds of Americans fought courageously ... for the independence of Cuba. ...

Original xeroxes of this oath, a letter to Eisenhower evoking his leadership in World War II, and the poignant notes the boys had sent to their families are all in the Herbert L. Matthews Papers, again indicating his role as facilitator.

79. Of course, the rebels' private perspective was rather different. Guevara remembered the boys as 'three pleasant characters who served to furnish our movement with a little advertising service, specially in the U.S. ... Two of them never heard a shot in the Sierra; worn out by the climate and the privations, they asked newspaperman Bob Taber to take them back. The other one fought at the battle El Uvero and later retired, quite ill, but at least he did participate in a battle. The boys were not ideologically prepared for a revolution; all they did was give vent to their spirit of adventure while in our company. We felt a sort of affection for them, but we were glad to see them go' (Guevara, *Episodes of the Revolutionary War*, pp. 49–54). Promoted to lieutenant, Ryan did a promotional tour of the States later in the year (Llerena, *Unsuspected Revolution*, p. 144).

80. Dubois, *Fidel Castro, Rebel*, p. 159.

81. Neill Macaulay, *A Rebel in Cuba*, New York: Quadrangle Books, 1970, p. 10. Elsewhere, Macaulay has written that 'for a while I thought about going to South America to look for lost trails and lost cities, but my application for a Fulbright grant to study archaeology in Peru was rejected while I was in Asia' (Macaulay, 'I Fought for Fidel', p. 80).

82. Macauley, *A Rebel in Cuba*, pp. 15–16.

83. Ibid., pp. 181, 183.

84. Macaulay, 'I Fought for Fidel', p. 92; letter, Macaulay to author, 8 April 1992.

85. Macauley, *A Rebel in Cuba*, pp. 13, 24.

86. Ibid., p. 99.

87. Letter, Macaulay to author, 26 February 1992.

88. As Professor Macaulay has pointed out to me, Walker pales by comparison with Europeans like Garibaldi or Lord Cochrane in South America, or the tradition of volunteer foreign legions (Irish, German and Italian) throughout Europe's revolutionary wars of the nineteenth century.

89. The most famous of these *expedicionarios* was General Frederick Funston, who made his name in Cuba in 1896–97, became a US Army counter-insurgency expert in the Philippines, and later led US troops in Mexico in 1914–17. See Thomas W. Crouch, *A Yankee Guerrillero: Frederick Funston and the Cuban Insurrection. 1896–1897*, Memphis, Tenn.: Memphis State University Press, 1975.

90. Macaulay, *A Rebel in Cuba*, pp. 22, 25.

91. *New York Times*, 6 September 1959. Quite a few US citizens were involved in less frontline work. Typical was the gun-running pilot Leslie Bradley, who explained his participation in terms of his rich Cuban friends: 'When I met Danny and his folks ... and they said they were working for the Revolution, I knew it wasn't a Communist revolution, and I didn't mind helping them' (*A Rebel in Cuba*, pp. 94–5). Also *Time*, 17 September 1958, on Charles Hormel, 'a rebel sympathizer

who married into a wealthy Cuban family 17 years ago', and ditched a plane full of guns off Oriente on his 28th flight; *New York Times*, 15 May 1958, on North Americans indicted in Texas for supplying arms; ibid., 1 April 1958, on three men arrested in Brooklyn for making bombs. Don Soldini remembers the US embassy asking him to identify dead US citizens from photographs: 'Two of them were burnt alive ... gasoline on the side of the ditch – it was typical.'

92. Matthews, *The Cuban Story*, p. 76. The Matthews Papers include a sheaf of grandiloquent signed-and-stamped military documents from the 'Second Front', prepared by Morgan in English. These offerings, such as a very detailed breakdown of the 'Estado Mayor' (General Staff) at the head of this tiny band, make plain how much rebellion sometimes has to do with play-acting, however lethal the theatrics become. Hugh Thomas and other writers suggest that the Frente Segundo del Escambray fighters were no better than 'semi-gangsters'. See also *New York Times*, 5 January 1959, on how Morgan and another North American, John Spiritto, were given permanent commands.

93. *New York Times*, 4 April 1958. The allegation that Batista was in bed with Cuba's Communists was based on their Popular Front alliance, which many Cubans and North Americans claimed had covertly survived. The hostile or simply confused attitude of the Partido Socialista Popular towards Castro's armed struggle through 1957 and parts of 1958 fueled this suspicion. There was a considerable degree of wish-fulfillment among Castro's supporters in this regard, but it is undeniable that the Rebel Leader himself had made these same charges publicly in the 15 July 1956 *Bohemia*, Cuba's most widely read newsmagazine. He cited the wartime alliance when Batista's 'electoral slogans hid behind the Hammer and Sickle', and alleged that 'half a dozen of his present ministers and confidential collaborators were outstanding members of the Communist Party' (quoted in Thomas, *Cuba: The Pursuit of Freedom*, p. 887). During the 1960s, New Leftists sometimes defended Castro by citing the PSP's supposed ties to Batista. See Maurice Zeitlin and Robert Scheer, *Cuba: Tragedy in Our Hemisphere*, New York: Grove Press, 1963, pp. 116–17, where the authors cite the PSP's 'obvious political opportunism', which defies any 'balanced reporting'. The most balanced view can be found in K. S. Karol, *Guerrillas in Power: The Course of the Cuban Revolution*, New York: Hill & Wang, 1970, pp. 151–5, which stresses the different worldviews and political styles of the PSP and the 26th of July Movement rather than the taint of collaboration with Batista to explain the lack of unity between the two.

94. Franqui, *Diary of the Cuban Revolution*, p. 289, presumably Evans Russell, named by Thomas in *Cuba: The Pursuit of Freedom*, p. 993 (the letter refers to another North American as well); Phillips, *Cuba: Island of Paradox*, p. 325; *Life*, 12 January 1959; *New York Times*, 27 and 29 November 1957. Other references of some interest include Daniel M. Friedenberg's account of how in 1957 he joined 'a guerrilla uprising in Manzanillo and served as a contact with Fidelista forces at Santiago de Cuba' (*Dissent*, Summer 1960), and very negative coverage of another Yankee executioner besides Macaulay, Herman Marks, who reputedly gave the *coup de grace* to 200 *batistianos* shot in the moat at La Cabana prison in early 1959 (AP story in *New York Times*, 31 March 1959).

95. Dubois, *Fidel Castro, Rebel*, pp. 278–9. At his father's appeal, Bartlett had been sent home, and was court-martialed, as was a Marine deserter, Gerry Holthaus, who became a lieutenant in the National Police before turning himself in at Guantánamo (*New York Times*, 17 October 1959).

96. See letter from the president of the Yale Political Union to Herbert L. Matthews, 12 November 1958, asking him to moderate the debate, in HLMP; Franqui, *Diary of the Cuban Revolution*, p. 292. For unclear reasons, this survey is presented as an 'Editor's Summary', with a few quotations.

97. Llerena, *Unsuspected Revolution*, p. 168.

98. Harold Flender, 'Cuba Libre', *The New Leader*, 3 March 1958. Many apprentice journalists went to Cuba, looking for a scoop. The already-cited J. L. Pimsleur had been 'recently an editor of the Columbia College *Spectator*', and the 8 April 1958 *New York Times* reported that two writers for the University of Michigan's *Michigan Daily* had been arrested for unclear reasons. The 15 April *Daily* clarifies that Barton Huthwaite and James Elsman, Jr 'spent their Spring vacation in Cuba attempting to get an interview with rebel leader Fidel Castro.' They made it to Santiago with the names of 'contacts' for the Sierra obtained in 'lower class bars' but were quickly arrested and expelled. The guarded character of their support for Castro comes through in an editorial. After assailing Batista as 'a tyrant, a crook, a murderer', they note that 'Castro raised some doubts in our minds as to his ultimate ambitions. But we are convinced that he is not now sympathetic to communism or socialism, and that he does not covet a dictatorship. ... In short, he is a liberal willing

to give his very life to wrest his country from the fear and tyranny of a dictator. He is worth taking a chance on. ... ' The presumptions of Cold War liberalism lead these two to the conclusion, therefore, that 'taking a chance' on Castro means that the US, 'in the name of our long-time concern for the Cuban people and in the name of American republicanism, intervene at first diplomatically and if necessary politically and militarily. ... '!

99. Letter, di Suvero to Matthews, 9 March 1957, in HMLP; see also Matthews's response, 18 March 1957, sternly stressing that the idea was 'utterly impossible'.

100. See W. J. Rorabaugh, *Berkeley at War: The 1960s*, New York: Oxford, 1989, p. 15, on SLATE's 1957 founding; also David Horowitz, *Student!*, New York: Ballantine Books, 1962. In addition, SLATE was the model for VOICE, the student party Tom Hayden founded at the University of Michigan that was SDS's nerve center. Michael Myerson, another early SLATE leader, has confirmed di Suvero's role as a SLATE founder.

101. All of the following quotations are taken from an interview with Soldini, 3 June 1992.

102. Fiorini worked under E. Howard Hunt in the CIA in the 1960s, and took his new name from a character in Hunt's novel *Bimini Run*. He was one of the Watergate burglars and has been repeatedly mentioned in connection with the assassination of John F. Kennedy, but that is another story. According to Soldini, 'He was no idealist. He was in it to make a buck' and 'became inspector of casinos right away', following Castro's victory. For a more heroic account of Fiorini's arms-smuggling, see one of the many mass-market pro-Castro books published in 1959, *Chicago Sun-Times* correspondent Ray Brennan's *Castro, Cuba and Justice*, pp. 189ff. According to Brennan, Fiorini had been a Marine Raider during World War II and fought in Cuba (where he too was tortured), because an uncle in Miami had been killed in a failed invasion attempt.

103. Thomas, *Cuba: The Pursuit of Freedom*, pp. 910, 973; Lazo, *Dagger in the Heart*, p. 127.

104. Glendon Swarthout, *Where the Boys Are*, New York: Random House, 1960, pp. 5–6. Swarthout was hardly the only writer to imagine young North Americans in Cuba during the revolution's early days. Novelists as diverse as Thomas Pynchon (*V*), Richard Fariña (*Been Down So Long It Looks Like Up to Me*), and Norman Lewis (*Cuban Passage*) also feature this touch of the picaresque. I thank Anne Rubinstein for bringing this point to my attention.

105. Ibid., p. 24.

106. Ibid., p. 44.

107. Ibid., p. 160.

108. Ibid., pp. 170, 165–6.

109. Ibid., pp. 189–90, 199–202.

110. Thomas, *Cuba: The Pursuit of Freedom*, p. 1062.

111. Peter Valenti, *Errol Flynn: A Bio-Bibliography*, Westport, Conn.: Greenwood Press, 1984, pp. 54, 165.

112. John Dorschner and Roberto Fabricio, *The Winds of December*, New York: Coward, McCann & Geoghegan, 1980, pp. 326, 437.

113. Recollections of Professors John McClure and John W. Chambers III, Rutgers University, August 1991.

4

1959: Whose Revolution Is It, Anyway?

The paradox of solidarity with the Cuban revolution over a generation is that the cast keeps changing. Nearly every segment of left liberalism claimed Cuba at one point or another, so that rather than continuity in who is 'pro-Castro', there have been episodic upsurges, notably at the beginning and end of the sixties. This history reflects, above all, the enmity towards Fidel within the national security apparatus and among US conservatives, who since 1961 have blocked the human connections upon which solidarity depends. It is also true that once in full control of the state, with a natural moat, material backing from the Soviet Union, Kennedy's promise not to invade, and the fervent support of the nonaligned bloc, the *fidelistas* did not need the solidarity of North Americans as much as other revolutionaries would later.

Over time, the disparate groups defending Castro have made a hodgepodge of strange bedfellows – anachronistic anti-imperialists and ardent Trotskyists early on, *New York Review of Books* intellectuals and Weatherpeople latterly; the single exception to this discontinuity has been the persistent current of solidarity within black America. There have also been distinct episodes in which Fidel appealed directly to the North American public, while potential supporters hung back: 1959 was one of these periods of transition, when most of the Cold War liberal activists, journalists and others who had formerly supported Cuba's cause retreated, while the organized left found its own reasons for talking loud but doing nothing. The most significant expression of solidarity during that long year lay outside the consciously political, among those alienated youths, African-Americans and others whose prairie-fire response to the Cubans' voluntarism has seemed to most historians only a disturbing oddity.

Long after Cuba was given up for good by most of the US 'political public', there still remained the nagging sense of a great opportunity lost, as various liberals and Social Democrats despairingly noted after the Bay of Pigs. This was the hope that Castro could have been another Tito, effectively repudiating the Soviet claim to defend the Third World, and somehow also 'our' Tito – an instrument to turn back the tide of ascending American militarism and Empire, to make the US a Good Neighbor again.

Yet it was never disputed by any party to this debate that for a good part of 1959, it seemed that the Cuban revolution and its larger-than-life Liberator were enjoying a genuine honeymoon with the North Americans. Though subsequently overshadowed by the chasm between US interests and Cuban independence, no one who lived through this apex of Yankee *fidelismo* has ever forgotten it. This infatuation was, of course, brief, and the permanent relationship quickly took on the sour taste of marital recrimination. But at least through Castro's barnstorming tour in April 1959 aimed directly at US opinion, when, in Hugh Thomas's words, 'unofficial North Americans indeed stretched out their hands to embrace a hero whom they had partly created, because of their own ardent demands for heroism', there was a noticeable divergence between the administration's public posture of wary tolerance (what William Appleman Williams called the 'passive-aggressive' phase) and widespread public enthusiasm.[1] The latter half of the year, however, was a sharp slope downwards, 'a duet in which each took actions to combat the threat from the other' and Castro's exoticism seemed ever more demonic.[2] By October 1959, when the State Department's liberals concurred with the decision to covertly remove Fidel, hardly any alternative voices were left within respectable politics or journalism.[3]

Given this increasingly vituperative confrontation, why was the Fair Play for Cuba Committee not formed until April 1960, a full year after Castro's visit to the US? Certainly, during this crucial Year One, a space for debate did remain tenuously open, even if no one filled it. The Cubans denied any socialist character to their revolution, even stamping all their mail to the US, in both English and Spanish, 'In Cuba, we are living happy now with humanism, no communism.'[4] But while some attempt at argument was made through the spring and summer, in the latter half of 1959 Cuba's remaining friends in US media and political circles made only scattered, ineffectual pleas for patience and understanding.

The most obvious explanation is sometimes the best – those who first stoked the fire of Yankee *fidelismo* were also the first to throw cold water upon the embers. The enthusiastic press drumbeat of 1957–58 was replaced by a chorus of sneers and abuse, epitomized by *Life*'s November 1959 description of Castro as 'the silly egomaniac who runs Cuba ... just another tinhorn tyrant.'[5] Given the monolithic character of the communications media in that period, such a seachange alone cut the legs out from underneath anyone attempting to defend Cuba's government. After all, the US press was hardly separate from a nonradical, vaguely liberal solidarity with the Cuban rebellion – it was the original site of this tenuous fellowship, and when the press turned on Castro, that solidarity evaporated in due course (or went underground). This burgeoning journalistic hostility did not directly reflect any official line.

In fact, during 1959–60 the press acted as a goad, spurring popular and con-gressional demands for a more activist, hardline policy against Castro. Ironic as it may be in retrospect, through the middle of 1960 the Eisenhower admini-stration's public face towards Cuba was one of the utmost restraint in the face of constant provocation, while it very privately shifted gears towards destabili-zation. One must conclude, therefore, that the reporters, editors and publish-ers who wrote or condoned pro-Castro coverage earlier did genuinely feel betrayed by Castro in power; evidently a large portion of the public agreed with this stance, in the absence of a counterargument.

It is as if North Americans discovered that Fidel really meant what he said about a great cleansing national revolution – or perhaps, in many cases, they had only listened selectively in the first place, picking out of his resonant dis-course the most appealing segments, such as promises of elections and the sort of pluralist society they believed existed at home. The resultant outrage helps explain why the 26th of July Movement's US partisans, in the press and out-side it, so quickly deserted from the fray: they had no understanding of how undeferential Castro would be when he no longer needed every ounce of US favor. However much Cold War liberals and plain Cold Warriors were pre-pared to support 'revolution' against corrupt dictators as necessary to blunt the appeal of Communism, evidently no one had contemplated what a true revolution would look like, even one avowedly nonsocialist like Cuba's: the unrestrained, disordered, thoroughly popular character of events as the Cuban masses flung themselves into motion. Quite suddenly, those ragged *guajiros*, whose devotion to Fidel had inspired such encomiums when he was only a guerrilla leader, became a threatening mob; the charismatic lawyer-rebel meta-morphosed into a ranting, unshaven demagogue.

Of course, the issue of Communism did intrude, as charges of Red sympa-thies were increasingly given credence in the press from late spring on, though much less among policymakers. But the idea of Castro as agent of the Soviet Union did not dominate that first year, because the Cubans had not yet made such an alliance.[6] As often as he was labelled a crypto-Red, Fidel was pilloried as a 'totalitarian', with numerous allusions to how Hitler and Mussolini had also worked a sinister magic upon their peoples through spellbinding oratory. Perhaps the most common charge was that he was simply crazy, a paranoiac with delusions of grandeur and ridiculously unfounded fears of the US.

In such an atmosphere of hysteria, individuals who retained their Castroist sympathies were easily intimidated, or simply ignored. Almost certainly, some significant number of ordinary citizens did retain an openness towards Fidel. The rapid blossoming of Fair Play for Cuba during 1960 demonstrates this, and Eisenhower noted grimly in his memoirs that 'admiration for Castro died slowly throughout the year 1959.'[7] Yankee *fidelismo* had lost its voice, though, and there was no precedent for creating new institutional expressions directly critical of Cold War premises (it is no accident that Fair Play began as an alternative media outlet run by professional reporters). The political world of 1959–60 was so circumscribed that, merely to survive, the moderate directors of the Committee for a Sane Nuclear Policy (SANE) felt compelled to abase themselves before the Senate's Internal Security Subcommittee and demonstratively purge themselves of people possibly 'soft' on Communism.

By 1960 anyone still professing faith in Castro's good intentions was baited as a sentimental fool at best, and a Communist sympathizer at worst, yet perversely this is when an anti-intervention coalition initiated by journalists and stray intellectuals finally assembled, in unplanned fits and starts. On the face of it, this solidarity beyond the pale was illogical or pathetic, but it had its own rationality. Therefore, rather than asking why Fair Play for Cuba was organized so late, it is more useful to ask why it was formed at all, at a point when the risks were already considerable. *The hiatus between the pro-Fidel bandwagon of 1957–58 and the prophetic minority movement of 1960–61 becomes crucial because it highlights who did demand 'fair play' for Cuba, and if this was part of a 'new' left, what was new about it.* To understand the character of this latter movement, therefore, it becomes necessary to trace not only the networks of private intervention and public sympathy during the guerrilla war, but to 'unpack' the year following Batista's fall. The much more radical solidarity with Cuba that flourished in the pre–*Port Huron Statement* stage of the New Left made an end run around both organized anti-Communist liberalism and the organized Old Left. But that coup, half-accident and half-design, would not have been either possible or necessary if these constituencies – one large and contending for national power, the other marginalized and fraying at the edges – had not each already found its own reason for leaving Cuba alone. This chapter is thus concerned with 1959 as a year of retreat and passivity on the one hand, and furious, decisive action on the other. As we shall see, abstention by past or future friends did not much faze the victorious revolutionaries, least of all Castro personally. With characteristic audacity, he set out to reach the North Americans himself.

Gaining and Losing the 'Mass Romantic Glow'

The press had only itself to blame if North Americans held onto an unreasoning taste for *fidelismo*. The fall of Batista and Castro's eight-day victory parade across the island was presented as an unmitigated triumph of the human spirit, of pure democracy over corrupt tyranny, and most especially of a distinctly American brand of masculine valor. *Life* put Fidel on the cover, with headlines blaring its approval of the 'Dynamic Boss' ('a bearded rebel scholar') and 'The Liberator's Triumphal March Through An Ecstatic Island'.[8] The rest of the journalistic establishment followed suit in similar awe-struck terms, as Jack Paar and Ed Sullivan, television's two most powerful hosts, immediately flew down to interview the whiskery hero, and 'Face the Nation' temporarily relocated to Havana.⁹ Perhaps the height of stardom was reached in early February when Edward R. Murrow's celebrity-interview show 'Person-To-Person' featured both Fidel and 'Fidel Junior' in their pajamas (with a puppy), from a luxurious Havana hotel suite. Looking almost cherubic, the modest revolutionary discussed his childhood and his facial hair, America's number one interest ('When we have fulfilled our promise of good government, then I will cut my beard'), and avowed that all he wanted was 'peace and progress' in the months ahead. In this rosy light and for a moment, nearly everyone was *fidelista*, even the Eisenhower administration, which rushed to recognize the provisional government, retroactively casting itself as a patron of democracy in Cuba.

Very soon though, this honeymoon began to wind down, as the centrifugal reality of what Herbert L. Matthews called 'a real revolution, not a changing of the guard, not a shuffling of leaders, not just the outs getting in, but a social revolution on the direct line of the French revolution of 1789' quickly spun off tensions in the US.¹⁰ The first sticking point was the methodical trial and execution of those responsible for Batista's fearsome repressive machine, which proceeded from the first days of January through the summer. Repeatedly, not only Castro but even the Catholic hierarchy justified the shooting of some hundreds of army and police personnel on political and moral grounds, to avoid the mob violence and long-term vendettas that had disrupted stable governance ever since the revolt against Machado in the 1930s. But the exemplary, ritual specificity of popular justice in Cuba – the confrontations with the families of those assassinated (in one case before a huge, shouting stadium audience, an incident well publicized in the US), the *batistiano* officers commanding their own firing squads – hinted at a fundamentally radical spirit, and as early as mid January 'a chorus of protest' was heard in the US Congress, with key Democrats like Representatives Wayne Hays and Emanuel Celler calling for a UN investigation and even a US embargo.¹¹

In a sense, the revolution became tainted in those first weeks or months, its 'mass romantic glow' lost, in Saul Landau's words, precisely because it proved to be a revolution and not the civic festival followed by a quick return to normalcy that was anticipated in the US.¹² The whiff of Jacobin solutions so close at hand suggested by the 'show trials', and Fidel's notorious gibe to reporters that if the US sent in the Marines there would be '200,000 dead gringos', provoked a growing paternal anger in the US in early 1959. Cartoonists depicted Cuba obscured by gunsmoke ('Pow! Pow! Pow!') under the heading 'Democracy Returns', and posed Fidel standing at 'The Familiar Fork' in the road between signs labelled 'Personal Ambition' and 'Representative Government'.¹³ Since 1957 and then especially in that extraordinary first week when he seemed in unbroken communion with the Cuban people – talking, listening and reaching into the vast crowds lining the victory march – Castro had taken on the monochromatic dimensions of a myth, the pure warrior with clean hands. Unavoidably, however, the implacable conviction to serve justice by settling all accounts, and the rowdy, raffish quality of the 26th of July Movement, clashed with North Americans' predilections for order and the appearance of legality. From another perspective, appearance really was the issue: those who lived through the late-sixties hatred of 'longhairs' that often approached vigilantism in the US will understand how unsettling were the Cuban beards. Anything less than early elections, the victory of a respectable, cleanshaven, middle-class government and the retirement of the Rebel Army from politics would probably have produced the same disenchantment. As Herbert L. Matthews summed up this period,

> the American press was praising and romanticizing Fidel Castro as if he were a knight in shining armor who had come to Havana on a white horse and who was going to make democracy, and bring social justice but otherwise let things go on as before. ... In reality, Americans were welcoming a figure who did not exist, expected what could not and would not happen, and then blamed Fidel Castro for their own blindness and ignorance.[14]

Increasingly, the rebels were seen as wild men, picturesque but embarrassingly crude in their approach to the responsibilities of power. This impression was only furthered by the late February 'goodwill visit on Washington's birthday' of a delegation headed by Major Camilo Cienfuegos, chief of staff of the Rebel Army.[15] Here were the ultimate *barbudos*, shaggy to a degree that North American hippies did not reach until the very end of the sixties: they stare out of newspaper photos like newly drafted Appalachian mountaineers in the big city, with vast, untrimmed beards and shapeless, pointy hats over drab fatigues. Though Cienfuegos was greeted with considerable fanfare and did all the right things, laying wreaths at the Tomb of the Unknown Soldier and the memorial to the battleship *Maine*, the message leaking from the incredulous prose of journalists following the revolutionaries around New York was that not *barbudos* but barbarians were at the gates.[16] Still, though the earlier trip had the air of an opera bouffe, with the ragged band's coming and going reported like a carnival sideshow, the undeniable celebrity of these rebels prepared the way for Fidel's grand tour two months later, and the rapport he managed to establish with North Americans as a most gentle barbarian.

For one remaining moment Castro managed to turn the weight of circumstance around, and to use his and the revolution's informality, the intense youthfulness noted by all observers, as a last gambit to recuperate the gringos – the people if not their government. In contrast with Cienfuegos's unfortunate sojourn, Fidel's trip across the Northeast in April 1959 became a galloping success, generating a bandwagon that for another fortnight dispelled the gathering storm. The visit was sparked by his acceptance in early March of an invitation to address the prestigious annual convention of the American Society of Newspaper Editors, apparently arranged by Jules Dubois, in a final demonstration of the revolution's special dispensation among the press.[17] At first the State Department let it be known that this was another witless breach of protocol, but the excitement when Castro announced he would come anyway caused the administration to roll out a miserly, unofficial welcome mat.[18] Fidel would not see Eisenhower himself, like an official head of state, but would have an 'informal' lunch with Nixon, and 'informal' meetings with Acting Secretary of State Christian Herter. However, the administration (and later commentators who endlessly debate whether the Cubans came seeking economic aid and, if so, whether it should have been offered to them) largely missed the main thrust of Castro's peaceable invasion. At the time, he was quite explicit. This was 'a truth operation' to bring the revolution to ordinary US citizens misled by a malevolent press, and perhaps thereby exert pressure in official circles.[19] As William Appleman Williams pointed out a few years later,

> Castro was very explicitly trying to use his visit to the United States as a means of building general support in the circles that do exert a measure of influence on official American policy. He was in this sense going to the people over the head of the official bankers in an effort to win popular backing – or at least sympathy – for more generous terms.[20]

By this standard, in his second major mission to the US, Fidel hardly came away empty-handed. In fact, the public adulation of the ex-guerrilla leader was so intense that even governors, mayors and congressmen bathed themselves in the glow of his publicity. In the long run, however, this evident personal popularity with a range of North Americans hardly dispelled the clouds of suspicion encircling the revolution. At best, Castro helped buy Cuba a few more months of ambiguity in the US lexicon of friend and foe. More important, he reinforced the subversive appeal of *fidelismo* to youth of all sorts here, which proved a more reliable surety than any warming by the State Department: as if to underline how real that appeal was, in a quantifiable or commodifiable sense, *Life* reported on 13 April that a US toy manufacturer had 100,000 Fidel cap-and-beard sets ready to hit the market. The accompanying photos of a gang of little boys running around the New Jersey woods pretending to ambush each other seem familiar to any North American of a certain age, except that instead of Davy Crockett coonskin caps or plastic GI Joe helmets, their khaki fatigue caps sport a 26th of July movement logo and the legend 'El Libertador'. Even odder, though, is that the caps' chin-straps are covered in thick black hair, for a moment creating the illusion that a host of tiny, grinning *barbudos* had sprouted from North American soil.

The effect of Castro's overpowering personality up close, or his presence here as represented through television, print, photograph, newsreel and word-of-mouth, was to suspend disbelief in the possibility of revolutionary virtue. For a week or two, he was again Everyone's Man from Havana, leaving admiration in his wake. To his wary hosts, the 1,500 editors assembled in Washington on 17 April, Castro affirmed, 'We are not Communists', and after two hours of explanation and exhortation, they gave him a prolonged standing ovation. Later that same day, after meeting various House and Senate committees, the Dixiecrat patriarch Senator Russell Long pronounced himself 'reassured', and a Republican Congressman from Pennsylvania, James Fulton, described himself as a 'nuevo amigo. ... I was neutral and suspicious before, but today I was very favorably impressed. I think we should help him.' Meanwhile, the real action was in the streets, with Fidel 'holding ... by its lapels' the staid, Jim Crow capital, hosting big parties at the Cuban embassy near Dupont Circle, sneaking out in the wee hours to a Chinese restaurant where he met students and appeared on a popular radio talk show, taking unscheduled strolls to shake hands, sign autographs and wave at buses filled with high school students shouting 'Hi, Fidel!', in general creating as much hubbub as possible. From the big tourist sites like Mount Vernon and the Jefferson Memorial to an elementary school playground, he engaged the crowds directly, at the Lincoln Memorial reading aloud in English the Gettysburg Address; an awards ceremony was even staged at the Cuban embassy, where hand-struck gold medals were presented to twelve top US journalists. The effect was summarized by one *New York Times* reporter as 'out of another century – the century of Sam Adams and Patrick Henry and Tom Paine and Thomas Jefferson.' For a moment, Fidel had 'stirred memories, long dimmed, of a revolutionary past.'[21]

Washington proved to be only a dry run for New York, with its huge Latino population plus large constituencies of liberals, students and even radicals. Castro was greeted at Penn Station by 20,000 people and perhaps twice that number cheered him at a night rally in Central Park where, following the playing of 'The Star-Spangled Banner', he was presented with ceremonial keys by a city commissioner, in an augury of how Third World pride would later alter urban politics. He made the rounds of elite institutions (the Ford Foundation, the Council on Foreign Relations), the press (the *Times*, *La Prensa*, *New York Post* publisher Dorothy Schiff, and Henry Luce), City Hall, the UN, the Empire State Building and, briefly, Columbia University, and was everywhere applauded. He even visited the Bronx Zoo and was photographed sticking his hand into the Bengal tiger's cage and eating an ice-cream cone.[22]

Yet, for all the furor of celebrity in New York, the natural base of both Cuban-American and Yankee *fidelismo*, it is of greater interest that Castro's two other stops were at universities. Evidently, his US representatives' reports of their reception on campus, and the efforts of young gringos to join his forces, had made an impression. But Fidel did not visit schools at random. Instead he chose Harvard and Princeton, two pinnacles of social and intellectual prestige for the Eastern Establishment (he also got off the train in New Haven for some gladhanding and quickly toured Columbia, underlining the elite focus). Of course, these institutions did invite Fidel, but amid the clamor of urgent appeals, it is his targetting of these particular student bodies that stands out – he could have expected as strong a response almost anywhere else. It proved a masterful strategy for demonstrating to the greater public that, even within the training-grounds of power, Cuba had enthusiastic US friends, since the Ivy League's response was nothing short of overwhelming.

The events at Princeton, in 1959 still a genteel male cloister focused on pantyraids and houseparty weekends where a reading by 'Beatnik' poets was a major curiosity, indicates the peculiar avenues to solidarity with Cuba, and the potential latent in the most unlikely places. Castro's invitation was secured not by some ardent student activist, or the Cubans themselves, but by local alumnus Roland T. Ely, class of '46, cousin of Enrique Menocal y Villalon, an aide of Manuel Urrutia during exile and the newly appointed Director General of Revenue and Taxation in the provisional government.[23] During the war against Batista, Ely had hosted Menocal and Urrutia on campus, taking them to a football game and having the latter speak at Lawrenceville, the nearby private boys school. After the victory, he flew down to Havana and met Fidel, bringing Princeton's invitation to lecture in an American Civilization Program seminar on 'The United States and the Revolutionary Spirit'. As it happened, the seminar with a closed audience of 300 (where Castro 'three times overruled Professor R. R. Palmer', the eminent scholar of revolutions) was the pretext for a riot by an exuberant mob of up to 2,000 students who repeatedly broke through state police lines, cheering wildly. As in Washington, Castro defied his nervous escorts and plunged into the crowd, telling his audience that he hoped 'undergraduates here and throughout the U.S. will support our country's young government' before roaring off to stay at Morven, the official mansion of Governor Robert Meyner. There he met not only the latter and his wife, but gave a press conference and was photographed with Pennsylvania's Democratic Senator Joseph Clark and former Secretary of State Dean Acheson, who happened to be speaking on campus that day and did not shrink from the linkage.[24] The next morning Fidel capped his gladhanding by telling a reputedly awed audience of 800 Lawrenceville boys and teachers that

> only young people are capable of the greatest sacrifice. Only young people are pure and dedicated. With few resources, fighting against an army without morals or ideals, we achieved our victory, believing in what we were doing. ...[25]

As he left, Castro exclaimed to a campus radio reporter that Princeton was 'a paradise for students, teachers and all those who want to study', and extended an open invitation to the upcoming July 26th festivities.[26]

After his whirlwind tour of New York, Fidel's stopover at Harvard was similar to his stay at Princeton, although on a larger scale. After a trip like 'a campaign stump tour by a political hopeful, complete with observation-car speeches and handshaking expeditions at Bridgeport, New Haven and Providence', and an impromptu swing through a jammed, applauding Harvard Yard, Fidel was wined and dined by Dean McGeorge Bundy at the Harvard Faculty Club. The latter, an archetype of the 'national security intellectual' on the Cambridge-Washington circuit and a key architect of both Kennedy's and Lyndon Johnson's foreign policies, then introduced the Cuban to a crowd of 8,700 students at Soldier Field. Castro expertly wooed his audience, promising them low-budget vacations for US youth, and attributing the revolution's extrajudicial character to lack of a constitutional tradition: 'You cannot speak of what Jefferson said if you are hungry. Hunger, too, is a tyrant.' The audience ate it up, especially when Bundy promised to satisfy 'his ambition' and grant the Harvard scholarship that Fidel ingenuously confessed he had failed to receive eleven years previously.[27]

When the Going Gets Rough: The Few Who Spoke Up

Once Fidel was out of sight, however, his all-too-solid presence was quickly forgotten, soon to be replaced by the cartoonists' and rightwingers' familiar caricature of a ranting, fuzzy-wuzzy Latin upstart, an amalgam of Santa Ana, Pancho Villa and a Hollywood Beatnik. Despite the sense on all sides that the Americans had been successfully won over by Castro's sheer charm, it took only his departure for matters to worsen radically, with Stuart Novins's CBS Special Report on 3 May asking the question 'Is Cuba Going Red?', and leaving no doubt as to the answer: 'It is today a total dictatorship and is rapidly becoming a Communist beachhead in the Caribbean.' CBS did allow Rep. Charles Porter and three Cuban diplomats to rebut Novins's charges two weeks later, but as the US government's position hardened rapidly following the Agrarian Reform in June, the revolution's downward spiral became paramount in virtually all press coverage.[28]

Soon, the numbers of those willing to publicly urge moderation diminished sharply, in the face of a consensus that Castro was deliberately picking a fight. By November, senior *New York Times* reporters (far more restrained than their colleagues elsewhere) were describing his 'systematic demolition' of 'friendly relations', and rabid 'anti-Americanism'.[29] In many venues, such as the Luce publications, the polemic took on a vicious tone, with leering suggestions that the Cuban leader was mentally unstable: editorial cartoonists pictured him floating dreamily in a cloud of his own cigar smoke, or stamping like a maddened imp on a huge Uncle Sam hat.[30] The forced resignation of President Manuel Urrutia in July and the October jailing of Major Huber Matos, when he attempted to rally his officers to an anti-Communist position, convinced the US government that it could no longer hope to influence the revolutionary government from within: these were major stories as evidence of Castro's encroaching police state. Even earlier, the June defection of Major Diaz Lanz, chief of the Rebel Air Force, and his charge before the Senate Internal Security Subcommittee that Castro was a dyed-in-the-wool Communist, drew a line in the sand for the unreconstructed McCarthyite Right. North American and Cuban perceptions of day-to-day realities began to diverge sharply: in the US, these events were treated as the purging of the true, pro-US revolutionaries; in Cuba, outside of the worried middle classes, they paled beside the great social and economic upheaval of daily life attending the Agrarian Reform.

What happened to all of Cuba's erstwhile friends when Castro was no longer the media's darling? Polling data reinforce the sense one gets from Fidel's in-person appearances in April that solidarity with Cuba was a bit more than a momentary fad, because North Americans were surprisingly slow to get on the anti-Castro bandwagon. In May, a national poll showed that 88 percent of the public knew who Castro was (extraordinary for a non-European leader), and 31 percent still had a favorable impression of him – a figure indicating a major erosion in his popularity in the US since January, but also a substantial reservoir of support.[31] Perhaps even more tantalizingly, during the same week as the July 26th festivities, Gallup asked the same questions: 78 percent of those polled had heard of Fidel, and among these half (48 percent) had an unfavorable opinion of him, with one in five (20 percent) still favorable; the remaining third (32 percent) were 'uncertain'.[32] These results bear out President Eisenhower's memory – an even split, halfway through 1959, between those who had made up their minds against Fidel and those who were still thinking about it, or retained their sympathy.

In the post-Vietnam era, this sort of division on a high-profile foreign policy issue would have been echoed by conflict in Congress and trench warfare in editorial columns, with various institutional forces in business, labor and the churches lining up pro and con. But in 1959, the public was presumed not to know its own mind, and the remaining disaggregated liberal supporters of Castro could draw little comfort from poll figures. Minus any measurable anti-interventionist bloc in either of the political parties, partisans of Cuba were smeared with little fear of reprisal. The first baiting of the once-impressive *fidelista* lobby began with a *Time* story denouncing Herbert L. Matthews as an habitual dupe of tyrants going back to the days of Mussolini.[33] From then on, major figures in what passed for the liberal camp generally kept their heads down, or spoke very carefully, with rare exceptions like ex-President Truman's comment in the summer, 'I think that Fidel Castro is a good young man, who has made mistakes but who seems to want to do the right thing for the Cuban people.'[34] No other Democrat of any prestige went this far after early 1959, as indicated by three of the Senate's leaders on foreign policy issues. In August, J. William Fulbright of Arkansas urged that the US demon-strate patience, and not confuse nationalism with Communism. In October, Mike Mansfield of Montana suggested that if Castro pursued better relations he would find us to be 'reasonable men'. In November, Paul Douglas of Illinois again hoped for patience with Castro and not a 'wholesale condemnation'.[35] Privately, such a gray eminence of Cold War politics as Dean Acheson might assure his friend Herbert Matthews in March that 'I am still with you on Cuba', and dismiss 'the prevailing guff', but such private words never translated into a public stance.[36]

In this context, the tiny number of gringos knowledgeable about Latin America, like those partisans of the Inter-American Association for Democracy and Freedom who perceived Castro's sledgehammer impact on hemispheric opinion, tried to mute the hysteria by placing *fidelismo* in context. Lacking any base independent from Cold War confines, they had little influence, given that after June 1959 much more powerful forces branded Cuba as a mortal threat. The liberals who had expressed solidarity with Cuba were restricted to pointing out, with increasingly threadbare reasoning, Castro's non-Communist statements and purportedly anti-Communist actions. Early on, the IADF's *Hemispherica* had editorialized on those cabinet officers, 'sober in their sense of responsibility', who would presumably offset the 'precipitate haste' of the Castroites, but by the fall, after the 'regrettable' dismissal of Urrutia, it was reduced to *realpolitik:* 'The question which should be asked by those who oppose Castro is "What are the alternatives?"'[37]

Those parts of the Democratic Left who had always been guarded about Castro debated the appropriate degree of hostility or patience, continuing to see the island mainly as a factor in the East–West struggle. *Dissent*, for instance, simply ignored all the furor over Cuba until mid 1960, other than one thoughtful piece by an Italian observer, Livio Stecchini, who early on defined the revolution as that of a 'bourgeoisie with 19th century ideals', with Fidel a Garibaldi-like figure.[38] *The New Leader* ignored Cuba for most of 1959 after an initial noncommittal report, until the veteran Mexican polemicist Victor Alba issued a nasty prognosis on 'The Struggle Inside Cuba', seeing the army as on the verge of establishing an 'open, "revolutionary" dictatorship', while the 'democratic forces' fought for time, with Fidel as a weak and vacillating figure in between.[39] Meanwhile, Herbert L. Matthews was still permitted to cover Cuba and write editorials for the *New York Times* as an honorable eccentric, and remained Castro's most steadfast journalistic friend, reporting on his continuing popularity with the masses as well the revolution's remaining middle-class, non-Communist credentials. By now, though, Matthews's persona was thoroughly bound up with Fidel's rise to power. He no longer led a pack of enthusiastic reporters, but stood alone as a Cassandra-like figure. The *Chicago Tribune*'s Jules Dubois, who after the victory 'so completely monopolized Fidel's time you would have thought they were lifelong buddies', took a little longer, but within months of his eulogistic April 1959 book, *Fidel Castro: Rebel, Liberator or Dictator?*, he too discovered that he had been betrayed, and began writing and giving speeches on Castro's treason and how 'the Communists had tried to lynch me in Cuba in October, 1959.'[40]

Most intriguing of all the fragments of support for the revolution, at various points during 1959 leaders of major Protestant denominations with congregations in Cuba spoke up forcefully, hinting at the faith-based refusal of Cold War conventions that one day would become endemic. And unlike more ideologically acclimated liberals and socialists, the tone of their comments suggested an enthusiastic and instinctual solidarity with what was actually taking place in Cuba – the eradication of illiteracy, the thousands of new schools, clinics and modern homes across the island, the breakdown of long-held habits of deference and passivity. As Castro left the US on 26 April, the Methodist Bishop John Wesley Lord of Reading, Pennsylvania denounced the proliferating insinuations of Communism, described the executions as the 'lesser of two evils', and praised Fidel outright, saying, 'Now is the time to help Castro and the Cuban people consolidate and make sure of the rights they have won.'[41] In late July, as anti-Castro rhetoric reached a new intensity after the removal of Urrutia and the first expropriations of US-owned farmland under the Agrarian Reform law, William H. Rhoades, executive secretary of the American Baptist Home Mission Societies, wrote the *New York Times* explicitly citing the Cuban Baptists' connection to the 26th of July Movement and expressing support for 'those who are apparently exerting every influence to bring a better way of life to the Cuban people'.[42] At the end of the year, while Louisiana Senator Allen Ellender called Castro 'a rabble rouser of the rankest kind' who 'cannot and should not be trusted' and moderate Republican Senator Kenneth Keating of New York alleged 'Communist penetration all the way to the top', Dr Arthur L. Miller, moderator of the General Assembly of the Presbyterian Church in the USA, returned from a ten-day investigation not only urging that the US be 'patient', but explicitly justifying the expropriation of US corporations like United Fruit, which had made 'huge profits' in Cuba.[43]

An interesting accompaniment to this Protestant sympathy can be found in the Jesuit magazine *America*, which waited until 1960 to denounce Castro, and at points was pulled towards an instinctual solidarity. Thus, in February 1959, Managing Editor Eugene K. Culhane, travelling across the island with one of the 26th of July Movement's chaplains, explained the executions of *batistianos* in the most sympathetic terms, and implicitly wedded the Church to the revolution through a series of vignettes – visiting with the anti-Batista Archbishop of Santiago, accompanying a rebel soldier on his return home, and meeting cabinet minister Rufo Lopez-Fresquet and his American-born wife after mass. In the spring, there was considerable comment about Castro's lack of couth, and *America* was not impressed by his April visit:

Castro looks young and seems callow. For his country's sake, the Cuban Premier ought to set out to create just the opposite impression. We suggest he put those fatigues in mothballs, get a shave and buy a necktie. We wish him well, but we would like to find it easier to do so.[44]

Over the summer, *America* expressed increasing anxiety over Castro, but then Culhane again went to Cuba, and reported on the Agrarian Reform effort not as the entering wedge of Soviet-style collectivization but 'Hope for the Cuban Farmer'. His pro-Castro tilt was indirect but clear; the revolution had given the *campesinos* 'a new sense of their dignity and a new sense of belonging'.[45] Back in the USA, Culhane and the magazine soon returned to the fold, and from 1960 on, like the rest of North American Catholicism, *America* was intensely anti-Castro, but from this indecision one can catch a glimpse of the unpredictable responses of US Catholic men and women religious in the midst of Latin American repression and revolution over the next decades.

The most prominent national figure who continued to project himself as Castro's champion after Batista's fall was the Reverend Adam Clayton Powell, Jr, long a scandal to many as one of two blacks sitting in Congress, and what was worse, a man who delighted in defying white society. What is especially revealing is that Powell was the only person supporting Castro who drew upon an established, overt base of sympathy – albeit one that remained invisible to white America, segregated nearly completely from the realities of the African-American community.

Even before Fidel got to Havana, Powell called for US recognition of the revolutionary government and the astronomical sum of $200 million in aid.[46] On 15 January, as his colleagues were denouncing the court-martials of *batistianos*, Powell defended their legitimacy and announced he was flying down. In Cuba, he stood beside Castro at an enormous rally in Havana and at the latter's first press conference, and was congratulated for his leadership in cutting aid to Batista. On Powell's return he proclaimed Fidel an 'idealist', again defending the executions and denouncing both the 'pro-Batista lobby' here (a not-too-subtle allusion to certain Deep South congressmen) and all US arms shipments to Latin dictators.[47] Later, he publicly urged Eisenhower on several occasions to invite Fidel to the White House, and was even blamed for Castro's decision to make his 'private' visit.[48]

Powell's flamboyant public friendship with Castro was short-lived, but it remains notable for its singularity and what it augured. As he told it, by March 1959 the drift towards Communism was so evident that, at the urging of high-placed Cubans, he flew down to warn Fidel, but Teresa Casuso (supposedly one of the Reds closest to Castro) blocked their meeting. On his return, Powell conspicuously washed his hands of Cuba. This version of events is difficult to credit, however, since a year later Casuso herself, by then Cuba's UN representative, became a highly publicized defector.[49] Whatever the real story, it is clear that Powell kept his head down thereafter. He did not appear with Fidel in Central Park that April, tempting as the prospect must have been. Brief as it was, this episode with Castro reverberates, since after 1 January 1959 no elected white liberal chose to stand as close to the Cubans, literally and metaphorically, as the man who was arguably, through his sheer ability to cause trouble, the most powerful black national leader of the 1950s.[50]

On the face of it, Powell's showmanship would seem merely part of the Harlem congressman's idiosyncratic record. But, like much else connected with solidarity with the Cuban revolution in the twilight of the 1950s, it sounds a prefigurative note, given the eventual rise of a black urban polity that anchored the firmly anti-interventionist left wing of the Democratic Party throughout the post-sixties era. For Powell was an excellent politician, attuned to his constituents and the shape of things to come. He had just beaten the combined efforts of Tammany Hall and the black establishment to oust him from Congress in 1958 using the same candidate, Earl Brown, who had unseated the black Communist Benjamin Davis from New York's City Council in 1949 (the offense was endorsing Eisenhower in 1956 when Stevenson refused to firmly back integration). His independence guaranteed by a personal electoral machine, Powell evidently perceived Castro's immense popularity with both African-Americans and New York's growing Latino population. In doing so, he anticipated a whole generation of municipal, state and federal black officials from the 1970s on, some progressive and some merely opportunistic, for whom solidarity with Third World leaders, from Nelson Mandela to Yasir Arafat, was not a threat but a guarantor of popular support. Later Powell would affirm his anti-Communism and therefore anti-Castroism, but in 1959 he spoke for many among the Northern black community who admired Castro's decisiveness in ending segregation, while governmental action in the US was agonizingly slow.

For Powell did not hail Castro in any void. With an eye to his standing as a broker with both parties, he was actually more conservative regarding Cuba than considerable sectors of the mainstream black community. On the face of it, this may seem like a wild claim. The caution of organizations such as the NAACP regarding the taint of Communism, and their unwillingness to criticize US foreign policy in any way, is well established: witness the public censuring of Martin Luther King, Jr by many black leaders in 1966 for his opposition to the Vietnam War, after great pressure to keep silent. But what must be remembered is that the NAACP, the Urban League and others represented black America to the white world, and perforce sought access to that unfriendly terrain on its own terms. Within the separate civil society that most African-Americans inhabited in the 1950s, if not later, norms were quite different, and that which infuriated the white North American public, its journalists and its elected representatives, was not presumed to be a bad thing.

The quickest route to discovering how different Cuba looked from a black perspective is through the black-owned weekly press, mainstay of black community life. In January 1959 the Baltimore *Afro-American*, the largest circulation black paper with four East Coast regional editions, sent its editor Cliff Mackay down to Cuba to cover this big story. Mackay stayed in Havana for weeks, reporting his daily wanderings in ways that reveal how Cuba had long had a distinct meaning for black people in the US as a multiracial society close to home. From the *Afro*'s point of view, Powell's presence with Castro was not a sidebar, but the main topic, and the former's appearances with Fidel were hailed with headlines like 'FANTASTIC! Inside Cuba – "Will Eliminate Discrimination"'.[51] Attacks by various Republicans on Powell were cause for only more glee, and the inference was clear that those who did not like Adam Clayton Powell, Jr, and would not vote for civil rights, were also anti-Castro.

What really caught Mackay's attention, though, was the 'bearded dark-skinned Cubans' in the 26th of July Movement standing 'shoulder to shoulder with their lighter brothers'.[52] This easy-going integration made a tremendous impression because black journalists like Mackay were aware of what white journalists usually ignored – the pervasive black and mulatto presence in Cuban life – and readily compared it with the situation at home. In this context, Fidel's stated commitment to racial democracy appeared meaningful, in contrast to the vague promises made in the US, simply because around him there were black officers and aides. The contrast was especially pointed because Batista in the past had been hailed in the US as an example of colored advancement. Thus a mixed-race dictator, who had exploited his nonwhite identity to build support among Cuba's poor, was overthrown by a white liberator who not only embraced Powell and cited the example of General Antonio Maceo, black hero of Cuba's war against Spain, but also promised 'real democracy, not the synthetic kind' and apparently practiced what he preached. Always the Cubans drove the point home, and the Yankees were more than willing to repeat it, as when the *Afro Magazine* ran a special feature on Gabino Ulacia, billed as 'Castro's Right Hand Man', who wanted to bring Arkansas' notorious Governor Orval Faubus to Havana because 'he get good example of democracy. Maybe, he stop making war on children.'[53]

Nothing highlights the gap between black and white perceptions, though, more than the issue of executions. This, after all, was what made liberals queasy, and one looks long and hard for enthusiastic endorsements of Cuba's firing squads in any white publication, even on the left. Yet the *Afro*'s featured columnist Ralph Matthews had no qualms in telling how he read 'with a great deal of relish the rather gory accounts.' This was, he said, a salutary development:

> Every white man who cuffs, beats, deprives and abuses even the lowest colored person, simply because he is white and the other colored, should have seared upon his consciousness the fact that it is possible for the tables to be turned. Castro has proved it in our time.[54]

Citing also the Russian and French revolutions as 'object lessons' that should be understood by 'every American', Matthews suggested that 'what is happening in Cuba is standard, and I believe acceptable revolutionary procedure – that is to make life as hellish to the losers as possible' (for example, the French 'have not done a real decent thing since' they sent 'heads rolling about the streets of Paris like billiard balls'). In his view, there had been two 'dismal failures' in US history: sparing the losers in our two revolutions, the Tories and the Southern Bourbons. It was the latter who were especially on his mind:

> Not one traitor was strung up and the whole nation has been made a laughing stock because the descendants of these scalawags have never laid down their arms, observed the rules of the country, admitted defeat or ceased to prosecute the rebellion at any time.
>
> What a price we have paid for this folly! A divided nation, a breeding ground for men like Faubus, Almond, Eastland and their ilk who make a shamble of constitutional law and mockery of democracy.
>
> A few good tomb stones distributed on a states rights basis would have spared us all this. ...[55]

These may appear to be exceptionally extreme statements, but they were voiced in the black equivalent of the *New York Times* – the stately mainstream – without blushing. More genteel assertions that Castro was doing what white North Americans would not were voiced throughout equally respectable publications, such as *Jet* and the *Pittsburgh Courier*, and indeed during 1960 and 1961 the *Afro-American* remained quite willing to print the highly opinionated reportage of William Worthy and Julian Mayfield, both closely associated with Fair Play for Cuba. Ralph Matthews was certainly no Communist, but his refreshingly outspoken radicalism underlines how 'left-wing' opinions were never absolutely stigmatized among African-Americans as they were in white America during the Cold War. And, as they had since the previous century, black Americans felt a strong solidarity with the colonial world, and quite easily recognized a colonial situation and the reality of national liberation. The point to be drawn from the *Afro-American*'s coverage, or from Powell's canny use of Cuba to advance his own cause, is not that African-Americans were somehow exceptional. Rather it should underline how blinkered and blocked and exceptionally illiberal were those liberals who had called for Cuban freedom but who recoiled when the Cubans started acting like a free people.

And Those Who Did Not: The Left Abstains

Any reader following this account may wonder about the absence of Cuba's seemingly natural defenders in the US, those few anti–Cold Warriors who affirmed that in some degree their government was imperialist, racist, and a major threat to the world's peace. Where was the left – or what was left of it, at least, not only in 1959 but before? To answer this question fairly, we should take into account the state of the left, its disabilities and prejudices, as well as how events seemed at the time, the 'pastness of the past'. There are a host of good reasons, ranging from the pervasive web of legal repression to plain fatigue, why abstention was the response when the Old Left faced the Cuban revolution. Still, one cannot help but feel that the Communists, post-Communists, independent socialists, anarcho-pacifists, Popular Front liberals and radical Christians who had hung on grimly from Truman through Eisenhower had lost their ability to judge events on their own terms, and were as imprisoned by Cold War verities as their archenemies. They had no way of dealing, politically or emotionally, with Fidel's sheer popularity here – like so many radicals before and since, they had internalized their own isolation. And so during 1957–58, when only diehard segregationists and McCarthyites stood up for Batista and damned Cuba's bearded rabblerousers as 'Communists', virtually all the existing radical ghettos, from Wallaceite progressives to unreconstructed Stalinists, looked upon Fidel with confusion or suspicion, if they looked at all.

If the radical press is any guide, the left often preferred to ignore Castro, even when Cuba was continually in the headlines. For a long time, the *National Guardian*, the remaining voice of the old Popular Front, saw him as just one part of the anti-Batista opposition, an 'ex-student leader' with no definite program; and its coverage of both Cuba and Castro was neither as frequent nor as sympathetic as that of the journalistic establishment.[56] From the end of 1957 through the spring of 1958, however, it became much more enthusiastic, noting a leftward turn by Castro, whom even 'conservatives in the US' had previously favored, as he dispensed with his 'retinue of politicians from Miami'. Fidel was recognized as heading the revolution, though he was still defined as a middle-class intellectual without the working-class base of the Communists in the Partido Socialista Popular (Popular Socialit Party, PSP).[57] Then, between late June 1958 and the revolutionary victory, there was not a single story on Cuba.

Similarly, the Communists' no-longer-daily *Worker* was friendly towards the 26th of July Movement in the early months of 1958, referring to the 'gallant Castro guerrillas' at one point and announcing a 'Rising Tide in Cuba', with coverage of *fidelista* activities in the US.[58] But after the failure of the general strike in April, *The Worker* tarred the 26th of July Movement as 'bungling ... terrorist, coup-ist', saying that the *New York Times* had 'exaggerated Castro's role'.[59] Then, until 1959, there was another near-silence on Cuba, perhaps an implicit backing-away as the rebellion's chances were seen to ebb.[60] The CP's lack of excitement about the Cuban revolution in its insurrectionary stage was highlighted by the other writing on Latin America that suffused its paper.

Nearly every week Jesús Colon's column profiled contemporary Communist doings from Argentina to Colombia, or offered memories of the bygone days of the Latino left in New York. The Venezuelan revolt, in which Communists played a strong public role, was heavily covered and praised, another ironic instance of how the Communists and their bitterest enemies, the anti-Communist Social Democrats, shadowed each other. Most revealingly, all through April and May 1958, Mike Gold, the *Worker*'s famous voice of proletarian sentimentalism since the 1920s, issued gushing travel pieces from a sojourn in Mexico, which he found a 'Zapata-land' redolent of 'ancient Indian sweetness'. Gold's nostalgia for the great days of Cárdenas and Mexico as the best kind of bourgeois revolution, as well as the willful illusion that 'Zapata lives on' in current Mexican politics, expresses more than any of the *Worker*'s cryptic silences why many North American Communists were ill at ease with Castro.[61] The latter, who could be cryptic himself, appeared to promise either much more or much less than the appropriate kind of bourgeois revolution for Cuba, and showed no need for a Communist Party to illuminate the path.

Yet for all their sectarian partisanship, at least *The Worker* and the *Guardian* retained enough of an internationalist commitment to cover Cuba and intermittently to recognize Castro's role. Elsewhere, at the various poles of dissent from Popular Frontist orthodoxy, the 26th of July Movement was wholly invisible. There was hardly a word on Cuba in the vibrant new pacifist monthly *Liberation* until mid 1959, remarkable given how the question of solidarity with the revolution later affected that magazine. Perhaps, like the Communists, these deeply committed 'peacemakers' were alienated by Castro's support from many gleeful Cold Warmakers here. As for the Socialist Workers Party (SWP), then the only other Marxist-Leninist group of any significance, after the failed general strike in Havana, it paused in its sporadic coverage of Trotskyism's South American progress to indict Fidel as the candidate of the US, an 'unprincipled ... opportunist', without working-class support.[62] Otherwise, the SWP had no interest in Cuba, and it took a long time for US Trotskyists to assign Fidel the honor of leading a 'permanent revolution'. *Monthly Review*, which had initiated the revival of Marxist theoretical investigation in the US and was later closely identified with Cuba, never mentioned the rebellion until after January 1959.

Most revealing of the breadth of doubt or plain ignorance was the perspective originally advanced in *The Nation*, only surviving bridge between liberalism and Popular Front leftism, in that both people close to the CP and outspoken anti-Communist liberals still wrote for it. Thanks to Carleton Beals, *The Nation* did become a major supporter of the 26th of July Movement before the victory over Batista. However, Beals himself, who personified independent radicalism regarding US overlordship of Latin America for many decades, was a primary source of the left's problem with Castro. Part One of his first big piece from Cuba on 29 June 1957 explicitly evoked his own anti-

125

Machado legacy from the thirties with the title 'The New Crime of Cuba'. But after detailing the corruption, terror and gaudy venality of Havana under Batista, he went on in Part Two in the same issue, 'Rebels Without a Cause', to indict contemporary rebel youth in terms more searing than those used by either the Marxists or the liberals, then or later. Beals described a movement of 'upper-class youths' with no ideology, 'terrorists' like the ABC under Machado with a 'fascist flavor'. These new Cuban revolutionaries were

> closer to Spanish Christian fascism than to any other body of principles ... in general, the opposition is racist, anti-American, anti-Protestant, vaguely anti-capitalist, but not heavily anti-Semitic. ... Nearly all of the Cuban students today and especially the terrorists are well to the right.[63]

For Beals, Fidel was merely one aspect of this generalized youthful nihilism. Ignoring the 26th of July Movement, he dealt with Castro solely as an individual *caudillo*, assessed as an enigma driven by a 'father-love, father-hate complex' because his father was a 'famous bandit of the Sierras'. Lacking any political program, he could be a liberator or 'more ruthless and less predictable than Batista'. The venerable journalist concluded, 'Whatever Castro is, the amorphous new generation rises behind him', in this context a rather chilling prospect.

Once Castro and his popular army rode into Havana minus any party or point-by-point program, suspicions among various parts of the left hardly abated. Perhaps reacting to the mass media's early spurt of Castrophilia, initial responses mixed a bemused enthusiasm with wariness and the same Eurocentric tendency to view Fidel as just another backward, flashy strongman as in the regular press. Instinctual categories asserted themselves. If this was a revolution, where were the true revolutionaries – where was the proletariat? In a mirror image of the journalistic establishment, which hailed Castro and certain 'moderates' around him while suspiciously assessing Raúl Castro or Che, both the *National Guardian* and *The Militant* noted Fidel's upper-class background and willingness to conciliate the US, and what the former called his 'ominous lack of program' and lack of a working-class orientation.[64] (In the latter half of 1959, however, the *Guardian* did shift gears to begin integrating the Cuban revolution into its developing appreciation for Third World particularity.

Meanwhile, the Communist Party USA instantly lined up with its Cuban confreres, and disingenuously became ardent public boosters of Castro. The writer Joe North, one-time editor of the *New Masses*, went to Havana and then rushed into print with a series of *Worker* articles that became a pamphlet, *Cuba's Revolution: I Saw the People's Victory* (and eventually a book, *Cuba: The Hope of a Hemisphere* in 1961), finally embarking on a long tour of the Party's remaining redoubts, all in the first half of 1959. But despite North's genuine sympathies, he and other CPers always emphasized the Popular Socialist Party as the backstop of the revolution – a kind of rearguard-vanguardism – and their praise of the *barbudos* was as paternalistic as others' dismissal. The CP may have moved quickly to exploit popular interest in Fidel's improbable triumph, but nothing had changed here, and US Communists continued to offer a ritualistic, self-serving brand of solidarity intended mainly to highlight the vital role played by Communists.[65]

Even this appearance of fraternity with Castro stands out by contrast with others. The Socialist Workers Party now gave its full attention – though hardly to praise. While acknowledging the people's 'Triumph in Cuba' (*The Militant*'s 12 January 1959 headline), nothing more illustrates many North American Marxists' myopia than the SWP's obdurate contempt for Castro throughout that year. Well into 1960, he remained unworthy of the Trotskyists' trust regardless of the nationalizations, denunciations of imperialism, arming of the people, distribution of land, destruction of the existing state apparatus and so on. Instead, the doctrinal monolith of Fourth Internationalism judged the Cuban revolution and found it wanting. The executions of *batistianos* were simply an attempt to 'appease' the masses and 'divert' the revolution. Fidel was 'consciously resisting the tendency to continue in a socialist direction'. If, as the year went by, it was grudgingly accepted that the 'revolution is deepening', this was threatened by its leader's 'jockeying vis-à-vis class pressures'. However much the Agrarian Reform was a blow to Wall Street, objectively it was only intended 'to promote a Cuban capitalist class'. At the end of the year, with the propaganda offensive against Cuba at fever pitch, *The Militant* straddled the fence, with headlines like 'Cuba Inches Ahead'. In January 1960 it proclaimed 'Cuba at Crossroads' in an authoritative editorial that described the revolution's greatest weakness as its 'petty-bourgeois leadership', and gave the Cubans detailed instructions on how to rectify themselves.[66]

In sum, for a year and more, admonitions of 'Hands Off Cuba!' and varying uninformed estimates of the provisional government appeared across the left's spectrum – but words alone, read only by the faithful, had no effect on the escalating tensions. As if summoned into battle once more, Carleton Beals did double or triple duty as a one-man defence committee, publishing fiery defences of Castro in *The Nation*, *Liberation* and also the voice of mainline Protestant liberalism, *Christian Century*, but his efforts could not substitute for an active campaign of solidarity. Nothing was done organizationally, no scarce political capital wasted, to combat the violent calumnies that by late 1959 made Cuba out to be a prison-island presided over by a frothing madman. Instead, the left's limited resources of people, time and money were directed towards safer issues where they could expect to find some common ground with those outside the radical ghetto, like civil rights and the new disarmament movement focused on banning the testing of nuclear weapons and opposition to mandatory civil defense exercises.

Considerations of sheer survival were presumably still foremost in the minds of those hardy leftists who had been avoiding open combat and certain defeat for a full decade of bipartisan witchhunts. To step out into the open was to invite reprisal at a time when, for instance, various Communist leaders were finishing jail terms under Smith Act convictions and the Attorney General's list of 'subversive organizations' was a real threat. Before the victory, Cuba evidently did not need the US left's solidarity. In 1959, the exceptionally high profile and stepped-up redbaiting that would have accompanied an aggressive solidarity with Castro must have seemed not merely unwise, but suicidal. Revolutionary Cuba had to fend for itself, as it had in the past, and the immediate task of supporting the revolutionary government devolved by default upon its still substantial base of Cuban-American sympathizers. Even in 1960, in a pitched battle between pro- and anti-Castro Cubans over the privilege of laying a wreath at José Martí's statue, the latter were vastly outnumbered.[67] The left made no effort to engage with these non-Communist stateside *fidelistas*, though this would not have been difficult – none of the New York–based publications carried advance notice or reports of their protests. Nor did any segment of the US left, at any point during 1959, engage in a serious examination of the revolution's political character to distinguish its radically democratic and practically socialist core, emerging as early as May 1959 in the plans for the Agrarian Reform. Instead, over a long period and with near-unanimity, the left abstained.

Why this laggardly response, when unlettered US teenagers had already perceived the Jacobin dynamic of *fidelismo*, and its less-containable aura of challenging all the modern notions of order, limits and the mundane? Many who saw the world from the perspective of the East, not the West, must have assumed that 'the friend of my enemy is likely to be my enemy too' because of the host of Cold War liberals who championed Castro as an alternative to Communism, and Fidel's continued positioning of himself as non-Communist, even anti-Communist, throughout 1959. However, this hardly explains the disinterest or antipathy of those who were no longer (or had never been) sympathetic to the Communist movement. The left's awkwardness regarding Cuba followed no clear ideological pattern because the problem of the Cuban revolution was more profound than whether or not Castro was just a hairy, sharpshooting Adlai Stevenson, as many liberals and some leftists had originally presumed. Fidel's supposed moderation, his constant evoking of a fuzzy 'Humanism' and his studied lack of specificity could not by themselves be grounds for mistrust, when so many in both the Popular Front left and the new peace movement pinned their hopes on the thoughtful but thoroughly anti-Communist liberalism of the Stevenson Democrats as the sole alternative to Republican brinksmanship. The lack of empathy for the 26th of July Movement rebels among people who defined themselves as active dissenters and were instinctively anti-imperialist reflected a cultural, discursive and stylistic disjuncture still not adequately recognized. The great fear was of action, of violence, unmediated by thought – what Marxist-Leninists call 'adventurism'.[68] Were these adolescent guerrillas seemingly so concerned with bravado and the romantic gesture really just *pistoleros* and terrorists with a left facade, a very real phenomenon in Cuba and the Caribbean since the 1930s? Revolutionaries were expected to couple a rigorous ideological self-definition with a class-based appeal and organizing methodology, as in Russia or China. But this older left model of programmatic, party-based revolution was anathema to the Cubans with their populist, youthful origins, and their frank assertion of political eclecticism. They upset the apple cart, harkening back to 1776 and 1789 more than to 1917, to Martí (or Villa) more than to Lenin, and what was worse, they hardly seemed to care, proclaiming their Humanism as something that transcended all existing ideologies and polarities. This iconoclasm endeared them to people not yet of 'the left' and indeed radicalized many, while genuinely alienating those whose lives were already defined by long-established categories of opposition.

The Cubans Go Looking

The record suggests that the 26th of July Movement and Castro personally were intensely aware of their problems in the US and tried desperately to reach North Americans long after Fidel's visit in the spring of 1959. In speeches, press conferences and interviews, he expressed his confidence that the mud would not stick, comparing his situation to the virulent attacks on Franklin Delano Roosevelt, even issuing a public appeal that Eleanor Roosevelt come to Cuba and intercede on behalf of truth and fair play. During the first 26th of July festivities, which coincided with the ousting of Manuel Urrutia, a special live television 'feed' was set up by NBC at Cuba's request, so that Castro could devote fifteen minutes from one of his marathon speeches to speak directly to the North Americans in English.[69] But minus appropriate mediation in the US, or Fidel's pressing the flesh in person, these appeals had virtually no effect. A door had closed on Cuba, in terms of a fair hearing, that would not open again until the post-Vietnam detente with the Third World in the 1970s. Still, it is remarkable how long Castro remained confident that the attacks on him were a temporary aberration. Given the intense relationships forged in later decades with a range of US journalists and others, he may never have accepted failure with the North American people, and retained more confidence in the latent possibilities here than many on the US left.

The Cubans' attempts to stimulate solidarity organizing in the US during 1959 indicate how seriously they took this task, and how uphill a task it was without a core of organizers. Soon after the victory, an 'Aid to Cuba' group was formed, involving Frances Grant of the IADF among others, but it was apparently stillborn. Then, during the summer, the new cultural attaChe at Cuba's UN Mission, Dr Berta Pla, collaborated with a group of North Americans and Cuban-Americans to form a a 'nonpolitical' group called Cuba's Friends in America, Inc. Its stated purpose was to provide material and medical aid to Cuba's children, starting with an old-clothes drive, but again no record exists of this group following one benefit dinner at the Belmont Hotel in New York on 26 July 1959.[70]

Two incidents stand out as particularly suggestive of the possibilities for solidarity that would finally germinate in 1960. The first was the spontaneous self-organization of a group of North Americans in the early spring to publish *History Will Absolve Me*, Fidel's famous defence speech from his 1953 trial that had sparked the entire 26th of July Movement. According to the pamphlet's foreword, six weeks before its publication on 23 April 1959, an unnamed 'American woman' had been given a copy of *La Historia Me Absolvera* by two young Cubans, a tourist guide and saleswoman, in a linen-and-jewelry shop. On her return to the States, it was read by dozens of her friends, each of whom asked themselves, 'Where was *I* while this was taking place?' Then, this group of anonymous middle-class New Yorkers drawn from the arts, academia and publishing – the foreword described them as 'a theatrical director, an assistant to the art editor of a medical magazine, a medical student, a song writer, a chemist, a journalist on a Spanish language newspaper, a singer, a writer for a medical magazine, an engineer, a radio script writer, a photographer, a secretary to the editor of an international magazine, a publicity representative for a publishing house, a ballet dancer, a professor of literature, a poet's wife, a secretary for an insurance company, an actor' – worked feverishly to translate it and present to their fellow citizens for the first time while Castro was himself in New York. Perhaps most significantly, though, internal evidence indicates that the actual translator was Robert Taber, who a year later would found the Fair Play for Cuba Committee.[71] One can only speculate why Fair Play, or something like it, was not founded much earlier, if there were already North Americans who were enthusiastic about the Cuban revolution and willing to act. Perhaps it was people like Taber who were most surprised by the rapid shift in the US towards hostility and support for counter-revolution.

The Cubans clearly cooperated with and supported this one-time publishing effort, as they had helped to organize the various unsuccessful humanitarian aid committees. The foreword to this 1959 edition of *History Will Absolve Me* thanks

Ambassador Carlos Lechuga, Cuba's Alternate Delegate to the United Nations; Luis Baralt, Cuban Consul General in New York, and Armando Bascal, head of the Cuban Tourist Commission in New York City, for encouragement in this very pleasant task.[72]

But their major effort went in a different and more practical direction. Noting potential allies and a possible tourist market of vast dimensions, the Cuban government made a direct appeal to the black community; not to its radical currents, but to its all-American mainstream – and who was more mainstream than the Brown Bomber, Joe Louis?[73]

As they later explained at a hearing of the Senate Internal Security Subcommittee, in December 1959 William Rowe, a former New York deputy police commissioner and one of Louis's 'partners' in a public relations firm, had been doing PR for the fiftieth anniversary celebration of New York's black weekly newspaper, the *Amsterdam News*. Al Lockhart, advertising director of the paper, approached Rowe, suggesting that he might join the firm and bring with him a 'big account'. He had just received a cablegram from the Cuban Tourist Commission, inviting him to come down and discuss a business proposition. Rowe, Lockhart and another member of the firm flew to Havana, where they were asked to invite thirty Americans to attend the victory celebration on New Year's Eve, all expenses paid. The Cubans had a very specific sort of Americans in mind: 'He asked if we could bring Roy Campanella, Jackie Robinson, Willie Mays and Joe Louis.'[74] All of the above were contacted, and for various reasons, most refused (Mays begging off at the last minute). But Louis and seventy-one others, including the publishers of various black papers like the *Chicago Defender*, the *Philadelphia Tribune* and the *Ohio Sentinel*, did go to Cuba in an interracial group, and were photographed and shown on US television enjoying a lavish New Year's with Fidel at the Havana Hilton.[75]

As the Subcommittee's counsel noted later, almost admiringly, 'It was an outstanding public relations stroke.' Rowe agreed, ruefully, 'Well, I would say so. As a public relations man, I thought it was a great job. I was only sorry I hadn't thought it up.' The Cubans' desire for 'good-neighborliness' without an explicitly radical content went beyond wining-and-dining. Apparently, their experiences since 1957 had convinced them that face-to-face dialogue would prove effective regardless of the background of the North Americans. The day after the big party Fidel himself showed up unannounced and talked with the North Americans in their bathing suits for hours, answering questions and urging them to stay longer and see more of Cuba, even chartering a special plane for those who would miss their flights: 'He discussed the relationship between America and Cuba and he gave us the impression that he was very sorry about this relationship and that things will be better', Rowe remembered.[76] Indeed, well into 1960 the Cubans continued to make massive efforts to attract US tourists.

There is a fitting image capturing this final attempt by the Cubans to make the touristic stimulate the political. Their hope had been that geographical contiguity plus good times might suffice to build friendship, but increasingly the future of solidarity with Cuba was an explicitly oppositional, intellectual and cosmopolitan engagement, attended by a certain chicness. The *New York*

Times noted that Mr and Mrs Joe Louis sat at the head table that New Year's Eve with Fidel Castro, and with them were Jean-Paul Sartre and Simone de Beauvoir. One imagines Fidel making the introductions, but after that the imagination balks. Did they dance? Discuss boxing? Somewhere in this unlikely encounter is the essence of that unpredictability or stylishness that made revolutionary Cuba so attractive to young people and the young at heart, even as the ground was laid for invasion during 1960, and the question became not 'what to do with Castro', but how best to get rid of him.

Notes

1. Thomas, *Cuba: The Pursuit of Freedom,* p. 1208; Williams, *The United States, Cuba and Castro,* New York: Monthly Review Press, 1962, p. 82. Williams's point was that 'passive behavior is often as damaging as overt action'.

2. Benjamin, *The United States and the Origins of the Cuban Revolution,* p. 185.

3. What the US did or did not do during 1959 is a perennial subject of debate among policymakers-in-hindsight and diplomatic historians. I do not pretend to resolve the question here. Morris Morley and Jules Benjamin concur that until the Agrarian Reform was promulgated on 3 June 1959, US hostility towards Castro had not solidified, though their emphases are somewhat at odds. Morley sees the initial US response as 'very, very wary', with 'a fair amount of panic' over Cuban instability under Castro (*Imperial State and Revolution,* p. 73). He notes that while the US orchestrated multilateral economic pressure to rein in the new government, until June some agencies and international banks still favored the carrot of aid so as to achieve leverage over an incipient nationalist regime. Benjamin goes into Washington's response in greater depth, pointing out that while the US was greatly concerned with the 'chaotic' and 'inexperienced' character of the provisional government, 'the first few months of the post-Batista era produced much frustration ... but no serious conflicts' and even 'moderate optimism in Washington.' The continued prominence of figures like Treasury Minister Rufo Lopez-Fresquet, who led a delegation to investigate Puerto Rico's Operation Bootstrap, 'was heartening to liberals in the State Department who were already looking for a "good" revolution in Latin America, one that with U.S. assistance might become a model of anti-communist, progressive capitalist development' (*The United States and the Origins of the Cuban Revolution,* pp. 167–70). Supporting the latter point of view is former cabinet minister Javier Pazo's recollection in 1963 that as late as May 1959 Castro had reasonable hopes of being Latin America's Nasser, someone with whom the US would deal, however grudgingly (cited in Zeitlin and Scheer, *Cuba: Tragedy in Our Hemisphere,* p. 63).

4. An envelope with this stamp can be found in the Herbert Matthews Papers.

5. *Life,* 16 November 1959.

6. Jules Benjamin underlines that the reason the Eisenhower administration decided Fidel must go, and began covert manipulations within Cuba and recruitment of exiles outside, had little directly to do with the Soviet threat, and everything to do with the US political-economic relationship to Latin America. An aggressively nationalist Cuba, seizing property and declaring its neutralism, was rightly judged to be a highly dangerous example for the hemisphere (see *The United States and the Origins of the Cuban Revolution,* p. 186; also Morley, *Imperial State and Revolution,* pp. 113–14).

7. Dwight Eisenhower, *Waging Peace, 1956–1961,* New York: Doubleday, 1965, p. 524n. It should be noted that Ike apparently never felt the slightest personal sympathy towards Castro; until the very end of 1958, he and Secretary of State Dulles had been too busy with larger matters to pay much attention.

8. *Life,* 12 and 19 January 1959.

9. Casuso, *Cuba and Castro,* p. 155; Dubois, *Fidel Castro,* p. 359. The 'Face the Nation' broadcast of 11 January is at the Museum of Radio and Television in New York (as are all the other television programs described here, from Taber's in 1957 to William Worthy's in 1960). It was

moderated by Stuart Novins, and the panelists were Jay Mallin of *Time*, Richard Bate of CBS, and William Ryan of the AP. Their questions were probing but friendly, focused on immediate issues like Castro's attitude to the Directorio Revolucionário, a rival rebel group that briefly sought a coalition, or towards Trujillo. Pressed on why there would be an eighteen-month wait for elections, Castro assured his listeners of pluralism: 'Of course! If we don't give freedom to all the political parties to organize, we are not a democratic country.'

10. Matthews, *The Cuban Story*, p. 89.

11. *New York Times*, 16 January 1959. Maurice Zeitlin and Robert Scheer pointed out a few years later that Castro's genius for making news worked against him here, as the spontaneous, dramatic quality of Cuban events was exploited as 'news', and spurred a chain reaction: CBS televised an actual execution in early January, and many were the photos of firing squads and 'mass graves' in US newspapers (*Cuba: Tragedy in Our Hemisphere*, pp. 79–80).

12. Landau, interview, 31 May 1989.

13. Editorial cartoons reprinted in *New York Times*, 18 January 1959.

14. Matthews, *The Cuban Story*, pp. 135–6.

15. *New York Times*, 23 February 1959: 1,500 Cubans greeted Cienfuegos's party; he attempted to lead them on a march from Idlewild Airport to Manhattan but was stopped by police.

16. See the *New York Times*, 24 February 1959, on the 'dismal, frustrating day' the nine rebels had in New York, dazed by the snow and eating Yankee food. On the 25th, Cienfuegos met with Mayor Robert Wagner and gave a speech at PS 20 in Flushing, the school attended by Fidelito Castro before the triumph.

17. Casuso, *Cuba and Castro*, p. 207; for a somewhat different account, see Peter Wyden, *Bay of Pigs: The Untold Story*, New York: Simon & Schuster, 1979, p. 26, on how this famous event originated in lunchtime brainstorming by various editors in early January, with Dubois as only an intermediary.

18. *New York Times*, 4 March 1959.

19. *New York Times*, 16 April 1959. This was the language Castro used to reporters before he boarded the plane in Havana. On landing at National Airport, he said he came 'to speak to the people of the United States'. A survey of his speeches to the Cuban people during that year indicates how the bad faith of the North American media was an ever more bitter theme.

20. Williams, *The United States, Cuba and Castro*, p. 100.

21. *New York Times*, 17, 18, 19 and 20 April 1959.

22. *New York Times*, 22, 23, 24, 25 and 26 April 1959.

23. *Daily Princetonian*, 17 April 1959. Ely would go on to a career as a scholar writing on the Cuban colonial economy (see his two articles in Robert Freeman Smith, ed., *Background to Revolution: The Development of Modern Cuba*, New York: Knopf, 1966.

24. *Daily Princetonian*, 21 and 23 April 1959 (the latter quoting the *Newark Evening News* on the number of students).

25. *Daily Princetonian*, 22 April 1959.

26. Ibid.

27. *Boston Globe*, 26 April 1959.

28. Novins quoted in Matthews, *The Cuban Story*, p. 119; *New York Times*, 18 May 1959.

29. *New York Times*, 1 and 8 November 1959.

30. Reprinted in *New York Times*, 24 May and 8 November 1959.

31. *New York Times*, 18 May 1959.

32. George H. Gallup, *The Gallup Poll: Public Opinion, 1935–1971*, vol. 3, *1959–1971*, New York: Random House, 1972, p. 1624.

33. Discussed in Matthews, *The Cuban Story*, pp. 296–7.

34. *New York Times*, 31 July 1959. In his role as the honest if cantankerous senior statesman, Truman could be outspoken like few others. The kindly words for Fidel were part of a longer syndicated article on how to better oppose the international Communist menace.

35. *New York Times*, 12 August and 30 October 1959; Douglas quoted in Welch, *Response to Revolution*, p. 113. Senator Wayne Morse, the most powerful friend of the insurgency before 1959, had wasted no time in denouncing the 'bloodbath' of the 26th of July Movement's firing squads in January, prompting an immediate response from Fidel, and thereafter was widely seen as one of those who felt Castro had betrayed the US trust (this long-distance confrontation and what it signaled is highlighted in Williams, *The United States, Cuba and Castro*, p. 31).

36. Letter, Acheson to Matthews, 19 March 1959, in HLMP.

37. *Hemispherica*, February and September 1959. In between, the tumult in Cuba versus smooth progress in Venezuela under Rómulo Betancourt was explained in terms of Cuba's lack of a political culture (March/April 1959). Setbacks for Communists and Antonio Varona's call for early elections were also positively noted (July/August 1959).

38. *Dissent*, Spring 1959.

39. *The New Leader*, 23 November 1959.

40. Carlos Franqui, *Family Portrait with Fidel: A Memoir*, New York: Random House, 1964, p. 11; Jules Dubois, *Operation America: The Communist Conspiracy in Latin America*, New York: Walker, 1963, p. xv.

41. *Boston Globe*, 27 April 1959.

42. *New York Times*, 28 July 1959.

43. *New York Times*, 18 December 1959; see also *Fair Play*, 3 June 1960, citing an article in a church magazine on a 30-member Presbyterian delegation's favorable view of the revolution. The Cubans were aware of this opening, as the next prominent revolutionaries to visit New York after Castro both came with religious connections: the Reverend Carlos Herrera, a Baptist seminary student and the 26th of July Movement's Protestant chaplain, interviewed by the *Times* at the American Baptists' headquarters in uniform (*Times*, 13 June 1959); Antonio Nuñez Jiménez, who addressed the 200 delegates of the World Harvest Evangelistic Association and the American Evangelical Association in New York (*Times*, 18 July 1959).

44. *America*, 14 February and 2 May 1959, the latter commenting on Castro's 'Meet the Press' interview of 19 April.

45. Ibid., 22 August 1959. Fair Play founder Alan Sagner was strongly influenced by these articles.

46. *New York Times*, 5 January 1959; Adam Clayton Powell, Jr, *Adam by Adam: The Autobiography of Adam Clayton Powell, Jr*, New York: Dial Press, 1971, p. 189.

47. *New York Times*, 25 and 28 January 1959; Powell, *Adam by Adam*, pp. 190–91, 193–4.

48. *New York Times*, 4 March 1959; Powell, *Adam by Adam*, p. 196, where these efforts are described as attempts to save Fidel from the Communists who are 'capturing' him with the goading of an unfair and hostile US press.

49. An angry comment by Herbert L. Matthews in a letter immediately after Powell's public break with Castro suggests a more complicated scenario: 'Powell muscled into the picture very ostentatiously at the beginning and more or less tried to take over the 26th of July Movement. In the early days they were all so ignorant and naive as to think that Powell really represented something important and idealistic. They have learned differently since. ...' (Matthews to W. P. Gray, *Life* International Editions, 23 March 1959, in HLMP).

50. Rep. Charles Porter, a much less influential figure, did go to Cuba that February and discuss development aid with leaders in Oriente (see *New York Times*, 24 February 1959). He continued to argue against the prevailing tide longer than anyone else in Congress, but with little effect.

51. *Afro-American*, 31 January 1959.

52. Ibid.

53. *Afro Magazine Section*, 7 February 1959.

54. *Afro-American*, 7 February 1959.

55. Ibid.

56. See *National Guardian*, 24 December 1956; also 18 February and 10 July 1957 for similar statements.

57. *National Guardian*, 2 December 1957, and 7, 14 and 21 April 1958 (all written by Elmer Bendiner).

58. *The Worker*, 18 January and 2 and 30 March (an article by Juan Marinello, head of the PSP, indicating the continuing close ties between the two parties), 13 and 20 April 1958.

59. *The Worker*, 4 May 1958.

60. Presumably the vagaries of *The Worker*'s coverage reflected the up-and-down relationship between the PSP and the 26th of July Movement in Cuba. For a detailed accounting, see Thomas, *Cuba: The Pursuit of Freedom*, pp. 943–4, 980–81, 1002, 1079, including the fact that even in November 1958, the PSP did not envision Batista's military collapse, instead hoping for a 'democratic coalition government'.

61. *The Worker,* 6, 13, 20, and 27 April, and 4 and 11 May 1958. This feeling for the Mexican revolution was quite sincere and it was evidently painful to see it domesticated for North Americans. Thus Gold attacked Brando's portrayal of Zapata, underlining how history rendered anachronistic the memories of an entire generation.

62. *The Militant,* 21 April 1958, though the same writer, Lillian Kiesel, had in the 24 February 1958 issue obliquely referred to the 26th of July Movement as 'liberation forces'.

63. Carleton Beals, 'Rebels Without a Cause', *Nation,* 29 June 1957.

64. See *National Guardian,* 19 January 1959, also the 12 January 1959 issue, which is positive about 'Fidel's Long March', but contrasts Castro, the 'son of a planter' with the working-class PSP, noting that 'US investors [are] unworried'. Lillian Kiesel's articles in *The Militant* were more frankly hostile to Castro: he was a middle-class, pro-US plantation owner, and the best that could be said was that 'people have a chance to choose now' (*Militant,* 12 January 1959). In the first month, while revolutionary groups under different commands competed for turf in Havana, the SWP supported the student-based Directorio Revolucionário (*Militant,* 19 January 1959).

65. Explaining why 'the Cuban Revolution was the farthest thing from their minds, probably', a student activist of that time from a CP-family background suggests that the guiding assumption among Party leaders was that socialism would come to Latin America *only* via the United States, a perspective he ascribed to 'big nation chauvinism' (Michael Myerson, interview, 16 May 1992).

66. *The Militant,* 26 January, 2 and 16 February; 30 March, 22 June, and 16 November 1959; and 18 January 1960. At best, Cuba was akin to the 'national independence revolution' led by Iraq's Ba'ath Socialist Party (30 March 1959). Peter Camejo, then a leader of the SWP's Young Socialist Alliance (YSA), reports that during 1959 one member of his party's leadership, Joseph Hansen (a former secretary to Leon Trotsky), held a minority pro-Castro position, which appealed to many in the newly formed YSA (interview, 17 February 1993).

67. *New York Times,* 29 January 1960, also 23 and 28 February, on hundreds of Cubans at the UN and the White House protesting US actions.

68. No one I have interviewed has very clear memories of the 1957–58 period, though many had read Herbert L. Matthews and shared the majority's vaguely pro-Fidel sentiments. This lack of memory is perhaps the best indicator of the left's distance from Cuba. One individual close to the CPUSA, while approving Fidel personally, remembers vigorous arguments during which people familiar with Cuba denounced him as an 'adventurer'.

69. *New York Times,* 27 and 28 July 1959; see also a 20 October story on Castro reassuring 2,000 delegates at the Havana convention of the American Society of Travel Agents and a 27 October story on his speech at a mass rally, following the bombing of Havana by a light plane flown from Florida, where he again appealed to the people of the US, comparing the incident to Pearl Harbor.

70. *New York Times,* 27 July 1959; letter, June Cobb to Frances Grant, 20 July 1959 and response, 21 July 1959, in FGP.

71. The 1959 edition (copy in author's possession) is physically identical to the later versions published by Lyle Stuart and containing Taber's introduction. Thomas also reports that Taber first translated *History Will Absolve Me* (*Cuba: The Pursuit of Freedom,* p. 848).

72. Fidel Castro, *History Will Absolve Me,* New York: Liberal Press, 1959, p. 8.

73. The Cubans had initiated a crash program in September 1959 to recoup the fall-off in tourism since the revolutionary victory. By the end of the year, however, total visitors were only one-fifth of 1958's total (Thomas, *Cuba: The Pursuit of Freedom,* pp. 1240, 1256).

74. U.S. Congress, Senate, Committee on the Judiciary, *Communist Threat to the United States Through the Caribbean, Hearing Before the Subcommittee to Investigate the Administration of the Internal Security Act and Other Internal Security Laws of the Committee on Judiciary of the United States Senate,* 87th Congress, First Session (Washington, D.C.: U.S. Government Printing Office, 1961), 5 June 1961, p. 772 (hereafter *Communist Threat, SISC*).

75. See *Chicago Defender,* 16 January 1960, for a photo spread on this junket, including 'Miss Amsterdam News' riding a tractor.

76. *Communist Threat, SISC,* p. 776.

5

Fair Play!

Four major episodes marked the history of the Fair Play for Cuba Committee (FPCC) following its initial organization in the spring of 1960: Fidel Castro's flamboyant pilgrimage to Harlem during his United Nations visit in September of that year; the publication of C. Wright Mills's *Listen, Yankee* later that fall and its runaway success; the huge FPCC Christmas Tour of North Americans, which resulted in the January 1961 ban on travel to Cuba; and nationwide protests when a long-rumored invasion came ashore at the Bay of Pigs on 17 April 1961. This sequence of events adequately describes the short-lived rise of a movement in defence of the Cuban revolution, before its precipitous decline due to the embargo on most contacts with the island, governmental assault at President Kennedy's personal direction, and internal feuding. Since the existence of a current of international solidarity at the dawn of the sixties is the most pivotal development here, however, this chapter focuses on how the 'fair play movement' actually formed during 1960, explaining who was involved and why.

The best gauge of Cuba's significance for the making of a New Left in the US is its effect on specific constituencies who formerly either resisted politicization, or pursued their objectives isolated from others. Across an exceptionally wide range of stances, Cuba served as a political touchstone – or as a *tabula rasa;* in all cases it was a springboard. The defence of the revolution's right to a fair hearing became a catalyst to action and part of a pragmatic ideological awareness rooted not in Talmudic disputation about the past, but in human connection with the onrushing tide of a revolution in motion. Like the mass sit-in movement of southern African-American students that broke out in these same months, Cuba provided both a vision of praxis and an unambiguous call to solidarity.

In January 1960, hardly anyone could have predicted the sudden emergence of a movement that by the end of the year was a focus of national attention. As relations went from bad to worse between Cuba and the US that winter, with the recall 'for consultations' of Ambassador Philip Bonsal, the still-myste-rious blowing up of the munitions-laden French ship *La Coubre* in Havana harbor and continuous sabotage by light planes flying from Florida, the same inaction persisted on the organized left as in 1959, punctuated only by a few outraged pleas for action by those with a personal affiliation to Cuba. One-time friends distanced themselves as sharply as possible, with Rep. Charles Porter denouncing Castro's charges of US involvement in the *La Coubre* inci-dent as 'ridiculous and hysterical' (the State Department officially refused to take offence because of what it delicately referred to as the 'emotional strain' burdening the Cuban leader).[1] Yet, unseen and unimagined, the previous three years of reportage, rumor and real-life drama had stimulated a hardly articu-lated sympathy for the new Cuba that, like the proverbial tinder, needed only the right spark. Just as the guerrilla struggle commenced with only the twelve ragged survivors of the *Granma* straggling into the hills, so a single *foco* of sufficient daring would substitute for organized structures, well-laid plans and the prior accumulation of forces.

Creating Fair Play: 'A Responsible Newspaperman and a Political Naif'

The founding of Fair Play for Cuba has the appearance of extreme contin-gency – the fortuitous event that brings two or three people together at the right time rather than any iron law of historical development.[2] Initially, it was only a tiny group tangentially connected through that threadbare champion of anti-imperialist liberal politics, *The Nation:* to the extent that Fair Play had ideological and political origins, they lay in neither the Old nor New Lefts, but in the Old Liberalism.[3] These founders were motivated not by radical inten-tions, but by a deep-seated if naive outrage that the achievements of people they admired could be willfully distorted, and in reaction they sought to tell truth in the face of power like so many ad hoc assemblages ever since. Spon-taneously, with little thought of the potential consequences and a greater faith in American common sense than must have seemed merited by the previous decade, they set themselves to tell the truth about the Cuban revolution, as if that alone would spark a renewed good-neighborliness in US foreign policy.

Properly speaking, FPCC had two primary founders. The first and best known was Robert Taber, the CBS reporter who made the primetime docu-mentary 'Rebels of the Sierra Maestra' back in 1957 and who in the interven-ing years had become increasingly close to the 26th of July Movement. In one sense, Taber was the central player in Fair Play's history, its preeminent leader and shaper. Yet in other ways he remains an enigmatic figure, an impression reinforced by his refusal in later life to discuss this history.[4] According to many who knew him, he was in no typical sense a political activist, or even someone with any defined ideological views on subjects other than the Cuban revolution, though an earlier stint covering the Guatemalan coup in 1954 and the Algerian insurgency apparently made a strong impression.[5] Taber's solidarity was a function of face-to-face knowledge of the 26th of July Movement and its chief, a loyalty that grew directly from his professional commitment as a journalist to the facts of those events that he observed first-hand. Much as orthodox Marxists once dismissed Fidel's own individualistic 'adventurism', one veteran New York leftist who worked with Taber remembered him as simply

> a good newspaperman. He was very excited about the Revolution. He had no deep political convictions of any sort. He was inclined to be romantic about the Revolution, rather than political. ... In my contact with him, it was just a one-issue position. He was very strong on Cuba, and very strong on Castro. Castro was his hero, not the Revolution, if you can make that distinction.[6]

Another partisan of the Old Left, a member of the Socialist Workers Party and one of Taber's closest collaborators in FPCC, used strikingly similar language: 'Taber was basically a nonpolitical person, a romantic with no ties to any group.'[7] But Fair Play's key student leader, Saul Landau, was most acute in suggesting that, given 'the extreme voluntarism of the Cuban Revolution', it was natural that Taber would see himself as 'Fidel's *comandante* in New York'.[8] As such, it is apparent that he got the job done, and for the Cubans at least, that was the sole qualification.

In various respects, then, Robert Taber resembles Herbert L. Matthews, with the crucial difference that the former's comparative youth and lack of political definition allowed him to act in ways that Matthews, however enduring his sympathy, would never have considered. Taber had already helped organize the first US publication of *History Will Absolve Me* in 1959, and in January 1960, goaded by what Castro called the 'calumnious campaign of the US press', he wrote a major defence of the revolution for *The Nation*, describing what was really happening in Cuba, as he saw it.[9]

It took someone else's initiative, however, to turn Taber's journalistic expertise and connections with the Cubans into a more practical project. The immediate catalyst for Fair Play was provided by Alan Sagner, a wealthy New Jersey contractor and reform Democratic leader active in the Rotary Club and the Jewish community, who 'more than any other person can be said to be the founder of the Fair Play for Cuba Committee', as Taber's coworker Richard Gibson told the FPCC national conference in July 1961.[10] Sagner took his liberalism far more seriously than most, and had long been a devotee of *I.F. Stone's Weekly* and *The Nation*. As long as Batista was in power, he refused to join his friends and relatives for the good times in Havana. 'It's where you went for gambling, drinking, drugs', he later remembered with a mixture of contempt and pride, 'I wouldn't go to Spain either.' In late 1959, he visited the new Cuba and was deeply impressed by the egalitarian idealism affecting even upper-class Cubans.[11] Inspired by Taber's piece in *The Nation*, Sagner called the magazine, got Taber's telephone number, and called to suggest that something ought to be done. The two then met in a Cuban restaurant in Manhattan in early February, along with Charles Santos-Buch, a Columbia University medical student from a family of prominent bourgeois *fidelistas*. In short order, they pulled in the two most venerable, certifiably non-Communist, liberal-left experts on Latin America: Waldo Frank, the avant-garde litterateur of the teens and later champion of Latin American culture in the US, who joined in the planning at a subsequent meeting at Taber's apartment; and Carleton Beals, solicited by Taber in a 9 February 1960 letter that gives a sense of the entire impromptu effort:

> A committee is being formed here in the city, for the express purpose of combatting some of the anti-Cuban (counterrevolutionary is perhaps the more accurate expression) propaganda with which we are being deluged. The prime mover is a man of whom I know literally nothing, a chap named Alan Sagner who is, I understand, a builder in the Livingston, N.J., area. He contacted me after reading my recent article in the *Nation*, and said he wanted to bring along Reverend Reed, executive secretary of council of churches in Long Branch, N.J., and could enlist some other people. His idea: to form a Fair Play for Cuba Committee, or some such name, to seek some prominent names in the country at large, and to launch a sort of counterpropaganda campaign, perhaps even send a fact-finding committee to Cuba, with adequate attendant fanfare, via ads in the *Times* and whatever other means might recommend themselves.[12]

For all intents and purposes, this little group, along with Richard Gibson and Ed Haddad, two of Taber's colleagues 'on the late-night shift in the newsroom of CBS Radio News', was the organizing committee for Fair Play for Cuba.[13] They quickly focused on placing a large advertisement in the *New York Times*, explaining the 'truth' about Cuba over the names of as many prominent intellectuals as could be enlisted. After a considerable effort to find sponsors willing to associate themselves with such a controversial project, and to raise the necessary money (which soon proved a sore subject), the advertisement appeared on 6 April 1960.

There are two striking things about this first appearance of the Fair Play for Cuba Committee. First, its tone, so different from the caution of both the ghettoized left and conventional liberalism: rather than the former's guarded vagueness – the language of those trying to come in from the cold – or the latter's genuflection to Cold War requirements, Fair Play's originators were forthright, angry and ringingly sincere. Over a headline, 'WHAT IS HAPPENING IN CUBA?', with the word 'REALLY' cheekily inserted, they arraigned the 'great news agencies and a powerful section of the U.S. press'. Three recent claims from authoritative sources were presented:

COMMUNISM: 'A pro-communist state has been established in Cuba with the clear objective of bargaining with Soviet Russia for the munitions of war...' [the *New York Journal-American*]
CONFISCATION: 'In Cuba, Castro is stealing American property with impunity.' [*U.S. News & World Report*]
CHAOS: 'All that now remains is for Castro to give the word, and the Terror, the ruthless hunting down and shooting of Fidel's opponents, will begin.' [*Newsweek*]

Each was refuted in turn with a blizzard of facts and no apologies, and then the revolutionaries' side of things was sardonically interpreted for a North American audience:

It is true that the young leaders of the Cuban Revolution have little patience with considerations of profit and loss, in the face of poverty and human need. Nor have they any saving experience with the amenities of public relations, or the intrigues of dollar diplomacy, or the sophistry of journalistic 'facts' which distort truth. But if so, they are in the American tradition. Certainly they deserve a hearing. This much the American tradition owes them. This much we, as Americans, owe them.

Equally interesting to most readers must have been FPCC's thirty original sponsors. Some were obscure: Sagner's physicist brother-in-law, who long after had great trouble getting a security clearance; a manufacturer he knew; and others who remain unknown to this day. But by far the largest identifiable group were prominent intellectuals: the novelists Norman Mailer, James Baldwin, Truman Capote and Dan Wakefield, the theater critic Kenneth Tynan, and looming above the rest, Jean-Paul Sartre and Simone de Beauvoir, all complemented by Frank as chairman and Beals as co-chairman. Only a few overtly political types were listed, such as Sidney Lens, an editor of *Liberation,* and the Reverend Donald Harrington, a bastion of New York's Liberal Party, SANE, and chairman of the prestigious American Committee on Africa. Certainly, these names were the names that *Times* readers might have recognized, but there were less obvious hints as to Fair Play's future orientation. African-Americans might have noticed that eight of the thirty were black, including not only Baldwin and Richard Gibson, but the novelists Julian Mayfield and John O. Killens, the historian John Henrik Clarke (who would later help edit the journal *Freedomways*), and the very controversial Southern activist Robert F. Williams, about whom more later.

What stands out in retrospect is the 'outsider' quality of this assemblage in all respects. Besides the lack of ties to established labor, political or civil rights institutions, there was hardly a fellow-traveller of the Old Left among them (at least among the Yanks; Sartre and de Beauvoir had a long, complex relationship with the French Communist Party, but their status in the US was as bohemian 'intellectuals' first of all). Indeed, this grouping had no discernible political orientation. Its self-description seems not disingenuous therefore, as is usual, but apt: 'a group of thinking individuals, holding a variety of political persuasions, representing no one but themselves, linked here by a single common concern – for the overriding principle of justice which is always at issue, wherever partisan interest clashes with simple truth.'

To everyone's surprise, coming out of nowhere in terms of any organized political constituency and appealing to no one in particular other than 'Americans', Taber's and Sagner's gambit was enormously successful in evoking a spontaneous grassroots response: 1,500 people wrote in, asking for information or to join the 'committee', which as yet was nothing more than a short list of names (many had not even seen the *Times* ad, but instead a 6 April UPI story reporting on its appearance that gave FPCC's address).[14] Little had been planned beyond a one-time appeal to reason, but spurred by this response, Taber and the others haltingly set about creating an organization, feeling their way like the amateurs they were. By the end of the month they had begun issuing a professional-looking weekly newsletter called *Fair Play*, but beyond these initial steps, there were few plans. An initial public meeting with Waldo Frank as speaker was held at Reverend Harrington's Community Church in Manhattan on 24 April, but the idea of creating a national organization of local chapters had not yet germinated. The first issue of *Fair Play* stressed that the founding members 'weren't much interested in being a committee', and defined FPCC's mission specifically as a counterweight to the established press:

> Our basic appeal was to the spirit of fair mindedness on which most Americans pride themselves. The spirit did not appear to be noticeably operative with regard to the Cuban Revolution. Had it been observed in the editorial columns of the newspapers and the reporting of the great wire services which wet nurse the newspapers and the radio and television newsrooms there would obviously have been no need for such a public appeal.[15]

While there was a very positive public response, there was an equally clear negative reaction. The Senate Internal Security Subcommittee chaired by Senator James Eastland (known as the Eastland Committee) subpoenaed Beals to testify on 29 April and Taber on 5 May, dragging up the former's associations with 'known Communists' during the 1930s and focusing on the funding for the *Times* ad with the latter. As early as 7 April UPI was reporting the charge by 'diplomatic sources' that FPCC had been set up by the Cuban consulate in New York, while the McCarthyite George Sokolsky immediately went to work in his *Journal-American* daily column.[16]

The alacrity of the right wing's riposte to Fair Play's very existence indicates the overriding problem for Taber and his colleagues, non- or anti-Communists all, as they attempted to negotiate the shoals of received opinion about the Cuban revolution. No matter what, they needed to avoid the issue of Communism and Communists: like SANE, the Fair Play for Cuba Committee was legally created as a closed corporation under the direct control of Taber and a few others so as to make it impervious to infiltration and take-over bids by outside forces. It had been a basic condition of Beals's support, as he made clear to his Senate interrogators, that there not be the slightest 'pink' taint. Nor was this a purely abstract question. Fair Play's early organizers were extremely wary of domination by the organized left, especially its Communist or post-Communist sectors, a wariness that the evidence suggests was prompted by the 26th of July Movement's long, uneasy relationship with the Cuban Communists and the lack of support by North American radicals since 1957. Castro, almost certainly in close contact with Taber, had some sense of US political geography from his various trips to the States, voracious reading and the reports of his farflung exile network. He apparently calculated that the isolated US left, with its demonstrated lack of interest and its condescension towards Latin America, would be more of an albatross than a source of strength, and counseled Taber to seek instead the favor of the liberal intelligentsia, who throughout the world had responded so favorably to Cuban style.

Yet who could Taber call upon, if FPCC was to be more than a nucleus of writers concentrated in Manhattan, given that liberal and bohemian intellectuals of the nonofficial variety were much less of a social force in the US than elsewhere? The original Fair Players found themselves in a quandary caused by their own success and its limits. Minus more coordinated efforts of people beyond the pale and in the hinterlands, leftist and otherwise, they had nowhere to turn, since the hoped-for support of institutional liberalism did not materialize, and the existing group of Yankee *fidelistas* was locked out of the power elite. Alan Sagner still recalls his own shock on arriving in Los Angeles for the Democratic Party's convention that July as head of New Jerseyans for Stevenson, only to find that the local newspapers would not accept a Fair Play advertisement appealing to the Democratic delegates with the headline 'Don't Let Cuba Become a Western Hungary'.[17] Yet the organized left apparently offered nothing but pitfalls. Out of these multiplying concerns and entanglements, with Taber holding onto Fidel's direct franchise to reach North American opinion by any means necessary, Fair Play came together rather slowly over several months – one indication being that its next *New York Times* ad during July was merely a reprint without comment of a *Nation* editorial, 'Go Slow, Goliath', a rather inadequate grasp at legitimacy.[18]

Quite suddenly, however, Fair Play picked up steam, spurred by a combination of the increasing showdown in US–Cuban relations and the entry of new forces. June 1960 was when the Eisenhower administration shifted decisively to open hostility.[19] When US-owned refineries in Cuba, acting at the State Department's direction, refused to process Soviet oil, with the expectation that this would bring Castro to heel, they were promptly nationalized – an unforgivable step. In response, the administration pressured Congress to cut off

Cuba's guaranteed quota of US sugar sales, the chief market for the island's one-crop economy for decades.[20] By this time, any remaining ambiguity in US public opinion was long gone. A book like Nathaniel Weyl's *Red Star over Cuba*, with its charges that Fidel had been a Soviet agent since 1948, and even worse, the oderiferous leader of a 'Cult of Uncleanliness' received respectful reviews in the press (Weyl claimed that Fidel's nickname at college was *bola de churre* or 'greaseball', due to revolting grossness, while Raúl Castro was arraigned as a mincing, effeminate devil).[21] In a July poll, Gallup found 81 percent of North Americans hostile to Castro, and only 1 in 50 admitting to positive feelings (another 17 percent were recorded as 'neutral' or holding no opinion).[22]

Such a drastic worsening of relations acted as a considerable spur to FPCC. On 8 July, a 'Letter from the Editor' announced that *Fair Play*'s publication would become less frequent, as Taber and his colleagues were 'turning our attention to other urgent matters. Among these is the organization of Fair Play local chapters', in addition to those already existing in Tampa, Chicago and New York. From then on, through the late summer of 1960 and into early 1961, FPCC evolved at a dizzying pace, with dozens of chapters formed in major cities and smaller college towns along the coasts and across the Midwest. In the latter case, for example, not only did local Fair Play committees draw upon the Old Left's remaining industrial sanctuaries in Chicago, Detroit and Cleveland, but students and political novices at schools like Antioch College in Yellow Springs, Ohio, the University of Michigan in Ann Arbor, Carleton College in Northfield, Minnesota, and Indiana University in Bloomington also jumped into the fray.

Along the way, FPCC found itself rapidly moving to the left, both because of Cuba's increasingly open radicalization and through the dynamic of being that strange new thing, an independent radical membership organization – not a coalition, a fictive 'letterhead committee' or a party's 'mass organization'. As such, it became increasingly hard to justify the claim to be solely an educational corrective to an unfair press, as FPCC originally defined its mission:

> To disseminate truth, to combat untruth, to publish the factual information which the U.S. mass media suppress, which the American public has the right to know, and in the process to combat the ignorance, the inadequate leadership, the blatantly distorted reporting which we believe to constitute not merely a grave injustice to the Cuban people and a serious threat to their dream of a better life, but a serious threat, as well, to the free traditions of our own people, our nation, our Hemisphere.[23]

Fair Play's newness is summed up by the disparate character of its key organizers during this hectic year, following Taber and Sagner: the Trotskyist cadre Berta Green; Richard Gibson, CBS's first black newsman; the Southern firebrand Robert F. Williams; the Marxist graduate student Saul Landau. Between them, these few exemplified the fractious new constituencies expressing solidarity with revolutionary Cuba, and the story of their involvement in Fair Play indicates the peculiar kind of 'united front' it became.

The Trotskyists Enter

As we have seen, many liberals once found in Castro an antidote to Marxism, while most Marxists in the US had been either hostile or blind to the import of the Cuban revolution. But later rather than sooner, Cuba became intensely appealing to those from the existing Old Left's forgotten byways who sought to fashion a purified Marxism-Leninism, or some form of Neo-Marxism. Entirely unanticipated, defence of the Cuban revolution spurred the first significant alliance of North American socialists since the 1930s, but one that functioned outside the leadership of what remained the largest socialist organization in the US, the battered but still-surviving Communist Party USA.[24]

Instead, a major part in Fair Play's history was taken by a much smaller group, the Socialist Workers Party (SWP), the largest organization of US Trotskyists since the 1930s. In later years and among themselves, SWP members have taken a proprietary attitude towards Fair Play, exaggerating their organization's role as if they alone had been the vanguard of solidarity with Cuba and forgetting their own hostility to *fidelismo* well into 1960.[25] Within limits, though, their presence was central, albeit far more accidental than most choose to remember. As with Taber, Sagner and others, the presence of a single person proved decisive. In this case, that person was Berta Green, who became the sparkplug of Fair Play's expansion as its sorely needed 'national administrator' in the late summer of 1960.[26] Unlike virtually everyone else, Green was both an experienced agitator and a committed Marxist, with a background in the hard school of the 1950s, when organizing in a factory town could get the organizer tarred and feathered. By the time Fair Play came around, she had put in years as an SWP cadre in Detroit and had recently moved to New York.[27]

As Green tells it, the story is surprisingly matter-of-fact. At the direction of her local SWP branch organizer, she attended an early meeting of Fair Play's New York chapter, where with little difficulty she was elected to the Steering Committee. From this base, she was soon successfully showing up what SWPers called the 'Stalinist types', who had responded to the public call of Fair Play in large numbers. In this case, the main factional opponents from the Trotskyist point of view were Victor Rabinowitz, a well-known leftwing lawyer with the firm of Boudin and Rabinowitz, and a young activist named Joanne Grant, then a staff writer for the *National Guardian,* who on 3 February 1960 had been named as a member of the Harlem Youth section of the CPUSA before the House Un-American Activities Committee.[28] Rabinowitz had been a main organizer of the New York Fair Play chapter, in conjunction with Taber, Sagner and others, and had helped to get Grant elected chapter secretary, with Richard Gibson as president and the liberal publisher Lyle Stuart as treasurer.[29]

Given Taber's sensitivity to FPCC's public profile, his discovery that a person publicly labelled a Communist had just been elected an officer of Fair Play's flagship chapter came as a rude shock. Someone explained the situation to him, and he called Rabinowitz that same night very late, 'rather agitated' in the latter's recollection. A painful process of self-purging began, which culminated in the departure of Grant and others perceived as part of the CPUSA's milieu – in her words, 'it was abandoned to the SWP'.[30] Meanwhile, Green had been making herself useful, taking advantage of what she regarded as Grant's deliberate dilatoriness in arranging the first public mass meeting for New York Fair Play, which took place on 21 July 1960 at Steinway Hall on 57th Street.[31] Green's diligence quickly drew Taber's attention and then, as she put it delicately later, 'I, of course, had to inform Taber at this point of my political affiliations.'[32] On discovering that she was more than just a particularly dedicated volunteer, a complicated maneuver unfolded. According to Green, Taber consulted with Fidel and then met with SWP leaders Farrell Dobbs, Tom Kerry and Joseph Hansen at her house, whereby a deal was sealed to throw the tiny party (then numbering only 400 cadre) into organizing Fair Play on a national scale, albeit in a covert and unacknowledged fashion, as required by the Cubans. In this novel fashion, Taber and the 26th of July Movement acquired the organizational resources that they otherwise lacked, and what they felt was needed – what Richard Gibson called 'a limited bulwark against' the vastly larger CPUSA (or those who shared its politics), then as later committed to a more behind-the-scenes and less confrontational style of organizing.[33] The result was that while CPers and other 'Stalinist types' who were hardly Communists might well have continued to seek influence among liberals, the Cubans and their closest US friends opted for intensive, high-profile organizing, denouncing the liberals if necessary.

The results of Taber's marriage of convenience with the SWP were rapidly apparent. Though Fair Play would undoubtedly have grown considerably during this period, it grew that much more because of the distinct organizational impetus it received from the Trotskyists. At Green's personal urging as much as through any party discipline, SWP members across the country initiated or helped form chapters in alliance with individuals and stray fractions of the old, not-so-old and completely new lefts.[34] In little more than six months, Fair Play was transformed: from three local chapters plus a claimed 2,000 members receiving the *Fair Play* bulletin, with no systematic program, to an organization claiming 7,000 members in twenty-seven 'adult chapters' and forty Student Councils capable of coordinating nationwide protests during the Bay of Pigs invasion. But much more was involved in this growth spurt than just

Green and the three full-time organizers donated by the SWP as Fair Play's travelling regional representatives for the East, Midwest and West Coast, or its other financial and organizational assistance. The Trotskyists were not the sole midwives to this mobilization. In fact, well before they made their intervention in FPCC, a very different effort was under way to capitalize on Fidel's appeal to African-Americans by a few activists at the forefront of an emerging black nationalism. Key to this strand of Fair Play's history, and its main public leader after Taber, was Richard Gibson.

'From One Liberator to Another': Afro-Cuban-American Solidarity

Gibson met Taber after the Urban League sponsored him as CBS News's first black journalist. He had earlier made his name in reporting on the Algerian uprising from 1955 to 1958 for Agence France Press in Paris, where his active solidarity with the rebels eventually cost him a job and led to a scandal still discussed in studies of the black American expatriate community.[35] After serving as president of the New York Fair Play chapter during 1960, Gibson succeeded Taber as acting executive secretary in January 1961 when the latter precipitously left for Cuba. Gibson's own flight to Algeria just ahead of a likely federal indictment in September 1962 signaled the practical eclipse of the Fair Play for Cuba Committee.[36]

Though he was hardly a popular figure with many of the whites involved, Gibson deserves the credit for making African-Americans some of the most prominent spokespersons in defence of the Cuban revolution and for FPCC. Throughout the organization's history, he aggressively linked various national liberation struggles to the struggle for equality in the US; during 1961–62, he did double duty as executive secretary of both FPCC and the New York–based Liberation Committee for Africa. The combination of an incipient black nationalism and what he later called a 'Fanonist expression of solidarity' with Cuba is one tangible sign of how the binary world of right and left, Communism and anti-Communism, was crumbling, and of Cuba's then very visible hand in making this transformation possible.[37]

From the beginning, Gibson, working closely with the Cubans, inserted a consciously black element into Fair Play's politics, as demonstrated by the eight signers of the original *New York Times* ad. Then, before the SWP's involvement and any systematic national recruitment, he helped organize the first full-scale Fair Play delegation to Cuba in late July 1960 as a nearly all-black group, including Robert F. Williams (who had already spent a week touring the island with Gibson and John Singleton in June), John Henrik Clarke, Julian Mayfield, Harold Cruse, and the poet LeRoi Jones, whose celebrated essay 'Cuba Libre' in *Evergreen Review* that fall was a gauntlet thrown down before the antipolitical ethos of the Beats. Even before this, on 4 July 1960, the

147

weekly Cuban literary magazine *Lunes de Revolución* came out with a special issue, 'Los Negros en U.S.A.', produced with the editorial cooperation of Gibson, Williams, Julian Mayfield and Taber; it included original contributions from LeRoi Jones, Langston Hughes, James Baldwin, Harold Cruse, John Henrik Clarke and Alice Childress. The magazine's visuals made the clearest possible analogy between reaction at home and abroad: photos of demonstrators in Little Rock, with placards like 'Governor Faubus, Save Our Christian America' and 'Race Mixing Is Communism', underscored by the caption 'Los racistas son tambien anticommunistas', and a cover comparing a slave poster, 'Virginia 1829', with a photo of a black schoolboy walking by a National Guardsman, 'Arkansas 1957'.

This appeal to black America did not come in a vacuum; the Cubans' efforts since January 1959 had paid off considerably in public goodwill. Then in June 1960, under great political and personal pressure (including usage of Joe Louis's income-tax troubles), Rowe-Louis-Fisher-Lockhart, Inc. cancelled its contract to promote black tourism in Cuba. Before that, the firm had run ads in the black press extolling Cuba as a 'first class vacation' where 'you will be treated as a first class citizen', and Joe Louis's rhetorical question, 'Where else can an American Negro go for a winter vacation?', received sustained coverage.[38] In the establishment media, the Brown Bomber's submission was cast as a victory for the US, but in the black press it stimulated considerable resentment, both because of Louis's humiliation, and because the Cuban contract had been the largest ever awarded a black public relations firm.[39] Meanwhile, a 31 July 1960 front-page story in the *New York Times*, 'Castro Seen Losing Bid to U.S. Negroes', attacked Robert F. Williams and asserted the NAACP's position that US blacks favored Batista over Castro because of the former's mixed-race background. The article noted that 'Negro leaders, like many white trade union and other leaders, have been put on the mailing list of *Revolucion*', as well as the fact that 'American Negro leaders' like Henry Lee Moon, NAACP director of public relations, had refused invitations to visit.

Fair Play's emphasis on 'Afro-Cuban-American' solidarity was not simply for media consumption, but was carried through in terms of organizing: one of the largest FPCC events of late 1960 was a Harlem rally on 17 November with Gibson; Robert Williams; William Worthy, star foreign correspondent of the Baltimore *Afro-American*; and Daniel Watts, president of the Liberation Committee for Africa.[40] Subsequently, Fair Play's two major national speakers tours during 1961 featured Williams and Worthy.

That Cuba's large black population strongly supported the revolution was key to this connection, but in addition Gibson and the others succeeded in explaining their solidarity in terms specific to the experience of blacks in the US. As Julian Mayfield put it in the *Afro-American*: 'The colored American should take a good look at the Cuban Revolution... it doesn't take decades of gentle persuasion to deal a death blow to white supremacy.'[41] Certainly, to

Fidel Castro in New York's Central Park during his 1955 fundraising tour of the United States.

Robert Taber interviews Fidel in his documentary 'Rebels of the Sierra Maestra: The Story of Cuba's Jungle Fighters', 1957.

Donald Soldini (right) with an *Ejercito Rebelde* unit in the Sierra Cristal, spring 1958.

Neill Macaulay on guard duty after the revolution's victory, spring 1959.

Neill Macaulay with the *Ejercito Re-belde* in the Organos Mountains, 1958.

Donald Soldini (middle) with Fidel Castro, spring 1959.

Ernest Hemingway meets Fidel, 1959.

Richard Gibson, Pinar del Rio, Cuba, 1960. (Photo by John Singleton)

Founding ad of the Fair Play for Cuba Committee, *New York Times*, 6 April 1960.

Fidel stayed at the Hotel Theresa in Harlem during a September 1960 meeting of the United Nations. Here he is greeted outside the Theresa by Jawaharlal Nehru and Krishna Menon of India. (AP WideWorld Photo)

CUBA LIBRE

by Leroi Jones

Photo by LEROY McLUCAS

Reprinted by permission of
EVERGREEN REVIEW

20 ¢

Published by **FAIR PLAY FOR CUBA COMMITTEE**
799 Broadway, New York 3, N.Y.

Cover of 'Cuba Libre' by LeRoi Jones, as published by the Fair Play for Cuba Committee, 1961. (Tamiment Library, New York University)

Robert F. Williams and attorney Vincent Hallinan, San Francisco,
March 1961. (Asher Harer Papers)

Lawrence Ferlinghetti reads 'One Thousand Fearful Words for Fidel Castro' at a Fair Play for Cuba forum in San Francisco, 14
January 1961. (Photo by Al Willis/Asher Harer Papers)

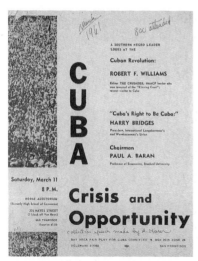

Leaflet for a Fair Play for Cuba forum with Robert F. Williams, Harry Bridges of the ILWU, and Marxist economist Paul Baran, 11 March 1961, in San Francisco: 800 attended. (Asher Harer Papers)

Fair Play demonstration against the Bay of Pigs invasion, San Francisco, 23 April 1961. (Photo by Harvey Richards/Asher Harer Papers)

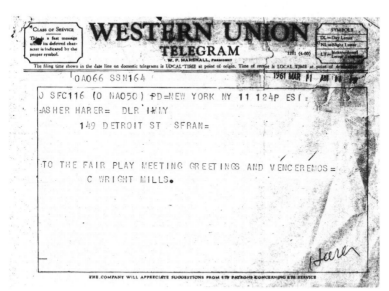

Telegram from C. Wright Mills: 'To the Fair Play Meeting Greetings and Véncerémos', 11 March 1961. (Asher Harer Papers)

Fair Play for Cuba picket line at the United Nations, New York, 15 April 1961. (GuardianPhoto)

Fair Play demonstration during the Cuban Missile Crisis, San Francisco, 27 October 1962. (Photo by Al Willis/Asher Harer Papers)

many Southern whites it seemed as if Castro, the Beatnik Communist, was 'bearding' them in exactly the same way as the earnestly nonviolent Northern agitators known as Freedom Riders. More than one Southerner asserted an explicit connection, as when Brigadier General T. B. Birdsong of the Mississippi Highway Patrol charged that two Fair Play members on a Freedom Ride in June 1961 had been trained in this nefarious technique at a 'Soviet-directed seminar' in Havana.[42] Infuriating some of the cautious Old Lefties around Fair Play, Gibson openly invited this linkage between the two insurgencies and their common enemy, while marking the difference between his and an older radicalism. As he told the Eastland Committee during the Bay of Pigs invasion, after trading insults and combatively taking the Fifth Amendment dozens of times, 'I am not a Communist at all. The color of my politics is not red, it is black.'[43]

That a new African-American militance would translate so readily into solidarity with Castro should hardly be surprising. The latter's dramatic gestures and the provisional government's concrete actions made a great impression on those who for years had been turning the other cheek and heeding the counsels of nonviolent moderation: the undeniable fact that Cuba abolished its own Jim Crow practices with no 'deliberation' and a maximum of 'speed'; the unmistakably black commander of the Rebel Army, Juan Almeida; Castro's biting attacks on the ringleaders of segregationist resistance, like Senator James Eastland, to whom most liberal Democrats still publicly genuflected because of their institutional clout. More than any other event, however, Fidel's ostentatious gesture of staying for a week in a Harlem hotel in late September 1960 placed him aggressively on the side of black America, as well as providing Fair Play for Cuba with an unexpected jump-start.

According to Berta Green, the move to the Hotel Theresa came about accidentally. Castro's arrival in New York to attend the opening session of the United Nations sparked intense publicity, and though he was still met at the airport by 3,000 fans, the overall tone was now raucously negative. To the *Daily News* for instance, which could hardly get enough, Fidel was 'The Bearded One', 'El Beardo' or simply 'The Beard', and Senator Barry Goldwater's comment that Fidel 'came over the hills looking like a knight in shining armor, and turned out to be a bum without a shave' was quoted approvingly in an editorial entitled 'Spoiled Brat With a Gun'.[44] The tabloids all spread the story that the Cubans were slaughtering, plucking, and cooking chickens in their midtown Manhattan hotel, the Sherbourne, a tale calculated to titillate the sensibilities of an urban audience (and well-remembered even today, though quite differently by blacks and whites), and the quality of the coverage in general can be gauged by this typical daily report:

> Girls, girls, girls have marched into the Cubans' suites. There have been blondes, brunettes, redheads and – a detective said – many known prostitutes. Along with the

girls has gone booze, booze, booze. ... Fidel himself had a visitor from 2 A.M. to 3:30 A.M. yesterday – an attractive bosomy blonde.[45]

Angered by these slurs and the Sherbourne's insistence upon a large security deposit, Castro complained to UN Secretary General Dag Hammerskjold that he would to sleep in Central Park if need be. Then Taber suggested that a move to Harlem would dramatize where Fidel was truly welcome in the US, and his idea was immediately implemented.

The resulting furor has lived on in the popular memory, much more than the more decorous visit only seventeen months before, and was given the Hollywood Cold War treatment in the 1969 Hitchcock film *Topaz*.[46] It produced a memorable series of images: in particular, Nikita Khrushchev's journey uptown to be photographed outside the Theresa, beaming in obvious delight, while 'thousands of spectators lined the sidewalks and cheered as Dr. Castro and Mr. Khrushchev walked to the curb, their arms around each other.'[47] Crowds ringed the hotel night and day, not only attracted by Castro's notoriety but genuinely excited by his attention to a largely invisible people; when Majors Juan Almeida and Antonio Nuñez Jiménez went on a stroll near the Theresa, they too 'received wild applause' from a crowd of up to 20,000, and even the *Times* ran a large photo of Foreign Minister Raúl Roa eating a hot dog at the Chock-Full-O'-Nuts on the corner (a similar photo ran as a five-column cover in *Revolución*, and a 'Solidarity Week with the Negro Peoples of the United States' was proclaimed in Cuba).[48]

How did Harlemites, or black North Americans in general, react to all this? Perhaps the most apt statement was by Jackie Robinson, then supporting Richard Nixon for president, who appeared at the Theresa to denounce Castro's 'propaganda', but admitted that the media spotlight Castro brought with him did 'give Harlem a real lift – a sense of pride'.[49] The *Afro-American* gloated over uptown's triumph over the downtown snobs and 'pansies' at the Sherbourne, reported Harlem's favorite number to play that week was Fidel's hotel room number, and editorialized that 'the blood of Fidel Castro is proud like that of his colored ancestors. He refuses to accept an inferior status, either for himself or for his country.'[50] By the end of the week, the *Times* showed a new respect for Castro's 'campaign for the support of American Negroes', with one reporter noting that

The comments of some residents near the Theresa and of police officials around the hotel suggest that Dr. Castro has earned considerable respect for his demonstrative opposition to racial discrimination.[51]

The Cubans showed a willingness to up the ante at every stage. When he was conspicuously excluded from a US-hosted lunch for Latin American delegations to the UN, Fidel returned to the Theresa and before television camerastreated its staff to steaks. Egypt's Nasser and India's Nehru, the two most prominent leaders of the emerging 'neutralist' nations, followed Khrushchev to Harlem, provoking more excitement, and a hastily organized Fair Play for Cuba reception received heavy coverage. C. Wright Mills, Allen Ginsberg, I. F. Stone and Henri Cartier-Bresson joined 250 other luminati of the left and the arts in the Theresa's ballroom, where Richard Gibson handed Fidel a small bust of Lincoln, ad-libbing 'from one Liberator to another' and Ginsberg asked security chief Major Ramiro Valdés, 'What does the Cuban Revolution think about marijuana?' The leftwing European journalist K. S. Karol has left the best impression of that night of early 'radical chic'. He remembered

> a fraternal and free-and-easy atmosphere, which formed a glaring contrast to that of all the diplomatic receptions – including the 'socialist' ones – I had attended on previous evenings in Manhattan. The proletarian staff of the hotel, the olive-green uniforms of the *guerrilleros*, the general lack of formality, all helped to emphasize the gaiety and the stimulating, if not revolutionary, character of the meeting. Fidel Castro arrived rather late, and was immediately surrounded by a group of Negroes, each as imposing in stature as Fidel himself. They flung themselves into his open arms. Everyone else then wanted to follow their example, and there were a few moments of pandemonium.[52]

Meanwhile, Harlem politics were in a minor uproar, as a local state senator and the Manhattan NAACP head committed the faux pas of meeting with Fidel, while the Reverend Adam Clayton Powell, Jr denounced him, saying his welcome would terminate 'the moment he launches any Communist-inspired activity or rioting in Harlem'.[53] Some of Powell's anger may have resulted from who Castro did reach out to: the *New York Times* reported in rather mysterious terms that 2,000 Black Muslims had rallied outside the Theresa, but readers of the black press knew that this was because the first black personality Castro met with was the Nation of Islam minister Malcolm X.[54] Gibson, who knew Malcolm from an earlier CBS assignment in Harlem, remembers this almost-chance encounter:

> I spotted him standing discreetly in the doorway of the bar on the righthand side of the lobby when we entered the Hotel Theresa. I waved to him and he came over. When Fidel learned that he was the leader of the Black Muslims in New York, he invited him to come upstairs with him. Malcolm apologized for not being able to do so immediately. He said he had to tell Brother Joseph, an aide of his, first and then he would come, within a few minutes. During that time, I contacted some black newspapers and alerted them. ... We got a great photo of Malcolm and Fidel embracing. Malcolm welcomed Fidel to Harlem with the words: 'No one knows the master as well as the servant.'[55]

All in all, it was a scandal and a success, sending a message at top volume that the *fidelistas* wanted as friends those US citizens who had historically been friendless, and demonstrating the Castro charisma once again. As Murray Kempton suggested in his 21 September *New York Post* column, describing how outside the hotel he saw black nationalists 'respectfully' arguing with Jackie Robinson, 'America had suddenly absorbed Fidel Castro; we were in a Southern town standing on the corner, quietly intimate, human again.'[56]

From Joe Louis on, the Cubans' notably successful wooing of black celebrities, tourists and radicals has been similar to Fidel's September 1960 Harlem sojourn. Through subsequent decades, it has periodically surfaced to be scorned by Cold War liberals, black as well as white, and the organized right, yet because of the deeply separate character of black life, the attraction of Cuba could not be exorcised.[57] A major splash was made by the reporter William Worthy, who had been a Nieman Fellow at Harvard, and who had broken the law by entering the People's Republic of China for CBS News in 1957. All through these years, Worthy continued to write militantly pro-Castro pieces for the *Afro-American*, yet he was still sought after by the mass media – presumably because of his unrivaled access to revolutionary leaders.[58] In December 1960, his cinema vérité documentary, 'Yanki, No!', dramatizing the spread of *fidelismo* in Latin America, was shown on ABC during prime time (his camera crew included the cream of sixties documentary-making: D. A. Pennebaker, Albert Maysles and Richard Leacock). Only months later, he made a national tour for Fair Play, while even more intriguingly, the Tuskegee Institute sent him on a 16-day jaunt through the South in February, which included his speaking to 2,000 students at Tuskegee itself.[59] In mid-1961 Worthy was indicted for illegally travelling to and from the island, spurring considerable anger against the Kennedy administration, which had not targetted white journalists violating similar bans, and inspiring a satirical Phil Ochs song, 'The Ballad of William Worthy': 'William Worthy isn't worthy to enter our door/He just came back from Cuba, he's not American anymore./But it seems awfully funny to hear the State Department say,/"You're living in the Free World, in the Free World you must stay."'

But one individual gave the link between Cuba and national liberation a harder edge than the failed attempts to promote black tourism or even the tableau of Fidel-in-Harlem. The rebellion and subsequent persecution of Robert F. Williams, and his own coupling of that defiance with Castro's example, culminating in asylum in Cuba in September 1961, made the most telling connection between the rising anger of African-Americans and the island revolution.

Williams was a Marine Corps veteran who in the late 1950s became a notorious figure for organizing National Rifle Association–affiliated 'rifle clubs' of blacks to practice self-defence in Monroe, North Carolina, where he was president of the local NAACP chapter. Though rarely mentioned in later histories of the civil rights movement, at the beginning of the sixties Williams was a more inflammatory figure to whites than Malcolm X; his threat came not from a Northern ghetto like the Muslims, but deep in the heart of Dixie. His challenge to the NAACP, which first removed him from office and then restored him after considerable protest in 1959, and his angry defiance of the entire white power structure of his state, citing the constitutional right to bear arms, were truly incendiary.[60]

Williams's solidarity with Cuba predated the Fair Play for Cuba Committee, and he was associated with the latter from its beginning.[61] Given that his was the only recognized, pro-integrationist critique of Martin Luther King, Jr's nonviolent strategy, this partisanship for Castro helped insert the Cuban revolution into the black political debate.[62] In his bluntly stated vision, Cuba's example was 'the new Sermon on the Mount ... a pilgrimage to the shrine of hope' to be proclaimed so that black people in the US could see the living hell of their own apartheid, and finally throw off the Uncle Tom leaders who, in his words, 'would lick any master's rump'.[63] There was nothing staged about this, and we should not doubt that Williams meant every word when he wrote in The Crusader after a trip to Havana that it was 'three weeks of the only true freedom I have ever known'.[64]

Rather quickly from late 1960 on, Williams's long crusade for school integration and access to public accommodations became inextricably tied to the defense of Cuba, not only in his public utterances but in the eyes of his white antagonists, apparently including Jesse Helms, the town's fire chief and father of the US senator.[65] Williams's insistence on not turning the other cheek but instead threatening to shoot those who tried to slap him down led to an extraordinarily tense situation, as he and his men repeatedly faced down sheriff's deputies and others with guns drawn. It was not only a few radicals who imagined Williams might become the 'Black Fidel Castro of the South', and to underscore the point, he invited Fidel to visit during the September 1960 UN trip, though the Cuban premier was barred by the State Department from leaving Manhattan.[66]

In August 1961, however, Cuba became more than just a part of Williams's gadfly persona. By that time a local race war was brewing in Monroe; in July, Williams and his family were denied passports to visit Cuba, a fact he bitterly noted in the context of four attempts on his life in the previous month.[67] What precipitated the final violent confrontation was when an interracial group of Freedom Riders, including James Foreman of SNCC, came to Monroe to demonstrate their nonviolent solidarity and overcome the mounting hostility and tension. In the ensuing picketing, dozens of black residents and Freedom Riders were beaten by crowds and then arrested, and the city became an armed camp. Increasingly large white mobs circled outnumbered black neighborhoods, giving and receiving fire for several days. After an incident in which Williams briefly took a white couple into his home to protect them from an angry crowd, he decided to slip through a police cordon and get out of town to defuse the situation. North Carolina promptly indicted him on a kidnapping charge. Amid a national manhunt by the FBI at the direction of Attorney General Robert Kennedy, he was spirited north to Canada by members of the Socialist Workers Party also active in Fair Play, and eventually made his way to Cuba via the US and Mexico.[68] Once home free, he became a figure of great celebrity on the island, living proof of the hypocrisy of the defender of the Free World. Williams played this role to the hilt, and then some. For several years, he published *The Crusader* 'in exile', shipping it to the US via Canada, and beamed a Radio Free Dixie into the Southern states, urging armed struggle. Eventually, he broke with the Cubans and ended up in China, where *The Crusader* took on an unremittingly savage tone, before returning to the US in 1969 and living quietly.

Robert Williams thus passed from the scene, but his example did not, inspiring a number of black activists to 'pick up the gun', notably the Revolutionary Action Movement, which he officially chaired from abroad, and to an extent, the Black Panther Party.[69] In later years, Black Panther leader Eldridge Cleaver and Assata Shakur, founder of the Black Liberation Army, were among the prominent black exiles given sanctuary in Cuba; Stokely Carmichael and Angela Davis made well-publicized trips there at the height of their fame. Combined with long-term Cuban solidarity in the form of aid, technicians and troops to beleaguered African revolutions from 1965 on, when Che Guevara fought in the Congo, through the South African army's decisive defeat at Cuito Carnivale in southern Angola in 1988, this record gave Cuba a prestige in parts of the black community that has been the revolution's most reliable line of defence in the US over the past generation. Though few remember it now, that solidarity can be traced back to the visible role of people like Gibson, Williams and others in Fair Play for Cuba, as well as the solidarity proclaimed by the Cubans with the struggle against racism in the United States in 1959 and continually demonstrated ever since.

'New Men' on Campus

Not only Trotskyists and some African-Americans came away from Cuba changed, with a vision of revolution and of their own consequentiality. In terms of actual recruitment, the Fair Play for Cuba Committee made its greatest impact on the first small levies of self-consciously 'new' leftists in the US. Among the thin strata of radicalized students and bohemians, already engaging with nuclear disarmament and civil rights, Cuba became another essential criterion of political commitment circa 1960. Some perceived that the revolution was taking on socialist characteristics while breaking with the Soviet practice of authoritarian social control. Many simply felt that this was 'their' revolution, in the way that earlier generations had gone to Spain or identified with the Bolsheviks. They agreed strongly with that anonymous, composite Cuban who told them, through C. Wright Mills, to put the Soviets behind them as either model or nemesis:

> We've not gone through all that terribly destructive process; we have not been wounded by it; and so we are free. We are revolutionaries of the post-Stalin era; we've never had any 'God That Failed'. We just don't belong to that lineage. We don't have all that cynicism and futility about what we're doing, and about what we feel must be done.
>
> That is the one big secret of the Cuban revolutionary.
>
> As young intellectuals, of course, we know something about all that disillusioning process from books ... but we never lived it. We are new men. That is why we are so original and so spontaneous and so unafraid to do what must be done in Cuba. There are no ex-radicals among us. We are new radicals. We really are, we think, a new left in the world.[70]

The 1958–59 school year had been the postwar nadir of campus politics, and as we have seen, students hardly took the lead in supporting Castro, though they did respond to the man in the flesh when he showed up in the Ivy League that spring. By the spring of 1960, however, things began to pick up, with a powerful wave of picketing at chain stores across the North in solidarity with the mass sit-in campaign led by students at the South's historic black schools.[71] In May, the student 'riot' in opposition to the House Un-American Activities Committee took place in San Francisco, while across the country the Student Peace Union came together as the first new large-scale campus organization in many years, rapidly attracting thousands of members. Many observers noted a growing tension over the Cold War and the issue of self-determination at home and abroad. At the time, David Horowitz of Berkeley's SLATE linked these issues in language similar to that used in the opinion columns of student papers across the country:

> The campus is the last refuge of true democracy in America. Only on the campuses was there widespread support of the right of self-determination for the Cuban people; only on the campuses has there been large-scale community action in the defence of free speech.[72]

In a sense, therefore, the full-scale confrontation between the United States and Cuba came along at just the right moment. As long as there was unlimited, cheap access to Havana, some fraction of US youth was likely to go looking for themselves. Even without Fair Play for Cuba, one could have predicted some student activism in favor of leaving the Cuban people alone, in the same way that students ardently desired to end the stultifying in loco parentis restrictions governing campus life, and were drawn to demonstrations supporting the right to sit at a lunch counter and drink a cup of coffee in peace.

Apparently the Cubans themselves thought in these terms, since they heavily promoted package tours to 'student colonies' in the summer of 1960, working directly with groups like the International Relations Club at Hunter College in the Bronx, which reported over 700 inquiries to a posted announcement, and through black and student newspapers, which commonly recycled press releases as news articles with convenient listings of where one could write for information.[73]

One such independent campus group, which went to Cuba for three weeks in July, was led by two graduate students, Robert Scheer and Marvin Gettleman, who later played prominent roles in the movement against the Vietnam War. This was hardly a solidarity trip, though, since 'anybody could get on this delegation', including some who were already, or became later, strongly anti-Castro. The two leaders themselves were wary of being taken in by official guided tours and 'Potemkin villages'. In Gettleman's remembrance,

> Bobby and I weren't going to let history repeat itself. We read everything we could get our hands on. There was a bibliography, an economic study of Cuba. We discovered the Foreign Broadcast Service reports. ... We were very skeptical and our intellectual guide was [New York Times reporter] Tad Szulc, who we saw as being above the battle.[74]

He and Scheer armed themselves with a list of negative claims regarding the revolution, which they proceeded to check on a case-by-case basis, the whole group of several dozen dispersing each day to cover different parts of the country, usually visiting cooperatives to observe the Agrarian Reform. Eventually, the shallowness of many of the assertions by Szulc and others, combined with uncontrived witnessing of popular commitment, turned Gettleman and Scheer away from neutrality, and both came home to be Fair Play leaders at their respective campuses, City College of New York and Berkeley (Scheer would co-author an important early New Left book with Maurice Zeitlin, Cuba: Tragedy in Our Hemisphere). One unannounced visit out in the countryside had a considerable effect:

> We get to this cooperative late in the afternoon. We picked it out from a map given to us by the government. It was a site we were encouraged to see, but not that day. We went there, and got in the middle of this debate that was going on. ... If I remember the argument correctly, the content was less important to me than the fact that it took place. I think the agronomist was arguing for diversified agriculture and the local guy, who was an incredibly forceful speaker and vehement and angry. ... He was the local leader of the clandestine union among the sugar cane workers, elected by his local people and in fact, the meeting was at his house. ... We went in. They barely glanced up at us. No sense that what they were doing had to be hidden in any way. The local guy was arguing. I remember he said, 'These are my comrades. This is what we do. We grow sugar. We should do this, we should do that. And we didn't fight

this revolution to have policy dictated to us from Havana.' Very, very vehement meeting. Yet on the other hand, the guy from – the expert sent by the government, had won over a number of the people. ... For us, it was a thrilling experience, it was the single thing that turned me around. Very emotional ... the experience of seeing people totally powerless taking their own lives in their own hands.[75]

Many others had similar personal revelations in that last spring and summer before the unforeseen travel ban. The future playwright Barbara Garson and her husband Marvin took a honeymoon with no political itinerary:

We wouldn't go on a Cuban government tour. They said, 'You can stay in this student whatchamacallit' – no, no, no, we wouldn't do that. We didn't trust them and so on. So we just hitchhiked all around Cuba, where everybody came running out of their houses, saying, 'Oh, we have to show you "la verdad de Cuba"', and they'd bring out their *Life* magazines and their *Readers Digests* and say, 'Oh, we know what they're saying about us.'[76]

Gradually, the urgency of ordinary Cubans' desire to be understood by North America drew them in, but it was the culture shock attendant upon returning to the US that willy-nilly radicalized the Garsons; they too joined FPCC:

I guess what really made Cuba make me political is that when I got back – we all know that newspapers lie, but to know it is one thing, and to have black and white in front of your face is just – you know, you're walking around spluttering.[77]

Contemporary testimony to this uncoordinated grassroots attraction can also be found, as in the September 1960 letter to Herbert L. Matthews from Christopher Salter, Oberlin's 'Latin America Representative', apparently a kind of junior student adviser. Writing on behalf of 'a small core of students that have recently been to Cuba and have returned favorably impressed', he explained his plans for 'an active informational campaign this year on the better side of Castro and Cuba', which he hoped Matthews would 'spearhead' by spending a weekend at Oberlin talking with 'the increasingly large number of students that are curious about Cuba in particular and the Caribbean in general.'[78] In one way or another, then, many of the young people who would come together in Fair Play for Cuba in the months leading up to the Bay of Pigs had already seen Cuba, or perhaps heard about it from friends and looked forward to their own investigation. This was, after all, the true spirit of the residual Anglo-American ideal of 'fair play', as it was still taught in those days: to judge for oneself, to reason calmly and without excessive passion, to try to see the other fellow's point of view – above all, to accept innocence until guilt was proven.[79]

One campus is particularly representative of how the Cuban revolution stood as example and goad to the early New Left – the University of Wisconsin at Madison. As one former student described it, by the time he got there in the fall of 1961, 'over everything was imprinted the influence of the Cuban revolution, its then "nonideological character", and the message that revolution was possible notwithstanding the disparity of forces.'[80]

Madison was that rare school at which some kind of coherent student movement existed and even began, in a small way, to flourish during the Eisenhower years, so that by the late 1950s there was not one, two or a dozen 'lefties' on campus, but a few hundred oriented around the Socialist Club. In several ways its influence was felt nationally in turning the nascent new radicalism towards *fidelismo*. Two products of Madison, the journal *Studies on the Left* and one of its editors, Saul Landau, intersected during 1960 with another signal development, C. Wright Mills's great political tract *Listen, Yankee* (discussed in Chapter 6). As before, solidarity was constructed through the central experience of going there. With Mills and Landau, as with many others, it was as if people were drawn to test themselves and their assumptions in this new world so close to home.

To get at the relation of Madison to Cuba in the making of the early New Left requires delineating, however, what the term 'New Left' actually meant in the late 1950s. The reference at the time was hardly obscure: in England, various Marxist intellectuals who had quit the Communist Party after the events of 1956 joined with other socialists in founding a project they dubbed a New Left, principally several journals, *The New Reasoner* and *Universities and Left Review*, which in 1959 merged to become the *New Left Review*. This process of reviving a critical, humanistic Marxism in turn sparked similar efforts in the US. The most important of these was *Studies on the Left*, begun in 1959 by a group of graduate students and Socialist Club leaders at Madison including Martin Sklar, Saul Landau, David Eakins and Eleanor Hakim, soon joined by the somewhat older James Weinstein. Many of the *Studies* founders were one-time members of the defunct Labor Youth League, who brought with them elements of the CP's internationalist and anti-imperialist tradition, and most had begun learning to rethink the history of the United States from the historian William Appleman Williams. *Studies* rapidly established itself as the nascent New Left's main theoretical and scholarly organ. Its importance in this germinative stage, however, has been effaced by the attention paid to the non-Marxist New Leftists associated with another key campus, Ann Arbor, where a different intellectual coterie led by Robert Alan Haber, coming from the other 'Old' Left tradition of social democracy, was birthing SDS. Not the least reason for *Studies*' (and Madison's) obscurity in later histories is the clear commitment to a rigorous socialist politics, and an equal emphasis upon the historical nature of US imperialism coupled with analysis of revolutionary developments in the Third World, in which Cuba was then foremost.

The tone was set by the third, 'Cuba issue' of *Studies on the Left* in late 1960, which amounted to a detailed manifesto of solidarity. A close-up photo of a Cuban crowd listening attentively to an unseen speaker, taken by Lee Baxandall during the speech by Fidel that became known as the First Declaration of Havana, made for a dramatic cover. The long editorial statement, 'The Cuban Revolution: The New Crisis in Cold War Ideology', began with the unequivocal declaration that 'the editors consider the Cuban Revolution to be the most important and least understood social development in the recent history of the Western Hemisphere', anatomized the crisis, and warned in conclusion that

It is already late for American intellectuals to challenge cold war ideology; further acquiescence to this attempt of cold war ideologues to crush the new humane society in Cuba might seriously thwart the chances of constructing a humane society in the United States.[81]

Then came an essay by Sartre, 'Ideology and Revolution', reprinted from *Lunes de Revolución,* on how the 26th of July Movement had redefined the nature of ideology, with these suggestive closing lines:

It is very certain that practice creates the idea which clarifies it. But we now know that it deals with a concrete and particular practice, which discovers and makes the Cuban man in action.[82]

A whole series of translated articles and speeches by Che Guevara followed, and then Landau's and Hakim's review of *Listen, Yankee* and Paul Sweezy and Leo Huberman's *Cuba: The Anatomy of a Revolution.*[83]

Studies' 'Cuba issue', the Sweezy and Huberman book (the first full examination of the revolution from a Marxist perspective, very widely read in 1960 and after) and *Listen, Yankee* together served as a clarion call to student radicals in the US, and by early 1961 a partisan line had been drawn, with far-reaching consequences. Already, however, one of *Studies'* editors had gone beyond scholarship to show the potential route from inquiry to action. Amidst the weighty documents in that issue of *Studies* was a small advertisement headlined 'Student Council Fair Play for Cuba Committee Sponsors A Christmas Tour To Cuba'. A careful reader would note that the editor of FPCC's Student Council bulletin (dubbed *Student Council,* of course) was Saul Landau.

Landau was hardly the only Madisonian to fly down to see the revolution. During 1959 and 1960, his wife Nina Serrano, James Weinstein and Lee Baxandall (who translated Che Guevara for *Studies* and worked for *Lunes de Revolución),* all went on their own and returned stirred and impressed.[84] But Landau stayed much longer and established a permanent relationship with the Cubans that lasted for decades, during which he made a notable series of films chronicling the revolution's trajectory; his original entree came from the fact that Raúlito Roa, UN delegate in New York and son of Cuba's foreign minister, was a *Studies on the Left* reader and gave him a scrawled letter of introduction that opened many doors. After four months in Cuba during the middle of 1960, during which he met C. Wright Mills, Landau returned to the US in September at Robert Taber's urging to organize campus Fair Play affiliates, meanwhile working as an editor at Ballantine Books, which brought out *Listen, Yankee* in paperback that November. With little trouble, FPCC's Student Councils rapidly took off as an ad hoc network linking the disconnected advocates for Cuba. Both Landau and Taber toured campuses across the Northeast and Midwest, a professional-looking *Student Council* bulletin began publication, Cuban films were widely distributed and, above all, there was heavy recruitment of students for a 'low-cost vacation tour', the prize that Fidel had been holding out to North American youth for a long time.[85]

It was the latter that was Landau's main accomplishment in fact, given the window left barely open before the 'chiclet curtain' came down between the US and Cuba. Though *Student Council* would claim in its first issue that more than twenty FPCC Student Councils were forming, and clearly the whirlwind speaking tours had an effect, there was no time to build an organization in the usual painstaking manner of those days, when official recognition (the right to host speakers and reserve rooms) was very difficult to gain at most schools, and even the most radical students were quite cautious. One can reasonably surmise that FPCC's progress that fall at the University of Chicago was typical. Robert Taber spoke there on 21 October under the sponsorship of the SWP's Young Socialist Alliance, telling his audience bluntly that 'Nixon and Kennedy should be hanged', and, according to a student reporter, 'tentative plans to set up a Fair Play for Cuba committee at the UC were made.' Other than printing a press release on the Christmas tour as a filler article, there was nothing more in public until the New Year – at least nothing else made it into the *Chicago Maroon*.[86] Other schools like Cornell displayed similar first steps towards controversy over Cuba.[87]

Anything more than polite, indoor meetings at such an early stage took place where there were homegrown traditions of activism, and FPCC served mainly as an outside reference or resource. At Berkeley, Robert Scheer and Maurice Zeitlin drew in their friends in SLATE to form their own 'Fair Play for Cuba Committee', the sole group to hold outdoor student rallies on Cuba during 1960, but which had only a distant relationship to the regular Bay Area FPCC chapter and national Fair Play.[88] At tiny Quaker-affiliated Swarthmore College outside Philadelphia, an intensive 'Cuba weekend' was held in December, while the student government debated whether to allow five students and one professor going down at Christmas the use of an official truck.[89] Outside of these few campuses, however, that fall saw only the most preliminary on-campus organizing around Cuba – arguments in editorial columns, or invitations to a friendly professor to give a talk. At the vast majority of campuses, of course, including later sixties' hotbeds like Columbia, even that minimal level of activism was not yet visible.[90]

The FPCC Christmas Tour, coordinated by Landau and Berta Green, changed all that. A mass exodus of young Yankees willing to listen, it was an emotional high point for Fair Play, helped coalesce its various fragments into a national organization, and briefly spurred an exceptional upsurge of local activity much more outspoken than anything before. This effort snowballed from the various attempts by the Cubans to get US students, along with African-Americans an obvious natural constituency, to come down and see for themselves. In the late fall of 1960, it gathered force in an increasingly tense atmosphere, with presidential candidates Nixon and Kennedy trying to out-do each other in anti-Castroism, and the first exposure of the long-planned invasion – Ronald Hilton's 19 November article in *The Nation*, 'Are We Training Cuban Guerrillas?', could not be completely ignored.[91]

In late October, the tour was announced as a luxurious holiday break: 'Christmas in Cuba ... easy living and a season in the sun. ... You'll *live it up*' the first leaflet promised.[92] Given that the all-inclusive package cost was only $100 from Miami and $220 from New York, FPCC rapidly found itself flooded with reservations, as its nascent chapters organized carpools (even a chartered plane with 80 Chicagoans), and students from all over the Northeast and Midwest planned to bus and hitchhike down.[93] Eventually 326 North Americans from as far afield as San Francisco, Los Angeles, Iowa, Kansas and Michigan left from New York and Miami on the 'informal good will delegation', amid intense pressure and celebrity.[94] In the final weeks, the State Department sternly warned that the trip was not sanctioned by the US government, the New York State Attorney General threatened fraud charges over the tour's promotion, and the Civil Aeronautics Board promised an investigation. Then, on the eve of the flight, the pilot of the Cubana Airlines plane was convinced to defect, and the assembled Fair Players had to wait as a new pilot was flown in. As they finally embarked, huge crowds of hostile Cuban exiles roared for the cameras, threw stones and picked fights as indifferent police looked on.[95]

Once in Cuba, the gringos had by all accounts a memorable time, travelling from one end of the island to the other. Landau's fellow Madisonian Anne Eakins, then married to a *Studies on the Left* editor, wrote a report for *Fair Play* about a typical day visiting cooperatives and the like, exclaiming at the end, 'Wouldn't it be great to live here?' In a more serious vein, another student commented, 'You know, they have transformed the human personality in less than two years. They have real human beings here. I didn't think it was possible in this world', while fifty *turistas* donated blood to victims of one of the frequent counter-revolutionary bombings, and seven went to the US embassy for a heated debate.[96] At the climax was a grand party hosted by Fidel himself, during which the news of Eisenhower's breaking diplomatic relations with

Cuba was announced.[97] And then no more. With the travel ban of 17 January 1961, it would be nine very long years before any sizable group of US citizens would see the revolutionary island for themselves (and the cane-cutting Venceremos Brigades that began arriving in early 1970 were as different from Fair Play for Cuba as the names suggest). In the short term, however, Fair Play's Christmas tour had dramatic results with US students, reflected in a rash of fiery 'I was there' campus newspaper articles, packed debates, rallies, and many more Student Councils. The topic of Castroism and the appropriate US response made the winter of 1961 rather hot at many schools, and generated considerable momentum in advance of late April's Bay of Pigs debacle.

Before closing this account of how FPCC came together during 1960, however, the question of why the *fidelista* revolution appealed to North American students needs to be addressed more fully. After all, those early New Leftists like Saul Landau and the *Studies on the Left* crowd, or for that matter Bob Scheer and the SLATEniks, were not the cheering Ivy Leaguers who admired Castro as a man of action, but rather an exceptionally serious bunch of young intellectuals; as we have seen, there was a deep desire on the left not to be taken in by any false gods or unverified claims. In and of itself, the legend of the armed struggle against Batista and the romantic revolutionism at which the Cubans excelled would not have been sufficient to attract the white campus nuclei of the US New Left, because this example was plainly inapplicable to Madison, Wisconsin or Berkeley, California in 1960. Instead, it was the Cubans' method, or rather their antimethodological method, that impressed skeptical students brought up on The End of Ideology and trying to find a way back. Certainly this is what Dale Johnson, writing in *Studies on the Left* in early 1961 'On the Ideology of the Campus Revolution', suggested in one of the most precise analyses of First Wave (1959–62) student radicalism. After surveying the wide range of organizing that had put Bay Area students in the forefront nationally (SDS founders Tom Hayden and Al Haber drove to Berkeley in July 1960 just to observe and soak up the ambience), he suggested that 'most important of all, there has been the impact of the Cuban Revolution' and the 'ideological similarities between the Cuban and the Campus revolutions.'

Both Cuban and Campus rebels are *strong* dissenters, firm in their convictions and willing to speak out and act militantly in spite of the mighty coercive powers of the American state. Both are pragmatic, always putting first things first, with rarely an eye to ultimate ends. In Cuba this takes the form of 'the year of agrarian reform', the 'year of education', the 'year of industrialization'. ... Here at home the pragmatic outlook is manifested in the multitude of single-issue groups devoted simply to getting things done in the most effective manner possible. ... Both Cuban and Campus Revolutions are inexperienced, groping movements sometimes stumbling, sometimes making mistakes of a tactical nature – with either too much anti-Americanism or too much fear of offending or alienating 'public opinion'. Most important, their motivating ideologies are neither socialism – Marxian or otherwise – nor liberalism, although they combine elements of both. Rather, the ideology of both the *Barbudos* of Cuba and the campus revolutionaries is a refreshing combination of humanism and rationalism. ... In at least one sense the Fidelista is very fortunate. He is confronted with the opportunity to steer Cuba's, and perhaps Latin America's, destiny upon the path which he chooses. So he sets about, rationally, to build a new society. Many students at U. of C., Stanford, San Francisco and San Jose State Colleges, at Wisconsin, and Chicago and NYU grasp and appreciate this attempt to direct human history, to take hold of one's environment and shape it, to institutionalize better human values. ...[98]

But a common ideological pragmatism coupled to the generational camaraderie of young intellectuals was only one part of Cuba's appeal. There is always a 'cruder', more subjective or simply popular side to any effective politics. To put it in the terms relevant to student organizing then and later, Madison and Berkeley and a few other schools were hip, and so was Fidel, and the two in 1960–61 appeared closely connected in their hipness to would-be bohemians or radicals elsewhere, the coffee-house and folk-music crowd burgeoning since the late 1950s. This association and its public quality was in the end more important than the hundreds of US students who actually visited revolutionary Cuba, and the sense of outcast solidarity was only heightened every time some powerful old man – a Senator or a Cardinal – called Fidel a 'bum' or a 'beatnik' or simply 'crazy'. The continual, obsessive dwelling on Castro's hairiness and lack of couth alone must have had a powerful effect, if one remembers the political weight attached to 'long hair' in the US well into the 1970s. What Fair Play for Cuba and its jerry-rigged Student Councils did, especially by going down to the island in such large numbers, what any new political upsurge does when it manages to break through the flat, horizonless plain of hegemonic discourse, was to make visible or audible an alternative position, and to do it with sufficient verve and self-confidence.

Before the later sixties' institutionalization of a mass 'counter-culture', it is difficult to demonstrate with any quantitative precision how something truly was hip at a particular moment. After all, even the Beats might well have labored in respectable obscurity (and perhaps never been 'the Beats' as such) if they had not sparked the interest of major media organs as an oddity, followed by considerable book sales.

Fortunately, Madison comes to the rescue with a fine example of how a new cultural style of all-encompassing irreverence played off of the Cuban mystique. The skit at the 1961 edition of that campus's annual 'Anti-Military Ball', held just before the Bay of Pigs landing, was entitled 'Boy Scouts in Cuba'. Written by Lee Baxandall, Marshall Brickman (later Woody Allen's collaborator) and Danny Kalb (later guitarist of the Blues Project), and acted by Socialist Club and *Studies on the Left* mainstays, it featured characters named Big

Fidel, Big Raúl and Big Che, parodying *Guys and Dolls,* the 1950s musical in which lovable gangsters and gamblers, including a threatening figure known as Big Julie, travel back and forth from Manhattan to Havana; the film version starred Frank Sinatra and Marlon Brando. As they await the invasion that evidently was no secret to anyone by that time, the revolutionary leaders discuss their plans. But this was hardly humorless idolatry at the feet of Third World despots, or simple-minded agitprop. Interrupted by his comrades' constant shouts that 'Kennedy is an imbecile!', Big Fidel declares, 'Our militia stand at their posts. They are ready to cast the harpoon of Cuban freedom into the tough shark of Yankee imperialism', and then makes a simple request:

> Big Che, I want you to clear all channels of radio and television for tonight. I must tell the Cuban people about the sadness of my heart [that is, that the Yankee shark has not shown up yet to be speared]. I shall have my feelings speak spontaneously to the populace. From eight until two thirty will be satisfactory, Big Che.[99]

But the Madisonians were even sharper and funnier regarding the wealthy exiles they pictured sitting in a Miami hotel lobby, looking at pictures of their former estates in *Revolución*:

> *Los maricones!* Everywhere in Miami, they are saying the discontent grows in Cuba. The *revolución* will not last. Why, when Castro opened the beaches to the workers one week ago, it is said the workers just *threw* themselves into the sea![100]

Best of all is a singing, dancing, maracas-shaking Adolf Berle, Cold War liberalism's gray eminence who was Kennedy's special adviser on Latin America, and widely known to be 'advising' the anti-Castro exiles. He gets to sing 'The Berle Song':

> A more patriotic teacher never
> Was in America found,
> To nobody second
> I'm certainly reckoned
> A professor heavenly bound.
> It is my chauvinistic endeavor
> To speak these words to all:
> Each backward nation
> Must yield its ration
> Of profit, however small![101]

There were undoubtedly people who would have found such flippancy an inexcusable deviation from serious political work, especially in April 1961, when the fate of the Cuban revolution hung in the balance. There are always those in any political camp for whom certain ideas and historical personages cannot be mocked, even affectionately, without giving aid and comfort to the enemy. But those who would argue that such summer-camp shenanigans merely demonstrate the New Left's dilettantism, its 'petty bourgeois' immaturity, should keep in mind that the Cubans, at least, would probably have appreciated the joke, including even Big Fidel and Big Raúl. After all, very early in 1959, when Comandante Raúl Castro was sounded out by a Hollywood screenwriter in Havana doing research for a film on the heroic Castro boys, his first question was, would they get Sinatra and Brando for the parts?

For generations, historians and journalists have liked to quote Marx to the effect that history repeats itself, the first time as tragedy and the second time as farce. What the Madisonians, other US students and the Cubans all seemed to understand was that the tragedy and the farce had become inextricably intertwined, and that the trick was to both enjoy and exploit this combustible mixture. Surely this is what Fidel was doing when, with evident relish, he told the United Nations in September 1960 that Kennedy was 'an ignorant and illiterate millionaire'. He was playing to a crowd that others could not see, transgressing in high style, with the beard, the cigar, the olive green fatigues and pistol, and most of all the harangues rich in invective. Some part of the crowd here, responding to this Dionysian symbolism, decided not just to 'play fair', but to join the play. Young people in the US already had a culture of rebellion of their own; they did not need Fidel for that. What he showed them was how political the hip could be, given half a chance.

Notes

1. *New York Times*, 6 March 1959.

2. 'A responsible journalist and a political naif' is Alan Sagner's description of Robert Taber and himself.

3. See David Halberstam, *The Best and the Brightest*, New York: Random House, 1972, p. 14, for a reference to this period and to how the 'old liberalism of the Thirties ... defiantly liberal-humanist' had been repudiated by politicians but 'not necessarily [by] liberal voters'.

4. Taber declined several requests for interviews or comments upon earlier versions of this text. Former colleagues suggest that his leadership of FPCC led to many years of harassment and blacklisting as a journalist. In a single, cautionary letter, he indicated that my account of FPCC's internal history was quite incomplete (about which he is surely right), because many of those involved 'have forgotten much, rewritten the script that we all carry in our heads to please themselves – or imagined auditors. They telescope time, contradict one another, make gross mistakes.' He added, 'One thinks of history as fiction: it is designed to give the shape and significance that the chaos of untutored raw experience seems to need – mainly for institutional and societal indoctrination. It is mostly false. The worst becomes doctrine.' Letter, Taber to Gosse, 23 January 1992.

5. See *Fair Play*, 2 September 1960, for a reference to Taber's being in Guatemala; his colleague Richard Gibson is the source for his experience in Algeria.

6. Interview with Victor Rabinowitz and Joanne Grant, 11 July 1990. Taber certainly was an experienced reporter. He told the Eastland Committee on 5 May 1960 that he had worked for CBS 'off and on' for ten years, and previously had written for various newspapers around New York, including Long Island's *Newsday*. See U.S. Congress, Senate, Committee on the Judiciary, *Fair Play for Cuba Committee, Hearings Before the Subcommittee to Investigate the Administration of the Internal Security Act and Other Internal Security Laws of the Committee on the Judiciary of the United States Senate*, 87th Congress, First Session, Washington, D.C.: U.S. Government Printing

Office, 1961, p. 13 (hereafter *Fair Play for Cuba Committee, SISC*).

7. This is a quote from a history of Fair Play and the SWP's involvement written by Berta Green for internal party education sometime in the 1970s, hereafter referred to as Berta Green Party History (BGPH).

8. Interview with Saul Landau, 31 May 1989. As Landau put it, the whole idea of Fair Play for Cuba was 'probably something Fidel said one day'.

9. *New York Times*, 31 December 1959; Robert Taber, 'Castro's Cuba', *The Nation*, 23 January 1960.

10. 'Report of Richard Gibson, Acting Executive Secretary, to the First National Conference of the Fair Play for Cuba Committee, July 1–2, 1961', in Berta Green Papers (hereafter BGP).

11. Interview with Alan Sagner, 25 June 1990.

12. This letter was handed over to the Eastland Committee by Beals. See *Fair Play for Cuba Committee, SISC*, 29 April 1960, p. 3. Despite an abject performance before the senators, Beals continued his association with FPCC, giving major speeches at events in New York and Chicago that fall (see *Fair Play*, 2 September 1960). Around the same time, Sagner gave his own public version of events. After describing how, 'in common with many other Americans I was disturbed and confused this winter by the unfavorable reports in the papers concerning Castro's Cuba', he explained his getting together with Taber and Frank: 'Our motive was one of simple humanitarianism for the Cuban people, who have suffered so long; but even more, the selfish devotion to our own nation, which was being led into following a policy that we felt in the long run would impair its peaceful and prosperous way of life. Waldo Frank, Taber and I wrote to people we knew personally, or knew about, who had a reputation for devotion to liberal causes, without regard to their political beliefs or even their views on Cuba. All we asked was their support of our position to present the facts that were not getting to the public. We have not taken a position of unqualified support of Castro's government, but are solely dedicated to the premise that small and underprivileged countries be allowed to solve their peculiar problems, both social and economic, without undue pressure' (a statement in response to the rightwing columnist George Sokolsky, reprinted in *Fair Play*, 6 May 1960).

13. Letter, Richard Gibson to Gosse, 24 September 1989.

14. *Fair Play*, 29 April 1960.

15. Ibid.

16. Ibid.

17. Sagner interview, 25 June 1990. The ad, asking for 'a new constructive clear-sighted foreign policy' in the language of liberalism, was distributed to delegates as 'An Open Letter' (in BGP).

18. *New York Times*, 20 July 1960.

19. Privately, of course, the shift had been taken much earlier, with Allen Dulles's approval in December 1959 of tentative plans for the 'elimination of Fidel Castro', and Ike's final go-ahead for an exile invasion in March 1960. Throughout the year, however, the president underscored to his subordinates that 'the main thing was not to let the U.S.'s hand show' (see Morley, *Imperial State and Revolution*, pp. 95–8).

20. In May 1960, the major oil corporations were told by the Department of State's Roy Rubottom that they 'should feel free to exert pressure on Castro', and subsequent high-level meetings underline how deliberate this strategy was (see Morley, *Imperial State and Revolution*, pp. 102–4). Originally, the Democrats on the House Agriculture Committee saw themselves representing consumers who would have to pay higher prices for sugar, and voted to keep the quota. However, in light of the refinery nationalizations and Republican Congressional Chairman William Miller labelling this vote 'pro-Castro' and a 'bonus for Communism', they rapidly changed their minds. Rep. Thomas Abernethy assured Secretary of State Herter, 'I would like to ask you, sir, what quantity can I vote for and not be regarded as being a Communist or voting for Communism? [Laughter] I am serious about this. It is not funny. I will vote for whatever you think, or whatever you assure me will not be a Communist vote' (quoted in Zeitlin and Scheer, *Cuba: Tragedy in Our Hemisphere*, pp. 179–80).

21. Nathaniel Weyl, *Red Star over Cuba: The Russian Assault on the Western Hemisphere*, New York: Devin-Adair, 1960, pp. 36, 50, 91.

22. Gallup, *The Gallup Poll*, vol. 3, *1935–1971*, pp. 1680–81.

23. *Fair Play*, 29 April 1960. These early issues consisted mainly of rebuttals to newspaper stories and reprints of articles that Taber found enlightening. In many ways, the earliest conception

of FPCC resembles the 'media watchdog' information centers later common on both right and left.

24. This prefigures the subsequent history of US radicalism, as the preponderance of non-party socialists and others since the 1960s, abetted by the multiplication of 'vanguards' or mini-parties, is the clearest point of demarcation from the old labor-left of the century's first half that was centered first by the Socialist Party and later by the Communist Party.

25. See the notes from an internal SWP class at UC-Berkeley on 17 December 1978. The lecturer, former FPCC leader Asher Harer, offered a chronology in which the SWP supported the struggle against Batista, despite Castro's being a 'bourgeois democrat', and then supported the revolution's 'positive acts' in 1959, eventually forming a 'defence committee – Fair Play for Cuba'. The party then arrived at the 'theoretical position' that it was a 'Workers and Peasants Government' that 'didn't know Trotsky's findings' about the Permanent Revolution. Still, he concluded, the 'law operated – Forced Rev. Forward'. Thus, the 26th of July Movement was made Trotskyist-in-spite-of-itself and the SWP's equivocal position towards Cuba was effaced.

26. This was her term; officially she was secretary of the New York chapter and, without any official title, worked full-time in the national office – which did not exist until she opened it in October 1960. The range of Green's tasks are indicated by a single item in her later notes, 'Some Aspects of FPCC Work': 'Organized fund-raising and fund-raising committees banquet, benefits, receptions, NY meetings; picket lines, buttons and leaflets, arranged posting of leaflets, ads etc. Spoke at public meetings when no one else available. Arranged literature publications, wrote chapter newsletter and natl newsletter, handled correspondence that required special attn., arranged for press releases at appropriate times (enlisted various people to help write releases, leaflets, etc.) Newspaper ads.'

27. BGPH, and interview with Berta Green, 6 July 1989. It should be noted that all other sources, written and oral, agree on her central role. I am also indebted to Asher Harer, who put me in contact with Berta Green and provided me with documents, hereafter cited as Asher Harer Papers (AHP).

28. See Grant's extremely close-mouthed appearance before the Eastland Committee (*Fair Play for Cuba Committee, SISC,* 10 October 1960, p. 74) where the earlier testimony about her is cited, along with her leadership in the US delegations for the 1957 and 1959 World Youth Festivals. Following the former a group of US students illegally went to the People's Republic of China, and subsequently Grant's passport was revoked (a picture of Grant and others singing songs with Chou En-Lai was included in the hearing record).

29. In 1961 Stuart published Taber's still useful account of the 1957–58 struggle, *M-26: Biography of a Revolution,* as well as a highly successful version of *History Will Absolve Me* with an introduction by Taber, and various other 'pro-Cuban' books, alongside his usual list of erotic novels and other outré materials, all of which led the Eastland Committee to make a quite explicit equation of FPCC with 'pornography' when they interrogated him years later; see U.S. Congress, Senate, Committee on the Judiciary, *Castro's Network in the United States (Fair Play for Cuba Committee), Hearing Before the Subcommittee to Investigate the Administration of the Internal Security Act and Other Internal Security Laws of the Committee on the Judiciary of the United States Senate,* 88th Congress, First Session, Washington, D.C.: U.S. Government Printing Office, 1963, 8 February 1963, pp. 325ff (hereafter *Castro's Network, SISC*).

30. This account is based on the Berta Green Party History, an interview with Green, a joint interview with Rabinowitz and Grant, and Stuart's very frank three-part series on FPCC in the September, October and November 1961 issues of his newspaper, *The Independent.* In essence, these sources agree, with the significant proviso that Rabinowitz vehemently denies that his involvement represented the CP's interests, since he was already distancing himself from the Party at this point ('I was acting all the time on my own. ... I was on speaking terms with lots of people who were personal friends, but so far as the organization was concerned, I was not connected with it in any organizational sense') though he found it quite understandable that both he and Grant 'were identified by Berta ... as CP. No question about that. I had been for many years very active in almost every Party operation that anyone can think of. ... There's no doubt that lots of people viewed me as a representative or speaking for, or aligned in some way with the Communist Party.' Rather than any factional defeat, Rabinowitz ascribes his own abrupt resignation from FPCC to the Cuban government's retaining his firm as their US lawyers, which he felt implied a possible conflict of interest. Evidently Grant and others did leave under some pressure and feeling considerable anger, though as she put it, 'We weren't an organized force working against them.' She went

on to a long involvement as activist, author and filmmaker with the Student Nonviolent Coordinating Committee and later civil rights and black organizing efforts.

31. According to the *New York Times*, 22 July 1960, 260 people attended this meeting, where Taber claimed FPCC had 2,000 members nationally.

32. BGPH.

33. Richard Gibson to author, 24 September 1989; BGPH; and Green interview. In the latter Green remarked that the SWP's leadership had not been interested in Fair Play, and only begrudgingly permitted her to take on a main role in its national operation (a point not made in the internal lecture when she was still a party member). It is important to note that the CP was not excluded from FPCC, but rather as an organization chose to stay away, though clearly many members or former members involved themselves anyway – which did lead to the sort of complicated factional conflict described here. Michael Myerson, then not a member but close to the CP, has suggested that the Party never pursued 'any major involvement in Fair Play' because of its basic suspicions regarding the Cubans, at least until the Missile Crisis in late 1962, when Castro became clearly aligned with the Soviet Union (Myerson interview, 16 May 1992). Victor Rabinowitz notes that 'directly contrary to what Green says ... I was looked upon with some disapproval by the Communist Party structure because I was consorting with or dealing with Green and Gibson, who were viewed as enemies.' Gibson reports that he often met with black Party leaders such as Claude Lightfoot and William Patterson, who he says remained critical of the Cubans, seeing affinities between *fidelismo* and 'Trotskyite adventurism'. He emphasizes that 'the Communists were personally invited by me to participate in FPCC as *loyal* partners'.

34. Supplemental notes from Berta Green entitled 'Some Aspects of FPCC Work' and 'FPCC and SWP' indicate that in fact much of her party was quite tardy in backing this effort. Not only did she have to 'discourage advances of many (SWP leaders apparently regarded my success at organizing FPCC a result of my imagined promiscuity)' but 'as more SWP members drawn into activity, official SWP bodies, esp. the NY local, resented this competition and regarded it as detrimental' to their other work (in BGP).

35. Gibson letter, 24 September 1989. He had begun as a trainee reporter with the *Afro-American* in Philadelphia, and then received a fellowship to study literature in Rome in 1951. Gibson's extensive European experience (he wrote a novel and did publicity work for the Italian film industry) and personal knowledge of the Algerian FLN gave him 'the experience that most black journalists could not then have got if they had remained in the States. I had languages, travel and media experience.' In a later letter, he admitted proudly to having been 'an agent of influence' of the FLN, which led to the so-called 'Gibson affair' (see Michel Fabré, *The Unfinished Quest of Richard Wright*, New York: William Morrow, 1973, for a very hostile account, considerably modified in Fabré's *From Harlem to Paris: Black American Writers in France*, Urbana, Ill.: University of Illinois Press, 1991). The overtones of this nasty fight in the expatriate community, involving Richard Wright and others, followed Gibson to New York and led some Communists to spread the story that he was an *agent provocateur*. In 1985 Gibson won an action for libel in London against Penguin Books because the book *Inside BOSS* by ex–South African spy Gordon Winter alleged that he had been utilized by the CIA (Gibson to author, 9 April 1992, including a copy of the court's finding).

36. He and Taber.were forced to resign from CBS in the summer of 1960, apparently due to pressure from the powerful Senator Harry Byrd of Virginia, but Gibson managed to hang onto a CBS Fellowship in African Affairs at Columbia University for the 1960–61 school year.

37. Gibson to author, 24 September 1989.

38. The ads are reprinted in *Communist Threat*, *SISC*, 5 June 1961, p. 322.

39. See *Chicago Defender*, 4 and 11 June 1960; *Fair Play*, 10 June 1960, includes a reprint of Jackie Robinson's column in the *New York Post* defending Louis, and much else.

40. 'Dear Friend' letter, 6 November 1960, from Berta Green, sent to New York FPCCers, plus Press Release, no date, claiming that more than 1,000 attended the event, in BGP.

41. Quoted in *Fair Play*, 25 October 1960.

42. FPCC Press Release, 30 June 1961, responding to a 29 June Associated Press story on Brigadier Birdsong's allegations.

43. *Fair Play for Cuba Committee*, *SISC*, 25 April 1961, p. 148.

44. *Daily News*, 21 September 1960. The contemporary public mood can be gauged by the *Daily News* report that Long Islanders protesting the Soviets' purchase of an estate and Khrush-

chev's arrival burned Fidel in effigy 'as an afterthought'.

45. Ibid., 24 September 1960.

46. The account below is based, in general, on daily accounts in the *New York Times*, 21 to 27 September 1960, in conjunction with the Baltimore *Afro-American*, 1 October 1960. Specific incidents not covered by the *Times* are noted separately.

47. *New York Times*, 21 September 1960.

48. The quotation and the crowd estimate are from the *Afro-American*, 1 October 1960.

49. *New York Times*, 21 September 1960.

50. *Afro-American*, 1 October 1960. Even among black journalists, however, reactions varied considerably. In this same issue of the *Afro*, one reporter, Ray Boone, actually provided more evidence of suspicion or plain disinterest in Castro than did the *Times*. Fidel paid serious attention to the black press, itself exceptional in those days, and proved a master of the appropriate one-liner: 'We feel here like we would in our country. ... I belong to the poor, humble people. ... I think this is a big lesson for people who practice discrimination.'

51. *Afro-American*, 21 and 25 September 1960.

52. *Fair Play*, 7 October 1960; Carlos Franqui, *Family Portrait with Fidel*, p. 90; Karol, *Guerrillas in Power*, p. 7.

53. *New York Times*, 26 September 1960. Powell had earlier announced that he was inviting Nasser, Kwame Nkrumah of Ghana and Sékou Touré of Guinea to visit him in Harlem in what the *Times* described as an effort to offset Castro's presence: none of them responded.

54. *Afro-American*, 1 October 1960.

55. Gibson to author, 5 August 1992. An FBI informant reported that Malcolm X belonged to a Harlem committee formed to greet any UN delegates from new African countries, and that he chose to put Castro under this rubric. A later report from someone 'who made available the names and addresses of individuals in New York City who currently are on the mailing list of the FPCC' noted that the Muslim minister's entry indicated that he was a member (see Clayborne Carson, ed., *Malcolm X: The FBI File*, New York: Carroll & Graf, 1991, pp. 198, 214). My account of black American solidarity with Cuba, including Malcolm X's role, is sharply at odds with the version of events by Carlos Moore, most recently in his book *Castro, the Blacks and Africa*, Los Angeles: Center for Afro-American Studies, University of California, 1988. Moore was an FPCC member in New York, and later worked with Robert F. Williams in Cuba. The problem with his various startling claims (for example, that Cuban Intelligence in the early 1960s had a 'clandestine effort' to recruit US blacks for sabotage) is a complete lack of evidence other than the author's memory of things people told him long ago, combined with many errors of fact – for example, that Josephine Baker and Richard Wright were members of FPCC, or that Roy Campanella and Jackie Robinson participated in the Christmas 1959 junket. Though Moore insists that Malcolm X was highly critical of the Cuban revolution, there is ample evidence that his solidarity stayed constant. During his Africa tour some years later, Malcolm went to the Cuban embassy in Ghana to talk over old times (Peter Goldman, *The Death and Life of Malcolm X*, Urbana, Ill.: University of Illinois Press, 1979, p. 175). A collection of his later speeches is filled with emphatically positive references to the Cuban revolution (George Breitman, ed., *Malcolm X Speaks*, New York: Grove Press, 1965, pp. 9, 44, 68, 150, 163, 220; also Bruce Perry, ed., *Malcolm X: The Last Speeches*, New York: Pathfinder, 1989, pp. 72–3, 162–3). Most obviously, at the 29 December 1964 public meeting of the Organization of Afro-American Unity at the Audubon Ballroom, Malcolm read a telegram from Che Guevara, an invited speaker who at the last moment could not come, and commented: 'I love a revolutionary.' He added, 'And you don't see any anti-Castro Cubans around here – we eat them up' (*Malcolm X Speaks*, p. 102). For a more detailed examination of the encounter between Castro and Malcolm X, with many fine photographs, see Rosemari Mealy, *Fidel and Malcolm X: Memories of a Meeting*, New York: Ocean Press, 1993.

56. Reprinted in Kempton, *America Comes of Middle Age: Columns 1950–1962*, New York: Viking, 1963, p. 115.

57. Clearly this drive was opposed, and those who enlisted did so knowing that there might be considerable repercussions. A decade's worth of FBI attention to James Baldwin was instigated by his signing the April 1960 *New York Times* advertisement for Fair Play as a favor to his associate from Paris, Richard Gibson (see James Campbell, *Talking at the Gates: A Life of James Baldwin*, New York: Viking, 1991, pp. 167–8). Similarly, Langston Hughes was extremely disturbed by a false report in the *New York Times*, *New York Post* and *Time* that he had dined with Castro at the

Theresa, and publicly denied any such association, later refusing to sign an ad denouncing the Bay of Pigs invasion despite a plea from old friend Nicolás Guillén (see Arnold Rampersad, *The Life of Langston Hughes,* vol. 2, *1941–1967: I Dream a World,* New York: Oxford, 1988, pp. 323, 330–31). Nonetheless, despite his later distancing, Hughes did earlier contribute a new poem to the special edition of *Lunes de Revolución,* 'Los Negroes En La U.S.A.'

58. In one six-month period, for instance, Worthy had major *Afro* articles charting Cuba's progress on 9 and 23 July, 17 and 24 September, and 31 December 1960, and 7 and 14 January 1961; for evidence that Worthy operated within a wider current, see also the respectful review by J. Saunders Redding of Huberman and Sweezy's *Anatomy of a Revolution* in the *Afro* on 27 August 1960, minus any Red-baiting, and the 23 July *Afro* editorial, 'Cuba Is Not Red': 'Remember the White Citizens Councils and the Seggies charge that the NAACP is Communist, when it isn't.'

59. *Cleveland Call and Post,* 11 February 1961.

60. In addition, the 1958 Monroe 'kissing case', in which two black boys were jailed for kissing a white female playmate, stirred national and international attention, and it was Williams's status as their defender that helped shield him from NAACP control. Monroe and surrounding Union County were clearly one of the South's activist centers in these years; when Richard Gibson called Williams in March 1960 to ask for his name on the *New York Times* FPCC advertisement, the latter was immersed in the sit-in campaign that had started in February; later that year he ran for mayor and received a startling 99 votes.

61. See the remarks in late 1959 issues of *The Crusader,* Williams's aptly named mimeo-graphed newsletter, which reached a national audience, both white and black: 'The American white man claims to be upset by the latest developments in Cuba. Only the fool can expect to exploit and oppress peoples over an extended period of time without provoking animosity and resistance' (11 November); 'Castro and all other colored rulers will do well to shun bigoted Uncle Sam's smiling false face and his racial claims of bondage' (28 November); also the very fierce 'U.S. Gunning for Castro' (2 December). One could argue that Castro was not in fact 'colored', but in terms of how he was coming to be seen in the US at that time, Williams's placing of all Latin Americans in that category seems more telling.

62. In October 1959 at New York's Community Church, for instance, *Liberation* sponsored a debate on the question of violence, pitting Williams and Conrad Lynn, the radical civil rights attorney, against Bayard Rustin and Dave Dellinger (*The Crusader,* 19 September 1959). Throughout Williams's later public identification with Fair Play for Cuba, the NAACP pressured him to resign because of the harm this controversy was doing the organization (see letter from Gloster B. Current, director of branches, in *The Crusader,* 8 April 1961).

63. *The Crusader,* 13 August 1960 and 29 April 1961. In case the point was not entirely clear, the former had a simple cartoon of a bearded man on the cover entitled 'Fidel Castro: Spirit of Christ'.

64. *The Crusader,* 30 July 1960. He had used virtually the same words in a 28 June 1960 postcard to Berta Green: 'Really enjoying the only freedom I have ever known' (in BGP). Apparently the integrated Cuban schools made a considerable impression, as Williams had been trying without success to get his three children into Monroe's superior all-white schools.

65. *The Crusader,* 19 September 1959.

66. *The Crusader,* 17 September 1960. The allusion to a 'Black Fidel Castro' is from the 11 November 1961 *Crusader,* restarted after Williams was in Cuba: a wistful reference to what might have been if Williams had been 'given more radical support'.

67. *The Crusader,* 24 July 1961.

68. This story is powerfully told in Williams's own *Negroes with Guns,* New York: Marzani & Munsell, 1961, which is essentially a series of interviews introduced by Truman Nelson, with many photographs. Harold Cruse also put Williams and the political currents that swirled around him at the center of his analysis of black New Left politics in *The Crisis of the Negro Intellectual,* New York: William Morrow, 1967, but leaves out Gibson's and FPCC's role, as will be discussed further below in relation to LeRoi Jones. The most complete version of Williams's life is Robert Carl Cohen, *Black Crusader: A Biography of Robert Franklin Williams,* Secaucus, N.J.: Lyle Stuart, 1972. The claim that it was SWPers who smuggled Williams out of the US comes from Berta Green, and differs from other versions, including Williams, as told to Cohen.

69. See *Encyclopedia of the American Left,* New York: Garland, 1990, pp. 48, 57, 95–6, 416, with various bibliographical citations.

70. C. Wright Mills, *Listen, Yankee,* New York: Ballantine Books, 1960, p. 43. It was Che Guevara, of course, who kept insistently calling for a 'new socialist man', so Mills certainly did not make this up on his own.

71. See O'Brien, 'The Development of a New Left, 1960–1965', for the best exposition of this crucial shift from apathy to activism. As he points out, the student arm of the Americans for Democratic Action disbanded in 1958, and the Communist Party did not even bother to form a new youth group in place of its dissolved Labor Youth League. As one indicator of how exceptionally reduced campus politics were in 1958–60, 'the most important radical youth organization in the U.S.', the newly revived Young Peoples Socialist League attached to the Socialist Party-Social Democratic Federation, had a grand total of 200 members (p. 60).

72. Horowitz, *Student,* p. 151.

73. See the promotional article in the *Chicago Defender,* 11 June 1960, suggesting that these colonies were designed for black students primarily, with a US address; also *New York Times,* 10 August 1960 ('Cuba Eases Rates for U.S. Students') for a report on the colonies and their promotion here. The latter noted that only one was operating, but more students were expected from Hunter and elsewhere. A 21 September 1960 *Times* article, 'Castro Is Seeking Negroes' Support', summed up the wide range of black activism and Cuban efforts involving Joe Louis, Robert F. Williams, Fair Play for Cuba, and even how *Lunes de Revolución*'s special issue was 'widely distributed throughout the country, in particular at Negro colleges and universities'. It stated that 'numerous student groups, usually mixed groups including Negroes, have visited Cuba as guests of the Government', listing Hunter, City College, Antioch, St Johns and Stanford. See also the *Daily Cardinal* of the University of Wisconsin at Madison, 21 July 1960, for an alarmed editorial 'Comment' about the volume of Cuban literature received, and a 21 September 1960 article ('Cuban Peasants Content, Visiting UW Student Says') about Seymour Arnstein, who spent a week with room and board paid; a similar article by Steven Kenin, in the *Temple University News,* 20 October 1960, was reprinted in FPCC's *Student Council,* 4 November 1960.

74. Interview with Marvin Gettleman, 14 January 1992.

75. Ibid.

76. Interview with Barbara Garson by Ronald Grele, 12 August 1984, in Oral History Research Office, Columbia University.

77. Ibid.

78. Letter, Christopher and Linda Salter to Matthews, 21 September 1960, in HLMP; see also the report by 'two young students' just returned from the island, Edward Friedman and Richard Kraus, in the Winter 1961 *Dissent,* probably the most pro-Castro piece that journal ever published.

79. It is worth noting that the idea of 'fair play' proved untranslatable. The Cubans usually referred to it as the Comité Pro Justo Trato Para (sometimes Hasta) Cuba, roughly the 'Committee for Just Treatment Towards Cuba'. This is a good literal translation, but it misses the resonances of gamesmanship and reciprocity, in the Protestant sense of doing unto others, summoned up in the almost archaic term 'fair play' (as in 'turn-about is fair play', or in the later, cruder North American idiom, 'what goes around comes around'). Justice is after all hardly synonymous with fairness, and 'treatment' is not at all the same as 'play'. In FPCC's original formulation, the name suggested that Yankees needed to be aware of what they had done to Cuba over the past sixty years, especially in backing Batista, so as to understand if not necessarily approve of Cuban anger and radicalism. It was on these terms that many liberals joined, out of a certain prickly solidarity that refused to define itself as 'pro-Castro'. 'If you go to Cuba today, no one will recognize it. Cubans never did, not having a counterpart for such a sporting expression. ... They could not, you see, consider the struggle against the colossus *yanqui* as a game'. Letter, Taber to Gosse, 23 January 1992.

80. Malcolm Sylvers, 'Memories from the Periphery', in Paul Buhle, ed., *History and the New Left: Madison, Wisconsin, 1950–1970,* Philadelphia, Temple University Press, 1990, p. 184. This collective memoir is an indispensable reference for the politics and the cultural ethos of the new university left in its formative stage.

81. *Studies on the Left,* vol. 1, no. 3 (1960), pp. 1, 3.

82. Ibid., p. 16.

83. Sweezy and Huberman had been staking out a premature New Leftism for a decade, but had little interest in Cuba during or after the guerrilla war until they visited Cuba in early 1960, intrigued by the Agrarian Reform. The subsequent articles in *Monthly Review*'s July/August 1960

issue was immediately issued in book form, and have gone through many editions. Before anybody else (and well before Castro), they unequivocally declared Cuba to be a socialist state, and this socialism-in-deed was anatomized as uniquely innovative and participatory. The most famous, controversial and revelatory passage of the book, however, was their assertion of what was already obvious: 'For the first time, a socialist revolution has been made without the Communist party.'

84. See their respective reminiscences in Buhle, ed., *History and the New Left.*

85. The third issue of *Student Council,* dated 9 December 1960, describes Landau speaking to crowds of 350 at Madison, 250 at the University of Minnesota, and 100 at the University of Iowa; the first issue (4 November) lists a very lengthy itinerary for Taber's appearances in the second half of October, also before large crowds.

86. *Chicago Maroon,* 28 October and 11 November 1960.

87. See a letter in the *Cornell Daily Sun,* 5 January 1961, describing in detail a 'public meeting' just before the Christmas break at which Landau spoke, along with a Cornell graduate student who had been to the island and showed his slides. Cornell was roughly equivalent to Chicago in intellectual prestige, and witnessed that fall only slightly more visible activism on Cuba. Some members of the *Sun's* editorial board, such as Robert Starobin and Peter Geismar, did battle with others taking an anti-Castro line, and Professor Walter LaFeber, a student of Appleman Williams, gave a talk on 'Foreign Policy in the 1960 Election', stressing that the US must learn 'how to live with radical revolution in an age of radical revolution' (see *Sun,* 28 and 29 September, 3 and 4 October, 17, 22, 29 and 30 November, 12 December). The same FPCC press release on the Christmas tour ran as an article on 28 November.

88. See the *Daily Californian,* 20 September 1960, on a SLATE noon rally attended by 250 students where the featured speaker was SWP presidential candidate Farrell Dobbs, whose campaign was vociferously pro-Castro, and 22 September 1960, on how the day before 'well over a hundred students crowded Stiles Hall ... to take part in the organization of the 'Student Fair Play for Cuba' committee ... completely independent of campus, national or political groups' (though it was suggested that this group 'may affiliate with the International Play Fair Committee headed by French philosopher Jean-Paul Satre [sic], French novelist Simone de Beauvoir, and Columbia University scholar C. Wright Mills'). Most later references to this Berkeley group describe it as the 'U.C. Cuba Forum' (as in Horowitz's *Student!*) or the 'Student Forum on Cuba', suggesting the need to maintain some distance from FPCC given the Berkeley administration's prohibitions on involvement with off-campus partisan issues, as well as the desire for autonomy.

89. Other than a few student letters, the *Swarthmore Phoenix* had nothing on Cuba until the issue of 6 December, which reported on a group petition to drive a truck to Miami and catch FPCC's chartered plane. A 9 December article on William Worthy coming to campus to discuss Cuba mentioned that this would be 'a preview of the upcoming Cuba weekend on 16–17 December', which included Fred Bronner of Columbia speaking Friday on the 'Historical Prerequisites of Revolution', plus two FPCC films *and* a speech by Leo Huberman of *Monthly Review,* followed by an unnamed 'journalist just returned' from Cuba on Saturday representing Fair Play. The students who were the leaders of this ad hoc Cuba group (including Ollie Fein, Charlotte Philips, Mimi Feingold and several others) are named as the key activists of the early sixties Swarthmore New Left in an unpublished paper by Douglas Rossinow of Johns Hopkins University (copy in author's possession).

90. Despite having a visible – and voluble – C. Wright Mills on campus, the Columbia College *Spectator* had no editorial polemics on Cuba nor did it report any relevant student activity until January 1961 (though the existence of an FPCC Student Council was reported in *Student Council*). Student newspapers can be an excellent source since they are often hungry for campus news in the most undiscriminating fashion, but they also typically reflect the predilections of one or a few editors. Relying solely on the *Daily Cardinal,* one would know nothing about Madison's Fair Players in fall 1960, other than the details of Landau's appearance before a big crowd on 31 October, where he was introduced by William Appleman Williams.

91. Since Hilton was the director of the Institute of Hispanic-American Studies at Stanford, his evidence was grudgingly given some credence, though it took months for the *New York Times* to actually cite it.

92. Leaflet in BGP.

93. *Fair Play,* 2 December 1960.

94. *Fair Play,* 16 December 1960.

95. Ibid., 31 December 1960; also Saul Landau, No "Fair Play" at Miami Airport', in the 13 January 1961 issue.

96. Ibid., 13 January 1961; *Afro-American*, 14 July 1961. According to Landau in this *Extra!* issue of *Fair Play*, most of the tour's members were students, accompanied by prominent Fair Players like Scott Nearing, Sidney Lens, Vincent Hallinan and Lyle Stuart (the latter two were named during Richard Tussey's interrogation before the Eastland Committee, *Fair Play for Cuba Committee, SISC*, 13 June 1961, p. 360). The image of such a diverse group of radicals partying together in Havana is odd, as if some perfect new unity was in the offing. The reality was rather grubbier: as Berta Green suggests, there was already jockeying for power. She remembered an FPCC leader from Chicago trying to organize a separate trip to the Sierra Maestra. For a fine, evocative description of Havana on that last Christmas, and the FPCC tour, see *Kulchur* editor Mark Schleifer's 'Cuban Notebook', *Monthly Review* (July/August 1961), pp. 72–83.

97. On the party, see Cedric Belfrage in the *National Guardian*, 16 January 1961. In the same issue, General Manager James McManus reported that with the FPCC tour and the *Guardian*'s tour as well, there were at least 600 Yankees spreading holiday good-will. See also the *New York Times*, 2 January 1961.

98. *Studies on the Left* vol. 2, no. 1 (May 1961), p. 74.

99. Reprinted in Buhle, ed., *History and the New Left*, pp. 286–8. Lee Baxandall states (p. 132) that this skit was on 9 April *1960*, when that is manifestly not the case. In the spring of 1960, JFK was not president, nor even the front-running Democratic candidate. I am presuming that the 9 April date is accurate, but for the next year, 1961.

100. Ibid., p. 287.

101. Ibid., p. 288.

6

Going South and Going Public

From its beginning, the base of the Fair Play for Cuba Committee was a hodgepodge of self-radicalizing liberals, black nationalists or those considered to be such, Trotskyists and other Old Leftists on their way into the New, and young people somewhere between a purified liberalism, neo-Marxism and all-purpose radicalism. Its civic persona, however, the face it presented to the world, was rather more uncomplicated and even elegant, thanks undoubtedly to Taber's and Fidel's calculation as to what would work in the US. Fair Play's constant assertion was to stand outside of partisan politics, as simply a band of truth-telling intellectuals – 'a group of distinguished writers, artists, journalists and professionals', in the standard formulation of FPCC press releases. It was hardly accidental that in his marathon UN speech on 21 September 1960, Castro singled out Waldo Frank and Carleton Beals, FPCC's titular chairmen, as examples of the kind of North Americans who honorably defended Cuba. This lack of ideological definition combined with the cosmopolitan aura of names like Sartre, de Beauvoir, Mailer, Capote and Baldwin was the secret of Fair Play's success, what made it so attractive to young people and such a hard target for the McCarthyite Right, what made it truly germinal to the New Left. From one perspective, these intellectuals lacked all intellectual rigor, but from another they had gained the advantages of pluralism and fluidity so signally lacking in either of the traditions, liberal and radical, that the New Left drew upon.

The reader will already have noted, however, that the Fair Play speakers' tours did not feature Truman Capote and Simone de Beauvoir, or some such luminary combination, and may conclude that the presence of 'intellectuals' was really so much window-dressing in the effort to build solidarity with Cuba. Beyond the usual mechanics of presentation, however, the Cuban revolution was a catalyst in the revival of an oppositional intelligentsia, 'a political public that may offer resistance to the NATO intellectuals', in Saul Landau's prescription.[1] Since what intellectuals properly do is produce ideas and narratives and images, such a watershed is naturally harder to measure than organizational growth. To demonstrate its substance, this chapter focuses on a few key texts that together defined a new, angry role for the critical thinker, no longer proudly alienated – 'in this world but not of it' – but engaged in a way we now take for granted. None of these is unknown: C. Wright Mills's *Listen, Yankee*; 'Cuba Libre' by LeRoi Jones and a variety of other Beat efforts such as the journal *Pa'lante*; finally, Norman Mailer's tortured attempts to reconcile his two 'existential heroes', Jack Kennedy and Fidel Castro. Yet this body of writing, nearly all of which appeared in the same few months of late 1960 and early 1961, has never been seen as a whole, a common moment, rather than as odd fragments in each writer's evolution. As much as the growth of FPCC as an organization, these texts establish Fidel Castro's curious presence in the mind of America at the dawn of the New Frontier. In each case, the writing itself is about the act of physically or metaphorically going to Cuba – 'going native' it would have been called in another imperial context – and how this voyage changed, purged and made anew the writer.

'I'll Show You How to Use Those Pistols': The Journey of C. Wright Mills

The first event here is C. Wright Mills's *Listen, Yankee:* the book itself, its bestselling status, how he came to write it and with whose help, and finally what it (almost) led to. Published in late November 1960, *Listen, Yankee* became the most famous example of 'going south' to soak up the revolution's sun, and it merits careful study. Its sheer popularity, as measured in sales figures and influence, mark it as one of the key radicalizing texts of this generation, ranking with *Howl!*, Martin Luther King's 'Letter from a Birmingham Jail', and *The Port Huron Statement*. More practically, it was also the first radical bestseller, foreshadowing *Soul on Ice, Sisterhood Is Powerful* and many more at the high tide of the sixties. In sum, then, *Listen, Yankee* establishes the New Left's connection to Cuba so explicitly that one is at a loss to explain its subsequent effacement. But this intervention by 'the only radical with a national reputation and a clean record', let alone Mills's membership in and the book's relationship to the Fair Play for Cuba Committee, is virtually unknown today, if current historiography is any guide.[2] *Listen, Yankee* exists only as a passing reference to a dying man's folly, cloaked in mystery or embarrassment, even in those books that otherwise celebrate Mills's intellectual and personal significance for SDS and others.

At the end of the 1950s, following a decade of trendsetting and widely read studies like *White Collar* and *The Power Elite*, Mills was weary of even his own unconventional brand of sociology and sought to go beyond the existing limits of intellectual dissent. He began to polemicize, writing 'Pagan Letter to the

Christian Clergy', *The Causes of World War III* and, above all, the 'Letter to the New Left', which first appeared in the *New Left Review* in the fall of 1960 as he was writing *Listen, Yankee,* and which came out in the US in *Studies in the Left* the next spring.

But this was not enough, given his self-definition, in Landau's words, as 'a strong man ... who would not abide the immorality over which he, as an individual, had no control.'[3] Mills decided that it was necessary to go into the world, never an easy choice for a North American scholar, least of all in an age dominated by the cant of objectivity and national consensus. At that point in US history, such a journey could only lead southwards: either below the Mason-Dixon line to the Jim Crow states, or even further, to Cuba. Mills chose the latter, because he found himself obliged to define where he stood on the revolution; he felt that one way or another he would be called to account, and ignorance was no excuse:

> Until the summer of 1960, I had never been in Cuba, nor even thought about it much. In fact, the previous fall, when I was in Brazil, and in the spring of 1960, when I was in Mexico for several months, I was embarrassed not to have any firm attitude towards the Cuban revolution. For in both Rio de Janeiro and Mexico City, Cuba was of course a major topic of discussion. But I did not know what was happening there, much less what I might think about it, and I was then busy with other studies.[4]

This astonishingly frank admission is perhaps the best explanation of why the North American left, in any of its guises, abstained on Cuba until Robert Taber, Alan Sagner and a few others stepped into the breech. Stunned by the moral and emotional demands of the Cold War, both pro-Soviet and anti-Communist radicals had lost their sense of responsibility and become fundamentally passive adherents of one or another camp, content to let others decide the line and issue the marching orders: 'I did not know what was happening there, much less what I might think about it.' But then Mills, through some personal process that remains mysterious, began to change. In a fashion characteristic of radicals in the later 1960s, this individual movement had the flavor of professional academic inquiry, in which Mills's disinclination to be simply a partisan disbeliever in the Old Left style is admitted:

> In the late spring of 1960, when I decided 'to look into Cuba', I first read everything I could find and summarized it: partly as information and partly in the form of questions to which I could find no answers in print. With these questions, and a few ideas on how to go about getting answers to them, I went to Cuba.
>
> That journey has forced me to the view – a view which for a long time I rejected – that much of whatever you have read recently about Cuba in the US press is far removed from the realities and the meaning of what is going on in Cuba today.[5]

Here is where the role of Fair Play for Cuba and a climate of solidarity developing among the new radical intellectuals become crucial. Without either of these, as stimulus and to smooth the way, Mills might have wanted to 'look into Cuba', but almost certainly would have gotten nowhere. In August of that year, he criss-crossed the island, interviewing 'rebel soldiers and intellectuals, officials, journalists and professors', including 'three and a half 18-hour days with Prime Minister Fidel Castro', he explains at the beginning of *Listen, Yankee*. Tucked away in the acknowledgements are Mills's thanks to 'Saul Landau, U.S.A., who shared with me the results of his own astute experience of Cuba; Robert Taber, U.S.A., who facilitated my trip to Cuba and my work while there.'[6] Actually, Taber had introduced Mills to Landau upon the former's arrival in Havana. Landau recalled that

> he wasted no time. After the briefest of amenities he began to pump me. About four hours later he had all I knew about Cuba. ... His bush jacket was stained under his arms. He reminded me of Hemingway.[7]

Taber had already agreed to spend two weeks guiding Mills around Cuba, presumably facilitating his exceptional access to revolutionary leaders by explaining the potential to influence large numbers in the US.[8] The relationships did not end there: Landau was Mills's editor at Ballantine Books that fall, while simultaneously setting in motion the campus network that would crystallize into action the excitement caused by *Listen, Yankee*, and in 1961 accompanied Mills on his final European *exilio* before the latter's premature death at age forty-six in March 1962.

By the time of his return from Cuba, Mills had conceived of a new kind of popular book, the kind of tract that would fit his new role as a freethinking agitator, in the manner of Tom Paine or William James.[9] In six weeks or less, working sixteen hours a day from copious tapes and notes, he had assembled *Listen, Yankee*, planned as a cheap (50 cents) paperback to ensure the widest possible distribution.[10] Very quickly in the fall and winter of 1960–61, it became a runaway hit, selling 400,000 copies, inspiring thousands of letters to Mills, and proving as much as all the Fair Play delegations, demonstrations and newspaper ads put together that in the marketplace of desire, Cuba retained a potent base of interest and hope in the US.

In retrospect, it is the narrative style of *Listen, Yankee* that proved most controversial. Book-ended by two 'Notes to the Reader', and a short but useful bibliography (listing *Fair Play* next to *Business Week, Foreign Affairs* and *The Wall Street Journal*), the core of the book is eight 'Letters' in which Mills speaks in the voice of the Cubans he had met. This proved to be one of the most nervy devices for bringing 'the other side' home in modern memory, and the main reason he was attacked for sinking to 'rhetorical wind' and 'narrative trickery'; the book has been, in effect, read out of his life's work by Mills's former admirers, whether his old friend Irving Howe in the early 1960s or his biographer, the latter-day neoconservative Irving Louis Horowitz, at the end of the 1980s.[11] Indeed, *Listen, Yankee* might have survived much better as part of the recognized Mills *oeuvre* if he had assumed a properly academic third-person voice, and assembled an apparatus of scholarly proof to establish the non-Communist orientation of the 26th of July Movement, the poor motives and bad faith of the exiles, and the real nature of the Cubans' relationship to the Soviets. Instead, he produced a witty, vernacular polemic, a kind of contructed 'oral history' long before that genre achieved scholarly legitimacy via books like Theodore Rosengarten's *All God's Dangers* or Nell Painter's *The Narrative of Hosea Hudson*, and a host of films built on careful editing of aged radicals' recollections like *The Wobblies, Rosie the Riveter, Union Maids* and *Seeing Red.*

A reading in the present, taking him at his word, suggests that Mills almost naively chose what seemed an appropriate methodology to secure his basic intent. In the prefatory 'Note to the Reader', he explained himself in scholarly tones: 'My major aim in this book is to present the voice of the Cuban revolutionary, as clearly and as emphatically as I can, and I have taken up this aim because of its absurd absence from the news of Cuba available in the United States today.'[12] Once one enters into the main body of the book, however, its sound shifts drastically, as Mills's Cuban says any number of things calculated to outrage the sensibilities of liberal intellectuals in the US:

> We Cuban revolutionaries don't really know just exactly *how* you could best go about this transforming of your Yankee imperialism. For us, with our problems, it was simple: In Cuba, we had to take to our 'Rocky Mountains' – you couldn't do that, could you? Not yet, we suppose.
>
> (We're joking – we suppose. But if in ten years, in five years – if things go as we think they might inside your country, if it comes to that, then know this, Yankee: some of us will be with you. God almighty, those are great mountains!)[13]

It is this snide, wisecracking informality that obviously sets *Listen, Yankee* off from any academic text, and has drawn the most contempt – plus the fact that this was 1960, not 1970, and with the sole exception of Robert F. Williams, not even the most angry young men talked about going into the hills here in this fashion, let alone eminent Ivy League professors. Still, this passage of *ex tempore* advice, for all its staginess, avoids the sentimental pathos that Hemingway imposed upon Latin revolutionaries in *For Whom the Bell Tolls* and elsewhere, and much of *Listen, Yankee* approximates the rapid-fire intimacy and asides of Castro's speeches, and the sound of 'everyday Spanish' as spoken by political agitators when translated into 'everyday English'. Perhaps the problem for Mills's critics was, ultimately, their provincialism and their discomfort with a Cuban voice. The language used in *Listen, Yankee* was all too American, in the broadest sense, for those large sections of the academic and even socialist intelligentsia whose Europhilism ran deep.

In the end it made no difference how much Mills returned to a quiet and reasoned tone in the final 'Note to the Reader', carefully establishing that however much he agreed with the Cubans and was 'for the revolution', he was still a Yankee, with his own concerns separate from theirs. He had committed an unpardonable offense, conduct unbecoming a member of his caste, by publicly shoving this rude, gossipy Cuban into the face of liberal America, an act equivalent to bringing a foulmouthed thug, shouting in some foreign language, into a faculty meeting and forcing one's colleagues to suspend their business and listen. It was degrading, though Mills himself never seemed to feel degraded, and hereafter reveled in his role as iconoclast. It seems that Cubans were meant to be seen and not heard – even undergraduates might read such a thing and, worse yet, quote it! Worst of all, Mills had put into his Cuban's mouth some acute commentary about those circles (Columbia University, *Dissent*, the New York intellectuals at large) with which he was long associated. After noting that youth from all over the world have come to see Cuba, his archetypal revolutionary repeatedly asks, where are the North American students?

> Maybe they've read too much of what some of your intellectuals have written about the Cuban revolution ... the highly intelligent, sophisticated reflections and reportage of liberals, and especially of those ex-radicals who at least verbally cling to socialist kinds of ideals, but when you get down to it do not dare to get their hands dirty and so refuse to confront the real issues and the terrible problems that every revolution in the hungry world poses and demands, the issues and the problems that we Cubans are facing.
>
> We have read what some of these weary, know-it-all, Yankee intellectuals have written about the Cuban revolution. The truth about them *is* simple: they have been hurt personally by their own past attempts to be political men in your country. And now they are living inside these old hurts, and they are blinded by them. It makes them live inside their own little hesitations and cruel fears, and at times grief, because they can make no real commitment.
>
> Who are they to assume such a posture before the facts of our revolution in Cuba? By what miraculous insight do they *know* that it must end in terror and grief, as they suggest it will? When they come to Cuba, when they think about Cuba, they're not experiencing anything or anybody in Cuba. They are experiencing, once again, for the hundredth time, the failure of themselves as political men and as intellectuals.[14]

These were hard words that cut close to the bone of the 'anti-Stalinist' left, and Mills would not be forgiven. He had in truth written a book as much about the US and Cold War liberalism as about Cuba, though it was hardly perceived at the time. But the damage was done, as copies proliferated on campuses, not coincidentally just as Fair Play for Cuba approached its zenith.

In tacit recognition of this surfacing of solidarity, an NBC television debate on US policy in Latin America was scheduled for the evening of 10 December 1960 between Mills and Adolf A. Berle, Jr, the pre-eminent New Deal intellectual, diplomat and imperialist; this was within days of ABC showing William Worthy's apocalyptic 'Yanki, No' film, also in prime time. Again, Mills's role here was not simply as an individual, but as the recognized spokesman for a recognizable constituency. According to Berta Green, NBC called the Fair Play for Cuba office seeking a speaker, and FPCC convinced Mills to take the 'pro-Castro' position in the debate. But hinting at the abortive quality of Cuba solidarity at the beginning of the sixties, Mills suffered a sudden heart attack before this perfect confrontation between the old and the new could take place. Instead, Rep. Charles Porter, just defeated for re-election and by no means 'pro-Castro', served as a pale substitute, with Professor Robert Alexander serving as moderator.

The unrealized potential of a prime time Berle-Mills confrontation underlines how in just two years Cuba had destabilized the evasive consensus binding many liberals, Social Democrats and radicals to the Democratic Party and the Cold War. In 1958, Berle had been the principal honoree at the annual New York banquet of the Inter-American Association for Democracy and Freedom (IADF), the organization which then counted itself the strongest US advocate of Fidel Castro, in which Robert Alexander (also a ranking leader of the Socialist Party) played a key role. By 1960, the ideological spectrum on Cuba had widened so rapidly that the IADF had moved completely into the camp of counter-revolution, after several months of evasion. In coded language it urged a less drastic intervention, with different actors, than the invasion the CIA was widely known to be assembling.[15] Berle, the hope of the liberals for an enlightened Latin American policy with the incoming Democratic administration, headed President-elect Kennedy's pre-inaugural Latin America Task Force, which also included Alexander. In the new administration, Berle continued to head this now official Task Force. His duties included ministering to the CIA-sponsored Cuban Revolutionary Council in the months before the Bay of Pigs, often assisted by another IADF stalwart, the historian Arthur Schlesinger, Jr, now special assistant to the president.

Subsequently, Mills continued to defend Cuba until his untimely death in 1962, though Harvey Swados was to claim in an oft-cited *Dissent* memorial for their erring comrade that he underwent an agonizing reappraisal at the end, given Castro's tilt towards Marxism-Leninism.[16] Yet even this question of Mills's final stance is effaced in historical treatments of his effect on the early New Left. He can hardly be left out completely. His influence as a radical thinker, seen by many as an alternative to Marx, is indisputable; Tom Hayden, in particular, wrote a master's thesis on Mills after leaving the presidency of SDS. Yet *Listen, Yankee* is made to stand alone outside the movement of which it was a part (when the book is mentioned at all), as an inexplicable fall from the heights of scholarship. In fact, his example in going to Cuba went far in sanctioning active solidarity, and this is the reason why *Listen, Yankee* made people uncomfortable then and is treated gingerly now. Even before the Vietnam War put an inchoate awareness of imperialism at the center of US politics, Irving Howe was holding Mills accountable for planting a pernicious seed as 'the idol of an international political tendency, the authoritarian left'.[17] Howe was surely right; minus the polite facade of his 'Notes to the Reader', Mills had meant every biting word and in that sense Saul Landau's epigraph a few years later that he 'died a revolutionary' was only a different way of saying the same thing. Trying to explain how 'the big thing in our consciousness' at Berkeley 'was the Cuban Revolution', Maurice Zeitlin later remembered how

> in this poll that SLATE took ... a quarter of the SLATEniks said, when asked to name out of the blue who most influenced them in their young life as students – it was C. Wright Mills. ... Here was this independent radical non-Communist, anti-Communist, civil libertarian revolutionary, armed struggle, anti-imperialist – I mean, he fit all the categories.[18]

Indeed, anyone doubting that the sociologist had truly set his mind to rabble-rousing should ponder a story from the Columbia College *Spectator* in late November 1960, describing how 'Mountains, machine pistols and Revolution go together these days' in Mills's classroom lectures, and quoting him giving some pungent advice:

> 'I don't know what you guys are waiting for', Mills, who hails from Waco, Texas, commented recently. 'You've got a beautiful set of mountains in those Rockies. I'll show you how to use those pistols. Why don't you get going?'[19]

In one sense this was sheer braggadocio, and ridiculous from a vantage point where we have learned to suspect masculinist self-assertion in any guise. Yet it is telling that Mills, no sentimentalist, could feel the need to say such things to his students, and that he was not saying them in a vacuum: Columbia men had ample opportunity to see the revolutionary mountains of Cuba that Christmas (though never again with such ease), and an FPCC chapter was then forming in their midst.[20] *Listen, Yankee* did what it set out to do: it caused people to listen. Mills put the intellectuals' formerly private dissent over Cuba into the mainstream and made it acceptable, perhaps even fashionable, to consider the Cubans' point of view, to hear their voices as more than an incomprehensible rant. This was 'fair play' with a vengeance. It has a final context, though, that needs to be remembered: Mills was probably the only person in the US who could have gotten away with such a performance. He had a bankable name and tenure in the Ivy League, a sizable fund of intellectual capital thrown away in one grand toss. Others with no such prestige paid a serious price. Samuel Shapiro, a young Latin Americanist publicly identified as a Fair

Play member, who wrote rather moderate articles explaining Castro in *The New Republic*, was denied reappointment at Michigan State University, and various other cases showed that summary academic punishment for pro-Castro opinions was still normal business.[21] McCarthyism may have formally ended, but it had a long afterlife, and these were years when unpopular politics could still cause career-threatening trouble. Therefore it is important to understand *Listen, Yankee* as not merely an *outré* gesture, but daring in the real sense. If Mills had lived, there would have been no turning back. In death, he deserves to be remembered for his own choices, and not those that others wished he had made.

'Camus' Rebel Down There': The Fancy of Poets

There is nothing equivalent to *Listen, Yankee* in the literary culture of the time, no grand statement of poetic or novelistic solidarity equivalent to that which Spain had inspired a generation earlier. Yet in the US the Cuban revolution did have a discernible effect upon those who had quite consciously defined themselves as rebels with no need of a cause, the so-called Beats whose 'rootlessness, unconventionality, perverse humor, and across-the-board rejection of American culture', in James O'Brien's words, had already 'portended a cultural crisis in the very heart of the middle-class' well before Castroism began to rile up certain campuses.[22]

In the long view, it may seem unexceptional that US poets, writers and other bohemians would flock to Cuba. The first glow of revolution has usually proved conducive to creative visions and aesthetic ferment, whatever comes later, and as far as that goes, literary Cuba was very lively in those early years, especially in the pages of *Lunes de Revolución*. But it bears remembering that the Beat Generation of 1950s America had been thoroughly antipolitical in its initial premises, interested exclusively in unmediated experience and perhaps liberation via sex, drink, drugs, bop and hitting the road, often to Mexico in fact. Some of the Beats were vaguely anarcho-pacifistic, but the prevailing cynicism towards political endeavors of North America's literary bohemia was summed up by one of LeRoi Jones's close friends, Gilbert Sorrentino, another young Village poet, whose response when Jones decided to go to Cuba was a terse, 'I don't trust guys in uniforms.'[23]

Jones himself was an unlikely dambreaker. 'In those days, I was not political in any conscious way, or formally political at any rate', as he put it in his memoir, and any 'political consciousness lurking' was 'somewhat submerged under the focus and banner of my attention then to Art!'[24] Jones first made his public entrance in the nearly all-white white poets' and painters' subculture of lower Manhattan and established himself as neither a black nor a political poet but a pure Beat. In 1958 he founded the magazine *Yugen* with Allen Ginsberg's assistance, which published a long list of new poets, some already famous and some who would be later.[25] Like many others, he was first impressed by Fidel in a purely personal, spontaneous fashion:

> This was 1959, the civil rights movement was rising with every headline, and for the last few months I had been fascinated by the headlines from Cuba. I had been raised on Errol Flynn's *Robin Hood* and the endless hero-actors fighting against injustice and leading the people to victory over tyrants. The Cuban thing seemed a case of classic Hollywood proportions.[26]

In a different context, Jones put this sort of attraction rather more caustically: 'He was kind of a *vaguely* romantic figure at that time. People talked *vaguely* about him.'[27] In any case, out of such imprecise sympathies and with no particular political intent – there was as yet no FPCC – Jones published a collection called *Fidel Castro, January 1, 1959* as the third 'blue plate special' of a small press he started that year. This was his sole affiliation or act of solidarity with Cuba until he was sitting around one Saturday in June 1960, drinking with the usual friends, when Richard Gibson called with an invitation to join a delegation to Cuba of black writers. Almost on a whim, feeling a creeping anomie with the bacchanalian life, Jones agreed. The result was an experience that changed him utterly, 'the turning point in my life', and a piece of writing that effectively said goodbye to Beatdom and augured the beginning of something else.[28]

Jones's long essay, 'Cuba Libre', did not appear in any out-of-the-way forum or simply spread by word of mouth. It ran in the November/December 1960 issue of *Evergreen Review*, the flagship journal of North America's avant-garde and a memorable outpost of transatlantic free thought, and it must have hit like a unexpected kick in the groin. With a rarely equaled talent for invective, he indicted himself, his former Village 'scene', at least half the members of the delegation, and ultimately all of US society, Beat and otherwise. Amid all of this sharp-eyed and sharp-tongued observation, he also managed to lay before the reader that awkward process of consciousness-raising that he and eventually thousands of North Americans would go through when they engaged personally with revolutionary situations in Latin America and the Third World. There are many other writings of this sort: Tom Hayden and Staughton Lynd's *The Other Side* about their 1965 trip to 'North' Vietnam; Marjorie and Thomas Melville's remarkable *Whose Earth? Whose People?* about two Maryknoll missionaries in Guatemala in the sixties; books by Salman Rushdie, Joan Didion, Peter Davis and many others about Central America in the 1980s. 'Cuba Libre' was the first, and perhaps the hardest, the angriest. It begins with an odd, tangled 'Preface':

> If we live all of our lives under lies, it becomes difficult to see *anything* if it does not

have anything to do with these lies. If it is, for example, true or, say, honest. The idea that things of this nature continue to exist is not ever brought forward in our minds. If they do, they seem, at their most sympathetic excursion, monstrous untruths. Bigger lies than our own. I am sorry. There are things, elements in the world, that continue to exist, for whatever time, completely liberated from our delusion.[29]

Then, under the mocking heading 'What I Brought to the Revolution', Jones tells how he was recruited by Gibson and his surprise at the very idea that a poet should go to Cuba: 'Being an American poet, I suppose, I thought my function was simply to talk about everything as if I knew ... it had never entered my mind that I might really like to find out for once what was actually happening someplace else in the world.'[30]

At the airport he meets the rest of the delegation, described in a series of vignettes as precise as they are unpleasant: 'One embarrassingly dull (white) communist, his professional Negro (*i.e.*, unstraightened hair, 1930's bohemian peasant blouses, etc., militant integrationist, etc.,) wife. ... One 1920's "New Negro" type African scholar.' But Jones is hardly less scathing about his own pretensions and *amour propre*, his pose as the man of letters unsullied by politics. On meeting the others, he was 'disappointed ... because there were no other, what I considered, "important" Negro writers.' And like many others before and after, he lands in Cuba 'extremely paranoid', armed with plans to avoid the official itinerary and see for himself: 'I was determined not to be "taken." ... I felt immediately sure that the make was on.'[31]

Gradually, Jones's disengagement and suspicion are mollified by the intensive cultural program of their host, the government's Casa de las Americas, and by the friendliness of the Cubans he meets, including Haydée Santamaria, Antonio Nuñez Jiménez and the poet Pablo Armando Fernandez. This warming is only a prelude, however, to the core of 'Cuba Libre', which builds steadily away from (and off of) Jones's depiction of his own world-weary, hipsterish disdain into something startlingly different. As he describes travelling into the Sierra Maestra with thousands of Cubans to celebrate the 26th of July at the revolution's birthplace, a series of epiphanies and then a final transformation take place. On a wild fourteen-hour train ride, Jones meets a Mexican woman, an economics graduate student and delegate to the Latin American Youth Congress in Havana, who challenges him as a poet and as a North American:

I tried to defend myself, 'Look, why jump on me? I understand what you're saying. I'm in complete agreement with you. I'm a poet ... what can I do? I write, that's all. I'm not even interested in politics.'

She jumped on me with both feet as did a group of Mexican poets in Habana. She called me a 'cowardly bourgeois individualist'. The poets, or at least one young wild-eyed Mexican poet, Jaime Shelley, almost left me in tears, stomping his foot on the floor, screaming: 'You want to cultivate your soul? In that ugliness you live in, you want to cultivate your soul? Well, we've got millions of starving people to feed, and that moves me enough to make poems out of.'[32]

Between this abuse, evidently relished in retrospect, and the feast-day joy which even unfriendly observers admit has always attended Cuban revolutionary holidays, Jones becomes more and more swept up, losing his reserve as the train is engulfed in *fidelismo*:

> What was it, a circus? That wild mad crowd. Social ideas? Could there be that much excitement generated through all the people? Damn, that people still *can* move. 'Cuba Sí, Yanqui No', I called at the girls as the train edged away.
>
> We stopped later at the town of Colon. There again the same mobs of cheering people. Camaguey. Santa Clara. At each town, the chanting crowds. The unbelievable joy and excitement. The same idea, and people made beautiful because of it. People moving, being moved. I was ecstatic and frightened. Something I had never seen before, exploding all around me. ...
>
> About two o'clock in the morning they shut the lights off in most of the coaches, and everybody went to sleep. I slept for only an hour or so and woke up just in time to see the red sun come up and the first early people come out of their small grass-roofed shacks beside the railroad tracks, and wave sleepily at the speeding train. I pressed my face against the window and waved back.[33]

Eventually, Jones climbs the mountain and finds himself sitting behind Fidel on the speakers' platform. Briefly they talk, with well-wishers and autograph-seekers pressing in, and then Jones watches Fidel orate and is, typically, moved and impressed. After the colorful ordeal of a night outdoors, they get off the mountain the next day, thirsty and dirty, and make it back to the train. Once again Jones talks to the Mexican economist for fifteen hours or more, as her fellows make a conga line up and down the train: 'She was gentler with me this time, calling me "Yanqui imperialist" only a few times.'[34] Though there are five more days on the tour, Jones ends the narrative here, with the 'painful' ideas the Sierra had inspired:

> The idea of 'revolution' had been foreign to me. It was one of those inconceivably 'romantic' and/or hopeless ideas that we Norteamericanos have been taught since public school to hold up to the cold light of 'reason.' That reason being whatever repugnant lie our usurious 'ruling class' had paid their journalists to disseminate. The reason that allows that voting, in a country where the parties are exactly the same, can be made to assume the gravity of actual moral engagement. The reason that permits a young intellectual to believe he has said something profound when he says, 'I don't trust men in uniforms.' The *residue* had settled on all our lives, and no one can function comfortably in this country without it. That thin crust of lie we cannot even detect in our own thinking. That rotting of the mind which had enabled us to think about Hiroshima as if someone else had done it, or to believe vaguely that the 'counter-revolution' in Guatemala was an 'internal' affair.[35]

His furious conclusion is like a gauntlet thrown in the face of close friends:

> The rebels among us have become merely people like myself who grow beards and will not participate in politics. Drugs, juvenile delinquency, complete isolation from the vapid mores of the country, a few current ways out. But name an alternative here. Something not inextricably bound up in a lie. Something not part of liberal stupidity or the actual filth of vested interest. There is none. It's much too late. We are an *old* people already. Even the vitality of our art is like bright flowers growing up through a rotting carcass.[36]

On his return, Jones found himself estranged – 'The arguments I'd had with my old poet comrades increased and intensified' – and 'Cuba Libre' was one product of this struggle, the other the prose piece *The System of Dante's Hell* and the poems that eventually appeared in *The Dead Lecturer*.[37] For a while, he lived a kind of double life as both poet and activist. After being arrested that summer during an impromptu Fair Play demonstration, he was elected president of FPCC's New York chapter in late 1961 as a compromise candidate, worked closely with Gibson, and helped initiate various short-lived attempts to pull together the 'downtown' black intellectuals, while writing *Blues People* and discovering a new and distinct reality as both black radical and black artist.[38]

Given Jones's own trajectory since then as a public figure on both the black and Marxist lefts, one can see in hindsight the problems with how Cuba politicized this particular poet, and he was a powerful enough writer to suggest many of them, despite himself – his undiminished arrogance towards other North Americans, including those leftists who had long 'participated in politics', however *gauche* their manners; the premonition at the essay's end of a Third Worldist dismissal of the United States ('we are an *old* people...'); the overtones of privileged tourism that always shadow trips of this kind, which to his credit Jones underlines. The contradictions of this brand of solidarity were anatomized, underlining how Jones's trip to Cuba has had a lasting resonance, in Harold Cruse's encyclopedic polemical history published seven years later, *The Crisis of the Negro Intellectual*. Cruse devoted a whole chapter to how Cuba, via Jones, spurred 'the new era of black ideological transformation, especially among the newest wave of black intellectuals':

> ...the ideology of a new revolutionary wave in the world at large, had lifted us out of the anonymity of lonely struggle in the United States to the glorified rank of visiting dignitaries. For Jones' impressionable generation this revolutionary indoctrination, this ideological enchantment, was almost irresistible. And here, vicariously, a crucial question was engendered: *What did it all mean and how did it relate to the Negro in America?* It did demonstrate incontrovertibly the relevance of force and violence to successful revolutions, especially abroad. Beyond that, neither Robert Williams who tried mightily, nor Jones' generation, have adequately explained it in Afro-American terms.[39]

As Cruse pointed out in damning detail, his question to both Williams and Jones ('What did it all mean and how did it relate to the Negro in America?') was never satisfactorily answered. Nor could it be, given that the sharp limitations on what solidarity with someone else's revolution could ever 'mean' for one's own struggle were hardly apparent in the early 1960s. It was inevitable, especially given Jones's generational contempt for what had come before, that he and others would lean on the Cuban example literally and try to be 'new men' themselves without ever becoming fully aware of the crisis they were entering.

Cruse's acid critique of Jones's experience in Cuba, however, had little to do with Jones's role in FPCC (which Cruse does not mention at all), or even the most immediate effect of 'Cuba Libre', which was not aimed at African-Americans, but at Jones's fellow poets, virtually all of them white. To the extent that Jones was known then, it was as a protégé of Allen Ginsberg and an habitué of the Cedar Tavern and similar places, and 'Cuba Libre' undoubtedly stimulated the impact of the revolution upon Bohemia, those who since the mid 1950s or before had lived a subversive individualism. Perhaps in 1960 Beatdom was simply coming to a dead end, but Cuba's very different brand of subversion played a considerable role. Any cause-and-effect is hardly clearcut, and Jones was a symptom as much as an instigator. The commitment of one relatively obscure poet would have meant little, but so many others followed Jones to Havana and took public stands that a distinctly 'Beat' air attached itself to the Fair Play movement, aided and abetted by the constant sneering references to 'that beatnik in Cuba'. Interestingly, these were to an exceptional extent the original Beats first published in *Evergreen* and associated with the City Lights bookstore and press in San Francisco. Ginsberg, their star, put their solidarity with Cuba on the map by showing up for Fair Play's reception for Castro at the Hotel Theresa in September 1960 – the mass media liked to put the two 'beards' together, and Ginsberg had perhaps the lushest and most notorious facial hair in North America proper.

The most explicit association of the Beats with Fair Play for Cuba, however, came through Lawrence Ferlinghetti, owner of City Lights, first publisher of *Howl!* and famous himself for *A Coney Island of the Mind* in 1958 (which eventually sold a half-million copies). Ferlinghetti had first heard about the Cuban revolution when he and Ginsberg were attending a cultural congress in Concepción, Chile in January 1959, and his interest steadily grew. Near the end of 1960, he went south, stopping first to see long-lost relatives in the Virgin Islands, and arriving in Cuba on 3 December, where he met Pablo Neruda and imbibed a heady climate of joyful popular sovereignty vastly different than the by-now hysterical US press reports. As he put it in 'Poet's Notes on Cuba', jottings that appeared in *Liberation* a few months later, 'Whole population seems "turned on," a kind of euphoria in the air ... Camus' Rebel down there.' Returning deeply impressed, Ferlinghetti immediately wrote and pub-

lished as a City Lights broadside his poem 'One Thousand Fearful Words for
Fidel Castro', reading it for the first time in public at the massive inaugural
rally of San Francisco Fair Play in January 1961.[40] Better than any flyer or
newspaper advertisement or memoir, it captures the mingling of hope, des-
peration and deep affection felt for Castro by many in the Fair Play movement. It is also noteworthy that it took an anarchist Beat to evoke the *fidelista*
resonances in North American history, as in Ferlinghetti's explicit homage to
Whitman and this country's nearly forgotten revolutionary tradition in the
poem's final stanzas:

> I was sitting in Mike's place, Fidel
> waiting for someone else to act
> like a good Liberal
> I hadn't quite finished reading Camus' *Rebel*
> so I couldn't quite recognize you, Fidel
> walking up and down your island
> when they came for you, Fidel
> 'My Country or Death' you told them
>
> Well you've got your little death, Fidel
> like old Honest Abe
> one of your boyhood heroes
> who also had his little Civil War
> and was a different kind of Liberator
> (since no one was shot in his war)
> and also was murdered
> in the course of human events
>
> Fidel... Fidel...
> your coffin passes by
> thru lanes and streets you never knew
> thru day and night, Fidel
> While lilacs last in the dooryard bloom, Fidel
> your futile trip is done
> yet is not done
> and is not futile
> I give you my sprig of laurel[41]

The culmination of this poetic solidarity was the founding of a League of
Militant Poets by leading New York Beats at a time when the 'fair play' movement was in rapid decline. The League published a journal called *Pa'lante:
Poetry Polity Prose of a New World* (the title is Cuban slang for 'Forward!'),
whose editor was the poet Howard Schulman, 'Advised' by Elizabeth Sutherland and José Yglesias. Its editorial statement in the first and only May 1962
issue grandly declared:

PA'LANTE is devoted to the American renaissance and the writing of a new world. This new world is the world of the future whose image may be found in the fraternal socialist countries.

PA'LANTE will be a meeting place. By publishing the guerilla [sic] writing of Latin America and new work from the socialist nations, it seeks to demolish the walls put up in fear between men's minds. By including the writing of young Americans, it affirms the bloom of art in our country as an indication of radical economic and social change to come. ...

America, we are Yankee poets who believe that socialism will make you more beautiful, hundreds of times richer, and sane. The form of communal society to which we aspire will revive your revolutionary tradition and enhance our creativity. Put your bombs away. Don't waste blood fighting history in Vietnam, Laos, Cuba. Turn with us to love, beauty, the dream of Whitman.[42]

Reading this statement, one would expect an exercise in well-meaning socialist realism, with perhaps a few avant-garde trappings: this was the period still of the Khrushchevite thaw in Soviet letters, when Solzhenitsyn's *One Day in the Life of Ivan Denisovich* was published and Yevtushenko was making a worldwide reputation as an honest voice from the 'fraternal socialist countries'. But the one issue of *Pa'lante* is a most unexpected experience. To begin with, there was something jarring about Leroy McLucas's cover photo of a trim, uniformed, almost glamorous Che Guevara, leaning against a counter somewhere with a drink at his lips and a big Western-style six-gun strapped to his waist; the pose recalled all those publicity shots of James Dean lounging enigmatically. Then, counterposed to leading Cuban poets like Nicolás Guillén and 'an authoritative Marxist document' from the First Congress of Cuban Artists and Writers, was a range of North American contributions exuding 'bourgeois decadence' and Beat weirdness, stylistically and otherwise. Michael McClure's 'Fidelio' praised the *lider maximo* with medieval imagery:

> Charming bearded singer! Make the beast's tune that precedes
> the triumphal ending of mankind's symphony.
> We hold our breath & listen to the roar.
> Your tongue is ruby meat and vibrates a new melody
> of new virtue to the starving and the poor
> Eyes are mild within your lion's face.
> A finish will come for the old lore;
> and with your clean arm and paw
> the clotted massy dishes will be swept
> and the world
> left as pure as an old dark table
> covered by a gleaming linen cloth
> so stark and warm
> it may reflect the high points of your song.[43]

Still, it is not inconceivable that however overwrought, a poem this hagiographic would have been reprinted in Moscow. John Wiener's prose piece 'Monday (In the jungle' most definitely would not. It begins

> My room. Elise drunk at the end of the bed. I watch like a hawk as she staggers from bed to table with Jim Beam in her hand. She holds it high to the male guests who ignore her. Keith has a needle in his left hand. They are shooting sleepers...[44]

Besides poems from LeRoi Jones, Joel Oppenheimer and Thomas McGrath and photographs by Robert Frank, the most notable selection is Allen Ginsberg's long 'Prose Contribution to the Cuban Revolution'. Written from Athens in October 1961, it starts with an explicit discussion of his happiness at finding a place where boys 'are friendly & they make love between men like in Plato, the whole classic love scene preserved intact with no faggotry involved ... where my feelings are not *queer* but something old out of old human love story.' Then Ginsberg gives a political, aesthetic and romantic autobiography as stream-of-consciousness meditation, ending with his antipathy to the idea of government itself, and criticisms of Cuban poetry and cultural politics – their antimarijuana policy in particular. He concludes that

> I'm NOT down on the Cubans or anti their revolution, it's just that it's important to make clear *in advance, in front,* what I feel about life. Big statements saying Viva Fidel are/would be/meaningless and just 2-dimensional politics. Publish as much of this letter as interests you, as prose contribution to the cuban Revolution.[45]

This fascinating attempt at a left-bohemian Popular Front proved abortive. New and Old Left might have found Cuba a common ground in some respects, but culture has always been the most difficult terrain on which to build alliances (a permanent section entitled 'A Museum of Decadent Art' was promised for the next issue). Still, it is interesting that even here there was a connection to Fair Play for Cuba: besides Jones's offering, the next issue promised a piece from Richard Gibson, 'The Revolution in the Americas'.

But, of course, none of this literary fervor involved really 'famous' writers. Leroi Jones might eventually become famous, but 'Cuba Libre' was an early step on that road. In terms of prestige, it would seem as if cultural solidarity with the Cuban revoluton was limited to the original Fair Play ad in the *New York Times* with its various big names, plus the vague sense that Ginsberg on the one hand and Hemingway on the other liked the *comandante*'s style. The latter still had tremendous prestige as a global icon, and had been closely associated with Cuba in the public mind since the 1930s. He lived on the island throughout the Batista years without complaint, but had quietly hinted his sympathy for Castro on occasion. Then, in 1960 Hemingway told a Mexican journalist that

I was disposed to join the guerrillas of Fidel Castro in the Sierra Maestra, but I suffered an accident in Africa which prevented me from making any rough movements. I regretted it very much, truthfully. I would have had a great theme for a good story. Perhaps I will do something with the moments we are living now in Cuba, but I haven't thought about it. I am not a theorist, I cannot give specific reasons, but I can say that I am totally in accord with Cuba and its revolution.[46]

If he had ever acted on this fantasy of going to the mountains, even fictively like Errol Flynn, Hemingway would have brought an exceptional aura of romantic celebrity to the *barbudos* – a generation of young collegians remembering Robert Jordan/Gary Cooper in *For Whom the Bell Tolls* might have tried to follow him, giving the US consulate in Santiago de Cuba problems it had never dreamed of. But he was by then an exhausted old man, trapped in his own myth and rapidly losing his mental balance, who preferred matadors to guerrillas. The above statement was ignored in the US, and reprinted only in *Fair Play*. The indefinable but sharp sense that *fidelismo* signaled a reassertion of creative and heroic masculinity in the widest sense needed a high-profile mediator here, someone like Mills, but who could go beyond the political. At an appropriate moment, this interlocutor found himself. Who better than Norman Mailer, the characteristic subjective voice in postwar North American literature and *enfant terrible* of hipster hedonism, to explain Castro's Homeric status?

Norman, Jack and Fidel

The key aspect of Mailer's involvement was that he alone was able to get at the covert affinity of Fidel Castro and Jack Kennedy, casting a light into the secret dreams of liberals everywhere in 1960 and the betrayal of the hopes they had for the 'New Frontier'. By itself, any writing about Fidel by the ideologist of Hipsterism would have been interesting; after all, only a few years earlier Mailer had seemed to call for a figure exactly like Castro to emerge, a hero who could combine the existentialist's emphasis on the spontaneous act with the revolutionary impulse to purposeful action: 'Existential politics is rooted in the concept of the hero, it would argue that the hero is the one kind of man who *never* develops by accident, that a hero is a consecutive set of brave and witty self-creations.'[47]

But Mailer's near-mystical addresses to and about Fidel, whom he apparently never met and who surely fits this bill as much as any 'man' in recent history, took place within the context of his very public examination of John F. Kennedy as a kind of 'Superman', and the last best hope for the US, support which the vainglorious writer would later claim tipped the 1960 election to JFK. A few months after Mailer put his name on the April 1960 Fair Play ad in the *New York Times,* he went to Los Angeles for the Democratic Convention. In mid-October 1960, his long article on the candidate, entitled 'Superman Comes to the Supermarket', appeared in *Esquire.* A brilliant mélange of observation on US politics and argument for Kennedy as Existential Hero, it has remained one of Mailer's best-known nonfiction works, often cited; as he said a couple of years later, while Kennedy was still alive, 'This piece had more effect than any other single work of mine.' At the time, though, it had a double or triple layer of meaning in terms of Mailer's own life, and the role he assigned to Fidel Castro. As he put it later, describing the connection between the renewal of 'existential politics' on the left and the Democratic candidate,

> It was Kennedy's potentiality to excite such activity which interested me most; that he was young, that he was physically handsome, and that his wife was attractive were not trifling accidental details but, rather, new major political facts. I knew if he became President, it would be an existential event: he would touch depths in American life which were uncharted. Regardless of his politics, and even then one could expect his politics would be as conventional as his personality was unconventional, indeed one could expect his politics to be pushed toward conventionality precisely to counteract his essential unconventionality, one knew nonetheless that regardless of his overt politics, America's tortured psychotic search for security would finally be torn loose from the feverish ghosts of its old generals, its MacArthurs and Eisenhowers – ghosts which Nixon could cling to – and we as a nation would finally be loose again in the historic seas of a national psyche which was willy-nilly and at last, again, adventurous. And that, I thought, that was the hope for America.[48]

The original *Esquire* article, before Mailer's doubts and the grave limitations of 'existential politics' were revealed at the Bay of Pigs, aptly fits the author's subsequent admission that it was 'an act of propaganda'. Rather like Mailer's later magazine pieces on Marilyn Monroe or Muhammad Ali, it is all about physicality and stardom: 'a subtle, not quite describable intensity, a suggestion of dry pent heat perhaps, his eyes large, the pupils grey, the whites prominent, almost shocking, his most forceful feature: he had the eyes of a mountaineer.' After comparing JFK's magnetism to that of Marlon Brando, the liberals' favorite actor, the candidate's unpredictability and extraordinarily good manners were sketched. Finally, Mailer lingered over the PT-109 story, musing that 'the heroism here is remarkable for its tenacity.'[49] After hinting as to why Kennedy the man, if not his politics, was admirable and above all attractive, Mailer closed by reaching for the jugular and the repellent essence of Nixon's appeal – his vulgarity:

> America was at last engaging the fate of its myth, its consciousness was about to be accelerated or cruelly depressed in its choice between two young men in their forties who, no matter how close, dull or indifferent their stated politics might be, were radical poles apart, for one was sober, the apotheosis of opportunistic lead, all ra-

dium spent, the other handsome as a prince in the unstated aristocracy of the American dream. So, finally, would come a choice which history had never presented to a nation before – one could vote for glamour or for ugliness. ...[50]

Not for nothing did Mailer label this flim-flammery as 'meretricious' in one of his unending self-critiques, but something else was going on even as the piece ran, a doubled process of mythmaking. That fall of 1960, Mailer was preparing to declare his own candidacy for mayor of New York in the next year's election. The intended centerpiece of his announcement in late November, after the presidential election, was an 'Open Letter to Fidel Castro', which would have come hot on the heels of 'Superman Comes to the Supermarket', and then JFK's razor-thin victory. But Mailer was drinking heavily and entering a briefly lunatic stage in his career. A few days before the planned press conference, after a huge, open party intended as a kick-off to the campaign, he stabbed his wife Adele Morales in a drunken rage and was taken to Bellevue Hospital and locked up for several months so as to avoid a felony charge. The mayoral run premised on the letter to Castro was of course shelved. Like the Mills/Berle television debate, one can only imagine the results if Mailer had kept his head and managed to make his candidacy for mayor of the nation's largest city a serious referendum on support for Castro and hipsters everywhere just as *Listen, Yankee* was cresting and Fair Play hit its stride. At the least, the 'pro-Castro' argument would have heated up among the sort of people who took Mailer seriously as a cultural spokesman, a considerable number in those days.

As it happens, Mailer's 'Open Letter to Fidel Castro' ended up serving another purpose, as part of a more immediate front of opposition to the Bay of Pigs invasion. It was eventually printed following an open letter to Kennedy himself in the 27 April 1961 *Village Voice* (after the *New York Times*, *New York Post* and *New York Herald-Tribune* had all refused the honor). The first letter mixed insult and flattery, as if Mailer really hoped that JFK would read the letter to Castro and profit from it:

Dear Jack:
... I may have made the error of sailing against the stereotype that you were a calculating untried over-ambitious and probably undeserving young stud who came from a very wealthy and much unloved family.

I took a hard skimming tack against the wind of that probability and ventured instead into the notion that you gave promise of becoming the first major American hero in more than a decade. I also upheld the private hope that you were – dare I use the word, it has become so abused – that you were Hip, that your sense of history was subtle because it extracted as much from flesh as fact. ...

Wasn't there anyone around to give you the lecture on Cuba? Don't you sense the enormity of your mistake – you invade a country without understanding its music.[51]

The November letter to Fidel, however, made any 'propaganda' Mailer had written about Kennedy seem like faint praise indeed, and if the president ever read it, surely he must have wondered what it was exactly that Mailer saw in him. Obviously intended as a dramatic speech, it began with Mailer's ringing declaration that 'Fidel Castro, I announce to the City of New York that you gave all of us who are alone in this country, and usually not speaking to one another, some sense that there were heroes left in the world.'[52] Then the novelist hit his stride, and regardless of the text's histrionic voice, what he said then seems like perhaps the most concrete description of what Castro originally signified for the Silent Generation, and why the hipster and intellectual milieus of young men on and off campus had tried to hang on to their solidarity with Fidel after 1959. After a brief but detailed history of the revolutionary war ('meant for the people of New York'), he summed up the effect of the triumph over Batista:

> It was not unheroic. Truth, it was worthy of Cortes.
>
> It was as if the ghost of Cortes had appeared in our century riding Zapata's white horse. You were the first and greatest hero to appear in the world since the Second War.
>
> Better than that, you had a face. One had friends with faces like yours. In silence, many of us gave you our support. In silence. We did not have an organization to address you, we talked very little about you, we said: 'Castro, good guy', and let it go, but all the while you were giving us the idea that everything was not hopeless. There has been a new spirit in America since you entered Havana. I think you must be given credit for some part of a new and better mood which has been coming to America. ... Like Bolivar, you were sending the wind of new rebellion in our lungs. You were making it possible to breathe again. You were aiding our war.[53]

Then, expressing the Third Camp politics of many on the New Left, Mailer expressed his fear that the Communists were indeed taking over, hoping to provoke the Yankees and 'create a new Korea'. He urged Fidel in the most heartfelt terms to stay independent of the Russians, since Khrushchev was a 'Commissar' and not a 'Revolutionary', and reiterated that the hopes of the world rested on Castro maintaining his integrity. But it is Mailer's practical suggestion to the Cuban leader that is most resonant of the now-faded world of male attachment and ritual in which it was not absurd to feel a profound link between Jack Kennedy and Fidel Castro, to respond to both, to want deeply for them to get together. Mailer urged Castro to appoint Ernest Hemingway as a kind of umpire before 'the culture of the world', to whom both Kennedy and the world would have to listen (Kennedy because he so deeply 'wishes to be considered a great man in the cultivated verdicts of history'). Let Hemingway travel around the island completely on his own, talk to him, and 'hope that he will write something about Cuba – whatever he says cannot be ignored in my country. ... He may even be preparing a ground on which you and our new President can meet.'[54]

To a later generation suspicious of rhetorical excess and oratory in any form, this last suggestion regarding the now-derided Hemingway, as well as the use of such 'Open Letters', may seem like so much Maileresque sound-and-fury, signifying nothing but the writer's self-promotion. Yet more than almost anyone else in the US, Mailer was engaging in a truly *fidelista* action. The intense engagement with the media, the absolute unconcern about charges of egotism or *caudillismo*, the public challenge to higher authority in exalted tones, a politics composed in equal mixture of stylishness and outrage – this was the stuff that had originally drawn young firebrands to Castro's tiny 26th of July Movement before and after the Moncada affair, and what kept the Cuban masses devoted in 1960 and long after. Ever since January 1959, Fidel had been issuing public appeals to the troublesome North Americans, asking for the intercession of the famous and trusted, and exploring his own moral quandaries in public. It seems fair to assume that Mailer responded to Fidel's technique and sought to emulate it in his own ill-starred political endeavors. For that matter the suggestion of Hemingway as the one person who could reach 'Jack' was hardly inappropriate. The very first lines of Kennedy's ghost-written bestseller, *Profiles in Courage*, had consciously evoked Hemingway's motto of 'grace under pressure', while the novelist's literary and personal reputation in Latin America exceeded even the mythic status he had achieved in this country: the shrine the Cuban government made of his house, the 'Finca Vigia', was no cynical exercise in public relations. Apparently even Fidel was awed, and refrained from seeking out the old man; they met only once, in 1959 when Castro won the annual deepsea-fishing competition sponsored by Hemingway, and the author presented the *comandante* with his trophy. Fidel instead had looked first to Eleanor Roosevelt, while early on inviting Waldo Frank to come to Cuba and write whatever he wanted in the hopes of reaching mainstream North America with a respected, non-Communist voice. By the time Frank's book, *Cuba: Prophetic Island*, appeared in 1961 it was much too late, however, and it served only to make Frank unpopular with former comrades.[55]

In the end, the most revealing thing about the 'Open Letter to Fidel Castro' is that it was already a historical document, a record of lost possibilities, by the time it appeared (as Mailer clearly recognized at the time). Whatever the apparent affinities between Castro and Kennedy, after the Bay of Pigs the distance between them became absolute. No matter how much some young people might still admire both men, perhaps entering the Peace Corps with the vain hope of serving two masters, no one could help but be aware of the wall that had come down between the liberal's dream of a Kennedy America in a Kennedy World and the revolutionary reality.

It was easy enough then, as it will be now, to dismiss Mailer's pairing of

Jack and Fidel (like the Corsican brothers in the old Douglas Fairbanks, Jr film, twins who war to the death until they realize their kinship). At first glance, it seems like a purely novelistic flight of fancy concerning two men who were literally mortal enemies: interesting and revealing perhaps, but hardly relevant to these protagonists' actual doings and motivations. It is a premise of this book, however, that 'politics', so-called, stem as much from crises of identity that are the real conditions of everyday life – of masculine solidarity and anxiety, for instance – as from consciously ideological intent and geopolitical and political-economic necessity.

In such a world, there could be no question of a fated contest between a Kennedy and a Castro. Just as Eisenhower's relation to Fidel was accepted as entirely impersonal and distant, the closeness in age, style and appeal between his successor and the Cuban leader doomed them to a *mano à mano* face-off, or (it was thought by more than a few, including Fidel himself) the possibility of fraternity. This was not simply a generational issue: no one would have expected the same from Richard Nixon, who was JFK's exact contemporary. It was the special character of Kennedy's virility, its outlaw tinge, so evident to the men around him that they kept referring to it both enviously and admiringly to explain his appeal, that dictated he pick Cuba as a contest of arms. Thus the famous, oft-repeated epigrams that litter this star-crossed trajectory: Joseph Alsop's pleased quip upon meeting Candidate Kennedy ('Isn't he marvelous! A Stevenson with balls'); Stevenson's own disgusted putdown of the Bay of Pigs ('the damnedest bunch of boy commandoes you've ever seen'); the shock of a CIA man standing on a Cuban beach when JFK vetoed a desperately needed US air strike ('it was like learning that Superman was a fairy'); Kennedy's own expostulation in the fall of 1962 when he discovered that Castro had Soviet missiles ('He can't do that to me!'); and the scene a year earlier when Kennedy, sitting in the Oval Office, smoked a cigar that Che Guevara had given Dick Goodwin during a private meeting at the Punta del Este conference. The final judgment was Lyndon Johnson's, when he discovered upon taking office that his martyred predecessor had let the long-distance gunfight get so out of hand that it had become a 'goddamn Murder Inc. in the Caribbean'.

So before moving on to this story's conclusion in the political crisis occasioned by the Kennedy administration's attempt to invade Cuba by proxy, it is well to consider the doubled images of insurgency, rebellion and mastery offered simultaneously to the world by these two young men in their prime. My argument is that Jack Kennedy and Fidel Castro made a similar appeal to similar people in this country (and outside it, if one considers the enormous popularity of both men with Latin America's poor), drawing on the same charisma of male revolt against the status quo, the same martial sexual charm, and even the same brand of verbal facility, however different the visual effect in practice between the Hispanic and Boston Irish *cum* Harvard forms of eloquence. To understand the reach of Fidel's popularity here, therefore, one needs to remember what worked for Kennedy – the tale of PT-109 derring-do, the gorgeous wife, the air of taut rakishness – and recognize in the Cuban a wilder, more exuberant version, without the limits of a stale, equivocating middle-of-the-road politics that Mailer anatomized in his most unabashedly pro-Kennedy piece. What Castro offered to young men, and to young women as well, was all the 'right stuff' they got with Kennedy – 'ask not what your country can do for you, but what you can do for your country', 'bear any burden, pay any price' – but without the compromises, with the risks left in.

Garry Wills has gone furthest into the meaning of this final burst of Yankee *fidelismo* in his book charting the dimensions of sex and power in 'the Kennedy imprisonment'. In Wills's view, there was 'a "frontier" love for guerrilla boldness' revealed by Jack Kennedy's hardly concealed satyriasis and flagrant contempt for the older hands of the Establishment, not only Eisenhower but men in his own administration like Adlai Stevenson, Chester Bowles and Dean Rusk. The Kennedy style of continual crisis and organized charisma, with its deliberate bypassing of established procedures and structures, became 'a raid of mobile "outsiders" on the settled government of America', or 'counter-insurgency at home', that undermined most of what Kennedy intended. And as Wills points out, this intensely voluntaristic ethos, with its casual use of the tropes of rebellion and solidarity in the Peace Corps and the claim to support the civil rights movement (however vitiated that claim was in reality), radicalized many young people despite itself. Even Robert Kennedy was pulled sharply to the left at the end of his life, when he commanded 'not only a government in exile, but also a kind of government in the hills, his own personal Sierra Maestra', becoming 'a hero to people whose earlier heroes were Ho, Mao, Fidel and Che'.[56]

Ultimately Wills makes the direct comparison, and concludes that in the contest of two such charismas, the Kennedys could not hope to win:

> Castro brought out every combative instinct of the Kennedys. He was a hero to the young and a charismatic leader in both the superficial and the profound sense. John Kennedy was attempting a 'charismatic' but very limited raid on certain aspects of America's bureaucratic legal order. Castro was charismatic in the fullest, most authentic way – he overthrew the old regime entirely and instituted a revolutionary order based on his personal authority. His 'little brother' Che was a rebel himself, off to other countries fomenting revolution. They had an all-out dash and vigor the Kennedys could only hope to imitate in covert and surreptitious ways.[57]

So even if the post–Bay of Pigs Operation Mongoose had succeeded and the revolutionary government self-destructed, with Fidel succumbing to one of the innumerable CIA schemes to poison his ice cream and the like, there can be little doubt that the verdict of history would find Castro a braver, tougher, more audacious man. No army of publicists and eminent friends of the family was needed to manufacture the hard reality behind the legend of the Sierra Maestra, or to write Castro's speeches for him. Kennedy could not make any such claim about his carefully scripted passage from feckless Harvard boy to presidential candidate. One cannot help suspecting that he knew as much, and that this terrible awareness after the humiliation of the Bay of Pigs led first to the rage of the unmanned killer (Robert McNamara's comment that 'we were hysterical' about Castro comes to mind), and later to the beginning of truer self-knowledge, looking towards possible reconciliation. Certainly for years after Castro spoke admiringly and in an extraordinarily forgiving tone, stressing that JFK had the highest ability of the political leader, the capacity to change his mind. But any such change came too late. The truest measure of a ruler is to command, and not be commanded by, events: despite the vast disparity in power, it was not Castro who was felled by an assassin's bullet. Even if we never know the exact truth about 22 November 1963, it seems safe to say that not only did an obsession with Cuba corrupt the presidency of John F. Kennedy: in the end it destroyed him.

Notes

1. Saul Landau, 'C. Wright Mills: The Last Six Months', *Ramparts*, August 1965, p. 54.
2. Ibid., p. 47.
3. Ibid., p. 54.
4. Mills, *Listen, Yankee*, p. 9.
5. Ibid.
6. Ibid., pp. 7, 11, 12.
7. Landau, 'C. Wright Mills: The Last Six Months', p. 46. Landau remembers Taber introducing Mills to him in a Havana hotel (interview with author, 29 January 1993).
8. See *Fair Play*, 2 September 1960, for a detailed account of Taber's travels with Mills. The 22 July *Fair Play* mentioned Mills as a prominent new member.
9. The comparison to Paine is by Saul Landau, in Buhle, ed., *History and the New Left*, p. 112; the alternative, William James, is in Irving Louis Horowitz, *C. Wright Mills: An American Utopian*, New York: Free Press, 1983, p. 294.
10. Landau, 'C. Wright Mills: The Last Six Months', p. 47. Landau remembered Mills speaking ecstatically of this then-novel marketing device for a book on a serious topic: 'We're going to break it into the mass market. They're going to *listen*. We've hit on the new technique.'
11. To Howe, *Listen, Yankee* and the earlier pamphlet *The Causes of World War III* were 'scandalous' because they were 'so shoddy in thought and method, so crowded with rhetorical wind, so grandiose in pretension and feeble in documentation, and so coy in their evasions ... especially ... the narrative trickery, so unworthy of a man like Mills, employed in the Cuban pamphlet', which Howe could not even bring himself to name; see Irving Howe, 'On the Career and Example of C. Wright Mills', reprinted from *Dissent* in *Steady Work*, New York: Harcourt, Brace, 1966, p. 252. Horowitz's *C. Wright Mills: An American Utopian*, pp. 293–302, is the fullest account to date of the writing of *Listen, Yankee*, though it too omits the FPCC connection.
12. Mills, *Listen, Yankee*, p. 8: see also his explanation that 'most of the words are mine – although not all of them; the arguments, the tone, the interpretations, the tang and feel – they are in the main directly Cuban. I have merely organized them – in the most direct and immediate fashion of which I am capable.'
13. Ibid., p. 166.

14. Ibid., pp. 149–50.

15. In April 1960, the IADF held its second inter-American conference in Maracay, Venezuela. With IADF founder Rómulo Betancourt now president of Venezuela, having overthrown the dictator Pérez Jiménez, this was expected to be a triumphal event, but a debate erupted over whether to condemn Cuba. As the Summer 1960 *Hemispherica* delicately phrased the matter: 'The problem of the Cuban Revolution was on everybody's mind, with the implications, however unjustified, of threatened intervention by the United States, not openly expressed.' The same issue reported that 'Cuban Anti-Castro Democrats Unite', with evident approval. By November 1960, *Hemispherica* was worried about 'rumors' of 'unilateral action' by the US, and commented in veiled terms about how the US should not be choosing the exiles' leaders: while the *batistianos* in Florida were 'unfortunately considered possible companions by some', the IADF's favorite, Aureliano Sanchez Arango, was never high on the CIA's list. Here and in January 1961, strong approval was also given to the Movemiento Revolucionario del Pueblo led by former *fidelistas* Manuel Ray, Felipe Pazos, Rufo López-Fresquet and Raúl Chibas, presented as the ones who really were fomenting insurrection inside Cuba. This conspiratorial tone continued, with references in the February/March *Hemispherica* to 'undercover ... kingmakers' intervening in refugee affairs. After the Bay of Pigs, an August 1961 editorial was more explicit: 'As early as last January, members of this Association personally expressed to several members of the new administration, our deep protest concerning the plans for the Cuban invasion and the sordid maneuvres of the Central Intelligence Agency officials charged with this responsibility.'

16. Harvey Swados, 'C. Wright Mills: A Personal Memoir', *Dissent* (Winter 1963), pp. 35–42. It is worth noting that in the Summer 1963 issue, the British socialist scholar Ralph Miliband, also a friend of Mills, vehemently disagreed with Swados: Mills 'did fear that the revolution might go sour', but did not undergo any 'last-minute conversion and repentance' over Castro. Landau concurs.

17. Howe, 'On the Career and Example of C. Wright Mills', p. 252.

18. Interview with Maurice Zeitlin by Ronald Giele, 3 January 1985, in Oral History Research Office, Columbia University.

19. *Columbia Spectator*, 29 November 1960.

20. The context for all this Hemingwayesque taunting was Mills's very unprofessorial status as a male rebel, like Taber a 'tough guy'. In the best-known photograph, reproduced in James Miller's *Democracy Is in the Streets*, he is riding a motorcycle, a gesture of some import in those buttoned-up days. The graver implications of Mills's personal vision of solidarity are evoked in his comment to the *Spectator* interviewer: 'I've decided that America is terribly boring.'

21. Welch, *Response to Revolution*, p. 214n13; also the *Chicago Maroon*, 21 April 1961, where Arthur MacEwan describes how his father, Dr Alan MacEwan, an assistant professor of plant physiology at the University of Arizona, was abruptly fired for 'incompetence' after taking his family to Cuba and giving speeches in Tucson in opposition to US policy.

22. O'Brien, 'The Development of the New Left', p. 32.

23. LeRoi Jones, 'Cuba Libre', reprinted in *Home: Social Essays*, New York: William Morrow, 1966, p. 20; Amiri Baraka, *The Autobiography of LeRoi Jones/Amiri Baraka*, New York: Freundlich, 1984, p. 161.

24. Ibid., p. 152.

25. See ibid., pp. 150–51, where he refers to it as *Zazen*, apparently a bit of mischief, as he also calls the well-known uptown journal where his wife worked *Sectarian Review*.

26. Ibid., p. 161.

27. Interview with Amiri Baraka, 19 July 1990.

28. Jones, *Autobiography*, p. 163.

29. Jones, 'Cuba Libre', p. 11.

30. Ibid., p. 12.

31. Ibid., pp. 13–14, 16–17. James Baldwin, Langston Hughes and John O. Killens were all replaced at the last minute. The 'African scholar' was apparently John Henrik Clarke, with whom Jones would later work in various political/cultural endeavors despite this unflattering characterization. Jones was more positive about some members of the group, such as a '1930's type Negro "essayist" who turned out to be marvelously un-lied to' (Harold Cruse) and Robert F. Williams, who clearly impressed Jones very much from the first. In his *Autobiography* (pp. 163–4), he also lists the painter Ed Clark, the novelist Sarah Wright and her husband, and Julian Mayfield and his

wife Ana Codero.

32. Jones, 'Cuba Libre', pp. 42–3; also Jones, *Autobiography*, pp. 164–5, where he identifies her by name as Rubi Betancourt: 'As much hot hatred as I could summon for the US, its white supremacy, its exploitation, its psychological torture of schizophrenic slaves like myself, I now had to bear the final indignity – which made my teeth grate violently, even in reflection – the indignity and humiliation of defending its ideology, which I was doing in the name of Art. Jesus Christ!'

33. Jones, 'Cuba Libre', pp. 43–4.

34. Ibid., p. 60.

35. Ibid., p. 61.

36. Ibid., p. 62.

37. Jones, *Autobiography*, p. 166.

38. See the *New York Times*, 27 July 1961, for the arrest of FPCC activists, including one 'Everett Jones'.

39. Harold Cruse, *The Crisis of the Negro Intellectual*, New York: William Morrow, 1967, pp. 356–7. The chapter entitled 'The Intellectuals and Force and Violence', pp. 347–81, delineates the relationship between Robert Williams, Cuba, and those young black radicals epitomized by Jones.

40. Neeli Cherkovski, *Ferlinghetti: A Biography*, Garden City, N.Y.: Doubleday, 1979, pp. 136–49; *Liberation* (March 1961), pp. 11, 14.

41. Lawrence Ferlinghetti, *Starting from San Francisco*, New York: New Directions, 1967, pp. 48–52.

42. *Pa'lante* (May 1962), p. 5. Elizabeth Sutherland, now Elizabeth Martínez, had been an editor at Simon & Schuster, assistant to the director of the photography department at the Museum of Modern Art, and books and arts editor at *The Nation*. Subsequently she has been a prominent Latina writer and activist (letter, Martínez to Gosse, 8 April 1992).

43. Ibid., p. 53.

44. Ibid., p. 56.

45. Ibid., pp. 61, 73.

46. Hemingway is quoted in *Fair Play*, 9 September 1960.

47. Norman Mailer, *The Presidential Papers*, New York: Putnam, 1963, p. 6. All of Mailer's writings on the politics of the New Frontier are usefully collected here, extensively annotated.

48. Ibid., pp. 26–7.

49. Ibid., pp. 47–8.

50. Ibid., p. 59.

51. Ibid., pp. 65–6.

52. Ibid., p. 67.

53. Ibid., pp. 68–9.

54. Ibid., pp. 74–5.

55. Only the left-wing publishers Marzani and Munsell would bring the book out, and the fact that it was strongly pro-Castro and that Frank had received a grant from the Cuban government outraged some. He was removed from the board of the anti-Communist Spanish Refugee Aid at the insistence of several major financial contributors in 1963, according to Nancy MacDonald's memoir *Homage to the Spanish Exiles: Voices of the Spanish Civil War*, New York: Human Sciences Press, 1987, p. 156.

56. Garry Wills, *The Kennedy Imprisonment*, pp. 147, 169, 207, 211.

57. Ibid., p. 211.

7

On the Beach

This book properly concludes with the US defeat at the Bay of Pigs in late April 1961, which military and diplomatic historians have come to regard as a 'perfect failure'.[1] After this climactic event, the die was cast, and the question of any possible toleration for the Cuban revolution was answered in the negative. The movement led by the Fair Play by Cuba Committee rapidly dissipated.

In one sense, the ignominious collapse of the CIA's exile brigade on the beach named Playa Girón was a decisive end to a particular vision of America that assumed an essential benevolence, an exceptional stance from which the US could safely decry the imperialism of others. In a larger sense, it was the beginning of a different world, one in which innocence was no longer presumed even by North Americans, and the sheep's clothing in which Cold War liberalism had come to power was rapidly discarded. At the time, the pacifist A. J. Muste, the only universally respected figure on the fractured left, summed up in a single, brutal phrase the invasion's significance: it was 'the death of the republic'. Reconstructing how 'the best and the brightest' started down the road to a much greater defeat in Indochina, the journalist David Halberstam captured how this 'shattering event' was an augury of something far worse: 'It would be said of John Kennedy and Lyndon Johnson that both had their Bay of Pigs, that the former's lasted four days and the latter's four years.'[2]

This book is about the United States at the height of the Cold War and the making of the New Left. The focus of its final chapter is how the Bay of Pigs altered the domestic political landscape, producing the first publicly visible dissent over imperial policies since the beginning of the Cold War. Although in hindsight two weeks of rallying by a few dozen, a few hundred or a few thousand people in twenty or thirty cities and college towns, accompanied by denunciations from leading liberals and academics, may seem like a pitiful response indeed, it was at the time completely exceptional.[3]

It is important to note at the outset that there was a double layer to the defeat in Cuba, which made it intensely personal for a generation of liberals who deeply believed they were opposing an empire rather than constructing one, and had assured themselves that once in control of the ship of state they would be the best friend of revolution in the developing world. It was the Republicans who symbolized the 'Ugly American', and part of Jack Kennedy's promise, as presented during the campaign by his call to Coretta Scott King while her husband languished in a Southern jail, was that he understood the cry of the oppressed, and would be their tribune.

Who Lost Cuba?

It is hardly incidental therefore that, early in 1960, Senator Kennedy had moved to guarantee his standing among liberals with a carefully phrased book, *The Strategy of Peace*, 'edited' by the eminent historian Allan Nevins (and ghostwritten by later US Senator Harris Wofford), with a particular section addressing Cuba in ambiguously sympathetic terms:

> The wild, angry, passionate course of the revolution in Cuba demonstrates that the shores of the American Hemisphere and the Caribbean islands are not immune to the ideas and forces causing similar storms on other continents. ... Just as we must recall our own revolutionary past in order to understand the spirit and the significance of the anticolonial uprisings in Asia and Africa, we should now reread the life of Simon Bolivar, the great 'Liberator' and sometimes 'Dictator' of South America, in order to comprehend the new contagion for liberty and reform now spreading south of our borders. ...
>
> Fidel Castro is part of the legacy of Bolivar, who led his men over the Andes Mountains, vowing 'war to the death' against Spanish rule, saying, 'Where the goat can pass, so can an army.' Castro is also part of the frustration of that earlier revolution which won its war against Spain but left largely untouched the indigenous feudal order. 'To serve a revolution is to plow the sea', Bolivar said in despair as he lived to see the failure of his efforts at social reform.
>
> Whether Castro would have taken a more rational course after his victory had the United States Government not backed the dictator Batista so long and so uncritically, and had it given the fiery young rebel a warmer welcome in his hour of triumph, especially on his trip to this country, we cannot be sure.[4]

For the time, this was as far to the left as any elected politician in the country could venture. In both tone and substance it clearly echoed Herbert L. Matthews, and implied that considerable blame in both the long and short term lay with the US, and not with Castro. How difficult it must have been for many liberals when the word began to seep out in late summer that on the hustings Senator Kennedy was speaking in quite a different voice, appealing to those audiences who, in their question cards handed up from the floor, wanted to hear what JFK would do about, or to, Castro.[5]

Here one must confront a comforting fable about Kennedy. It is an established fact that on Cuba and other aspects of foreign policy, he cut sharply to Nixon's right, squashing the suggestion that Democrats were 'soft' on fighting the Cold War. Among these maneuvers, none is more famous than his demand in late October 1960, before his final debate with Richard Nixon, that the US government 'strengthen the non-Batista democratic anti-Castro forces in exile, and in Cuba itself, who offer eventual hope of overthrowing Castro.'

Kennedy's most prominent defender, Arthur Schlesinger, Jr, a campaign aide and later special assistant to the president, has argued that this upping of the ante was an accident, a complication of deadheat pressure in the campaign's final weeks and a press release put out in the candidate's name without his knowledge.[6] However, given Kevin Tierney's detailed analysis of Kennedy's speeches from August through early November 1960, claims for JFK's lack of conscious intent regarding the call to overthrow Castro cannot hold water.[7] In fact, the Massachusetts senator had played hardball from early on, declaring as the campaign opened that Cuba was 'a chink in our defensive armor. ... For the first time in the history of the United States, an enemy stands poised at the throat of the United States.'[8] He placed Nixon on the defensive with continual rhetorical assaults like, 'If you can't stand up to Castro, how can you be expected to stand up to Khrushchev?', so that on 1 October, the Republican found himself (in latter-day terms anyway) on Kennedy's left, taking the non-interventionist position in two Midwestern speeches:

> Should the United States have dealt with the Cuban people who have been the victims of Castro's demagoguery, as Khrushchev dealt with the Hungarian patriots in the streets of Budapest?. ... We can be proud that the United States is not ... using its muscle ... against a very small country.[9]

Kennedy in turn did not shrink from declaring on 3 October that

> we will hold out the hand of friendship to those who have been driven out of Cuba by Castro. ... There are undoubtedly those in the mountains now who are growing beards in preparation for undoing Mr. Castro. I think we should observe with at least some interest their progress.[10]

Although JFK's main theme over several months was the Republicans' 'softness' on Castro, he also periodically revived the essential liberal claim that Eisenhower's deepest sin was in tolerating 'the brutal, bloody, and despotic dictatorship of Fulgenio Batista', and affirmed that the 26th of July Movement in its original form had 'reflected the deepest aspirations of the Cuban people' before 'Castro and his gang ... betrayed the ideals of the Cuban Revolution.' Reeling off statistics on how much of Cuba was owned by US corporations, Kennedy would emphasize before some audiences that cold-hearted US economic dominance combined with the Republicans' indifference to tyranny this close to home had led the Cuban people to believe that North Americans did not really care about them: 'It was our policies – not Castro's – that first began to turn our former good neighbors against us. And Fidel Castro seized on this.'[11] The effect of this neat double-game was to lay claim to those voters fighting mad over Castro's defiance of the US and in no mind to listen to Nixon's protestations about international law, while simultaneously reaching out to those who believed that Ike had brought on revolution by coddling Batista so that Big Business could make a buck.

Castro was mainly a stick with which to beat Nixon with during the campaign, but Kennedy must have known he would be held to account for repeated claims that he would correct 'the most glaring failure of American foreign policy ... a Communist menace that has been permitted to rise under our very noses, only ninety miles from our shores.'[12] Clearly, it had helped him win the election, to the extent that Nixon in the last days proposed a fifth debate exclusively on the subject of Cuba, hoping to turn the tide by showing how his opponent had callowly shot from the hip with his demand that the US *openly* fund counter-revolution, rather than the less overt Guatemala-style pressure tactics that Nixon proposed. The campaign controversy also directly contributed to hardening Eisenhower's policy. Only a week before Kennedy's call for funding anti-Castro guerrillas, the administration announced an economic embargo, the last step before the total break that came in January. As the *Wall Street Journal* declared on 20 October,

> Politically the action amounts to a reply for Vice President Nixon against charges of his democratic rival for the presidency, Senator John F. Kennedy, that the Republican Administration is soft on the Castro regime. Mr. Nixon can now say the U.S. is cracking down and intends to continue such a policy.[13]

Nonetheless, among the Cubans and their remaining US friends, hope sprang eternal. When Kennedy became bellicose, the Cubans pinned their hopes on Adlai Stevenson, praising him immoderately as 'a man of great culture, wisdom and knowledge' because on 25 October Stevenson criticized the embargo and, implicitly, Kennedy's 'hard' position in a campaign speech.[14] Castro himself responded to Kennedy's inauguration by declaring that Cuba would 'begin anew' with the new administration, and earlier Robert Taber optimistically described the postelection appointments of the liberal foreign policy 'team' of Secretary of State Dean Rusk, Undersecretary Chester Bowles and UN Ambassador Stevenson as a possible 'winter thaw ... in the offing', arguing that

> the task for Fair Play during the intervening weeks will be to rally American liberal opinion to make an overwhelming demand on the new President for such negotiations. ... There is reason to hope, despite the record, that he and the team of advisors

with whom he has had the good sense or good luck to surround himself may be listening. And that is the first real ray of hope we have had to report since *Fair Play* was founded. Happy New Year![15]

As it turns out, the residue of trust that Cuban and North American radicals retained for the party of Franklin Delano Roosevelt proved grievously misplaced.

A Flowering of Fair Play

In a certain sense, the nationwide response to the US-sponsored invasion of Cuba provided a satisfying closure for the Fair Play for Cuba Committee. Though FPCC would soldier on for years in a few places, it had nowhere to go but downhill after the Bay of Pigs. The lifeline to Cuba was cut with the travel ban, likely federal indictment had already sent Robert Taber and Saul Landau out of the country, and its heterogeneous base made a tempting target for the FBI. On the surface, however, Fair Play went from strength to strength in the winter and early spring of 1961, as the Christmas tour produced what Berta Green later called 'a small army' of organizers, and new chapters appeared at a steady rate. Already by November 1960 the *New York Times* had published a detailed article on the who, what and where of this new organization, listing most of the prominent local and national leaders, and quoting Green extensively (one paradox of the early 1960s is that leftwing efforts then, however small, received much more publicity than the much larger radical movements of the postsixties decades).[16]

What did the Fair Play chapters actually do, beyond organizing themselves publicly, often enough to provoke local inquisitions? At first glance, it appears to have been simply the mundane business of oppositional politics: speakers, slideshows, films, pickets, potlucks and fundraising parties. It should be remembered, however, how liberating these activities were after what I. F. Stone called the 'Haunted Fifties', especially for the college students and postcollegiate intellectuals who were Fair Play's main base. Many cities and campuses had seen nothing like this in years, and protests or even indoor events by Fair Play chapters supporting the 'anti-American' Castro sometimes met with physical intimidation from Cuban exiles and legal harassment. But how widespread was this activity in truth – how big was Fair Play?

As with virtually all radical groups, there are many possible yardsticks, and ambiguity in terms of announced membership versus the available evidence. In late 1960 and early 1961, FPCC leaders claimed 5,000, then 6,000, then 7,000 members and up to twenty-seven 'adult' chapters and forty 'Student Councils'. If anything like this actually was in place, it was very impressive; after several years of recruitment with support from established organizations like the League for Industrial Democracy and the United Auto Workers, SDS at Port Huron comprised at best ten small campus chapters (several dormant) and a few hundred card-carrying members.

The only precise record of FPCC's base was given, under extreme duress, by Acting Executive Secretary Richard Gibson on 16 May 1961 to the Eastland Committee: he listed twenty-three chapters in Lynn (Massachusetts), Boston, Hartford, New Haven, New York, Brooklyn, Queens, Newark, Bergen County (New Jersey), Philadelphia, Baltimore, Washington, D.C., Tampa, Cleveland, Detroit, Chicago, Denver, Seattle, San Francisco, Palo Alto, Santa Clara, Los Angeles and San Diego; in addition thirty-seven FPCC Student Councils were named at Bennington, Goddard, Harvard, the Massachusetts Institute of Technology, Boston University, Brandeis, Tufts, Brown, Yale, City College of New York, Brooklyn College, Queens College, St John's, Columbia, Cornell, the University of Virginia, Fisk, Indiana University, Oberlin, Antioch, Ohio University, Wayne State, the University of Michigan, the University of Chicago, Roosevelt University, the University of Wisconsin, Grinnell, Carleton, the University of Minnesota, the University of Kansas, the University of Colorado, the University of Washington, Reed, Berkeley, Stanford, UCLA, and Los Angeles City College.[17] Even if close to twenty of these Student Councils were to some degree adjuncts of existing chapters in New York, Boston, Chicago, San Francisco, Los Angeles and elsewhere, it still suggests the ability to coordinate action on a national basis.

Anchoring this apparent breadth were New York and San Francisco, respectively the past and future cultural centers of the US left, where Fair Play's presence approximated the new kind of left social movement later prevalent, operating in the interstices of formal politics rather than within institutions like trade unions. In both places, FPCC supporters numbered in the thousands, with a rich and ongoing intraorganizational life.[18] Nor was this essentially a paper membership of donors supporting a small activist core, the norm in later years. Enough of older left traditions survived that a large percentage were active to some degree; if the difference between the 'old left' and the 'new social movement' aspects of FPCC appear to be blurred in this depiction, that is deliberate. In San Francisco and New York at least (as at Madison), the survival of the former was a precondition for the strength of the latter.

In New York, for instance, by the first half of 1961 FPCC had separate organizations in four of the five boroughs, a chapter newsletter, constant parties, dinners, dances and even 'swinging' boat trips, Spanish classes, a Speaker's Bureau, Trade Union Committee, and more.[19] Its political composition was also strikingly heterogenous for that time. The nominating committee's proposal for the chapter's Executive Committee in late 1961 included LeRoi Jones as the new president replacing Richard Gibson, the pacifist leader Dave Dellinger as member-at-large, and the Trotskyist cadre Nat Weinstein as Brooklyn branch representative.[20]

San Francisco FPCC started later (though Berkeley students had been organizing since September 1960), initiated by Socialist Workers Party members
and some 'independents', people formerly in or close to the CPUSA like Al
Saxton, George Hitchcock and the prominent leftwing lawyer Vincent Hallinan.[21] A provisional organizing committee received its charter in the late fall,
and publicly launched itself when 1,100 people attended (and another 200
were turned away from) an indoor rally on 14 January 1961, where Lawrence
Ferlinghetti read his famous poem, 'One Thousand Fearful Words for Fidel
Castro', and notables like Paul Sweezy spoke, with prominent liberal professor
Marshall Windmiller chairing.[22] Starting from this base, FPCC in the Bay Area
stayed strong throughout 1962–63 while the national organization withered,
only dissolving itself after the assassination of John F. Kennedy. With a healthy
treasury, continuous display advertisements in the local papers, the widespread circulation of films and speakers throughout Northern California and
even beyond, and a continual round of local film festivals and forums linking
such disparate figures as Mike Tigar, chairman of UC-Berkeley's SLATE, a still-
powerful Harry Bridges (whose longshoremen protected FPCC events and
who, through the ILWU's relationship with the Democratic Party, ensured a
tolerant police attitude), Stanford Professor Paul Baran, the sole tenured
Marxist economist in the country, and the actor Sterling Hayden, Bay Area
FPCC fully justified the self-description by one of its leaders as 'the only game
in town'.[23]

Seen only in terms of the largest cities, one could summarize Fair Play's
success as a limited renascence of the existing radical base with an admixture
of younger liberals and African-Americans, though Taber's leadership does not
fit any category of the Old Left, harkening back instead to the days of John
Reed in the teens or Carleton Beals in the twenties. It is, in fact, a thesis of this
book that such a restructuring of the 'old' is a big part of the 'new' radicalism.
At the same time, however, there was a quite separate process taking place on
campuses that was even more illustrative of how the New Left created itself.

Here is where it is useful to talk about a 'fair play movement' rather than
just the Fair Play for Cuba Committee, because among students, formal affinity with a national group like FPCC was often tenuous, a tendency towards
self-conscious organizational autonomy not confined to those years. It would
take an intensive search to check the content of FPCC's claim to more than
three dozen affiliated Student Councils. Were these sometimes a few individuals who over the course of a semester or two tried to pull together an initial
organizing committee, as one suspects? On the other hand, certainly there
were schools where the level of active organizational commitment to FPCC
was considerably greater, especially given the difficulty in chartering official
campus organizations. At the City College of New York, for instance, the local
Fair Players, operating under that name, waged a well-publicized fight with
the CCNY administration in late 1960 when they invited Raúl Roa, Jr to speak

on campus. Since FPCC was not a recognized group, the Eugene Debs Club agreed to be official sponsor, but the latter's faculty advisor, Professor of English John M. Hutchins, refused to sign the appropriate forms, declaring Roa an 'unwashed ape' and telling the campus paper that 'there are some opinions that are so haywire that educational institutions would frown on them.' During the resulting furor, the Department of Student Life invoked obscure technicalities to stop Roa's appearance, but speak he finally did, leading the student government to change its rules in the name of academic freedom.[24]

What is clear is that, following the first tentative stirrings in the fall and a surge of students onto the Christmas tour, activism that was variously 'pro-Castro' or pro-'fair play', with some orientation to national FPCC, did grow dramatically at a core of campuses, not incidentally many of those that played leading roles throughout the next decade. The furor at these schools during the invasion and its immediate aftermath, from 17 April into early May, had no institutional precedent in open opposition to US foreign policy among young people after World War II. It needs to be assessed as both a spontaneous response, and also the fruit of considerable debate stirred up in the preceding year by FPCC.

In this case, the term *debate* is not simply a metaphor for public disagreement, but the preferred vehicle through which budding campus radicals felt their way around the minefield of obstacles to any organized discussion over 'noncampus' issues. A survey of those schools covered in Chapter 5 reveals the degree of activity, and its characteristic forms of formal debate, lecture and printed polemic. At Columbia College on 9 January, the Debate Council sponsored a disputation on the question, 'Resolved: The United States should work for Castro's overthrow', with Melvin Urofsky, '61, his brother Roger, '63, and Jack Samet, '61, arguing in the negative. Later in the spring, I. F. Stone keynoted the campus newspaper's annual dinner, declaring that Cuba was the *real* 'New Frontier' in the Americas.[25] At Swarthmore, students just returned from Cuba held a lecture in mid January, which quickly turned into an impromptu debate, as heckling from the floor spurred 'animated and lengthy discussion', followed by a vitriolic war of words in the *Swarthmore Phoenix*'s letters page.[26] January was also quite busy at Cornell, with enthusiastic first-hand reports on Cuba by graduate student and FPCC contact Alphonso Pinckney provoking more Red-baiting. On 12 January, Professor Douglas Dowd, who later played a major role in the antiwar movement, gave a lecture in which he unequivocally declared his support for the revolution, and on 13 January four students debated, with two Cubans on opposite sides.[27] Similarly, at Madison, after nine students returned from the Christmas tour, the Young Democrats sponsored a debate with two prominent campus radicals, Jim McWilliams and Dick Ward, versus a journalism student who had gone on the tour for a local paper and an anti-Castro Cuban, which degenerated into a near-screaming match involving vociferously pro-Castro Latin Americans in the audience.[28]

Almost certainly, one could go on to catalogue similar debates at schools around the country, including most of those where FPCC claimed Student Councils. The *Student Council* bulletin hailed widespread results stemming from the Christmas delegations and high-profile attractions like Robert F. Williams's national speaking tour for Fair Play in March: 100 students at a first organizing meeting at the University of Minnesota on 25 January; SWPer and Midwest FPCC representative Ed Shaw in an ADA-sponsored debate at the University of Pittsburgh before 350 people; Maurice Zeitlin speaking outside to 600 students at Berkeley for four hours (prompting a gentle gibe about taking Fidel's example too literally); a march of Yale students on 16 January protesting the cut-off of diplomatic relations, and the beginnings of organized FPCC activity at other schools such as the University of Kansas, Carleton, Brown, Stanford and the University of Washington.[29]

All of this – crowds in the hundreds, the nasty letters calling these youth Commie dupes, the shouting matches – was the prelude to the Bay of Pigs, and the shock when the forewarned and yet unimaginable happened: the Yankee's Budapest, the frank display of what Senator J. William Fulbright would later label 'the arrogance of power'. Looking back, what is hard to understand is how this discussion percolated in the leading universities while there was virtually no disagreement in the nation's political mainstream over the wall of hostility settling into place against Cuba, though the coming invasion was evident to any assiduous newspaper reader. This does not mean that debate among the youth and the intellectuals and others had no meaning, like the proverbial falling tree unheard. The reverberations reached high enough to set off alarm bells for those with a sense of history like Schlesinger, who confided to JFK just before the invasion his fear that 'the Russians would enlist volunteers in José Martí and probably even Abraham Lincoln Brigades'.[30] The absence of impact on the policymaking process indicates that the monolith of official opinion needed considerably more in the way of battering from outside and internal fissuring to show any cracks. It needed, in other words, the impact of bodybags coming home to every small town in the US, as in 1966 and 1967, or the sheer failure of a Bay of Pigs, when the cracking was also real, if very brief. On the face of things, the engine of US diplomacy backed by bipartisan consensus moved forward, from one president to the next, with nary a hitch. When Eisenhower cut all relations with Cuba in early January, only Senator Albert Gore of Tennessee spoke up to suggest it was 'inadvisable' to take such a step on the eve of a change in administrations.[31] On 10 January 1961 the *New York Times* finally reported very elliptically on the evidence of something fishy involving landing strips and jungle training camps in Guatemala, nearly two months after *The Nation* broke the story in the US. Other major papers had similar articles before and after, and by late January even *Time* was referring to the CIA giving $500,000 a month to the exile 'Frente', but no one in Washington was prepared to take the bit by the teeth and question the new administration on its plans – a textbook example of how something can be known yet secret at the same time.[32] Throughout February and March and into April various plans for smaller and larger landings at different sites were floated internally, while this condition of official disavowal and near-unanimous complicity persisted. After Vietnam, someone would have blown the whistle on such a dubious scheme, or at least the competing assessments would have been fought out in the open via leaks and exposés. In that era a discreet silence was observed, as well as mental self-censorship. Many eminent officials like Stevenson and United States Information Agency head Edward R. Murrow were told nothing at all, and apparently refused to countenance the considerable evidence of a massive CIA operation until the last moment.[33] As Hugh Thomas dryly observed, 'In Europe such revelations as these about a government's intentions would have caused a storm. In the US the constitutional organization of opposition was harder.'[34]

By himself, Fulbright as chairman of the Senate Foreign Relations Committee fought a private battle within the councils of power to stop the invasion, warning JFK in a long memorandum, and at a subsequent high-level meeting to which he was the invited dissenter, that Cuba was only 'a thorn in the flesh', not 'a dagger in the heart':

> To give this activity even covert support is of a piece with the hypocrisy and cynicism for which the United States is constantly denouncing the Soviet Union in the United Nations and elsewhere. The point will not be lost on the rest of the world – nor on our own consciences.[35]

The scenes of Kennedy going around his war room asking for yes or no votes on the invasion plan, with most of the New Frontiersmen speaking up strongly for it – an aged Adolf Berle snarling 'let 'er rip', while the Joint Chiefs of Staff were prudently noncommittal – have been retold many times in the literature on the Bay of Pigs, usually emphasizing the president's Hamlet-like anguish over whether to scuttle this inheritance from Ike. There is a strong element of apologetics to this writing, as if the unannounced invasion of a small country with which the United States was not at war by the greatest military power in history somehow 'just happened' through bureaucratic inertia, confusion and bad advice. The stress is very much on the people who knew better and wished in retrospect they had spoken up a bit more firmly, from Kennedy himself on down.

In fact, like Vietnam, the Bay of Pigs was 'the very definition of the New Frontier', in Garry Wills's phrase, however much, like Vietnam, it proved an orphan after the fact. Eisenhower might have authorized it, and was certainly no more of a friend to Cuba than JFK, but it was JFK's 'urge to power and fear of failure', and his aggressiveness towards Cuba during the 1960 campaign, that made the invasion 'inevitable', as William Appleman Williams described it in his 1962 post-mortem.[36] To get at the emblematic rather than exceptional character of the Bay of Pigs for Cold War liberalism, we have to consider the political campaign preceding the invasion, framing it as a natural extension of liberalism's impulse to global reform. Indeed, this is part of the schizoid atmosphere of the times, with official Washington again and again denying any intention to intervene in Cuba, while simultaneously presenting a host of reasons for doing so. After the inauguration, a propaganda offensive aimed at the administration's core constituency of Northern Democrats took off rapidly. The anchor of this campaign was the massively ballyhooed Alliance for Progress, pitched as a preemptive strike of limited social revolution to forestall Castroite Communism. The oligarchies throughout Latin America would be persuaded or enticed into granting land reform, democratic elections and a host of other good things. Nor was this an entirely hypocritical posture, since as Castro himself said later,

> to effect social reform which would improve the condition of the masses in Latin America ... was a politically wise concept put forth to hold back the time of revolution. ... One has to admit the idea of the Alliance for Progress was an intelligent one; however, an utopian one.[37]

The Bay of Pigs was framed within this larger reformist context, which at the Alliance's unveiling in mid March 1960 appeared to answer all the dreams (and was largely based upon the ideas) of the hemisphere's 'Democratic Left'. A small stick next to a large carrot, the invasion to expel Castroism as an extra-hemispheric intrusion was premised on the claim that the US was the savior of the true, democratic Cuban revolution against Soviet imperialism and Cuban quislings. Such an elaborate explanation for what in any other context was old-fashioned 'gunboat diplomacy' needed a supple historical and political argument. State Department boilerplate about the Soviet menace would not suffice, if the exiles' insertion was to be presented as an effort at reform. On 3 April, just two weeks before the landing craft entered the Baya de Cochinos, the administration's 'White Paper' on Cuba appeared to great approval. Written by Arthur Schlesinger, Jr, it presented itself as a critique of Castroism from the left (even very selectively quoting I. F. Stone to buttress its argument that Cuba was turning to the Soviets), and repeated Kennedy's admission during the campaign that the US had backed Batista. Schlesinger in fact sent a draft of it to JFK with an explanation that

> the function of this document, I take it, is to win over those who had some initial sympathy for the Cuban Revolution, to give them reasons for changing their minds and thus provide them a bridge by which they can accept the necessity of hemisphere condemnation of Castro.[38]

Meanwhile, to deconstruct the myth of *fidelismo* for a more specialized audience, the prestigious London magazine *Encounter* – main covert CIA front among the transatlantic intelligentsia – asked the redoubtable scholar of US Communism, Theodore Draper, for an in-depth assessment of the character of the Cuban Revolution that would confound and convince the non-Communist left, especially those who might be wavering on Cuba.[39]

Taking on in detail all of the various liberal and radical defenders of the revolution – Mills, Huberman and Sweezy, Matthews, the Englishman Paul Johnson in *The New Statesman* – and for balance the extreme rightwing narrative of Nathaniel Weyl, Draper presented a Marxist analysis of Castro's revolution as one of those

> bastard and spurious 'socialisms' born of Leninism's convergence with the status anxiety of the underdeveloped world: Instead of the proletariat, they issue out of the middle class, but of that portion in revolt against the failure of the middle class. These sons and daughters of the bourgeoisie gravitate irresistibly towards the ideology of socialism, but they can make use only of those aspects of socialism which conditions permit them to utilise. They cannot be faithful to the fundamental ideas of the socialist tradition – that the proletariat should liberate itself, that there are prerequisites for socialism, especially an advanced industrial economy, and that socialism must fulfil and complement political democracy.[40]

For Draper, then, Castroism was one more stage of the story of how Communists had traduced Marx, but it was also a distinctly new progression beyond the renegade National Communism of Tito or Mao Tse-tung, into the ideologically inchoate nationalism of Ghana's Kwame Nkhrumah or Guinea's Sékou Touré, with Fidel personally 'as much demagogue as idealist, as much adventurer as revolutionary, as much anarchist as Communist or anything else.'[41] The title of this still-influential essay bore home Draper's ultimate message for any leftist reader: 'Castro's Cuba: A Revolution Betrayed?', a conscious echo of Trotsky's massive 1937 indictment of Stalinism, *The Revolution Betrayed*, implicitly offering a way to be honorably anti-Castro. As we shall see, it did not take long for a socialist position to cohere in support of the counter-revolution.

By the time the invasion forces landed before dawn on Monday, 17 April, a current of tension and suppressed hysteria akin to the approach of war was felt in the US. The respectable press reported a claim that pro-Castro Cubans in south Florida were plotting to kidnap little Caroline Kennedy.[42] Both *The New Republic* and the *New York Times* spiked big stories with detailed evidence of the CIA's plan, though the *Times* did report on 11 April that a serious internal debate over what to do regarding Cuba had 'oddly enough ... divided many old friends in the process'. At a 12 April press conference, Kennedy told a series of bold-faced lies about his commitment to nonintervention in Cuba and respect for international law and went unchallenged, despite the rumors sweeping Washington and the open discussion of the invasion in Miami, as last-minute volunteers were funneled into Brigade 2506 and the addresses of recruiting offices ran openly in both Spanish- and English-language daily papers in New York.[43] The axis of the entire plan, though, was that the landing's galvanizing shock, married to the efforts of clandestine counter-revolutionaries and progaganda mimicking the homegrown *fidelista* feel (for example, the offshore Radio Swan's staged amateurism, with chairs audibly scraping on floors) would set off a popular uprising. Anyone wanting to understand the CIA's projection of what would happen needed only to look at the Associated Press lead story following the invasion's disastrous first day:

> Anti-Castro forces struck their long-awaited invasion blow for liberation of Cuba Monday and claimed immediate successes.
>
> The counter-revolutionary blows went in by air and sea with help from uncounted Castro foes rising inside Cuba.
>
> Bearded Prime Minister Fidel Castro, his red-tinged government at stake, kept silent on how the battle was going after announcing the initial landings, and denouncing the United States for causing them. ...
>
> Amid a fever of rebel reports and rumors, anti-Castro spokesmen claimed thousands of Castro's militiamen had deserted him at the first shot and that the first thrust of the invaders carried to the area of Colon, astride central Cuba's main east-west highway.[44]

As is obvious, something very different took place. The Cuban revolutionary government was quite capable of reading the same Guatemalan newspapers that the US press chose to ignore, and knew their historical precedents – in particular, the recent Guatemalan example. They had 'armed the people', organizing a massive militia, and were primed to quell any attempts at internal subversion by detaining every possible counter-revolutionary at the first news of an attack. The overwhelming popular response suggests that many Cubans had been waiting a long time for such an opportunity to repel a foreign intruder, and even with a less-prepared government, the invaders would never have had a chance. The exiles begin skirmishing with local militia as soon as they waded ashore, and within a day tens of thousands of troops converged on the beachhead with Castro in the lead, while Cuban pilots flying a few propeller-driven trainers (hardly the 'Soviet MiGs' that the CIA's PR men claimed) played havoc with the Agency's overextended fleet of World War II–era bombers. The invasion force of 1,400 men never got off the beach, and quite clearly they never really expected to fight it out on their own, nor to 'exfiltrate' out of the swampland landing zone and become a guerrilla force. As all the official studies soon made clear, the exiles' North American handlers, in good or bad faith, had given assurances that Kennedy would never allow them to lose, and they could expect US help to whatever degree was needed. Faced with the terrible truth that they were not a scouting force for the Marines, Brigade 2506 quickly collapsed, surrendering after three days with less than a hundred dead and all heavy weapons intact – an ignominious defeat that no amount of teeth-gnashing bellicosity in later decades could conceal.

'If That Isn't Organized Protest, What Is?'

The Bay of Pigs had two measurable effects upon the domestic politics of the United States. First, it sparked the kind of outright public protest that since the Cold War's beginning had been deemed un-American, unpatriotic and un-acceptable regarding any aspect of US foreign policy. Second, it split apart the formerly solid front of liberalism by hitting at the root of its postwar anti-Communist consensus, so that for the first time, a wide range of liberal Democrats and their socialist and peace activist allies took to openly quarrel-ling with each other over whether the first Democratic president since Harry Truman had done right, or should be supported even if he had done wrong.

At home, it took only hours for serious anger to bubble over into the streets under the auspices of Fair Play for Cuba. Not surprisingly, New York and San Francisco led the way in terms of large-scale responses. Actions with up to 2,000 people outside the United Nations began the same day as the invasion and lasted throughout the entire week of the crisis, culminating in a rally of perhaps 5,000 in Union Square on 21 April – the largest leftwing demonstra-tion there or anywhere else in the US since the execution of the Rosenbergs, and one also unprecedented in that a young Communist and a young Trotsky-ist shared the same public podium, brought together by the 26th of July.[45] That same day, FPCC ran 'An Appeal to Americans' in the *Times* that had been turned down by four Chicago papers and the *St Louis Post-Dispatch*. After excoriating Rusk and the CIA in particular, it concluded:

> For our part, our consciences demand that we denounce before the world the intervention of our government in Cuba's domestic affairs. We here state that we will do all in our power to safeguard the integrity of the legitimate government of Cuba, and that we will work to preserve the integrity of our own and, when it is necessary, recall it to its duties and obligations.
>
> If this be treason, we stand condemned.[46]

Meanwhile, San Francisco saw demonstrations in which students played a leading role. Coordinated actions on various Bay Area campuses on 19 April were followed by a student-only rally of 2,000 in Union Square on 20 April, and an equally large all-ages Fair Play demonstration at the Civic Center on 22 April, where protesters picketed the Federal Building and then spontaneously took to the streets of the downtown area to march to the offices of Hearst's virulently anti-Castro *San Francisco Examiner*, an unheard thing to do in those days – as one SWP and FPCC leader remembered it, the 'young hotheads' were 'ready to go. They started the march down Market Street and so, we said, well, "Here it goes".'[47] This was also the rally at which C. Wright Mills's terse, apocalyptic condemnation of Cold War liberalism, with its premonitory challenge to go the limit, was read aloud:

> Kennedy and Co. have returned to barbarism. Schlesinger and Co. have disgraced us intellectually and morally. I feel a desperate shame for my country. Sorry I cannot be with you. Were I physically able to do so, I would at this moment be fighting alongside Fidel Castro.[48]

Fair Play's real test of strength, however, was the extent to which actions immediately took place elsewhere. Many hundreds turned up for protests in Chicago, Los Angeles, Washington, D.C. and Boston, but smaller protests were reported across the US, in Tampa, Philadelphia, Detroit, Cleveland, New Haven, Seattle and Baltimore. From our post-Vietnam vantage point, the numbers participating seem so small as to be inconsequential – *Fair Play* reported 100 in Tampa, 150 in Detroit, 200 in Boston, and 300 in Chicago on 20 April in a driving rain – but that is not how these rallies and marches were seen at the time. To many in the hardly silent conservative majority, this was an intolerable revival of a radicalism they had thought long extinguished. When a few dozen Fair Players from Ohio's tiny Antioch College left their campus and went to the state capitol in Columbus to picket, they excited statewide outrage, physical assaults, threats from their own college's trustees, and national attention, as former members fondly recall; this experience was repeated across the country.[49] Indeed, many chapters reported open violence against peaceful demonstrators by anti-Castroites and other harassment during and after the invasion: meeting-hall bookings were cancelled in Los Angeles, Detroit, Newark and Tampa; the Chicago chapter was evicted from its headquarters; the Seattle Student Council had to fight simply for the right to have a picket; Fair Players in Rockford, Illinois were first assaulted by a civilian (as was a picket line in Philadelphia) and then arrested by police; in Providence, police dispersed a demonstration by a dozen Brown University FPCC members 'before it got under way'.[50]

As can already be seen, the most powerful indication of dissent came from students. In relation to the size of the surrounding communities, the crowds attending campus rallies and debates dwarfed anything else in the country, and these events were no longer inside, decorously under wraps, but outdoors and vociferous in the fashion associated with what came later in the decade. And since many of these schools were out in the hinterlands, blame could no longer be assigned to the residual strength of the Reds, as the *Times* did with its claim that at the big Union Square rally of several thousand people in New

York, 'most' of those present 'were recognized as faithful attendants at local Communist Party affairs'.[51] Though this fervor burned itself out quickly with the end of the school year, for a moment it did seem as if FPCC was making 'deep inroads into the political life of colleges in all parts of the country', as the Young Americans for Freedom anxiously warned that spring.[52]

The largest disturbances ensued where Cuba was already a major topic of student polemics, including Cornell, Swarthmore, Madison, Berkeley, City College, Yale, the University of Michigan and Oberlin.[53] At Cornell on 20 April, 400 students met for what one disgusted conservative called a 'fire-eating rally' on the steps of Willard Straight Hall, while the university chimesmaster made his own comment by playing patriotic tunes on the campus bells.[54] At Swarthmore, the campus newspaper's headline on 21 April read 'Cuba Affair Stirs Swarthmore' as one student reported on the violent public response when he and 11 others went into Philadelphia for a 19 April Fair Play picket (others went on to FPCC's White House action of 800 on 22 April). The Off-Campus Affairs Committee passed a resolution opposing the intervention, which an emergency meeting of the Student Council approved and decided to submit to the student body as a referendum: it lost by a vote of 346 to 265.[55] At Madison, the New Left and New Right got into a full-fledged fight. A 19 April petition from the Fair Players in the Socialist Club was met by violent abuse, and a 21 April protest rally was moved indoors to a theater because of a counter-protest by the fraternities, centers of proinvasion sentiment – the hanging of Castro in effigy indicates the tone. Even so, 20 boisterous 'Goldwater conservatives' then disrupted this meeting of a 1,000 people for thirty minutes, refusing to let Socialist Club leaders Ron Radosh, Jim McWilliams and Arnold Lockshin proceed. Finally, Ed Garvey, former president of the Wisconsin Student Association, stepped in to mediate, and a shouting-match argument transpired. Subsequently, the debate over this 'mobbing' by the Conservative Club, which one liberal letter-writer called 'Leninist Rightism', occupied the pages of the *Cardinal* for many weeks, and the ebullient Goldwaterites even briefly formed their own Freedom Fighters for Cuba committee.[56]

However, the largest student response to the Bay of Pigs undoubtedly came in the San Francisco Bay Area. Besides the events already described, at Berkeley, 'nearly a thousand' students met at noon on 17 April, within hours of the invasion, and listened to speakers Maurice Zeitlin and Don Warden, a third-year law student, until 3 p.m. The next evening, 60 students from five campuses formed the 'Bay Area Student Committee to Oppose U.S. Intervention in Cuba', which sponsored the two massive citywide student rallies that UC-Berkeley President Clark Kerr denounced as 'not the work of students'.[57] Around San Francisco at least, it felt as if a Rubicon had been crossed. As Dale Johnson explained in a hurried postscript to his *Studies on the Left* article, 'On the Ideology of the Campus Revolution',

The American intervention in Cuba ... has had a tremendous impact on both the size of the student movement and its ideology, at least in the Bay Area. Many student 'hangers-on' and potential rebels have been activated by the gross nature of the irrationality in high places. Most important, however, is the fact that U.S. imperialistic ventures have served to *radicalize* the dissenters. For example: (a) the concept of demonstration has been altered to include 'dramatic non-violent acts of civil disobedience'; (b) new and truly radical students have gained leadership positions and the old activists have moved to the left along with their student base of support.[58]

Much of this student activism was only indirectly related to Fair Play for Cuba, but African-American responses to the Bay of Pigs came more explicitly under FPCC's instigation. The prime example of the latter is 'A Declaration of Conscience by Afro-Americans', which appeared in the *Afro-American* on 22 April 1961 and in the *New York Post* three days later. Initiated by Richard Gibson, signed by twenty-seven others (including W. E. B. Du Bois who, with his wife, Shirley Graham Du Bois, had recently joined FPCC's Brooklyn branch), and labelled a Fair Play advertisement, it hammered home how liberation in Cuba was tied to fighting the 'segs' at home:

> Because we have known oppression, because we have suffered more than other Americans, because we are still fighting for our liberation from tyranny, we Afro-Americans have the right and the duty to raise our voices in protest against the forces of oppression that now seek to crush a free people linked to us by bonds of blood and by a common heritage. ...
> Now our brothers are threatened again – this time by a gang of ousted white Cuban politicians who find segregated Miami more congenial than integrated Havana. ...
> Afro-Americans won't be fooled. The enemies of the Cubans are our enemies, the Jim Crow bosses of this land where we are still denied our rights. The Cubans are our friends. The Cubans are the enemies of our enemies.

One week later in the *Afro-American*, William Worthy compared the US in Cuba to other colonial powers frightened by what they feared was 'an incoming tide of black supremacy', and intimated a later wave of African-American anger in his own personal reaction to the invasion: 'Home is home, I long have told myself. Yet with every passing month I anticipate fewer and fewer regrets about handing in my Jim Crow resignation from this moral wilderness.'[59] Such hardbitten vitriol was hardly unique. Charles H. Loeb, the publisher of another major black paper, the *Cleveland Call and Post*, opined on the same day that

> It never occurred to our arm-chair diplomats that the pressures exerted on Castro might have come from the people rather than from the always-convenient Soviets. They wanted land, so Castro gave them land. They wanted status, so Castro pro-

moted hundreds from peonage to politics; from privation to privilege. They wanted control of their own industries, so Castro had to seize it from those who really controlled it – the American money interests who owned it, and the Cuban opportunists who manipulated it for their American bosses.

This, frankly represents Castro's blackest crime, and any except an opinionated, color-prejudiced fool, could see it if he half looked. But nobody wanted to see it – and what's worse, nobody who saw it could talk too freely about it without fear of retaliation from official segments of the United States.[60]

From Monroe, North Carolina, Robert F. Williams dispatched an open telegram to Cuba's Foreign Minister Raúl Roa, then denouncing the US before the United Nations. Mocking Kennedy's justifications for the intervention 'in the cause of freedom', he asked Roa to 'Please convey to Mr. Adlai Stevenson this message':

Now that the United States has proclaimed military support for people willing to rebel against oppression, oppressed Negroes in the South urgently request tanks, artillery, bombs, money, use of American airfields and white mercenaries to crush the racist tyrants who have betrayed the American Revolution and Civil War. We also request prayers for this noble undertaking.[61]

This jibe would have had all the effect of a lone hand trying to clap, but that Roa read it aloud to the Political Committee of the UN General Assembly during the tense debate on the evening of 20 April, when the outcome of the invasion was still in doubt. As if to cement the point, Gibson first told the Senate's Internal Security Subcommittee on 25 April that 'On behalf of the Fair Play for Cuba Committee, and speaking personally for myself and for many other American Negroes, I can only express delight at the utter and dismal defeat of this act of international banditry', and then read them the texts of 'The Declaration of Conscience' and Williams's message to Roa.[62] The *Times* gave prominence to both Gibson's appearance and a report on 9 May that the Immigration and Naturalization Service had barred him from exiting the country (a report quickly denied). Meanwhile it was also widely reported that Robert Taber had been wounded at the beachhead while covering the fighting for *Revolución*.[63]

The hipsters made their own splash, and naturally Norman Mailer managed to turn it into a literary vignette. At the end of the invasion week, just before the *Village Voice* ran his man-to-man letters to Castro and JFK, Mailer and the editors of five literary magazines staged their own picket at the UN. Later, in a long article on Jacqueline Kennedy, Mailer described how one particularly flamboyant protester had carried a sign with the peculiar message, 'Jacqueline, Vous Avez Perdu Vos Artistes'. Negligible as this may seem, there is little question that the self-created Camelot on Pennsylvania Avenue dearly loved its reputation as a haven for the cultured. Apparently Mrs Kennedy was quite offended at Mailer's sly story, and refused him an interview despite their earlier friendliness during her husband's campaign.[64] Mailer also spoke during the Bay of Pigs at a major 'Symposium on Cuba' in New York, with Murray Kempton and Michael Harrington; between them, these three men represented the three distinct positions among the liberal intelligentsia not only at that moment, but as they would play out over the coming generation.[65]

Meanwhile, Fair Play for Cuba's doings were causing high-level disquiet, with *Fair Play* reporting exultantly in early May that CIA Director Allen Dulles had attacked the committee in an off-the-record briefing. Four years later, in the bestselling memoir of his White House duty, *A Thousand Days*, Arthur Schlesinger, Jr still remembered all the details of the wave of protest as '... some on the left, more than one might have thought, now saw full vindication of their pre-election doubts about Kennedy.' In an excellent precís of events during the week of the invasion, he cited the reactions of graduate students and his colleagues at Harvard such as H. Stuart Hughes and Barrington Moore, Jr, the telegram indicting him from C. Wright Mills, and how 'Protest meetings erupted on a dozen campuses' and 'A Fair Play for Cuba rally at Union Square in New York on April 21 drew three thousand people.'[66]

There are many such hints of unease among the political classes, but the best bit of contemporary evidence for the upsurge's felt impact was recorded in Arthur Krock's magisterial *Times* column in late May, when the heat had barely cooled. Krock was one of those disturbed by the lack of *realpolitik* among the intellectuals. To buttress his point, he quoted comments made 'from his State Department desk' by William Yandell Elliot, the Williams Professor of Government at Harvard (like many others from Cambridge, Elliot had moved south with the new administration). Expressing disgust at Harvard's 'Cuba protest meeting' of 400 students and faculty, which had adopted an 'Open Letter' to Kennedy, Elliot noted that this convocation had been 'one of 134 similar meetings all over the United States', a remarkable figure that in itself suggests close monitoring by an anxious government. But it was Elliot's conclusion that should be underscored: '*if that isn't organized protest, what is?*'[67] As with Lyndon Johnson later, he saw only one possibility: the Communists were up to their old tricks, stirring up trouble among the gullible. But something else was happening that at the time seemed impossible or irrational. No party, organized force or group – not even Fair Play, however much credit it deserved for pulling together a national network and getting people to the island – was orchestrating this measurable tremor of protest; rather we can say with some confidence that during the Bay of Pigs (as with the disarmament protests and civil rights agitation gearing up at the same time), a new US left was making itself.

However much they did not appreciate the inner workings of that New Left, Elliot and Schlesinger understood their times better than many do even in hindsight, and the notice they gave to this level of 'organized protest' should be taken seriously. One result of the sixties was that disenchanted radicals, the press and just about everyone else became blasé about demonstrations, marches and protests: by the late 1980s, even large-scale arrests for civil disobedience rarely merited national news coverage. In the post-Vietnam years from Presidents Carter to Bush, a persistent level of public agitation against US military interventionism was expected, and from this vantage point 15,000 or so marchers over the course of two weeks seems a feeble response to a historic event like the Bay of Pigs. But there was no reason to expect any protest at all in 1961. The valid reference point is not Vietnam later in the decade, but the absence of dissent over the remarkably similar proxy intervention by the CIA in Guatemala in 1954. In the latter case, the historian cannot find more than a wall graffitti in San Francisco and a few dozen Communists and their friends picketing the UN in New York. The April 1961 rallies and pickets led by Fair Play for Cuba form a powerful contrast to the debacle in 1954, and indeed are comparable in impact and scale to the famous April 1965 Washington antiwar rally organized by SDS, when an unprecedented 25,000 marchers gathered after months of escalation that, unlike Cuba or Guatemala, involved the massive commitment of US ground troops.

The Liberals' 'Dirty Business'

Beyond these hectic free-for-alls with unruly youth and assorted peaceniks as a nagging thorn in the side, there was a layer of criticism of the Kennedyites from closer to home that blended practicality and morality and was hardly 'pro-Castro'. This current of anger within the institutions and private worlds of anti-Communist liberalism foretold a future schism – the Democrats' breakup when men like Hubert Humphrey, Gene McCarthy and George McGovern nearly destroyed each other and their party over Vietnam. Nor did the disagreements with the premises of Kennedy's 'little war in Cuba' follow an obvious pattern. It was hardly left versus right within the Democratic Party: J. William Fulbright, who alone fought to block the invasion, was also a Southern Democrat and a states-righter, while the men who wrote the manifestoes and soothed the would-be leaders of the 'provisional government' were archetypal Northern liberals, heirs of Franklin Roosevelt like Schlesinger, Berle and JFK himself.

At the time, the veteran leftists Carl Marzani and Robert Light argued that one result of the Bay of Pigs disaster was that 'some sectors of the ruling class are beginning to take stock.' Suggesting that this 'low' in 1961 from the high of 1945 was understood as 'disastrous' even for 'the narrower class interests of the ruling groups themselves', they declared that 'Cuba has brought out into the open a debate which has been going on among the power elite in the privacy of their homes, offices and clubs', citing Walter Lippmann, the *New York Times* and other mainstays of the Eastern Establishment.[68] The left's job, then, was to 'widen and deepen the debate between the re-adjusters and the standpatters, to isolate such powerful forces as Standard Oil and the Pentagon which will not budge a millimeter':

> The contemporary King Canutes have already suffered a major defeat in the very fact that a debate has begun. ... It is our belief that events will force this debate to go deeper and deeper and to penetrate into all layers of the American population.[69]

Reading the most famous among the political pundits of the day, those whose reputations have lasted because they were willing to go beyond the columnist's usual role of sounding board or loudspeaker, one finds considerable evidence for the thesis that the Bay of Pigs set off alarms among the 'power elite'. The essence of these doubts about the pursuit of empire on such foolhardy terms was voiced by Walter Lippmann, who who 'more than any other man determined critical Washington's taste buds', and had heavily promoted Jack Kennedy's candidacy in 1960.[70] Lippmann's acid conclusion in his column of 27 April 1961 indicates the extent to which the new president had crossed a line:

> Have they thought what a little war in Cuba would be like after the Marines had captured Havana and a few cities and had then to govern a revolutionary peasantry? Our people have to fix it in their minds that the world-wide revolution cannot be stopped and settled by the U.S. Marines.[71]

And if anyone doubted that Lippmann was deliberately casting the United States as an imperial power and raising the need for an anti-imperial readjustment, he continued his excoriations on 18 May, attacking 'the Dulles system of Asian protectorates' now 'crumbling' in Iran, South Korea, Laos and Vietnam:

> These American client states are not only corrupt but they are intolerably reactionary. ... Our present experience on the periphery of Asia is the American equivalent of what the British and French are experiencing during the dissolution of their colonial empires.[72]

In similar fashion, a few days after the invaders surrendered, Drew Pearson pointed out that Castro was widely supported because 'the landless peasants of Cuba – who can be the biggest asset to a revolutionary force – now have land. So they're for Castro ...', a claim until then made only by the Cassandra-like Herbert L. Matthews.[73]

Murray Kempton, the liberal's liberal writing in the *New York Post*, hit hardest of all on 19 April. After noting how 'the French ... rejoiced that we now have an Algeria' and 'the British were glad to know we had found a Kenya', he compared the sordidness of 'this dirty business' to the war the US had provoked with Mexico in 1846, citing Lincoln's courage in denouncing that war versus the cravenness of the present:

> The debate in the United States followed the lines customary in our debate: (1) it did not exist; (2) what faint quivers there were appear to have been resolved by the reflection that Castro betrayed the revolution. Ask no more why we do not give BARs [Browning Automatic Rifles] to people attempting to overthrow Trujillo; Trujillo never betrayed a revolution.[74]

Kempton then imagined a satiric dialogue with a close friend, in which they played the parts of Emerson and Thoreau when the latter, in opposing the Mexican War, had invented the concept of 'civil disobedience':

> I do not propose to go to jail over this matter – assuming that the rulers of the earth would condescend to send me – and thus our grandchildren will miss the catch in the throat which otherwise would dampen their eyes at the news that a man I revere had said to me, 'What are you doing in jail, uh, Murray?' and I firmly and bravely gave reply, 'And what are you doing out there, Arthur Schlesinger, Jr., and what would your father think if he could see you?'[75]

He concluded by drawing a sharp distinction between what anti-Castro Cubans might choose to do ('Under ordinary circumstances, being no Fidelista, I should wish them well'), and what it meant for the US to sponsor and direct such an invasion: 'There is every excuse for them; but there is no excuse for Allen Dulles and John F. Kennedy. If you think there is, you are, believe me, wrong.'[76]

Beyond these individual voices sounding the tocsin, various sectors of traditional Establishment liberalism manifested considerable distress over the invasion. On 26 April, the General Board of Christian Social Concerns of the Methodist Church, one of the largest Protestant denominations, declared itself opposed to all forms of intervention and urged the US to reopen diplomatic relations with Cuba.[77] The Unitarians, a smaller denomination with a long tradition in New England reform, followed suit in 'overwhelmingly' opposing US intervention in Cuba in mid May.[78] The fourteenth annual convention of the Americans for Democratic Action, vital center of Cold War liberalism since its 1947 founding, was torn by disagreement between those who supported the invasion, led by ADA founder Schlesinger, and a group led by *New York Post* editor James Wechsler, who wanted to condemn it outright.[79] Even the legal profession spoke up, when 132 attorneys sent the president a 29-page brief demonstrating the unlawfulness of supporting military action from the US against a sovereign nation; signers included major corporate lawyers; four former judges; Arthur Larson, the ex-director of the US Information Agency; and many law school professors, such as Yale's Thomas Emerson and Fowler Harper.[80]

The greatest stir was created when mainstream academia, rarely associated with 'fair play' towards Cuba or anywhere else in these years, made its own bid of disapproval. In later years, it is a given that leftwing ideas enjoy some currency in the US academy, but in the postwar decades, an opposite assumption was common and for good reason. The humanities and social sciences had enlisted en masse in the Cold War, just as they had signed up for the earlier war against Hitler. The Northeastern elite schools in particular still saw themselves as guardians of conservative tradition and high culture. Thus it was a genuine shock to the system when not one but three different 'open letters' came out of the Ivy League in quick succession during May 1961: first a Harvard *pronunciamento* signed by 70 (which, as we have seen, caused the greatest stir), then a historians' letter initiated by Carl Schorske of Princeton and signed by 181 professors in forty-one different departments, finally a Princeton-only letter signed by 38 members of the faculty. The Cuban Revolutionary Council went through a great show of denouncing the Harvard professors in the press, and four of the latter (Eric Bentley, David Riesman, H. Stuart Hughes and Donald Fleming) promptly agreed to debate 'on television and elsewhere', while a countergroup formed at Princeton, and declared over 43 professors' names that 'those who would have us adhere, without exception, to a unilateral position of nonintervention condemn us to a steady erosion of the free world.' Here as elsewhere the precedent invoked to justify the invasion was the appeasement of Fascism in the thirties.[81]

This degree of dissent within aboveground politics crested at a certain point, however, outmatched at all times by a fierce barrage from those advocating immediate retaliation for Castro's temerity, including powerful figures in both parties. On 1 May alone, following the invasion's failure, Republican Senator Hugh Scott and Democrats Styles Bridges and Herman Talmadge spoke out urging a full-scale war, and Nixon carefully maneuvered throughout, saying both that he would back the president and that the price of his bipartisanship was going all the way to remove the cancer of Castroism.[82] This push for a military solution placed a continual pressure upon 'responsible' liberals to back JFK as the voice of moderation. Still, it is sobering that so few newspapers went as far as the *St Louis Post-Dispatch*, which suggested it was 'unwise' to back counter-revolutionaries with so little support among the populace, but praised JFK for avoiding 'open intervention by American troops', or the *Detroit News*, which noted delicately that

> The world thinks the big fellow is seeking to re-establish his influence in the little fellow's back yard. The main lesson is: never get into a situation like this if you can't or won't follow through.[83]

Even these hesitant gestures towards nonintervention found no echo in Congress. On 17 May, the House voted 401 to 2 for a motion declaring Castro 'a clear and present danger' to the Americas. The lonely dissenters were Clare Hoffman, Republican of Michigan, and Frank Kowalski, Democrat of Connecticut. Similarly, in the Senate, besides Fulbright, only the iconoclastic Wayne Morse was willing to declare the invasion 'a colossal mistake' in itself, and not merely because it was bungled.[84]

To the extent that public opinion can be measured by polling, the results were more ambiguous. Certainly most North Americans seemed hostile to Castro. A Gallup Poll taken the week after the Bay of Pigs showed that only one in seven thought that he could win a free election in Cuba, though even that 14 percent is noticeably high for such a reviled figure; Gallup had stopped asking if anyone 'approved' of Fidel. What is truly notable is that an overwhelming majority (63 percent to 24 percent) opposed the use of US troops, and the public split evenly (44 percent yea to 41 percent nay) on whether the US should give money and guns to the counter-revolutionaries. Nearly a quarter also thought an embargo a bad idea.[85] Obviously, polls can be both taken and read in various ways to support a preferred conclusion, and a private survey sponsored by the administration in May 1961 showed that more than nine in ten 'endorsed the attempt of Cuban refugees to get rid of Castro'.[86] Still, the remarkable consistency over the next two years in the majorities opposing the use of US troops suggests a distaste for intervention among ordinary voters, even if that meant tolerating Castro, and it is not unreasonable to conclude that Kennedy's approval ratings went up after the invasion at least in part because he was perceived as avoiding any rash escalation.[87]

Disgust from Lippmann, contention within the ADA and the professoriate, and a surprising moderation among the public only hints at a deeper discontent. Obviously enough, there were no resignations from the administration, or the promotion of opposition caucuses and quixotic candidacies as during Vietnam, when even the 1972 Republican presidential primaries were disturbed by an antiwar standard bearer, Rep. Paul McCloskey. In charting how the Bay of Pigs called forth the first muted trumpets of a new anti-imperialism, one cannot look for a contemporary body-count, measurable in congressional votes or immediate policy shifts. Instead, the major effect of this humiliation was to accelerate the push for counterinsurgency and covert action in Cuba and elsewhere. The Kennedys gave the green light to a CIA campaign of sabotage and guerrilla war against Castro, which, when exposed in the 1970s, helped sustain an anti-intervention consensus in Congress and the public. And rather than pulling back from overextended commitments in Southeast Asia, JFK pushed forward, with only the most circumstantial evidence suggesting that he contemplated withdrawal after the 1964 elections. Indeed, it is easier to demonstrate that in late 1963, Kennedy was considering a *modus vivendi* with Fidel.

Nonetheless, among a considerable number of Democrats a verdict was privately pronounced that the gross violation of international and US law at the Bay of Pigs was not only mistaken but flawed in a deeper sense. If no one of note moved explicitly towards the politics of Fair Play for Cuba, by now out on the edge of militant solidarity, ethical objections were voiced across a wide spectrum, a foreboding that Kennedy really did not give a damn about playing fair with Castro or anybody else. This fear of imperial hubris about 'the rights and wrongs of public morality' and the need for 'a basic moral reference point' in dealing with weaker nations, the subtext of Fulbright, Lippmann and Kempton, is made explicit in a May 1961 diary entry by Under-Secretary of State Chester Bowles:

> The question which concerns me most about this new Administration is whether it lacks a genuine sense of conviction about what is right and what is wrong. I realize in posing the question I am raising an extremely serious point. Nevertheless I feel it must be faced.
>
> Anyone in public life who has strong convictions about the rights and wrongs of public morality, both domestic and international, has a very great advantage in times of strain, since his instincts on what to do are clear and immediate. Lacking such a framework of moral conviction or sense of what is right and what is wrong, he is forced to lean almost entirely upon his mental processes; he adds up the plusses and the minuses of any question and comes up with a conclusion. Under normal conditions, when he is not tired or frustrated, this pragmatic approach should successfully bring him out on the right side of the question.
>
> What worries me are the conclusions that such an individual may reach when he is tired, angry, frustrated, or emotionally affected. The Cuban fiasco demonstrates how far astray a man as brillant and well intentioned as Kennedy can go who lacks a basic moral reference point.[88]

Publicly Bowles spoke for the administration's small coterie of doves in more elliptical language. A late May radio address blended practicality, implicit morality and disdainful *noblesse oblige*: 'It would be very wrong if we get trapped into a fight between the United States of America, with its 180 million people, and Mr. Castro and his beard, and whatever number of the Cuban people want to fight with him.'[89]

Similarly, at the end of June Fulbright warned that the US should not 'disfigure our national style' and try to 'beat the Communists at their own game', and in July Stevenson returned from Latin America reporting the widespread feeling that 'the Cuban peasant has acquired his place in the sun', therefore the US should avoid 'investing Fidelismo with an aura of martyrdom' by more direct intervention.[90] Regardless of how it was phrased, the Kennedy men had little tolerance for such subtleties and strong-armed their internal dissenters, with Pierre Salinger calling Bowles 'yellow-bellied', and others spreading the word that Stevenson 'wanted a Munich'.[91] These Rough Rider tactics must also have caused some disquiet, but like so much else it was buried. The time had not come for public schisms, which required as goad the quagmire resulting when the US finally tried 'to govern a revolutionary peasantry'.

From such anecdotal shards as church resolutions and statements both public and private one can assemble a circumstantial case that the Bay of Pigs spurred anti-interventionist feeling among the Democrats' liberal base in the middle classes; certainly the party's labor wing showed no similar discontent, but that is another story. There is also is the commonsense conviction that the antiwar movement erupting in slow-motion after 1965, and which in 1967–68 overthrew a president from within his own party, was not a species of mass conversion but the surfacing of widespread 'peace' sentiments always present among liberals, if repressed in a Cold War context. However, to really argue that distaste for empire as a significant current of Democratic politics was not the result of Vietnam, but predated it, wants more measurable proof. This current did not yet exist in Congress during the Bay of Pigs, nor for long thereafter, given the overwhelming support for the Gulf of Tonkin Resolution in 1964 and similar measures. Notwithstanding this impasse, the political structure of the United States extends below the federal level, and in later decades, activists made good use of allies in city halls and state legislatures to signal displeasure with foreign policy. In the years when Castro was the whipping boy of Cold Warriors of all persuasions, however, these venues remained closed.

What is left then are the political parties, the great incubators and conductors of tension in US politics. In the early 1960s, a New Right was germinating within the Republicans that in time would move the GOP and the United States in a new direction, with Barry Goldwater as its first standard-bearer against statist liberalism, whether that of Nelson Rockefeller or the Kennedys. The Democrats appeared more cohesive, except for their old problem of a Southern wing that was the nation's anchor of conservatism. On the face of things, his party backed JFK monolithically on Cuba, if congressional votes or statements are any measure, with only Wayne Morse offering direct public criticism. Yet substantial statistical evidence suggests that among leading local Democrats outside the South, a strong minority were well to the left of anyone in Congress in opposing JFK's 'get-tough' policy. In this respect, Fair Play for Cuba founder Alan Sagner was not a lone wolf, but only ahead of his time. Indeed, once he left FPCC sometime before the Bay of Pigs, Sagner went back to being a party insider at both state and national levels for the next three decades.[92]

In mid 1963, soon after the Cuban Missile Crisis, when hostility to Castro was at its peak, a group of social scientists surveyed attitudes on 'coping with Cuba' among 'members of state and county central committees of the Democratic and Republican parties' in five large Western counties: San Francisco, Santa Clara and Los Angeles counties in California; Boulder, Colorado; and Kings County, Washington, which includes Seattle.[93] The local Republicans' 'policy preferences' demonstrate the pressure for more direct intervention, with a plurality (46 percent) favoring invasion of Cuba with US troops, the strongest of the five options presented, and most of the rest (40 percent) endorsing another US-supported exile invasion. The Democrats were another story, and agreed on little except their support for a president of their own party. Fully one-third – the largest single group – favored 'Economic aid to Cuba', the most liberal option presented, in a context where 'economic aid' clearly indicated a radical reversal in policy; another 14 percent supported a 'Conciliatory status quo'. Ranged against this plurality of 47 percent who supported a peaceful accommodation with Castro were more than a quarter who wanted another invasion, either with US troops (9 percent) or exiles (17 percent), and 27 percent who supported 'Further economic sanctions', Kennedy's avowed policy.

From the survey's careful correlation of responses to a wide range of questions, it is clear that the group advocating 'economic aid' formed a coherent ideological bloc in the party. They were most likely to envision an invasion of Cuba leading to all-out nuclear war, most worried about their chances of surviving such a war, gave 100 percent approval to 'increased support to the US Arms Control and Disarmament Agency' and the lowest rates of support (18 percent) to 'increasing the defense budget' and 'federal funds to construct fallout shelters'. Regarding Cuba specifically, these peace Democrats were the only ones, among all those polled, who gave Castro an average rating on the 'good-bad' scale of recent world leaders that did not place him in the company of Hitler and Stalin (though he did not cross over the median into approval, unlike Khrushchev). Nine in ten recognized that 'the majority of the Cuban people prefer Castro to Batista' and 97 percent agreed that the US 'is at least partly responsible for the bad relations between Cuba and the United States.' By comparison, 70 percent of the many Republicans (and some Democrats) who wanted to send in the Marines assumed that the Cuban people preferred Batista.

The peace bloc's despair regarding their preferred policy's chance of adoption is especially striking. While overwhelming majorities of the Democrats who advocated a new exile invasion or further economic sanctions expected their choice to go forward (76 percent and 70 percent, respectively), only one in ten of those who wanted an 'open door' for the Cuban revolution thought that there was a chance of this happening, despite their potential strength as a group. This negative assessment helps explain liberal acquiescence to a policy of status-quo hostility that they did not support – lesser-evil politics with a vengeance, in what the studies' authors called a 'pall of pessimism', with a resonance wider than just Cuba. There was another subtext here, which clarifies the absence of open intra-party struggle. As the authors of the study put it, 'Cuba appears to be a spectacularly divisive question, more so among Democrats than Republicans.' For every liberal who imagined a rapprochement, a Cold Warrior applauded Kennedy's stated resolve to quarantine and, in some dim future, get rid of Fidel. Many of the former must have sensed how any public battle over interventionism abroad would tear the party apart, helping to create the conditions for a new conservative alignment in national politics drawing in many Democratic voters. They were right.

'Until We Have Done with the American Empire Altogether...': Dilemmas on the Left

As one moves across the Democratic Party, responses to the Bay of Pigs are quite unpredictable, from Fulbright's warnings publicized after the fact and the surprising vigor of the Ivy League's dissent to the stiff-upper-lip discipline of Stevenson and the many loyal Stevensonians, presumably including the Westerners described above – though Stevenson's denial of the obvious at the UN cost him dearly in stature: as H. Stuart Hughes remarked on 23 April, it was mortifying 'to see this man who has been a great American reduced to the level of a shyster lawyer.'[94] A more coherent response might be expected, however, on the Democrats' putative left, shading into unequivocal support for Castro on the 'far left' with FPCC and assorted militants around it.[95] This was not the case, and instead of a spectrum one finds contention and disarray. What is central to this confusion is that the anti-Communist or 'anti-Stalinist' leftists in the milieu of the old Socialist Party were typically less forthright in protesting the Bay of Pigs than many of the liberals in the Democratic Party. Given the importance of this milieu to the early New Left, as demonstrated by Maurice Isserman and others, and the influence of the Young Peoples' Socialist League on campuses and in the Student Peace Union, the largest radical youth organization of 1960–62, the failure by North American Socialists to firmly oppose intervention in Cuba was a significant event.

Until the invasion itself, the recently renamed Socialist Party-Social Democratic Federation (SP-SDF) had a measured Third Camp position in public, appearing favorable to the Cuban revolution without declaring any unconditional solidarity: 'There can be many opinions among socialists and liberals on the nature of the Castro regime', but '*no difference* among us as to intervention' [emphasis in original].[96] Some of the most unfettered debates over what was happening on the island took place in *New America*, the SP-SDF's new weekly newspaper edited by Michael Harrington. Late in 1960, for instance, the paper opened 'a discussion on Cuba' with FPCCer William Worthy comparing the US attitude towards Castro to the aversion felt by a 'psychopathic and vengeful Stalin' for Tito, while Victor Alba argued that there was no revolution in Cuba at all, only 'paternalist demagoguery'.[97] In March 1961, the Socialists' National Committee 'called upon the United States government to resume diplomatic relations' and 'repudiate any invasion plans', noting that US hostility was pushing Castro into the Soviets' arms. Only after affirming 'solidarity with the basic aims of the Revolution, and the fight against corporate power and imperialism in Latin America', in the 'context of support to the anti-imperialist fight', were objections made to the curtailment of free speech and labor rights and the abrogation of elections.[98]

Once the exiles began landing at Playa Girón, though, the Socialists began to bob and weave, speaking in several contradictory voices at the same time, both anti-CIA and anti-Castro (or anti-invasion and pro-exile), apparently trying to satisfy disparate internal constituencies. Norman Thomas, the party's leading figure for decades and still widely respected among liberal Democrats, came out furthest to the left, initiating an 'open letter' from forty-nine 'writers, trade unionists and political figures', the strongest action taken by US Socialists. Signed by a very impressive roster, including Norman Podhoretz, Philip Rahv, Edmund Wilson, Van Wyck Brooks, Arthur Miller and A. Philip Randolph, it unambiguously opposed the invasion, stating that although the revolution had 'turned upon its original democratic aims', 'any further intervention will be regarded as a naked, open reactionary attack of imperialism.'[99]

Many in or close to the SP-SDF, however, like those at *The New Leader* heavily promoting Theodore Draper's savaging of *fidelismo*, tilted towards solidarity with the counter-revolutionaries. The most nuanced version of this argument, underlining the contortions required for democratic socialists who 'chose the West', came from *Dissent*, which in June 1961 sent a free Special Supplement to its readers, 'Cuba – The Invasion and The Consequences', by Michael Walzer. This cogent analysis began with the proposition that Latin America was our colonial empire, equivalent to those of the French and British in Africa and Asia, however much we lacked their imperial 'idealism'. Yet Walzer did not advocate the genteel anti-imperialism of those French intellectuals who backed Pierre Mendès-France in accepting Dienbienphu, or the British liberals and socialists who agitated for Indian independence. After dismissing the 'criminal stupidity' of the invasion, he argued that the US could only overturn Castro through a commitment to 'democratic radicalism':

> ... revolt must begin with the newly-mobilized groups – the men in the militia, the peasants on the farms, the workers in the state-controlled unions. It must begin with their disillusionment and it must be based on their discontent. ... This, indeed, is Fidel Castro's achievement – that the struggle against him cannot be won unless it can take on a 'progressive' form.[100]

Walzer then discussed in subtle fashion the ferment among liberals and non-Communist leftists and the demand for a reexamination of Cold War premises, which he evidently recognized led irresistibly towards a solidarity that *Dissent* could not share. In an oddly pleading voice, he called for

a certain turning away from the morbid anti-Americanism prevalent among many radicals today. These men insist that we must see ourselves as others see us – convicted, then, of irrevocable ugliness and stupidity. But it is willfully naive to suggest that this way of seeing does not also involve distortions. ... It is simply not possible to accept *and to live with* the idea that incidents like the Guatemalan *putsch* and the Cuban invasion are inevitable, that the United States is trapped forever in its role as defender of the *status quo*.[101]

The internal tension in this argument is emphasized by Walzer's recognition that 'in a crude, but persistent and convincing manner, American behavior in the Caribbean has conformed to the expectations of the Marxist intellectuals', since 'the CIA is an actor also in the mythic drama of pseudo-Marx'. He concluded by urging that the Alliance for Progress underwrite nationalizations of North American businesses throughout Latin America, to prove 'our own willingness to support radical social change', while we bought off the US corporations nationalized in Cuba, gave up Guantánamo, asked Brazil to mediate, opened relations, and offered aid (with plenty of strings attached), a program little different from that of Fair Play, though the ultimate goals certainly differed. Such a 'flexible' policy would allow us to encourage the best 'democratic and anti-totalitarian elements among the revolutionaries', and if civil war or a faction fight broke out, would ensure that 'we can act quickly and consistently to provide support for the democratic forces.' Looking back, Walzer averred that all of the trouble might have been avoided if Ike had 'spoken to the world from a Cuban village ... followed in his journey by hundreds of young Americans – teachers, medical internees, student engineers, agricultural experts', surely as much of a 'mythic drama' as anything Wright Mills envisioned.[102]

Harrington's *New America* attempted to straddle all of the above positions, and ended up contradicting itself. The 5 May 1961 editorial, 'Listen Mr. Kennedy!', obviously alluded to Mills, and warned that if JFK sent in troops, 'Havana would be America's Budapest.' It quickly added, however, that 'in saying this we do not procede from an endorsement of the Castro regime', and after citing Theodore Draper on the latter's Communist character, something other than a strict non-interventionism became apparent. The CIA's most grievous error was not in trying to overthrow Castro, but in refusing to back the 'Fidelistas without Fidel' among the exiles in Miami, rather than the *batistianos* who led the Brigade 2506. Implicitly, the United States should have supported action by 'the left wing of the anti-Castro opposition.' Yet before any reader could conclude that the SP-SDF endorsed another, better invasion, Harrington muddied the waters with a host of ambiguities:

> But even if the CIA had not blundered as it did, we would still have opposed American intervention. ... We want democracy. Yet, the struggle for this goal can only win if it comes from inside of Cuba. ... In saying this, we do not condemn those democrats and trade unionists in Cuba who have taken the path of open opposition.

Neither do we censure those who work for change by other means. ... Cubans must settle questions of tactics; Cubans, and not the CIA or anybody else in Washington, must establish policy and control their movement.[103]

Meanwhile, *New America* ignored the host of protest activities, with or without Fair Play for Cuba involvement, and while proclaiming the SP-SDF's active opposition to the invasion, conspicuously did not encourage its readers to join with others – in real terms a formula for inaction. Socialists did hold a few of their own protests, but even these sent mixed messages. At the largest, on 18 April in Berkeley where the leftwing SP-SDF branch was a real force, party leader Max Shachtman shocked many of his comrades by a nimble endorsement of the invasion.[104]

One could go on describing what some will regard as the political sins of North American Socialists regarding Cuba, but like detailing what North American Communists said over the years about the Soviet Union, this would be flogging a dead horse. That the SP-SDF was unable to move beyond an obsessive anti-Communism should come as no surprise, since this dynamic already shapes the core narrative of the New Left. Many books have examined how the Students for a Democratic Society fought a bitter battle from 1962 on with their Socialist controllers in the League for Industrial Democracy over the SDSers' 'softness' on Communism, until finally breaking all remaining ties in 1965 just as SDS burst onto the national stage with its forceful, nonexclusionary leadership of the antiwar movement. The earlier division over Cuba is only a small part of this story, but nonetheless a telling one. In 1961, the Socialists were only beginning to realize their differences on the global role of the US, and could not anticipate their party's final breakup in 1972, when opposing factions (led, ironically, by Shachtman and his one-time protégé Harrington) split over support of Richard Nixon or George McGovern. Already, though, the eminent John Roche, Morris Hillquit Professor of Labor and Social Thought at Brandeis, had resigned from the SP-SDF because of the Norman Thomas letter. In a missive to the *Times* he denounced 'liberal isolationism', saying that 'Hands Off Cuba' now was equivalent to 'Hands Off Nazi Germany' in the thirties. In 1962 Roche would handily defeat Morris Rubin, editor of *The Progressive*, for the presidency of ADA.[105]

The evolution of US pacifists over Cuba contrasts sharply with the Socialists' trajectory. These two wings of non-Communist radicalism moved in opposite directions, foreshadowing the SP-SDF's later marginality, while the amorphous, pacifist-led 'peace movement' became the umbrella under which most of the New Left gathered. By 1962 the Socialist leadership advocated aid to guerrillas in Cuba and promoted anti-Castro exiles in their publications, becoming indistinguishable from Cold War liberalism on foreign policy issues at precisely the moment when that distinction acquired political salience.[106]

The main body of the peace movement, however, refused to take sides and either kept a judicious silence or engaged in what Richard Welch has described as 'a modest educational campaign' in favor of nonintervention, involving pamphlets and the occasional conference.[107] More important, a noticeable minority of pacifists, grouped around the magazine *Liberation* and the Committee for Non-Violent Action (CNVA), stepped into the breach created by the marginalization of FPCC after the Bay of Pigs. Other than the briefly notorious student delegations to 'break the travel ban', organized by the Progressive Labor Party in 1963-64, these radical peaceworkers carried out the only serious efforts to bridge the gap with Cuba between the Missile Crisis in late 1962 and the rise of an antiwar movement in the late 1960s. In terms of their commitment to ethical politics writ big, to putting one's body on the line and refusing to choose between the Cold War camps, the 'nonviolent action movement' is widely recognized as the most direct precursor of New Leftist ideological and political practice. Yet its involvement with Cuba came later than the rest of the organized left. Perhaps many instinctively recognized that this revolution, born of violence and fiercely anti-imperialist, might divide their beloved community, or push it into a more complex politics.

Throughout 1960, *Liberation,* effectively the united front of the peace movement, engaged in a low-key fashion with Cuba and made no reference to the burgeoning movement around FPCC. The same month that Fair Play was founded, three different 'Reflections on Cuba' were printed, ranging from Robert Alexander's 'Contradictions of the Castro Regime', which urged solidarity by the Democratic Left in the US to offset the increasing influence of the Communists, to the artist Douglas Gorsline's enthusiastic claim that Cuba 'positively reeks of freedom', denouncing the 'ethically timid' non-Communist left for its inability to solidarize with the revolution.[108] Everything changed with Dave Dellinger's long essay, 'Cuba: America's Lost Plantation', which appeared in the December 1960 and January and March 1961 issues, subsequently reaching a broad liberal, peace, religious and international audience through reprintings in the *Catholic Worker,* Lyle Stuart's monthly *The Independent,* the *New Left Review* and as a popular pamphlet, all invested with Dellinger's moral authority as a hardcore resister during and after World War II, and as an organizer of CNVA. Dellinger gave the Cuban experiment a historical resonance that spoke directly to those who would go into the New Left seeking to find a humane revolution by celebrating instead of denying *fidelismo's* radical character. He compared the ethos of the island to his experiences in Spain in 1936, in terms of the egalitarian spirit he found everywhere – an example rarely invoked, either because of the Spanish struggle's divided legacy or simple historical myopia. Above all, he emphasized the absence of hierarchies and dogmas and the participation by the Cuban masses in their own history-making, while identifying the 'liberals', in Cuba and the US, as the real counter-revolutionaries.

'Cuba: America's Lost Plantation' was received with 'unusually large and almost unified enthusiasm' by *Liberation*'s readers, and damned only by a few (notably James Peck) as a capitulation to the 'Russian brand of imperialism' and a sell-out of everything the magazine had stood for.[109] It also split *Liberation* in the months leading up to the Bay of Pigs, pushing some pacifists to a clearer definition of a new solidarity politics than was available anywhere else until much later. As Dellinger put it during the Missile Crisis, 'We cannot make nonviolence historically relevant until we have done with the American empire altogether and align ourselves unequivocally with the dispossessed and under-privileged peoples of the earth.'[110]

The debate began when the March 1961 issue announced a long-running 'serious disagreement' on Cuba between Roy Finch and the other four editors – A. J. Muste, Bayard Rustin, Sidney Lens and Dellinger, evidently brought to the fore by the latter's recent articles. Characteristically, all parties articulated their differences calmly and with respect for each other, despite the stakes involved. As was his right, Finch published an interview conducted with several self-exiled Cuban anarchists by Russell Blackwell of the New York–based Libertarian League, in which detailed allegations of Communist police terror against the libertarian left were made. He also quoted Camus on 'totalitarianism' as the ultimate evil, and averred that the revolution had been 'stolen from the Cuban people'. In the next issue Dellinger responded, rebutting Blackwell and citing his own commitment to antitotalitarianism and arguing that Cuba was genuinely in the Third Camp, as well as an 'organically democratic revolution'. At the end of his article, 'The Campaign Against Castro', he also proposed a pacifist work-camp in Cuba as a way making peace and beginning 'a new tradition', but this level of organized direct action was deferred for another generation and another revolution in Latin America. Meanwhile, Dellinger and Finch's co-editors and many readers were being drawn in, with Sidney Lens taking a less emphatically pro-Cuba position, but still maintaining that the revolution was overall an 'institution for social good', like the union movement or Christianity. Of the five, Dellinger was the most convinced partisan, but evidently he carried the day with Lens, Muste and even Bayard Rustin (later on a defining figure of neoconservatism), who had also gone to Cuba around this time. In the May 1961 issue of *Liberation* Finch announced his resignation, declaring Cuba a 'state capitalist' dictatorship that should be non-violently 'overthrown'.

Of course, this debate within the pacifist community took place in the countdown to the invasion, with Finch's resignation announced in its immediate aftermath. Pushed by the Bay of Pigs, the debate was transformed into action, and some of the main pillars of the 'peace movement' immediately formed their own coalition with the name Non-Violent Committee for Cuban Independence (NVCCI), suggesting more than just 'peace'. This ad hoc group's program, and its membership of key leaders, indicates the impact of Dellinger's articles upon a whole constituency. The *Catholic Worker*, Committee for

Non-Violent Action, Peacemakers and even the venerable War Resisters League were the NVCCI's organizational sponsors, and its individual members were Dellinger, Jim Peck, Barbara Deming, Richard Gilpin, A. J. Muste, George Willoughby, Ralph DiGia, Al Uhrie, Robert Steed and Robert Swann, with the last two and Dellinger designated a 'tactical leadership'. Its four-point program called for ending all forms of intervention in Cuba, economic and technical aid from the US, the abolition of the CIA, and a request that 'Dr. Castro and the Cuban people ... look with compassion and forgiveness upon the misguided invaders.'[111]

Anticipating a long history of civil disobedience at national targets identified with military interventionism, NVCCI conducted a two-week fast and vigil outside CIA headquarters, then within the District of Columbia, from 30 April to 13 May 1961. Such an action appears in hindsight eminently predictable, but in 1961 it was unprecedented. To be sure, pacifists had sailed into nuclear test zones at sea and climbed the fences at Strategic Air Command bases, but never had they targetted such a sensitive political installation; it would not be until 1967 that the Pentagon became a target. Further clarifying its political stance, the NVCCI collaborated closely with Fair Play for Cuba in this effort, as it became a centerpiece of the latter's East Coast response to the invasion, with each weekend demonstrators bused in to join the lonely, hungry group sitting on the sidewalk on Judiciary Square in downtown Washington.[112]

This episode involving various pacifist groups and many of the movement's most respected figures may seem isolated, but its repercussions were severe, given that the nation's largest peace organization, the Committee for a Sane Nuclear Policy – which advocated what some have called 'nuclear pacifism' because of its exclusive attention to ending the threat of atomic warfare – took no action at all during the invasion, and the sole response of the peace movement outside the NVCCI was a Fellowship of Reconciliation appeal that ran as a *New York Times* advertisement on 23 April 1961. Over the signatures of Erich Fromm, C. Wright Mills, Sidney Lens, A. J. Muste, Kermit Eby, Norman Thomas, Robert Gilmore of Turn Towards Peace and FOR's Alfred Hassler, it skirted the issue of Cuba itself but strongly condemned the intervention as a violation of law, with a headline reading 'WE CANNOT CONDONE THIS ACT!'

> Whatever you may feel about Fidel Castro and his regime, do you not share with us a deep feeling of shame that our government has pursued and is pursuing such a policy? We cannot condone it. ... If we are to survive and prosper, there must be somewhere a stop to the deadly cycle of violence and counter-violence. To break that cycle, there is no better place, no more opportune time, than here, now, in Cuba.

Hesitancy or outright refusal to link disarmament to anti-interventionism was not unique to that period. At every stage of the Cold War, major elements of the peace movement pursued a tightly defined, single-issue focus for sound

practical reasons. The Bay of Pigs invasion does have an unnoticed significance in the history of peace politics, however, because it was the first time
that this tension became visible. In the most fundamental way, a line had been
drawn in public, and people began to be pulled across it. A. J. Muste summed
up the meaning of the invasion for peace activists, and perhaps for the United
States as a whole, in his May 1961 *Liberation* editorial, 'Death of the Republic'.
To Muste, there was a fundamental breakdown in the idea of 'America' if a
significant number of liberals, pacifists and socialists could acquiesce by word
or inaction to something as flagrantly wrong as the Bay of Pigs: the 'young
men's era' promised by Kennedy was forever gone, and now came 'the open
advent of the American Empire'. Muste's thesis proved prescient, and the final
act of his long political life was to assemble the component parts of the grand
coalition against the Vietnam war in 1966–67, ending permanently the Cold
War division of liberalism and the left.[113]

The last important radical pacifist to come forward to defend Fidel, and the
only exponent of an explicitly Christian solidarity with the revolution, was
Dorothy Day. Though her *Catholic Worker* had run several articles by William
Worthy during 1960 and reprinted Dellinger's essay in its February 1961 issue,
and the Catholic Worker organization had helped sponsor the Non-Violent
Committee for Cuban Independence, with Robert Steed part of its three-man
leadership, Day herself had been silent. Then, after the Bay of Pigs, she began
to speak out in a prophetic voice. It must have been difficult to do so: the
largely Spanish-dominated Church in Cuba had come into sharp conflict with
the revolution in 1961, and Castro had expelled dozens of priests as 'Falangist'
counter-revolutionaries, while in certain instances (heavily reported in the
US) *fidelista* crowds had surrounded churches identified as counter-revolutionary and harassed believers. Conservative Catholic publications and some
readers sharply attacked the *Catholic Worker* for running pro-Castro pieces
(though Thomas Merton wrote to commend her), but this only led Day to
ruminate more deeply on where faith led.[114]

Characteristically, Day's long, highly personal response, 'About Cuba', in the
July/August 1961 *Catholic Worker*, hardly shied away from the implications of
solidarity and anti-imperialism. After reviewing her own history since the
twenties, when she had interviewed Sandino, and pausing to defend the centrality of Communists to building the CIO during the thirties, Day stated
plainly that it was 'hard', but that she had no choice but to side with 'the per-
secutors of the church' in Cuba, and specifically with Fidel Castro, because he
was on the side of the poor. Then, to underline the true significance of her
stand, she described visiting with migrant workers in California who were trying to unionize and had been Red-baited and cast out by their Church. After
more discussion of her travels and like experiences, and many asides (for example, a recent postcard from her old friend Mike Gold, and some thoughts
on the humanity Communists and Catholics shared), she reiterated firmly,

'We are on the side of the revolution. ... God bless Castro and all those who are seeking Christ in the poor.'

From then on, year after year, Day continued her discussion about the spiritual character of the Cuban revolution and its moral equivalence with her highly orthodox conception of faith. In late 1962, she went to Cuba, as Dellinger also continued to do, and examined for her 70,000 readers the changes in the revolution as it officially became Communist. Over the next generation, many other devout Catholics – notably the women religious among whom Day's example may have had a special significance – joined what had been her solitary pilgrimage towards a Church of the Poor in the Americas. In 1961, though, she stood virtually alone in defending Castro as a better Catholic than most, though after the Bay of Pigs the now intensely anti-Castro Jesuit magazine *America* did print an article indicating how the example of Cuba was gnawing upon others' consciences. In 'How We Look to Others', Father George H. Dunne focused on Che Guevara as a man inspired by a profound idealism – 'the inability himself to feel free so long as the peasant masses were poor, hungry and illiterate.' Suggesting that in the eyes of the world, the image of America was increasingly the 'hard-faced' bean-growers who would not let migrant workers' children go to school, or 'the hate-contorted faces of New Orleans housewives screaming epithets into the ears of a bewildered Negro child', Dunne pleaded that

> what is needed is the image of an angry people, people who react, not blasphemously like Guevara, but like Christ in the temple, against a social structure which creates, perpetuates or tolerates human misery anywhere. ... We had better find a way to do away with the bean-grower mentality and become a people who, like Karl Marx, can never feel free as long as Guatemala children or West Virginia children or Indian children have bloated bellies, or Mexican-American children slave in the fields, or Negro children are treated like medieval lepers.[115]

The pacifists and faith activists may have arrived late, but they were the last to leave. Long after FPCC had faded to a glimmer and the organized left had moved on to greener pastures, the nonviolent radicals continued to talk, think, write and agitate about Cuba. A new surge of activity arose following the October 1962 showdown over Soviet medium-range missiles on the island, at what was otherwise the nadir of relations between the two countries. This 'missile crisis' was a rallying point for the peace movement's cautious mainstream led by SANE, but effaced what was left of self-conscious solidarity à la Fair Play for Cuba. Indeed, the signal thing about the Cuban Missile Crisis is that it was so much about 'missiles' and so little about Cuba. The demonstrations, open letters and newspaper advertisements focused on the US and the USSR, virtually ignoring the revolutionary island, not surprising since Cuba had been temporarily reduced to the superpowers' plaything. FPCC's remnants were unable to play any significant part in the coalitions that formed, with San Francisco a major exception.[116]

Yet somehow the call for 'fair play' was revived in a different form following the Missile Crisis, though perhaps appealing to the same sectors of the Old Liberalism. At a meeting convened by the Fellowship of Reconciliation on 10–11 November 1962, leaders of all sections of the peace movement, including SANE, agreed to take action on Cuba and Latin America. An ambitious future program was described, involving delegations to the island from the American Friends Service Committee and the Committee for Non-Violent Action, with the former considering 'service projects' like its grassroots community efforts in Mexico, while both the Women's International League for Peace and Freedom and SANE claimed to be 'working with Cuban representatives in the United Nations ... to produce strategies that will relieve some of the immediate points of tension.' These peace leaders also agreed on the idea of a conference of US and Cuban intellectuals 'to discuss ways of improving relationships' and called for meetings throughout the United States to 'discuss the problems of peace in Cuba and Latin America.' Finally, it was agreed to explore, through FOR,

> the possible desireability of creating some new kind of 'Committee on Latin America' to function in the United States as a clearing house for information and communication between the North Americans and Latin Americans, and with the role of interpreting the revolutionary needs of Latin America to the North American people.[117]

Not surprisingly, most of these ideas came to naught, an almost inevitable result given the climate, when even venerable groups like FOR and the Friends were treated, at best, as honorable cranks by elected officials, and anti-Castro rancor was such that the emphatically non-Communist Carlos Fuentes was denied a visa to enter the US for a television debate on Cuba with presidential aide Richard Goodwin.[118] In such an atmosphere, 'interpreting the revolutionary needs of Latin America to the North American people' was a fool's errand, and bringing US and Cuban intellectuals together nearly impossible. It would require a greater imperial crisis to generate the conditions for not one but many 'Committees on Latin America', as well as mass delegations and systematic engagement with the US-based representatives of revolutionary governments and movements.

The peace movement did not simply offer rhetorical gestures, though. Its most radical sectors moved forward on the above-described plan, with considerable anger against the 'Uncle Tom-ism' of those who refused to act on Cuba.[119] In mid 1963, after months of preparation (including a campaign of aggressive 'reconciliation' with Miami's exiles by seven quixotic peaceworkers), CNVA kicked off a Québec-Washington-Guantánamo Peace Walk, akin to its

1961 San Francisco-to-Moscow walk, which had attracted considerable inter-national attention. Coordinated by Brad Lyttle, thirteen walkers left Canada in late May and were joined by several small feeder groups in the North before entering the South, then at the height of violent white reaction against the civil rights movement. When the interracial group of nearly two dozen finally reached Albany, Georgia in early 1964, a town where Martin Luther King, Jr had already lost a hard fight in 1962, their push for peace with Cuba became subsumed into the larger struggle for racial equality, as had happened earlier in Monroe, North Carolina. After forty-nine days in jail, drawn-out fasts, trials and considerable national attention, the pacifists got out of Albany, and made it to Miami, though few people remember that their part in the famous 'Al-bany Movement' was actually connected to solidarity with the Cuban revolu-tion. Finally, on 27 October 1964, seventeen months after it began, the Québec-Washington-Guantánamo Peace Walk ended with the summary arrest of the remaining walkers as they tried to set sail for the island.[120] This seem-ingly ignominious end, typifying the symbolic politics pursued by pacifists through good times and bad (Thomas Merton had hailed the Walk in *Libera-tion* because of its apolitical purity and lack of concern with temporal affect), came only a few days before Lyndon Johnson's massive electoral sweep as a peace candidate, while the war in Vietnam quietly moved into high gear. Soli-darity or simple friendship with Cuba was, for the moment, a lost cause, and CNVA's failure to reach Guantánamo seemed to be the final whimper with which that hope died.

On the Trail of the Assassin...

In fact, the call for 'fair play' had exploded somewhat earlier in thoroughly shocking fashion, not with a whimper, but the biggest bang in modern US history. Though its founders and nearly all of the members were long gone, the Fair Play for Cuba Committee came back to public life spectacularly, albeit most unpleasantly, in the immediate aftermath of 22 November 1963. Before this book ends as it must, however, with the artificial closure imposed by the Lee Harvey Oswald affair, it is important to record the stages of FPCC's slide into obscurity, as a reminder of the real limitations on permissible dissent faced by the early New Left.

FPCC did not fall apart as a national organization immediately following the Bay of Pigs, but in late 1961 it began to enter the half-life, neither defunct nor active in any consequential sense, which is the fate of radical groups that outlive their moment. Though a substantial national conference was held in July and various chapters continued activity on their own, by the end of that year, the national office phone was disconnected, the *Fair Play* bulletin no longer appeared, and the local chapter base was shrinking.[121]

There are too many good reasons for this fading away to ascribe it to any one factor. Patently, Cuba lessened as an issue because of the likelihood that the US, having failed once, would not intervene directly again. Given the Cubans' real fears and Republican drumbeating, however, the possibility of another invasion could not be discounted. But each time FPCC warned the public of an imminent war, it sounded more and more like the boy who cried wolf, with that permanently fevered tone that many associate with the radical-as-lunatic fringe. Meanwhile, the crisis in Southern 'race relations' more and more dominated the consciousness of whatever Radical America there was, from Communists to SDSers to pacifists and former beatniks. For good reason, daiquiri-laden goodwill tours, even when packed with political discussion, paled beside the possibility of death or dismemberment on a Freedom Ride. For a little while in 1960, Cuba and the Southern struggle could be seen as complementary commitments. Now the encounter with Cuba was part of fast-receding past, while 'going South' right here at home was the future of radical engagement, of solidarity.

Equally important as this political evolution away from Cuba was the revolution's increasingly tight connection to the Soviet Union, highlighted by Fidel's proclamation in December 1961 that he was a Marxist-Leninist. It was infinitely harder to demand 'fair play' for a supposed Russian satellite, the distinction between alliance and clientage never very clear to North Americans, than for a nonaligned, non-Communist island. Ever since 1959, people as disparate as Herbert L. Matthews, Robert Taber, Alan Sagner, Berta Green, Richard Gibson, C. Wright Mills, Carleton Beals, William Worthy and Saul Landau had contrasted *fidelismo* favorably with the Soviet model of authoritarian social engineering, citing Fidel's own statements as proof, and defending whatever engagement there was with local and foreign Communism as the fault of the US, a temporary necessity forced upon the 26th of July Movement. However valid and effective these arguments were at the time, events had left them behind. The eclipse of Cuba's 'humanist' phase and the move to a unified party centralizing all political power – though not yet an official Communist Party, the ORI, or Integrated Revolutionary Organizations, would do until one came along – removed most of the political rationale for FPCC as a coalition with an open door to those who could imagine Cuba as a Caribbean New Deal, a liberals' revolution.

Matters more immediate to FPCC's internal functioning also came to the fore. At loggerheads with Richard Gibson both personally and politically, the SWP began pulling out its cadres in the fall of 1961.[122] Factional rivalries intensified, to the disgust of younger New Leftists without this baggage, while many liberals who had joined earlier pulled back. As Asher Harer remembered it, there were numerous causes of Fair Play's decline:

Differences began to develop, even at that time, 1961, with various chapters, and individual Fair Play for Cuba committees. In San Francisco, an opposition developed, which said that we were playing the role of a Cuban cheering committee, a Cuban revolution cheering committee and weren't keeping our proper distance from the revolution. ... The liberals who had come in just on the basis of 'fair play' for Cuba – you know, just sort of a civil liberties angle on an international scale – began to drift away, or find differences in the organization and began to debate these differences. The Cubans, as the revolution developed, the real revolutionary Cubans went back to Cuba. And very few of them remained around here, which further weakened Fair Play for Cuba. And also, as the Soviet Union entered more and more into the picture, and the revolution deepened in Cuba, the red-baiting began to step up. And it became quite severe.[123]

Of course, such disarray was ripe for government provocateurs, and they weighed in heavily. A pungent example is the letter, headed 'Foul Play for Cuba', presumably part of the FBI's massive COINTELPRO operation against the SWP and anything connected to it:

> The FPCC is at present in a 'holding condition', its finances are shaky and its influence is on the wane. We all had hoped the FP would become a guiding beacon in the new frontier. Today it is only a flickering taillight in the wilderness. Why has'nt [sic] this organization fulfilled its original great promise as the leader of a ground swell protesting the blatant scheming of the US State Department to undermine the Cuban revolution? Why?? Richard Gibson has failed us!!
>
> When Gibson forced Berta Green out of the National Office, lethargy moved in. Berta's keen grasp of the political overtones of the Cuban revolution, her industry and her administrative talent made her a natural leader of the FP and an inspiration to all of us who came in contact with her.... Nevertheless, when Gibson's scholarship at Columbia University expired, he immediately put himself on the FP payroll and shortly thereafter told Berta the FP financial situation did not permit keeping her.
>
> Gibson is a man who can stretch the truth! For example, why has he never identified the people behind the scenes who really control the FP. ... Of course, Gibson has his own political ambitions as a Negro Nationalist and has been able to further these ambitions by using the FP. He operated in a completely uncontrolled fashion. Who else would have dared to use the 'Fair Play', a publication supposedly devoted to improving US-Cuban relations, as a vehicle to rally support for the Negro Nationalist cause, as Gibson did in the Robert F. Williams case. ...
>
> Gibson must go!![124]

These internal problems were ultimately secondary to FPCC's external difficulties. In light of the tempest stirred up by the Bay of Pigs, these problems now came from the highest possible level. On 22 April 1961, when FPCC-led public protests against the invasion were daily occurrences, the National Security Council met and President Kennedy ordered the Attorney General and the Director of Central Intelligence to 'examine the possibility of stepping up coverage of Castro activities in the United States.'[125] On 27 April, J. Edgar Hoover issued a general order to his agents to report on pro-Castro agitation, noting that Fair Play for Cuba's actions showed 'the capacity of a nationality group organization to mobilize its efforts in such a situation so as to arrange demonstrations and influence public opinion', far too much capacity, in other words.[126]

For those hostile to FPCC, the resulting string of congressional inquiries was the main event during the rest of the year. Among the organized liberals or the larger public, it was a clear stop-sign indicating an illicit taint. In tandem with Castro's engagement with the USSR, 'pro-Castro' became the literal equivalent of 'pro-Communist'. Of course, neither the Internal Security Subcommittee headed by Senator James Eastland nor the FBI needed encouragement to interrogate those who criticized US foreign policy. Hoover had ordered an investigation into 'pro-Castro' groups in November 1960 so that the relevant individuals could be placed on his official Security Index of individuals to be detained in time of war, while in January 1961, the Justice Department had ordered FPCC leaders to register under the Foreign Agent Registration Act, though it never attempted to enforce compliance when they refused.[127]

During 1961, however, the Eastland Committee took the lead. It had probed FPCC earlier, but the grilling went into higher gear just as the travel ban was announced, so that the most damaging allegation had already surfaced before Kennedy took office. In early January 1961, Charles Santos-Buch, who had worked with Taber and Sagner to found FPCC, gave detailed testimony that the bulk of the funds for the original *New York Times* advertisement in April 1960 had come from Raúl Roa, Jr, Cuba's UN delegate.[128] This charge of direct foreign patronage unquestionably caused serious damage to FPCC's reputation, particularly since Taber was in Cuba and refused to return to testify, and the subcommittee threw into the hopper allegations that he had absconded with $19,000 withdrawn in cash just before leaving, apparently the collective airfare for the Christmas delegation. Then, just after the Bay of Pigs, Gibson was summoned twice, on 25 April and 16 May 1961. As we have seen, he gave as good as he got and managed to turn the hearings into an attack on his questioners. Following this set-to, the committee settled down to picking apart FPCC chapters, with various leaders' pasts exposed and, in several cases, jobs lost as well. In June and July 1961, a steady stream of local Fair Players who were past or present Communists and SWP members were ordered to Washington and asked questions to which they could give no answers. The senators was very concerned about the 'united front' apparently developing between the two parties. For some reason, the focus was mainly on the Midwest FPCC chapters – Detroit, Chicago and Cleveland, perhaps because this was where the Old Left's role was most predominant; it is noticeable that no members or leaders of FPCC's Student Councils were called despite their public prominence on the Christmas trip and during the Bay of Pigs protests.[129]

By now officially resigned from his post, Robert Taber finally appeared in early 1962 at a hearing devoted to dredging up his teenage criminal record dating from 1939.[130] Subsequently, various other persons with FPCC connections were summoned, sometimes with unintentionally hilarious results, as in the furious dispute between Lyle Stuart and his inquisitors over whether the 'erotica' he published had any connection to his pro-Castro activities. Having effectively disrupted the organization during 1961, the Eastland Committee began to look into small related groups, such as the Medical Aid for Cuba Committee and the Friends of British Guiana, and into illegal travel to Cuba.

Richard Gibson lingered on as executive secretary for a long time, until finally he left as well. In September 1962, the Friends Committee on National Legislation in Washington, D.C. warned him of imminent indictment as an unregistered foreign agent. He left the country legally through Canada and made his way to Algiers, where he would help edit the journal *Révolution Africaine*, before taking up a career in international public relations. He did not return to the US at all for some years, echoing similar unpleasant travails facing others once prominent in Fair Play.[131]

By 1963, if not before, FPCC was no more than an alternative identity for the SWP's Young Socialist Alliance in most places. At Indiana University in Bloomington, a tiny FPCC/YSA group was actually indicted for 'sedition' in the spring of 1963 because of the protest it organized during the Cuban Missile Crisis, a case which took years to resolve.[132] After Gibson's departure, V. T. 'Ted' Lee had taken over what remained of the national organization, with the Cubans' approval. He was the former head of the large Fair Play chapter in Tampa, which had grown dramatically during 1961–62 when the rest of the organization was declining, presumably because of the continued militance of Tampa's pro-Castro Cubans.[133] But Lee had little to do, as a one-man operation without any resources, and he restricted himself to issuing increasingly intemperate appeals and warnings. Ever more obscure, FPCC soldiered on; and then came November 1963 and a few seconds of infamy in Dallas.

There is no need to add anything further to the ever-expanding mountain of text and imagery surrounding the assassination of John F. Kennedy, much of which obsessively dissects Lee Harvey Oswald as mystery man, or front man, or patsy. For the purposes of this account, what matters is that on 23 November 1963, every newspaper in the country reported that a 'pro-Castro Red', a member of the Fair Play for Cuba Committee, had killed the president. The story of Oswald's *fidelismo* rapidly declined in importance after that, perhaps not incidentally, since it was too shoddy to stand up for long – the FPCC office he rented in New Orleans, for instance, was in the same building as Louisiana's main anti-Castro exile group – but the damage was done. While Richard Gibson presented himself at the US embassy in Paris to tell them what he did not know, Ted Lee issued a final, frantic press release on 26 November deploring 'the terrible wilderness of hatred and political intrigue' that had engulfed his cause. Not only the organization but the cause of fair play and equality between the peoples of Cuba and the United States vanished forthwith, leaving a trail of innuendo and suspicion that has not abated yet.[134] It is my hope that this book will restore not only the memory but the good name of that cause, and of all those I have dubbed the Yankee *fidelistas*. Whatever or whoever he was, Lee Harvey Oswald was not of their company, and his story is not theirs, though in death he claimed the final bow.

Notes

1. Trumbull Higgins, *The Perfect Failure: Kennedy, Eisenhower and the CIA at the Bay of Pigs*, New York: Norton, 1987.

2. Halberstam, *The Best and the Brightest*, p. 66.

3. It is important here to distinguish opposition to empire from opposition to militarism, which considerably predates Fair Play for Cuba. As various scholars have shown, the peace movement began to revive organizationally from 1955 on, both the traditional organizations such as the War Resisters League and Fellowship of Reconciliation, and newer ones like the Committee for Non-Violent Action and the Committee for a Sane Nuclear Policy. Though the more radical of these groups carried out a host of creative protests focused on the sites of nuclear war-making, no connections were made to US policy in the colonial and underdeveloped world. See Isserman, *If I Had a Hammer*, and Charles DeBenedetti with Charles Chatfield, *An American Ordeal: The Antiwar Movement of the Vietnam Era*, Syracuse, N.Y.: Syracuse University Press, 1990, for excellent examinations, respectively, of how the new agitation for disarmament helped beget both the New Left and, eventually, the Vietnam antiwar movement.

4. John F. Kennedy, *The Strategy for Peace*, Allan Nevins, ed., New York: Popular Library, 1961, pp. 167–8.

5. See Peter Wyden, *Bay of Pigs*, p. 65, for Richard Goodwin's claim regarding the audience question cards.

6. In *A Thousand Days*, pp. 72–3, Schlesinger treats the call for aid to anti-Castro guerrillas as an aberration spurred by fear of Nixon's 'inroads among suburban Catholics, to whom anti-communism made a strong appeal.' Goodwin wrote the press release and it was approved by Theodore Sorensen and Pierre Salinger while the candidate slept. Because of an 'immediate uproar among his liberal and intellectual supporters', 'Kennedy thereafter dropped Cuba and concentrated for the rest of the campaign on his central themes.' Unfortunately, while Schlesinger is certainly sincere in treating Cuba as a purely tactical issue for Kennedy (a way of playing the Cuba card as Republicans had played the China card), his account downplays the prominence Kennedy gave to Castro from the beginning, though later he mentions that 'Cuba, of course, was a highly tempting issue; and as the pace of the campaign quickened, politics began to clash with Kennedy's innate sense of responsibility. ... He began to succumb to temptation' (p. 224 *passim*).

7. Kevin Tierney, 'American-Cuban Relations, 1957–1963' (Ph.D. dissertation, Syracuse University, 1979), pp. 118–50, traces in detail Kennedy's speeches on the issue. In *The United States, Cuba and Castro*, William Appleman Williams addressed how, in subtle modulations of one standard speech passage describing how the US ambassador under Batista was the second most powerful man in Cuba, JFK skated over time from a vague anti-imperialism to demanding that imperial control be reinstated (p. 150).

8. Tierney, 'American-Cuban Relations', p. 125; see also *Fair Play*, 2 September 1960.

9. Tierney, 'American-Cuban Relations', p. 133.

10. Ibid., p. 134. For another instance in which Kennedy clearly called for aid to Cuban counter-revolutionaries well before late October, see Thomas, *Cuba: The Pursuit of Freedom*, p. 1296, quoting a 23 September speech: 'The forces fighting for freedom in exile and in the mountains of Cuba should be sustained.'

11. Tierney, 'American-Cuban Relations', p. 135, for a speech that Kennedy delivered on 6

October in Cincinnati.

12. Ibid., p. 134.

13. Quoted in Zeitlin and Scheer, *Cuba: Tragedy in Our Hemisphere*, p. 189.

14. Tierney, 'American-Cuban Relations', p. 150; Zeitlin and Scheer, *Cuba: Tragedy in our Hemisphere*, p. 191; Thomas, *Cuba: The Pursuit of Freedom*, p. 1300.

15. *Fair Play*, 16 December 1960; *New York Times*, 21 January 1961.

16. *New York Times*, 20 November 1960. Green was very forthcoming with reporter Peter Kihss, breaking another taboo of the Old Left: she claimed 3,000 adult and 2,500 student members, as well another 4,500 subscribers to *Fair Play*. Sagner, Gibson and 'Mrs. Elizabeth Barad, New York attorney' were named as members of a National Executive Committee, which seems to have existed only on paper. Among the chapter leaders named were a mix of people formerly close to the CP, such as Vincent Hallinan in San Francisco (1952 Progressive Party candidate and attorney for Harry Bridges's International Longshoremen's and Warehousemen's Union) and 'theater owner' John Rossen in Chicago, as well as several SWPers, such as Ed Shaw in Detroit and Richard Tussey in Cleveland. Green also cited FPCC's prominent individual members, including C. Wright Mills, William Worthy, I. F. Stone, Leo Huberman, Scott Nearing and Robert F. Williams.

17. *Fair Play for Cuba Committee, SISC,* 16 May 1961, pp. 181–2. The senators also recorded a telegram received after the hearing from the president of Grinnell College, Howard R. Bowen, assuring them that there never had been a Fair Play for Cuba Committee at his school.

18. The number of voting delegates assigned San Francisco and New York at Fair Play's one national conference held in July 1961 (five and eighteen, respectively, out of a total of sixty) suggests perhaps 500 individual members of national Fair Play in the Bay Area, and 1,800 in New York (for San Francisco, see the official national conference call from Richard Gibson, 'To All Fair Play Chapters', dated 15 May 1961, with the number '5' filled in by hand for the chapter's allotted delegates, in Asher Harer Papers; for New York, see 5 June 1961 'Dear Friend' letter from Berta Green, chapter secretary, inviting all members to meeting to elect eighteen delegates, in Berta Green Papers). In other words, one-third to two-fifths of the members were concentrated in these two cities, assuming of course that the several thousand student members were counted towards the adult chapters, as appears to have been the case. The Student Councils received 'fraternal' nonvoting status, with one observer each.

19. See November 1960 flyer promoting NY-FPCC's Spanish classes on the Upper West Side of Manhattan, where people would read *Revolución* and begin corresponding with Cuban 'pen pals'; 'Would You Like to Help?', volunteer sign-up sheet for the New York and National FPCC office, listing local subcommittees; flyer for 14 July 1961 film showing in Brighton Beach; flyer for 15 July 1961 Boat Festival with LeRoi Jones's group On Guard For Freedom, 'a "swinging salute" to Afro-Cuban and Afro-American Unity'; flyer for 22 July 1961 'M-26-7 Dance' in Flatbush; and the 16 February, 15 and 27 March, and 12 May 1961 New York chapter newsletters listing dozens of public events around the city; all in Berta Green Papers (BGP).

20. Flyer, 'Attention All Members!!! Yearly Membership Meeting!!!', for 9 November 1961 meeting, in BGP.

21. This account is largely based on two taped 'educationals' that Asher Harer gave to the San Francisco branch of the SWP on 2 and 9 March 1980, in my possession. According to Harer, FPCC was the main vehicle whereby the SWP drew in the 'periphery' it had developed since 1956 among ex-CPers and others. Saxton became chapter president, Harer was executive secretary; a former SWPer, the 'Cochranite' Carl Andersen, was secretary-treasurer; and various others like Hallinan sat on the executive committee. Harer also recounted how in late 1960 the ex-Communists setting up the Progressive Labor Party had tried to appropriate the Fair Play name, but the tight corporate structure Taber had set up and Harer's possession of the only official charter abrogated this competition. James Petras was the SWP's key activist in the Fair Play chapter at Berkeley, which, though quite autonomous, was also duly chartered (there were Student Councils as well at San Francisco State and San Francisco City College).

22. Cited in 'Fair Play Chapter Notes - Number 1', 28 January 1961, in BGP.

23. Besides details given in Harer's talks, see also flyer for an 11 March 1961 indoor rally, 'Cuba – Crisis and Opportunity', with Robert F. Williams, Harry Bridges, and Baran as chair, which also lists a 10 March event with Williams and Tigar; flyer for a 16–18 November 1961 'Cuban Film Festival', with speakers including Tigar; flyer for a 7 December 1962 event, 'Truth Needs No Passport', with William Worthy and Carlton Goodlett, publisher of the *Sun-Reporter* newspaper, also

Hayden and Baran; all in Asher Harer Papers. The quotation is something that Harer remembers Saxton saying, to describe how FPCC became the locus for all of the Bay Area's diffuse radical traditions.

24. *Student Council*, 9 December 1960; see also the issue of 24 March 1961, for how this very active chapter's joint 'Fiesta' with Columbia College FPCC was a sellout. As an example of how hard it can be to find where Fair Play's Student Councils did or did not function, it was never mentioned in the Columbia College *Spectator*, despite the fact that Robert F. Williams spoke on campus under its auspices, as reported in the 25 February 1961 *Student Council*.

25. *Columbia Spectator*, 9 and 10 January, 17 March 1961.

26. *Swarthmore Phoenix*, 17 January; also 10, 17 and 24 February and 3 March 1961 for letters, and Blake Smith's article, 'Cuban Farmers Enthusiastic', 17 March.

27. *Cornell Sun*, 10, 11, 12, 13, 16 and 17 January 1961; also *Student Council*, 25 February, where Pinckney reports that FPCC was now officially recognized at Cornell (though never mentioned in the *Sun*). Until the Bay of Pigs, other issues came to fore at this activist campus, but the main one – a February vigil in mourning for the Congo's murdered Prime Minister Patrice Lumumba hooted down by the school's rightwing students – was not unrelated to 'fair play' for Cuba.

28. *Daily Cardinal*, 5 January, 23 and 24 February 1961.

29. *Student Council*, 11 and 25 February, 24 March 1961.

30. Wyden, *Bay of Pigs*, p. 152.

31. *New York Times*, 7 January 1961.

32. See Victor Bernstein and Jesse Gordon, 'The Press and the Bay of Pigs', *Columbia University Forum* (Fall 1967), pp. 4–13, for an excellent analysis of how the press refused to report most of what it knew, which also details how much did leak through. Bernstein and Gordon were, respectively, the managing editor and an editorial consultant of *The Nation*, and had tried very hard to get the *Times* and the wire services to pick up Ronald Hilton's exposé in the 19 November 1960 *Nation*, itself based on a major story in one of Guatemala's leading newspapers, *La Hora*, whose publisher sat in the cabinet of President Miguel Ydígoras.

33. See Wyden, *Bay of Pigs*, pp. 144–6, 152–3 on how these two men were cut out of the decision-making process, and their horrified reactions upon finding out.

34. Thomas, *Cuba: The Pursuit of Freedom*, p. 1305.

35. Quoted in Wyden, *Bay of Pigs*, pp. 122–3.

36. Wills, *The Kennedy Imprisonment*, p. 231; Williams, *The United States, Cuba and Castro*, pp. 148, 145. Williams was convinced that Ike was both wiser, in that he would never have let such an ill-starred plan go forward, and more moral, in that he would never have risked mens' lives and a wider war so cavalierly. There are some who find eccentric Williams's stated preference for conservatives like Eisenhower and Fulbright (or Hoover) over liberals like Kennedy or Woodrow Wilson. It should not be obscure. Williams believed, with considerable evidence, such as Ike's refusal to intervene at Dienbienphu, that true conservatives were more likely to accurately gauge the price of empire.

37. This quotation is from a 1975 interview with Castro by Frank Mankiewicz, quoted in Arthur Schlesinger, Jr, *Robert F. Kennedy and His Times*, New York: Boston: Houghton-Mifflin, 1978, p. 577.

38. Memorandum, Schlesinger to the President, 25 March 1961, quoted in Welch, *Response to Revolution*, p. 204n31). Welch has a considerably more detailed discussion of the 'White Paper' and related issues.

39. See Draper to Herbert L. Matthews, 28 February 1961, which mentions how *Encounter* editor Melvin Lasky solicited the piece – 'the idea was not mine' – in Herbert L. Matthews Papers. Presumably Draper's article, which appeared in the March 1961 *Encounter*, was actually available in late February, which is why Draper wrote this letter to Matthews, whom he had criticized for an obtuse refusal to accept Castro's drift to Communism.

40. Theodore Draper, 'Castro's Cuba – A Revolution Betrayed?', *Encounter* (March 1961), pp. 21–2, 23.

41. Ibid., p. 23.

42. *New York Times*, 1 April 1961.

43. Bernstein and Gordon, 'The Press and the Bay of Pigs', p. 9.

44. This is the version of the AP story that ran in the *Cornell Sun* on 18 April 1961. It was hardly the most jingoistic, as one Miami paper carried the banner headline 'CUBAN NAVY IN

REVOLT', and elsewhere it was reported that Raúl Castro had surrendered amidst a popular uprising (see Bernstein and Gordon, 'The Press and the Bay of Pigs', p. 11).

45. The 26th of July Movement's speaker was Julio Medina, its most prominent New York leader. The SWP's Young Socialist Alliance was represented by Peter Camejo, later prominent in the antiwar movement, and Mike Stein spoke for the CP's low-key new youth group Advance. On the protests, see *Fair Play*, 10 May 1961; also *New York Times*, 18 April (reporting nearly a thousand demonstrators in New York with two arrests); 19 April (500 more at the UN); 20 April (an AP report on 2,000 marchers in San Francisco); 21 April (a report that FPCCers in New York were working 'behind chained doors packaging circulars'); 22 April (more than 2,000 at Union Square on 21 April; *Fair Play* claimed 5,000).

46. *New York Times*, 21 April 1961.

47. Asher Harer, talk to San Francisco Branch, SWP, 2 March 1980.

48. *Fair Play*, 5 June 1961.

49. *New York Times*, 19 April 1961; also interviews with Peter Irons, 7 December 1988, and Jeff Mackler, 10 January 1989, former members of FPCC at Antioch. The Antioch chapter seems to have been fairly typical. It involved three groups – independents like Irons, young Trotskyists like Mackler (who went on to be an SWP leader, and with Nat Weinstein, led the breakaway group Socialist Action in the 1980s), and 'red diaper babies' like Joni Rabinowitz, daughter of Victor Rabinowitz, who were considered sympathetic to the CPUSA. One of the two main groups on this small, historically radical campus (the other focused on civil rights), Antioch FPCC received a major impetus from a tour by Peter Camejo and existed through the 1962 Missile Crisis.

50. *Fair Play*, 10 May 1961; *Fair Play Supplement*, with 5 June 1961 *Fair Play* issue; for Providence incident, see *New York Times*, 23 April 1961.

51. *New York Times*, 22 April 1961.

52. This quotation from YAF's *New Guard* was gleefully reprinted in *Student Council*, 22 May 1961.

53. See the various earlier cited issues of *Fair Play* and *Student Council*, 22 May 1961, for dates and fragmentary details of local actions at all these campuses.

54. *Cornell Sun*, 21 April 1961. This ad hoc debate was called via leaflets distributed the day before by a new student radical magazine, *Controversy*. The characterization of the debate is from a column by Robert E. McDowell, Jr in the 25 April *Sun*, which frankly described foreign policy as 'a dirty game ... in which superior power, not superior morals, decides the winner.' The campus seemed entirely taken up with Cuba during the invasion, if the war of words between right, center and left in its paper is an indication. Later in the week, an overflow audience attended a forum, 'The Crisis in Cuban Policy', with Professors Mario Einaudi, Alfred Kahn, Walter Berns and Walter LaFeber.

55. *Swarthmore Phoenix*, 21, 25 and 28 April 1961. At Columbia, the Student Board NSA (National Student Association) Committee conducted a poll the week of the invasion, eliciting 364 replies: 56 in favor of 'training anti-Castro forces', 296 against; 111 for providing arms, 242 against. Two members of this committee, Eric Foner, '63 and Jonah Raskin, '63, were elected to the Columbia University Student Council shortly thereafter. Highlighting the single-issue foci of New Left politics even then (and the ways in which 'peace politics' were segregated from other issues), the main on-campus activity in this period at Columbia was a 1 May protest against mandatory civil defence, as 600 gathered at the center of campus, with no reference to the invasion (*Spectator*, 25 April, 1 and 5 May 1961).

56. *Daily Cardinal*, 19, 22, 25, 26, 27, 28 and 29 April; 2, 4 and 5 May 1961. A letter from the campus conservatives' chief, Anthony Cadden, in the last named issue above, captures the flavor of this cultural slugfest, with his characterization of 'pro-Castro beatniks' caught in 'the dim forests of their long black beards'. See also the Socialists' repeated references to the rightists as beer-drinking yahoos, as in Radosh's long editorial column of 26 April.

57. Horowitz, *Student*, pp. 144–7.

58. *Studies on the Left* (May 1961), p. 75.

59. *Afro-American*, 29 April 1961.

60. *Cleveland Call and Post*, 29 April 1961. This is Loeb's regular column, 'World On View'. He went on to note that 'Negro editors who returned from Cuban jaunts with high praise for Castro's efforts suddenly found themselves under critical observation by the FBI and allied "intelligence agents".'

61. Quoted in Gibson's testimony in *Fair Play for Cuba Committee, SISC,* 25 April 1961, pp. 170–71.

62. Ibid., pp. 168, 170.

63. *New York Times,* 9 and 10 May 1961.

64. *New York Times,* 23 April 1961; Mailer, *The Presidential Papers,* pp. 78–9, 89–90. The journals were *Kulchur, Second Coming, Provincetown Review, Birth* and LeRoi Jones's *Yugen.*

65. *New America,* 19 May 1961.

66. Schlesinger, *A Thousand Days,* pp. 285–6.

67. *New York Times,* 26 May 1961; the figure for the number attending the Harvard meeting is drawn from Robert Light and Carl Marzani, *Cuba Versus CIA,* New York: Marzani & Munsell, 1961, p. 43.

68. Light and Marzani, *Cuba Versus CIA,* pp. 68, 71–2.

69. Ibid., pp. 69–70.

70. Halberstam, *The Best and the Brightest,* p. 26.

71. Quoted in *Fair Play,* 10 May 1961.

72. Quoted in Light and Marzani, *Cuba Versus CIA,* p. 69.

73. Quoted in Zeitlin and Scheer, *Cuba: Tragedy in Our Hemisphere,* p. 210.

74. Kempton, *America Comes of Middle Age,* p. 118

75. Ibid.

76. Ibid., p. 119.

77. *Fair Play,* 5 June 1961.

78. An AP story in the *New York Times,* 14 May 1961.

79. *New York Times,* 14 May 1961; *New America,* 2 June 1961. According to the latter, the resolution that was finally passed 'denounced the fiasco of the recent intervention, deplored Castro's drift into a totalitarian dictatorship and Soviet penetration, and recognized the need for revolutionary changes in Latin America.' A close voice vote defeated an amendment opposing any 'punitive action' in the future by the Organization of American States. The majority position stated only that 'Nor is the present the time' for such action.

80. *New York Times,* 21 May 1961 (the *Times* identified the initiators, Leo J. Linder and Abraham Pomerantz, as 'New York corporation lawyers'; a print of the brief is in the FPCC Vertical File at the Tamiment Library).

81. *New York Times,* 10, 14, 16 and 19 May 1961.

82. *New York Times,* 1 and 6 May 1961.

83. Editorials in a sampling of press opinion, *New York Times,* 23 April 1961.

84. *New York Times,* 18 May and 25 April.

85. Gallup, *The Gallup Poll,* vol. 3, *1959–1971,* pp. 1717–8, 1721. This poll, taken between 28 April and 3 May 1961, also showed high approval of President Kennedy's 'handling the situation in Cuba' (61 percent versus 15 percent) and even greater support for the US working 'with Central and South American countries – through the UN – to decide what policy we should follow with regard to Cuba' (70 percent against 15 percent).

86. Sindlinger Poll response quoted in Welch, *Response to Revolution,* p. 103.

87. The percentage of North Americans who supported or opposed an invasion of Cuba with US troops stayed remarkably constant, even during and after the Missile Crisis. In a 20–25 September 1962 Gallup Poll, when the news about Soviet missiles in Cuba was breaking, an invasion was opposed by a margin of 57 percent to 36 percent, even if guaranteed not to bring about World War III. Told to presume that war with Cuba *did* mean war with Russia, those opposing invasion increased to 69 percent versus 19 percent. This latter figure, along with the 7–12 February 1963 poll in which 20 percent favored invasion versus 64 percent against, suggests that a consistent hard core of one in five citizens wanted to get rid of Fidel at any cost, while an equally solid majority of three in five (or more) adults had deep reservations about a land war involving US troops under any circumstances; however, equally large majorities regarded Castro as a threat to world peace. Polls like this are frustrating, because they rarely pose the kinds of questions that historians would like to ask. Gallup never asked the electorate whether the US should pursue an accommodation with Castro, so we have only fragmentary evidence of any willingness to make a deal for peace – the already-cited 23 percent who, during the Bay of Pigs, opposed an embargo of Cuba, or the 22 percent who picked 'hands off Cuba' as the best response at the beginning of the Missile Crisis in September 1962. Gallup, *The Gallup Poll,* vol. 3, *1959–1971,* p. 1787.

88. Halberstam, *The Best and the Brightest*, p. 69. Bowles is an important protagonist in Halberstam's book, as the key representative of the Old Liberalism that the Kennedys used but scorned. On 25 January 1959, he had published a letter in the *Times* calling for the most vigorous US support to the Cuban revolution and an acceptance of how revolutionary it would need to be.

89. *New York Times*, 29 May 1961.

90. *New York Times*, 30 June and 25 July 1961.

91. Quoted in Paterson, 'Fixation with Cuba', p. 136, and Wills, *The Kennedy Imprisonment*, p. 267.

92. He was treasurer of the New Jersey Democratic Party, commissioner of transportation under Governor Brendan Byrne in the 1970s, and chairman of the Port Authority of New York and New Jersey in 1977–85, as well as a member of IMPAC, the group of key national Democratic fundraisers formed in the late 1980s. As to why his colleagues tolerated his connections with FPCC, as well as similar efforts later, he has suggested, 'If you reach a certain level, there's no profit in going after you. You see, my Democratic bona fides were established. ... We've been in the trenches together. I might be a jerk because I "like Castro," they think I'm a little crazy, but I'm not suspect' (interview, 25 June 1990).

93. These individuals were either holders of elected office and nominees for same, or directly appointed by those holding office at the state and local level. With 38 percent of Democrats and 43 percent of Republicans responding, a total of 123 and 102 officials in the respective parties were reached, a sample the authors described as 'biased toward the more active, influential members.' See Paul Ekman et al., 'Coping with Cuba: Divergent Policy Preferences of State Political Leaders', *Journal of Conflict Resolution* (June 1966), pp. 180–97. A few months before, in a March 1963 Gallup Poll, 24 percent of the public named Cuba as the country's most important problem, second only to the 39 percent who named 'Other international problems, Berlin, Laos, etc.' (Gallup, *The Gallup Poll:* volume 3, *1959–1971*, p. 1812). For an insightful contemporary discussion of the fate of 'peace candidates', mainly Democrats running for the House (which, however, avoids any attention to Cuba and Castro), see Paul Booth, *Peace Politics: A Study of the American Peace Movement and the Politics of the 1962 Congressional Elections*, Ann Arbor, Mich.: Peace Research and Education Project, February 1964.

94. This comment was made at a Quaker meeting in Cambridge, quoted in Light and Marzani, *Cuba Versus CIA*, p. 43.

95. The reader may notice the lack of mention of the Communist Party USA during this discussion of the run-up to the Bay of Pigs and the invasion itself. As before, the CP acted mainly as a passive fellow traveller towards the Cuban revolution itself and any solidarity in the US; its main foreign-policy focus as an organization was elsewhere, reflecting both an orientation towards the needs of the Soviet Union and the Gus Hall leadership's distrust of Castro. Communist publications cast opposition to the invasion as part of the fight for 'peaceful coexistence' with the socialist world, in which the main danger was the 'Right Wing Republican Party'. For the CP's relatively benign attitude towards JFK, which contrasts sharply with the anger felt by others, see the pamphlet by James Allen, *The Lessons of Cuba*, New York: New Century, 1961.

96. Editorial in *New America*, 15 November 1960; the awkward name resulted from absorbing two earlier split-offs and the wild-card Trotskyists of Max Shachtman's Independent Socialist League in 1958.

97. Ibid., 1 November 1960.

98. Ibid., 10 March 1961.

99. *New America*, 19 May 1961; *New York Times*, 4 May 1961. Thomas was also a leader of the IADF, which was favored by many more rightwing figures in the party, such as Robert Alexander, a National Executive Committee member. Presumably because of the negative response to the invasion among IADF founders like Pepe Figueres, the organization's official response was to 'deplore US backing of the invasion, and any use of force', and, while expressing sympathy for the exiles, to call for a 'modus vivendi' with Havana (see draft of IADF statement in Frances R. Grant Papers). See Schwarz, *Liberal*, p. 334, for a description of Figueres dining with Berle and Schlesinger when news came of the exiles' landing, and his shocked, despairing reaction.

100. *Dissent*, June 1961 (Supplement), pp. 4–5.

101. Ibid., p. 6.

102. Ibid., pp. 7, 8, 9, 14.

103. *New America*, 5 May 1961.

104. See *Two Views of the Cuban Invasion*, a pamphlet self-published by Berkeley SP-SDF leader Hal Draper in May 1961, containing the transcript of Shachtman's remarks, and Draper's angry commentary. In this speech, Shachtman made various gestures towards neutrality, using phrases like 'no American intervention in Cuba!' and 'hands off Cuba' (p. 2) to indicate that the US should not intervene directly while the Cuban people decided the issue for themselves. However, he also made clear his unequivocal support for the 'good stout working-class fighters' and 'revolutionary democrats ... good nationalists' among the invaders, regardless of their relationship to the CIA: 'I hope for their success, and their expansion of the program of the Cuban revolution' (p. 3). Cuba was not like Guatemala because 'in Cuba, there is a *popular* force opposed to Castro. ... A popular, democratic movement' (p. 3), opposing 'an authoritarian, middle-class government, which is increasingly in the hands of an anti-socialist totalitarian force, the Communists' (p. 4), who 'have taken over more and more, here, there and the other, in their devilishly quiet and efficient way' p. 5). What Draper called 'Stalinophobia' is indicated by the argument that 'there isn't a hell of a lot of choice between a Batista-type revolution and a Communist Party despotism' (p. 5).

105. *New York Times,* 9 May 1961; *New America,* 26 May 1962.

106. See, for instance, *New America,* 15 October 1962: 'American socialists welcome and support democratic opposition to the Castro regime. But to give moral and material aid to democratic opponents of Castro, one must accept the elementary idea that theirs' and theirs' alone is the decision of the kind of government and society they are fighting for. ... We wholeheartedly support the Cuban underground.' The 10 November issue, published at the height of the Missile Crisis, included an article by Antonio de la Carrera of the Junta Revolucionário Cubana on his group's plans for guerrilla war and need for help; see also article by Carrera, 6 February 1963, attacking I. F. Stone for 'Castro travelling'. The Young Peoples' Socialist League published a pamphlet, *Yanqui No! Castro No! Cuba Si!* by Sergio Junco, identified as 'a Cuban socialist', assisted by Nick Howard (New York: YPSL, 1 May 1962, reprinted from the British magazine *International Socialism*), which denounced 'American imperialism' but argued that 'no support should be given to a totalitarian regime which is not progressive. ... Outside "critical support" would objectively help Castro.' The SP-SDF was hardly monolithic, of course, and Norman Thomas, though at no point after early 1959 a fellow-traveller of Castro's, would still put his name on a public letter in February 1962 pledging to defy the final stage of the trade embargo announced by JFK, which banned even humanitarian food and medicine shipments (see *New York Times,* 4 February 1962; joining Thomas were James Baldwin, James Peck of CORE and sixteen others).

107. See Welch, *Response to Revolution,* pp. 133–4; also the American Friends Service Committee publications, *Understanding Cuba,* Philadelphia: AFSC, November 1960, with articles by Professor Hiram Hilty of Guilford College and Herbert L. Matthews; and *Let's Talk about Cuba,* Philadelphia: AFSC, 1963, a 'Historical Introduction' by Professor William Bristol of Union College. One example of something more than print agitation is described in a 10 April 1961 memorandum from Matthews to his publisher, describing his speaking at an AFSC conference on Latin America in Wichita, Kansas, where he was heard by a large, respectful audience despite heavy harassment from local John Birchers, in HLMP.

108. *Liberation,* April 1960. Interestingly, since its founding, the magazine and its editors had engaged strongly with anticolonial struggles in Africa, where the US interest was more ambiguous, and imperialism (French, British, Portuguese or Afrikaner) was an undisputed fact. See the December 1959 editorial 'Anti-Bomb – Anti-Colonial' reporting Bayard Rustin and A. J. Muste's presence in Algeria protesting French atomic tests, and the Kenyan George Philip Ochola's piece, 'Why Mau Mau?' in the January 1960 issue.

109. See the numerous letters in the February, March and April 1961 *Liberation*. The first quotation is from the editorial in the February issue, and the second is from Peck's April letter.

110. *Liberation,* October 1962. Similarly, Staughton Lynd attacked the 'libertarian' argument against Castro in the June/July 1961 *Liberation,* comparing it to William Lloyd Garrison's antipolitical radicalism before the Civil War. Lynd, equating solidarity with Cuba to Lincoln's pragmatic engagement with the possible, which made his achievement much greater than Garrison's, called others to stand together with the unpacifistic Cubans: 'their violence ...[is] more purposeful, more hopeful, more open to ultimate moderation and humanizing, than the violence of those who oppose them. ... To proclaim anathemas on the worldwide struggle of exploited men to rise from their knees to their feet is the one sin above all others to be feared.'

111. 'Program of the Non-Violent Committee for Cuban Independence', and accompanying Press Release, in FPCC Vertical File, Tamiment Library.

112. *Fair Play*, 10 May 1961, which also included a 29 April letter to Castro from Deming, Dellinger and Waldo Frank, asking him to abolish the death penalty and spare the invaders, in light of the fundamental 26th of July Movement slogan, 'Revolución Es Construir'. See also *New York Times*, 1 May 1961, on the action's first day with 90 people; Press Release, 11 May 1961, from FPCC on the 13 May rally of Fair Players in Washington, in BGP; Fair Play leaflet promoting rallies on 6 and 13 May, with phone contacts listed for Washington, Baltimore, Boston, Connecticut and Philadelphia, in FPCC Vertical File, Tamiment Library. A postscript included with the pamphlet version of Dellinger's *Cuba: America's Lost Plantation* described how seven of those sitting in out-side the agency were arrested on the vigil's third day, and how at the finale on 13 May, 250 people joined the picket and then marched to the White House, where 400 rallied.

113. In her excellent *Abraham Went Out: A Biography of A. J. Muste*, Philadelphia: Temple University Press, 1981, pp. 184–5, Jo Ann Ooiman Robinson explains how Muste defined himself regarding the 'contradictions' between Castroism and pacifism: though 'careful to avoid association with uncritically pro-Castro groups such as the Fair Play for Cuba Committee', 'he was so secure in his own pacifism that he could negotiate a stance of qualified support for a figure such as Castro.' See also Muste, *Cuba: An Analysis of American and Soviet Foreign Policy*, Nyack, N.Y.: War Resisters League, 1962, written just before the Missile Crisis, in which he comments that 'the peace move-ment as a whole has so far failed to mount a campaign against U.S. Cuban policy and seems inclined to congratulate itself that Kennedy is showing such moderation.'

114. Nancy L. Roberts, *Dorothy Day and the 'Catholic Worker'*, Albany, N.Y.: State University of New York Press, 1984, pp. 155–6; William D. Miller, *A Harsh and Dreadful Love: Dorothy Day and the Catholic Worker Movement*, New York: Liveright, 1973, pp. 303–9.

115. *America*, 6 May 1961.

116. According to Asher Harer, FPCC led a rally of 3,500 in front of San Francisco's City Hall, in coalition with all other groups in the Bay Area except one: 'SANE wanted a condemnation of both sides. They said "we don't want a demonstration that centers around 'hands off Cuba', we want a demonstration which says – I don't know where Russia was at that time – but a condem-nation of Russia, and a condemnation of the United States, and a condemnation of Cuba, and the whole damn thing." But we wouldn't go for that, so they walked out' (talk to SWP branch, 2 March 1980). In New York, in contrast, Fair Play's rally of perhaps 2,000 people on 27 October was dwarfed by the SANE-led demonstration of 8,000 or more the next day (see *New York Times*, 28 and 29 October 1962). There is no record of Fair Players organizing protests anywhere else, with the exception noted below of Indiana University.

117. See *Next Steps on Cuba and Latin America*, Nyack, N.Y.: Fellowship of Reconciliation, 1962, described as 'A Statement of Principles and Program growing out of a consultation of rep-resentatives of several United States peace organizations' and listing Robert Gilmore (Turn Toward Peace), Alfred Hassler (FOR), Homer Jack (SANE), Sidney Lens, Stewart Meacham (American Friends Service Committee), Frances Nealy (Friends Committee on National Legislation), Enrique Noble of Goucher College, Mildred Olmsted (Women's International League for Peace and Free-dom), William Wingell (Friends Peace Committee), and Charles Laughlin (Student Peace Union).

118. *New York Times*, 7 April 1962.

119. See the June 1963 *Liberation* editorial, 'Uncle Tom-ism in the Peace Movement', arguing that 'freedom, equality and independence for the United States' erstwhile economic colony' should have the same moral urgency for peace workers as the showdown then taking place in Birmingham, Alabama.

120. This brief summary of a grueling campaign is based on Robinson, *Abraham Went Out*, pp. 125, 185–6; also *Liberation* throughout 1963–64. A sense of what the walkers faced is conveyed by their release from jail in Macon, Georgia after JFK's assassination because, in Dave Dellinger's words, 'Authorities felt that they could not be responsible for their continued safety in view of the notion, current in Macon at the time, that both the assassin and the walkers were "pro-Castro Communists".'

121. On the phone and general disarray, see Lyle Stuart's testimony, *Fair Play for Cuba, SISC*, 8 February 1963. The National Conference was covered in the *New York Times*, 4 July 1961, which reported sixty delegates and several hundred guests. According to documents in the Berta Green Papers, an ambitious program was sketched and a National Advisory Council formed with repre-

sentatives of chapters and Student Councils. The last *Fair Play* appeared on 28 October 1961, with a headline 'US Prepares Second Invasion of Cuba!' and a by-now constant request for funds. During 1962, Castro's and others' speeches were still issued as pamphlets, plus a crude bulletin, the *Cuban Press Survey*, the FPCC Vertical File at the Tamiment Library contains many of these materials, as well as a Spring 1963 National Office 'Literature Catalogue', and a Baltimore FPCC leaflet for a talk by National Chairman V. T. Lee on 17 May 1963, almost the only evidence of FPCC's continued existence during that year. The limited scale of FPCC's activity during 1962 is indicated by a mailing sent out following the Missile Crisis, describing how after the Bay of Pigs a 'lull set in'. With renewed help, Lee reported that 40,000 leaflets were mailed out in late October 1962, and *Fair Play* organized a rally of 2,000 in New York 'in its own name'; he also admitted that this was the first national mailing to members in a year.

122. As Berta Green later matter-of-factly told her comrades: 'About a year after our entry into the FPCC, the SWP decided we would have to begin to withdraw and this marked the beginning of the demise of FP. ... The ban on travel to Cuba deprived the Committee of its most important activity. The party wanted to utilize the *Militant* to carry Fidel's speeches since under Gibson's supervision the FP was no longer publishing as much material' (BGPH). Green left first, and reported in her later 'Notes' that Gibson had asked the SWP to pull her out because of their personal friction; the *New York Times* reported this 'rift' on 12 October 1961.

123. Asher Harer, talk to SWP branch, 9 March 1980.

124. Copy in BGP. Virtually every thing contained in this screed has some relation to reality; clearly the writer had access to private communications, and was able to make use of the fears of many white liberals and white Old Leftists regarding 'Negro Nationalism' and Negroes in general. Many other letters with a remarkably similar tone are reproduced in Nelson Blackstock, *COIN-TELPRO: The FBI's Secret War on Political Freedom,* New York: Pathfinder, 1975.

125. This directive became National Security Action Memorandum 45 on 25 April 1961; see Edward B. Claflin, ed., *JFK Wants to Know: Memos From the President's Office, 1961–1963,* New York: William Morrow, 1991, p. 63.

126. Athan Theoharis, *Spying on Americans: Political Surveillance from Hoover to the Huston Plan,* Philadelphia: Temple University Press, 1978, p. 172.

127. Ibid., p. 258n41; the 13 January 1961 order to FPCC to register as a foreign agent is mentioned during John Rossen's appearance before the Eastland Committee (see *Fair Play for Cuba Committee, SISC,* 14 July 1961, p. 76). The notebooks of Fair Play's lawyer, Stanley Faulkner, describe extensive meetings on this matter in January 1961 attended by Richard Gibson, Jeanne Taber, Saul Landau, Berta Green and the SWP leader and FPCC Regional Representative George Weissman. The idea of legally dissolving the committee was abandoned when they discovered FPCC could be ordered to register anyway after the fact (copy of Faulkner's notebook in my possession; this was when Weissman ordered Green to destroy most of the national records to protect everyone involved). The climate of acceptable repression against *fidelista* Cubans in the US, which included widespread violence in neighborhoods from Tampa to Hoboken, is suggested by the National Labor Relations Board decision in early 1962 that 'pro-Castro' affiliations were a legitimate basis for dismissal in a south Florida case (*New York Times,* 25 April 1962). Heavy FBI attention to FPCC is indicated by my failed attempts since 1988 to gain access to the Bureau's files through the Freedom of Information Act. In various telephone conversations, I was told that they wanted to avoid handling my request, since it involved many thousands of pages; because most of the information was obtained in ways (presumably informers, break-ins, phone taps and mail covers) that assured nearly all of it would be deleted, these files would be useless for my purposes. I was offered, but declined, expedited handling of many other requests in exchange for withdrawing the FPCC application. As of mid 1993, the FBI has not processed any part of my request.

128. *Fair Play for Cuba Committee, SISC,* 10 January 1961.

129. *Fair Play for Cuba Committee, SISC,* 12 and 13 June 1961 (Cleveland, with Herman Kirsch, Richard and Jean Tussey, Max Levey, Tad Tekla); 15 June 1961 (Detroit, with Stanley Kowalski of the Detroit Red Squad followed by Ed Shaw, Joseph Bernstein, Nate Rosenshine, Rose Bernstein, Arnold Sabaroff, Dave Wellman and Martin Miller); 13 and 14 July 1961 (Chicago, with John Rossen, Boris Ross, Richard Criley).

130. *Fair Play for Cuba Committee, SISC,* 10 April 1962.

131. Letter, Gibson to Gosse, 24 September 1989.

132. *National Guardian,* 14 March 1963. Reportedly there had been twenty demonstrators on

24 October 1962, who were mobbed by some in the surrounding crowd of a thousand.

133. See the copious documentation on Tampa FPCC included with Lee's testimony, *Communist Threat Through the Caribbean, SISC,* 14 February 1963.

134. FPCC Press Release, 26 November 1963, in FPCC Vertical File, Tamiment Library.

Conclusion

In the American Grain

In looking back at this book and the theses implied throughout, and on occasion baldly stated, I cannot help but notice how much they echo main points about the sixties that are, or should be, already familiar: that the subjectivity of the New Left drew more from liberalism than from the 'Old', already-existing Left; that it was grounded in a deep if inchoate sympathy with the resistance of long-exploited peoples and was based on interaction with those peoples, who were themselves part of the New Left, its 'mass base' if you will; that at the core of this interaction were volcanic tensions over gender roles among middle-class white people. All of these ideas are advanced in what remains the most useful book for understanding the connections between the different movements of the sixties, Sara Evans's *Personal Politics: The Roots of Women's Liberation in the Civil Rights Movement and the New Left.*

So, in a sense all this book does is 'put Cuba back in', and if it achieves that much, I will be content. The history of the sixties' social explosions was thoroughly overdetermined, and if it seems that Cuba comes to the foreground here to the exclusion of everything else, that is an author's typical folly. I reiterate that, for all the solidarity felt towards Fidel among youth and younger liberals, the main action between 1955 and 1965 remained in Dixie, and no one who understands the true history of the time should doubt that SNCC was the pre-eminent 'founding organization' of the US New Left, far more than Fair Play for Cuba, and for that matter far more than SDS, which needs to be re-examined as essentially a white youth's solidarity organization with the black student struggle that, characteristically and understandably, attempted to vault from its 'solidarity' role into a larger space. (After 1965, the 'main action' was in the antiwar movement, and it becomes folly to assign a central role to any one organization rather than to the shifting coalitions and alignments against the war.)

Having said this, I still wish to reiterate three main points.

First, that many of the most widely held ideas about radicalism in that fif-

255

teen or even twenty-year period we call 'the sixties' are received opinions, at best partially true, that cannot and do not explain large areas of activism and public ferment. There is a particular context here in which Cuba is singularly relevant. For many years scholars have insisted that one must write about black and white radicalism during the Cold War era separately, as wholly distinct movements. Therefore many people have analyzed the New Left, or even the sixties as a whole, without writing at all about black activism (or more generally, the mobilization of peoples of color, which includes but is hardly reducible to the black freedom struggle). Too often, this radicalizing of whole sectors of the population is treated as an external factor to the history of the New Left. The reasons for this omission are complicated. In some cases, it is the result of a conscious assumption of humility and some understandable caution by writers who do not wish to usurp the history of others and drown out their voices. In other instances, it seems to be a conscious political choice, and should be evaluated as such. The practical result is a long series of books on the New Left as nothing more than a movement of white students.

Recently this perspective has come under sustained attack. Many scholars and activists, not limited to people of color or women, are now calling for a history of the sixties that knits together the pieces of the whole and does not scant, displace or exaggerate any single part. The story of the 'fair play movement' around Cuba is intended as a contribution to this new direction. It is a clear refutation of any thesis equating the New Left with white youth alone, since this movement included among its chief leaders and best-known spokespeople black activists both famous and obscure, young and not-young. Even more important, though, is the fact that it was black America that provided some of the strongest support to Castro both when he was in favor with US liberals, and when he was not.

What united the disparate forces demanding 'fair play' for Cuba, what brought together black and white, was serious opposition to the United States role as counter-revolutionary guardian of the Free World, its imperial role. Here is where one must confront another common thesis about the sixties. It has long been axiomatic that until the large-scale commitment of ground troops in Vietnam, there was no meaningful domestic opposition to US globalism. The only exception to this historiographical generalization is recent scholarship that covers the revival of the disarmament movement from 1955 on, but the Cuban revolution and the Fair Play for Cuba Committee do not appear in this scholarship either. Obviously, an exceptionally strong pro–Cold War consensus did cloak the actions of Congress, and frame the electorate's choices, from 1947 through the late sixties. Nonetheless, this study of North American reactions to the Cuban revolution, and Cold War politics in general, suggests that doubts, tensions and struggles over America's global role were never absent from US political culture. However, I do not advance the Fair Play for Cuba Committee's one year of celebrity and success in 1960–61 as proof that the Cold War consensus was always a fragile one: Fair Play was not the instigator but rather the result of divisions over foreign policy that had surfaced within the mainstream of Cold War liberalism considerably earlier.

Locating the earliest source of consequential opposition to an imperial foreign policy after World War II among liberals rather than self-avowed radicals suggests this book's second conclusion. Just as it is not possible to separate black from white radicalism during the Cold War era, I would argue that it is not possible to write seriously about American radicalism in this period without simultaneously writing about American liberalism, and vice versa, so closely are these two impulses, cultures and traditions intertwined. Appearances may be quite different, of course, especially before and during the sixties, when liberals went to great lengths to demonstrate their moderation, and certain kinds of New Leftists made a whole politics out of 'liberal-bashing'. However, Cold War liberalism, with its hard edge of nationalistic anti-Communism, was rather more of an exception than a permanent pattern in the modern history of the liberal tradition. It did not claim the progressive mantle for very long, in retrospect, before transmuting into neoconservatism, and this book attempts to show that among the legions of diehard Democrats who backed figures like Adlai Stevenson were many who silently tolerated but never truly accepted the dicta of America's hegemonic mission. It was, after all, not a leftist who proposed and named the Fair Play for Cuba Committee, but rather a pillar of the reform Democrats in a major industrial state, Alan Sagner.

So, clearly my New Left is quite different from the usual version, which is characterized by the spectrum running from Tom Hayden to Abbie Hoffman, and I am quite aware that this constitutes a revision. The New Left posited here naturally includes students, but a much more ideologically and geographically diverse bunch of youth. It also incorporates the 'Old Liberalism' plus much of the Old Left – even the CPUSA, to the extent that its ordinary members and sympathizers (whatever their leaders' decisions) participated quite actively in Cuba solidarity work, just as they did in civil rights, disarmament and antiwar activism throughout the decade. It is black and white, liberal and radical, student and adult, religious and secular. In fact, if you consider as I do that Dorothy Day is a quintessential 'New' Leftist leader, then the New Left encompasses not only the middle-aged but even the generation from the twenties. *What makes it truly 'New' is not who is included, as individuals, organizations or social groups, but the structural form this left takes – its pluralist, informal and highly sectoralized or ad hoc character.*

This New Left is summed up to a considerable degree in the term used by SDS's intellectual mentor, the philosopher Arnold Kaufman who was also faculty advisor to the University of Michigan's Fair Play chapter in 1960. In 1968, he described the tumult around him as centered by a 'radical liberalism'.[1] This is a very useful term for understanding not just the ideology of the sixties, but also the actual breaking up of Cold War liberalism's consensus, a slow-motion schism in which the Cuban revolution played an important role. And if we think of the evolution of the Democratic Party in the twenty years between George McGovern and Bill Clinton, a period when the persistent 'ultra-liberalism' of its activist base was the bane of party leaders and pundits, it should be clear that the New Right born simultaneously in the early sixties is not entirely demagogic when it denounces the 'radical liberals' infesting what is still the largest party.

It is the third and last thesis of this book that I find most intriguing and most problematic, and that takes it beyond a story of practical politics, liberals and radicals warring and allying with each other. It seems ever more apparent that, at least in a postindustrial nation like the US, the most fertile seedbed and the unbidden partner of 'hard', instrumental, ideologically serious politics is the unserious, evanescent and impermanent world of popular or mass culture. Looking at the US response to the Cuban rebellion in the Eisenhower years drives this point home with a vengeance.

So what should we make of the 'Yankee *fidelismo*' that is described here in what may seem like overly affectionate detail? From our own, later, standpoint, and from a feminist perspective, it is hardly something to celebrate, this vicarious gunplay and lust for violent transformation. Boys who long to be Fidel, to join his band and carve a girl's name on the stock of their carbines, to ride into Havana on a tank to the adulation of crowds, may grow into men who associate social change with the all-encompassing force and charisma of a Maximum Leader, and either seek that role for themselves or seek it in other men.

I hope it is clear that because this book describes with a measure of fellow-feeling the impulse to go to Cuba to take up arms and remake oneself in the mountains, that it does not constitute an endorsement of the politics of voluntarism tied to *machismo*. Yet I cannot forgo the conclusion that men and women must constitute themselves politically from where they do stand, with its attendant ideology and understanding of the world, its language – and no other. Then, to the extent that is possible, as all of us do, they 'make the road by walking'. So it must be reiterated that young men (as well as young women) had many reasons to feel beleaguered and adrift in Eisenhower's America, and in need of a heroic struggle for justice, and simply of a hero.

Which brings us to the final point regarding this book. Concerns that it takes an insufficiently critical approach to gender issues will inevitably come back to the figure that looms above this narrative – Fidel Castro. It may be that history has no more need of heroes, and that the desire to be, or find, a hero is part of the cultural lag and detrita of thousands of years that we must now slough off. However, despite recurrent trumpetings of an 'end of ideology' or an 'end of history', it is by no means proven that we have no further need of revolution, and therefore of revolutionaries – people who are willing to make history within, and even despite, the conditions that history has dictated to them. Since 1959, in the United States as well as elsewhere in the hemisphere, the revolution in Cuba has been a catalyst, not to engagement with Fidel as revolutionary idol and saint, but to connecting with a much deeper truth, the lives of daily oppression and resistance suffered by those who lack all charisma save their God-given grace. Many thousands of North Americans have left their country and themselves and then returned, made wholer. This is the final significance of Cuba and *fidelismo* for the North American left, a left that continues to exist and go forward, despite all premature reports of its demise. The Cuban revolution is a historical fact that will always exist as such, regardless of any immediate outcome; Fidel Castro is the revolutionary who, more than any other, 'made' that revolution, using in the most deeply intuitive way the resources left him by a patriarchal culture imbued with a deep sense of nationhood. In the end, as a historian trying to understand the revolutionary character of his country's past and probable future, I am left with Ferlinghetti's words, and Whitman's:

> While lilacs last in the dooryard bloom, Fidel
> your futile trip is done
> yet is not done
> and is not futile
> I give you my sprig of laurel

Notes

1. Arnold S. Kaufman, *The Radical Liberal: New Man in American Politics,* New York: Atherton, 1968.

Appendix

A Brief Chronology

9 March 1952	Former president Fulgencio Batista seizes power in Cuba, suppresses political parties.
26 July 1953	Student militants led by Fidel Castro fail in attempt to take Moncada fort in Santiago de Oriente and set off a popular rebellion; most of those caught are killed. At his trial on 16 October, Castro gives 'History Will Absolve Me' speech.
June 1954	CIA-organized Liberation Army stages 'invasion' of Guatemala, instigating coup against elected government of Jacobo Arbenz.
May 1955	Following a general amnesty, Castro and supporters form 26th of July Movement, go to Mexico to begin planning insurrection.
October 1955	Castro tours Cuban communities on US East Coast, organizing support.
2 December 1956	82 members of 26th of July Movement land from the yacht *Granma* in Oriente province; a dozen survivors reach the Sierra Maestra; Cuban government claims Castro is killed.
24–26 Feb. 1957	Series by Herbert L. Matthews in the *New York Times* proves Castro is alive, inspiring Cuban supporters and US press.
March 1957	Three sons of US servicemen at Guantánamo base join rebel band in Sierra Maestra.
19 May 1957	Robert Taber's documentary, 'Rebels of the Sierra Maestra: The Story of Cuba's Jungle Fighters', airs on CBS.

March 1958	Denunciations of US support for Batista in Congress lead to Eisenhower administration embargo on further weapons shipments to Cuba.
April 1958	General strike by 26th of July Movement in Havana fails.
July 1958	US servicemen and civilians taken hostage by Raúl Castro's column in Sierra Cristal.
December 1958	Eisenhower's private envoy fails in last-minute attempts to convince Batista to resign in favor of a coalition government to exclude Castro. 26th of July Movement begins final offensive.
1 January 1959	In New Year's first hours, Batista flees Cuba; 26th of July Movement assumes power.
15 April 1959	Fidel Castro arrives in United States on 'truth operation', tours Washington, D.C., New York City, and Harvard and Princeton universities.
3 June 1959	Agrarian Reform law promulgated, ending period of ambiguity in US–Cuban relations; State Department protests, demands immediate full compensation.
18–24 July 1959	Castro resigns as premier to force resignation of Provisional President Manuel Urrutia, then resumes office.
13 August 1959	Major William Morgan of US plays leading role in blocking exile landing from Dominican Republic; hailed by Castro, loses US citizenship.
22 October 1959	Arrest of anti-Communist Major Huber Matos and a group of his officers.
November 1959	US begins covert hostilities against Cuba, including support for exile groups in Florida; consensus reached among policymakers to remove Castro.
23 January 1960	Robert Taber's article in The Nation leads to organization of Fair Play for Cuba Committee (FPCC) by Taber and Alan Sagner.
February 1960	Deputy Premier Anastas Mikoyan of USSR visits island; Cuba and Soviet Union sign agreement to barter Soviet industrial goods for 5 million tons of sugar over five years.
4 March 1960	Munitions ship La Coubre explodes in Havana harbor, US withdraws ambassador 'for consultations' in response

to Castro's charges of US involvement.

17 March 1960	Eisenhower approves plan for exile invasion.
6 April 1960	*New York Times* advertisement announces formation of FPCC.
7 May 1960	Cuba and Soviet Union establish diplomatic relations.
June–July 1960	US-owned refineries refuse to refine Soviet oil, are nationalized. Most of Cuba's guaranteed quota of sugar sales to US is cut. Soviet Union pledges support for Cuba against any aggression. FPCC delegation of African-Americans including Robert F. Williams, LeRoi Jones and Harold Cruse visits Cuba.
August 1960	Democratic presidential candidate John F. Kennedy begins attacks on Republican 'softness' towards Castro. Socialist Workers Party enters FPCC after negotiations with Taber.
September 1960	During attendance at meeting of UN General Assembly, Castro stays at Theresa Hotel in Harlem, greets world leaders.
13 October 1960	Cuba nationalizes all major enterprises still in private hands.
19 October 1960	Eisenhower administration announces embargo on trade with Cuba as Kennedy continues to attack Republican presidential candidate Nixon for losing Cuba, calls for aid to counter-revolutionaries on island.
24 October 1960	Final expropriation of 166 remaining US-owned businesses.
November 1960	Kennedy elected. C. Wright Mills's *Listen, Yankee* published. Candidacy for mayor of New York City by Norman Mailer on pro-Fidel platform aborted. LeRoi Jones's essay 'Cuba Libre' appears in *Evergreen*. Ronald Hilton article in 19 November *Nation* exposes US-run training camps for exile invasion in Guatemala.
23 December 1960	FPCC delegation of 326 people departs from Miami on 'Christmas Tour'.
January 1961	US breaks diplomatic relations with Cuba, bans travel to island. FPCC ordered to register as foreign agent, refuses. Charges in hearing of Senate Internal Security Subcommittee that Cuban government paid for 6 April 1960

Times ad. Taber stays in Cuba to avoid indictment.

March 1961	Alliance for Progress announced. Theodore Draper's 'Castro's Cuba: A Revolution Betrayed?' appears in *Encounter*.
3 April 1961	Kennedy administration releases 'White Paper on Cuba', written by Arthur Schlesinger, Jr, accusing Castro of betraying revolution.
15 April 1961	Havana bombed in preparation for exile invasion; US Ambassador to UN Adlai Stevenson claims raid is by defectors from Cuban Air Force. Castro declares for first time that revolution is 'socialist'.
17 April 1961	Brigade 2506 lands at Playa Girón in the Bay of Pigs on Cuba's south coast. Defeated in three days by Cuban militia as Kennedy refuses to authorize US air strikes. Protest meetings and rallies across US.
August 1961	Robert F. Williams receives asylum in Cuba. FPCC begins rapid decline.
2 December 1961	Fidel Castro declares 'I am a Marxist-Leninist.'
September 1962	Richard Gibson, Taber's successor as executive secretary of FPCC, flees US.
October 1962	Cuban Missile Crisis.
May 1963	Committee for Non-Violent Action begins Québec-to-Guantánamo Peace Walk.
22 November 1963	Lee Harvey Oswald, purported member of FPCC, charged with shooting Kennedy.

Index

THE HAYMARKET SERIES

Already Published

THE INVENTION OF THE WHITE RACE: Racial Oppression and Social Control
by Theodore Allen

MARXISM IN THE USA: Remapping the History of the American Left *by Paul Buhle*

FIRE IN THE AMERICAS: Forging a Revolutionary Agenda *by Roger Burbach
and Orlando Núñez*

THE FINAL FRONTIER: The Rise and Fall of the American Rocket State *by Dale Carter*

CORRUPTIONS OF EMPIRE: Life Studies and the Reagan Era *by Alexander Cockburn*

THE SOCIAL ORIGINS OF PRIVATE LIFE: A History of American Families, 1600–1900
by Stephanie Coontz

WAR AND TELEVISION *by Bruce Cumings*

IT'S NOT ABOUT A SALARY: Hip Hop in Los Angeles from the Watts Prophets to
the Freestyle Fellowship *by Brian Cross*

CITY OF QUARTZ: Excavating the Future in Los Angeles *by Mike Davis*

PRISONERS OF THE AMERICAN DREAM: Politics and Economy in the History of the
US Working Class *by Mike Davis*

MECHANIC ACCENTS: Dime Novels and Working-Class Culture in America
by Michael Denning

NO CRYSTAL STAIR: African Americans in the City of Angels *by Lynell George*

RACE, POLITICS, AND ECONOMIC DEVELOPMENT: Community Perspectives
edited by James Jennings

POSTMODERNISM AND ITS DISCONTENTS: Theories, Practices *edited by E. Ann Kaplan*

RANK-AND-FILE REBELLION: Teamsters for a Democratic Union *by Dan La Botz*

BLACK AMERICAN POLITICS: From the Washington Marches to Jesse Jackson
by Manning Marable

THE OTHER SIDE: Los Angeles from Both Sides of the Border *by Rubén Martínez*

AN INJURY TO ALL: The Decline of American Unionism *by Kim Moody*

YOUTH, IDENTITY, POWER: The Chicano Movement *by Carlos Muñoz, Jr.*

ANOTHER TALE TO TELL: Politics and Narrative in Postmodern Culture *by Fred Pfeil*

THE WAGES OF WHITENESS: Race and the Making of the American Working Class
by David R. Roediger

OUR OWN TIME: A History of American Labor and the Working Day
by David R. Roediger and Philip S. Foner

STRANGE WEATHER: Culture, Science and Technology in the Age of Limits
by Andrew Ross

THE RISE AND FALL OF THE WHITE REPUBLIC: Class Politics and Mass Culture in Nineteenth-Century America *by Alexander Saxton*

UNFINISHED BUSINESS: Twenty Years of Socialist Review *edited by the Socialist Review Collective*

BLACK MACHO AND THE MYTH OF THE SUPERWOMAN *by Michele Wallace*

INVISIBILITY BLUES: From Pop to Theory *by Michele Wallace*

PROFESSORS, POLITICS AND POP *by Jon Wiener*

THE LEFT AND THE DEMOCRATS *The Year Left 1*

TOWARDS A RAINBOW SOCIALISM *The Year Left 2*

RESHAPING THE US LEFT: Popular Struggles in the 1980s *The Year Left 3*

FIRE IN THE HEARTH: The Radical Politics of Place in America *The Year Left 4*

Forthcoming

THE ARCHITECTURE OF COMPANY TOWNS *by Margaret Cameron*

THE MERCURY THEATER: Orson Welles and the Popular Front *by Michael Denning*

JAMAICA 1945–1984 *by Winston James*

BLACK RADICAL TRADITIONS *by Cynthia Hamilton*

WHITE GUYS *by Fred Pfeil*

AMERICAN DOCUMENTARY FILM *by Paula Rabinowitz*

TOWARDS THE ABOLITION OF WHITENESS: Essays on Race, Politics and Working-Class History *by David R. Roediger*

FEMINISM IN THE AMERICAS *The Year Left 5*